COLORADO
By the Numbers

A reference, almanac and guide
to the Highest State

by Doug Freed

Virga Publishing, 2003

Cover Design & Graphics by Patricia Johnston

Library of Congress Control Number 2003114709

ISBN 0-9747164-0-5

First Edition   December, 2003

Additional copies of this book are available by mail.
Send $14.95, plus $3.50 tax, postage and handling to:
Virga Publishing, P.O. Box 2959
Grand Junction, CO 81502 • 970-242-0417
Or visit www.Coloradobythenumbers.com

Publisher's Cataloging-in-Publication
(*Provided by Quality Books, Inc.*)

Freed, Doug.
    Colorado by the numbers : a reference, almanac and guide
to the highest state / by Doug Freed. -- 1st ed.
    p. cm.
    Includes bibliographical references and index.
    LCCN 2003114709
    ISBN 0-9747164-0-5

    1. Colorado--Miscellanea. 2. Colorado--Statistics.
I. Title

F776.5.F74 2003   978.8
                                       QBI03-200895

Printed in the U.S.A. by Morris Publishing, Kearney, NE
1-800-650-7888

In memory of Kurt E. Lankford
Greatly admired, greatly loved.

Table of Contents

Illustrations and Photographs

Acknowledgements

I enjoyed a great deal of assistance in researching and preparing this book. I had many editors, even though most didn't know they were filling that role. For more than two years I talked of this book, thinking out loud, asking questions, seeking opinions. Those around me certainly grew tired of it all. Thank you for your tolerance, and thank you for helping me more than you could know. My wife, Shannon, leads the pack in the category of moral support and proved an able copy editor. My good friend Greg Doubek endured many phone conversations as I thought through sections of this book.

Assistance of a more concrete nature came from some professional colleagues, Bud Wells, David Iler and Karrie Mowen. To Craig Gaskill and Greg Doubek, and all those who reviewed sections of the book, please know that your efforts greatly improved the quality of this book.

I had help from artists, and cartographers, engineers and attorneys. Thanks to all of you.

Then there are those who came before me. The researchers, writers, scholars and adventurers who wrote the many excellent books on our state I used for research. I merely stood on the shoulders of others to compile the information for this book.

Any failings, errors or shortcomings in this book are mine alone.

64th county too young for data

The city of Broomfield in 1998 had an estimated population of 36,790. The city was unique in that its 27.5 square miles were spread across four separate counties. Jurisdictional problems were common, as were problems in accessing services. Residents sought relief from the confusion through a constitutional amendment creating a City and County of Broomfield. The amendment passed on Nov. 3, 1998. Following a three-year transition and organizational period, the state's 64th county – The City and County of Broomfield – was officially up and running Nov. 15, 2001.

In this book you will find scores of statistics broken down county by county. The City and County of Broomfield is not included. The county in most cases is simply too young to have its own data. I have included it where possible. Where it is not seen in a list, data was not available.

Preface

The effort behind this book is not to define Colorado, but to describe it. The spectacular geography and physiography of our state has long lent itself to grand efforts of poetry, painting, prose or song. The difference here is in the medium. With a little prose and a lot of numbers, I hope to lend a new perspective to what we call Colorado. It is my greatest hope this different perspective leads to a better understanding of the Highest State.

I started my research because I saw the need for a good writer's reference for my home state. I continued the research because I realized it could be a book for all those who love this place, for all its great diversity and richness.

President Theodore Roosevelt said the beauty of Colorado is enough to bankrupt the English language. Perhaps that is why I turned to numbers.

Foreword

By John Hickenlooper
Mayor, City & County of Denver

When asked to describe a trip to Colorado, President Teddy Roosevelt said, "The scenery bankrupts the English language."

Denver Mayor John Hickenlooper

It was that statement that helped inspire Doug Freed to write this book. If the story of Colorado could not be told in words, perhaps it could be told in numbers. And so Doug collected an unprecedented amount of facts, figures and statistics that together paint a new look at Colorado and the people who have called this state home.

But this is no mere collection of dry stats. Through the accumulation of data emerges a picture of Colorado that captures the vast resources and spectacular beauty of the state, while also telling of the ambition and courage of the Coloradans who helped tame the wilderness.

Colorado began with some strokes of a pen on February 28, 1861, when a group of Washington politicians decided that the new Colorado territory should be a symmetrical, 4-degree Latitude by 7-degree Longitude quadrangle. It was to be one of three politically created states where the borders are straight lines, chosen arbitrarily rather than following natural landmarks.

Ah, but what wonderful natural landmarks were included within Colorado's lucky borders. Here was to be the highest and largest inland sand dunes in North America, the steepest sheer rock canyon wall in the nation at the Black Canyon of the Gunnison, the most beautiful of the ancient Anasazi cliff dwellings in Mesa Verde, and the towering red sandstone pinnacles of Colorado National Monument.

And then, of course, there were mountains. America's highest state was to get all 54 of the Rocky Mountain peaks that soar to 14,000 feet with a bonus of 584 additional ranked mountains that climb to13,000 feet.

While the mountains made Colorado beautiful, they did present a formidable barrier to travelers in the 19th century. Lewis and Clark took the easy way west, bypassing Colorado, as did the Santa Fe Trail, the Oregon Trail and the first transcontinental railroad. By all reasoning, the dominant cities and growth of the Rocky Mountain region should have sprung up along these early routes.

Instead, it was Colorado that grew. Today, Colorado's population is greater than neighboring Utah's and New Mexico's combined; the City & County of Denver alone has more residents than all of Wyoming.

How this growth occurred is the story of human contributions to Colorado, and Doug Freed tells it with descriptions of both the people who came here and the engineering marvels they created.

For the railroads to head west from Denver, men had to dig the longest railroad tunnel in North America – the great Moffat Tunnel. For cars to go over the mountains, Coloradans built the highest auto tunnel in the world, the Eisenhower Tunnel, slicing through the Continental Divide at 11,000 feet. Today, 72,699 miles of roads criss-cross Colorado's mountains and plains.

When man could fly over the mountains, Denver built the world's second largest airport – a facility so huge it is twice the size of New York's Manhattan Island.

To make Colorado habitable, men not only had to move mountains, they also had to move water uphill. Only one-half of one percent of Colorado is covered with water, making it the state's most precious commodity. Even more challenging, 80 percent of Colorado's population lives in the arid Front Range, which is home to only 25 percent of the state's water.

The solution has been to build nearly 2,000 reservoirs and 40 water diversion projects, including the little known Roberts Tunnel – the longest major underground water tunnel in the world, which at 23.3 miles is nearly as long as the Chunnel between England and France.

From weather to wildlife, from people to places, Doug Freed has used numbers to create a vivid description of Colorado. Throughout this book are hundreds of gems that make the wonders of Colorado more accessible, while adding a valuable resource to the literature of the state.

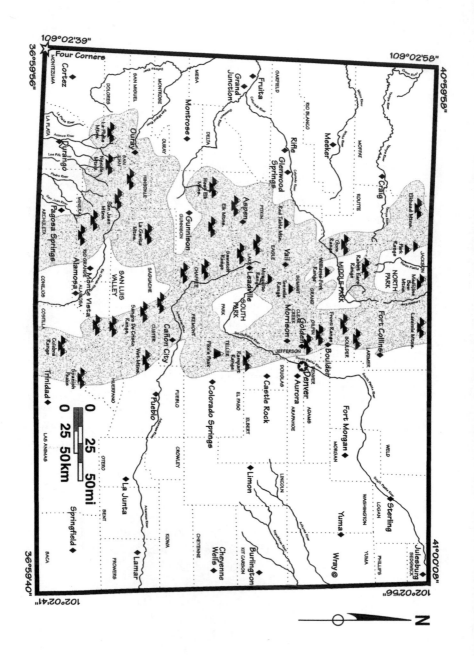

X

CHAPTER

1 Geography and Physiography

Colorado organized as a territory, boundaries set: February 28, 1861.
Colorado obtains statehood: August 1, 1876.

North boundary: 41º latitude.   **North-South Distance:** 276 miles
South boundary: 37º latitude.
West boundary: 102º 03' 02"   **East-West Distance:** 387 miles.
East boundary: 109º 03' 02"

Colorado is a straight-line state. Its boundaries are entirely political, and follow straight lines rather than natural landmarks. The state is a symmetrical 4-degree-Latitude by 7-degree-Longitude quadrangle. Only two other states – Wyoming and Utah – are straight-line states, having not a single boundary delineated by nature.

Total Area: 104,247 square miles. (approx. 270,000 Km²)

High Point: Mount Elbert, Lake County. 14,433 feet (4,398 meters)
Low Point: Arickaree River at Kansas border, Yuma County.
   3,315 feet (1,010 meters).
The United States Geological Survey lists Colorado's low point as 3,350 feet in Prowers County where the Arkansas River crosses the Colorado-Kansas border. Dale Sanderson, of Denver, a cartographer for Qwest Communications in Denver, researched USGS maps to discover the new Arickaree River low point.

Even at 3,315 feet, Colorado has the highest low point of the 50 states. Wyoming is second at 3,099, where the Belle Fourche River enters South Dakota.

1

Geographical center of state: In Spinney Mountain Reservoir, 30 miles northwest of Pikes Peak in Park County. Take a boat.

Distance from West Coast: 995 miles (1,600 km).
Distance from East Coast: 1,989 miles (3,200 km).

Mean elevation: 6,800 feet (1,020 m).

Number of separate peaks 14,000 feet or higher: 54.
Number of separate peaks 13,000 feet or higher: 584. (See Appendix)
Excluding Alaska, three-fourths of the nation's land area 10,000 feet or higher is in Colorado.

Temperatures typically drop 3.3 to 3.6 degrees F for every 1,000 feet elevation gain, or about 1.8 to 2 degrees C for every 300 meters.

Any area 9,000 feet or higher will experience a very short growing season. Frost can occur any day of the year at 9,000 feet. Fraser, in the upper reaches of Middle Park, is credited with having the shortest growing season in the state, averaging 48 frost-free days a year. Denver, only 50 miles away as the crow flies, enjoys warm summer nights and 211 days of frost-free weather. On the Continental Divide between the two is Berthoud Pass, 11,310 feet, where the annual average high temperature is 40 degrees and the record high is only 76. Compare that to Denver's average high of 64 degrees and record high of 104. Fruita, near the Utah border in the Grand Valley, enjoys the state's longest growing seasons.

Average humidity: 38% (measured at noon).

Higher elevations are analogous to northern latitudes. In a 16-mile drive from Colorado Springs to the summit of Pikes Peak, one passes through four separate ecosystems: Grassland, Montane Forest, Subalpine Forest and Alpine Tundra. To pass through similar life zones without gaining altitude, one would have to travel as far north as Northern Alaska or Canada. Many of the plants and animals living in Colorado between 9,000 and 11,500 feet, in the spruce-fir forest life-zones, thrive at 1,000 feet in northern Canada. The low tundra vegetation above timberline (approx. 11,000 feet) is similar to plant life found in the Arctic tundra.

Atmospheric Pressure / Boiling Temperature of Water
Sea level average: 29.92 inches of mercury.
    Boiling temperature of water: 212° F.
Denver, 5,280 feet: 24.89 inches of mercury.
    Boiling temperature of water: 202.9°F.
10,000 feet: 20 inches mercury.
    Boiling temperature of water: 193.7°F.

Major River Drainages: 10
North Platte, South Platte, Republican, Arkansas, Rio Grande, San Juan, Dolores, Colorado, White, Yampa.

Since water cannot flow uphill, and since Colorado is the Highest State, virtually all of Colorado's water flows out of the state. Of the 10 major river drainages listed above, all have headwaters in Colorado. The only water flowing in to Colorado is from the Green and Little Snake Rivers in the northwest corner of the state, and the Cimarron River, which cuts across the extreme southeast corner. The Green enters from Utah, and loops through Brown's Hole for 39 miles before leaving once again for Utah. The Little Snake headwaters in Wyoming but flows there only briefly before entering Colorado. It flows to the Yampa and back out of the state. The Cimarron enters Colorado, flows 45 miles, then exits to Kansas.

Number of Naturally Occurring Lakes: 2,286
Total surface area of naturally occurring lakes: 20,333 acres, 31.77square miles.
Percent of land area as natural lake: .029 of 1%
89% of Colorado's naturally-occurring lakes are above 9,000 feet.

"Headwaters Hill," is the unofficial name of a mountain in south central Colorado that serves as a Triple Divide. Water from this mountain flows to three different river drainages: the Gunnison, Rio Grande and Arkansas Rivers. There are only two other known triple divides in the United States – one in Wyoming, another in northern Montana. Only in Montana is it a true triple divide with water flowing to the Atlantic, Pacific and Arctic Oceans.

Physiographic Regions: 5

Great Plains, Southern Rocky Mountains, Colorado Plateau, Middle Rocky Mountains, Wyoming Basin.

Geographers describe physical land forms in terms of Physiographic regions. The Great Plains, Southern Rocky Mountains and Colorado Plateau comprise the vast majority of Colorado's land area, but the Middle Rocky Mountains and Wyoming Basin are evident in northwest Colorado.

Despite Colorado's fame as a mountainous state, the Great Plains comprise roughly two-fifths of the state's land area – some 40,000 square miles. This approximates the amount of land given over to the mountainous Southern Rocky Mountains.

The western-most one-fifth of the state is part of the Colorado Plateau, marked by mesas and canyons.

Major Ecosystems: 8

	% of State	Precip Range	Elevation Ft.	Mean temp
Grassland	35-40	10-18 inches	4,000-10,000	51.8 F (11C)
Montane Forest	10	15-25 inches	5,600-9,000	44.6 F (7 C)
Subalpine Forest	15	20-40 inches	9,000-11,000	35.6 F (2 C)
Alpine Tundra	5	24-48 inches	11,400 +	26.6 F (-3 C)
Montane Shrubland	5-10	13-17 inches	5,500-8,500	44.6 F (7C)
Piñon-Juniper Woodland	10-15	10-18 inches	5,500-8,000	50 F (10C)
Semidesert Shrubland	15	6-15 inches	4,000-8,000	42.8 F (6C)
Riparian Lands	1-2		up to 11,000	

Riparian lands represent less than 3% of Colorado's land area, yet 90% of its wildlife is found there.

Approximately 40% of Colorado is forested.

Species of Mammals:	130 (four introduced)
Species of Birds:	460 (264 breeding)
Species of Plants:	3,000
Species of Insects:	50,000 to 100,000
Species of Fish:	87 (54 native; 33 introduced)
Species of Amphibians / Reptiles:	67

30 species of Colorado plants are classified as noxious weeds, which compares to 1,200 noxious weeds worldwide and 140 in the U.S.

Threatened and Endangered Wildlife

Animals listed as either Colorado Endangered (CE); Colorado Threatened (CT); Colorado Special Concern (CC); Federally Endangered (FE); Federally Threatened (FT); Federal Candidate for Listing (FC).

COMMON NAME	SCIENTIFIC NAME	STATUS
Fish		
Arkansas Darter	Etheostoma cragini	CT, FC
Bonytail	Gila elegans	CE, FE
Colorado Pikeminnow (Squawfish)	Ptychocheilus lucius	CE, FE
Greenback Cutthroat Trout	Oncorhynchus clarki stomias	CT, FT
Humpback Chub	Gila cypha	CT, FE
Rio Grande Sucker	Catostomus plebeius	CE
Razorback Sucker	Xyrauchen texanus	CE, FE
Lake Chub	Couesius plumbeus	CE
Plains Minnow	Hybognathus placitius	CE
Suckermouth Minnow	Phenacobius mirabilis	CE
Northern Redbelly Dace	Phoxinus eos	CE
Southern Redbelly Dace	Phoxinus erythrogaster	CE
Brassy Minnow	Hybognathus hankinsoni	CT
Common Shiner	Luxilus cornutus	CT
Bluehead Sucker	Catostomus discobolus	CC
Flannelmouth Sucker	Catostomus latipinnis	CC
Mountain Sucker	Catostomus playtrhynchus	CC
Plains Orangethroat Darter	Etheostoma spectibile	CC
Iowa Darter	Etheostoma exile	CC
Plains Topminnow	Fundulus sciadicus	CC
Rio Grande Chub	Gila pandora	CC
Colorado Roundtail Chub	Gila robusta	CC
Speckled Chub	Macrhybopsis aestivalis tetranemus	CC
River Shiner	Notropis blennius	CC
Stonecat	Noturus flavus	CC
Colorado River Cutthroat Trout	Oncorhynchus clarki pleuriticus	CC
Rio Grande Cutthroat Trout	Oncorhynchus clarki virginalis	CC
Flathead Chub	Platygobio gracilus	CC
Amphibians		
Boreal Toad	Bufo boreas boreas	CE, FC
Northern Cricket Frog	Acris crepitans	CC
Great Plains Narrowmouth Toad	Gastrophryne olivacea	CC
Canyon Treefrog	Hyla arenicolor	CC
Northern Leopard Frog	Rana pipiens	CC

Threatened and Endangered Wildlife *continued*

Common Name	Scientific Name	Status
Plains Leopard Frog	Rana blairi	CC
Couch's Spadefoot	Scaphiopus couchii	CC
Great Basin Spadefoot	Spea intermontana	CC
New Mexico Spadefoot	Spea multiplicata	CC

REPTILES

Midget Faded Rattlesnake	Crotalus viridis concolor	CC
Longnose Leopard Lizard	Gambelia wislizenii	CC
Yellow Mud Turtle	Kinosternon flavescens	CC
Common Kingsnake	Lampropeltis getula	CC
Texas Blind Snake	Leptotyphlops dulcis	CC
Texas Horned Lizard	Phrynosoma cornutum	CC
Desert Spiny Lizard	Sceloporus magister	CC
Massasauga	Sistrurus catenatus	CC

MOLLUSKS

Rocky Mountain Capshell	Acroloxus coloradensis	CC

BIRDS

American Peregrine Falcon	Falco peregrinus anatum	CC
Whooping Crane	Grus americana tabida	FE, CE
Least Tern	Sterna antillarum athalassos	FE, CE
Southwestern Willow Flycatcher	Empidonax traillii extimus	FE, CE
Plains Sharp-tailed Grouse	Tympanuchus phasianellus jamesii	CE
Piping Plover	Charadrius melodus circumcinctus	FT, CT
Bald Eagle	Haliaeetus leucocephalus	FT, CT
Mexican Spotted Owl	Strix occidentalis lucida	FT, CT
Western Burrowing Owl	Athene cunicularia	CT
Greater Sandhill Crane	Grus canadensis	CC
Lesser Prairie Chicken	Tympanuchus pallidicinctus	CT
Barrow's Goldeneye	Bucephala islandica	CC
Ferruginous Hawk	Buteo regalis	CC
Gunnison Sage Grouse	Centrocercus urophasianus subspp.	CC
Northern Sage Grouse	Centrocercus urophasianus subspp.	CC
Western Snowy Plover	Charadrius alexandrinus	CC
Mountain Plover	Charadrium montana	CC
Long-Billed Curlew	Numenius americanus	CC

Threatened and Endangered Wildlife *continued*

Common Name	Scientific Name	Status
White Pelican	Pelecanus erythrorhynchos	CC

MAMMALS

Gray Wolf	Canis lupus	FE, CE
Black-Footed Ferret	Mustela nigripes	FE, CE
Grizzly Bear	Ursus arctos	FT, CE
Preble's Meadow Jumping Mouse	Zapus hudsonius preblei	FT, CT
Canadian Lynx	Lynx canadensis	FT, CE
Wolverine	Gulo gulo luscus	CE
River Otter	Lutra canadensis	CE
Kit Fox	Vulpes macrotis	CE
Swift Fox	Vulpes velox	CC
Black-Tailed Priarie Dog	Cynomys ludovicianus	CC

Full Moons, 2004 to 2013

Source: U.S. Naval Observatory. Times in Greenwich Mean Time, 7 hours later than MST.

	2004	2005	2006	2007	2008	2009	2010	2011	2012	2013
Jan	7	25	14	3	22	11	29	19	9	27
Feb	6	24	13	2	21	9	28	18	7	25
March	6	25	14	3	21	11	29	19	8	27
April	5	24	13	2	20	9	28	18	6	25
May	4	23	13	2/30	20	9	27	17	6	25
June	3	22	11	30	18	7	26	15	4	23
July	2/31	21	11	30	18	7	25	15	3	22
Aug	29	19	9	28	16	6	24	13	2/31	21
Sept	28	18	7	26	15	4	23	12	30	19
Oct	27	17	7	25	14	2	22	12	29	18
Nov	26	16	5	24	13	2	21	10	28	17
Dec	26	15	5	23	12	31	21	10	28	17

Solar Eclipse

April 19, 2004, partial
Oct. 14, 2004, partial
April 8, 2005, annular-total
Oct. 3, 2005, annular
March 29, 2006, total
Sept. 22, 2006, annular

Lunar Eclipse

May 4, 2004, total
Oct. 28, 2004, total
April 24, 2005, penumbral
Oct. 17, 2005, partial
March 14-15, 2006, penumbral
Sept. 17, 2006, partial

Sunrise, Sunset Times
Denver, Colorado

All times Mountain Standard Time. Add one hour for Daylight Savings Time.
Source: U.S. Naval Observatory

	Jan.		Feb.		March		April		May		June	
Date	Rise	Set	Rise	Set	Rise	Set	Rise	Set	Rise	Set	Rise	Set
01	0721	1646	0708	1719	0632	1753	0543	1824	0501	1855	0434	1922
02	0721	1647	0701	1720	0632	1753	0543	1825	0500	1855	0434	1922
03	0721	1648	0707	1722	0631	1754	0542	1826	0459	1856	0433	1923
04	0721	1649	0706	1723	0629	1755	0540	1827	0457	1857	0433	1924
05	0722	1650	0705	1724	0628	1756	0538	1828	0456	1858	0433	1924
06	0721	1650	0703	1725	0626	1757	0537	1829	0455	1859	0432	1925
07	0721	1651	0702	1727	0625	1758	0535	1830	0454	1900	0432	1926
08	0721	1652	0701	1728	0623	1759	0534	1831	0453	1901	0432	1926
09	0721	1653	0700	1729	0622	1800	0532	1832	0452	1902	0432	1927
10	0721	1654	0659	1730	0620	1801	0531	1833	0451	1903	0432	1927
11	0721	1955	0658	1731	0618	1802	0529	1834	0450	1904	0431	1928
12	0721	1656	0657	1732	0617	1803	0528	1835	0449	1905	0431	1928
13	0720	1657	0656	1734	0615	1804	0526	1836	0448	1906	0431	1929
14	0720	1700	0653	1736	0614	1806	0525	1837	0447	1906	0431	1930
15	0720	1700	0653	1736	0612	1807	0523	1838	0446	1907	0431	1930
16	0719	1701	0652	1737	0611	1808	0522	1839	0445	1908	0431	1930
17	0719	1702	0650	1738	0609	1809	0520	1840	0444	1909	0431	1930
18	0718	1703	0649	1739	0607	1810	0519	1841	0443	1910	0431	1930
19	0718	1704	0648	1741	0606	1811	0517	1842	0442	1911	0432	1931
20	0717	1705	0647	1742	0604	1812	0516	1843	0441	1912	0432	1931
21	0717	1706	0645	1743	0602	1813	0514	1844	0441	1913	0432	1931
22	0716	1708	0644	1744	0601	1814	0513	1845	0440	1914	0432	1932
23	0715	1709	0642	1745	0559	1815	0512	1846	0439	1915	0432	1932
24	0715	1710	0641	1746	0558	1816	0510	1847	0438	1915	0433	1932
25	0714	1711	0640	1747	0556	1817	0509	1848	0438	1916	0433	1932
26	0713	1712	0638	1748	0554	1818	0507	1849	0437	1917	0433	1932
27	0713	1713	0637	1750	0553	1819	0506	1850	0437	1918	0434	1932
28	0712	1715	0635	1751	0551	1820	0505	1851	0436	1919	0434	1932
29	0711	1716	0635	1752	0550	1821	0504	1852	0435	1919	0434	1932
30	0710	1717			0548	1822	0502	1853	0435	1920	0435	1932
31	0709	1718			0546	1823			0434	1921		

Sunrise, Sunset Times
Denver, Colorado

All times Mountain Standard Time. Add one hour for Daylight Savings Time.

Date	July Rise	July Set	Aug. Rise	Aug. Set	Sept. Rise	Sept. Set	Oct. Rise	Oct. Set	Nov. Rise	Nov. Set	Dec. Rise	Dec. Set
01	0435	1932	0458	1913	0528	1832	0556	1743	0628	1658	0702	1636
02	0436	1932	0459	1912	0528	1830	0557	1741	0629	1657	0703	1636
03	0436	1932	0500	1911	0529	1829	0558	1740	0631	1656	0704	1636
04	0437	1931	0501	1910	0530	1827	0559	1738	0632	1655	0705	1636
05	0437	1931	0502	1909	0531	1825	0600	1737	0633	1654	0706	1635
06	0438	1931	0503	1908	0532	1824	0601	1735	0634	1652	0706	1635
07	0439	1931	0504	1907	0533	1822	0602	1733	0635	1652	0707	1635
08	0439	1930	0505	1906	0534	1821	0603	1732	0636	1651	0708	1635
09	0440	1930	0506	1904	0535	1819	0604	1730	0637	1650	0709	1635
10	0441	1930	0507	1903	0536	1817	0605	1729	0639	1649	0710	1035
11	0441	1929	0508	1902	0537	1816	0606	1727	0640	1648	0711	1636
12	0442	1929	0509	1901	0538	1814	0607	1726	0641	1647	0712	1636
13	0443	1928	0510	1859	0539	1812	0608	1724	0642	1646	0712	1636
14	0443	1928	0511	1858	0540	1811	0609	1723	0643	1645	0713	1636
15	0444	1927	0512	1857	0541	1809	0610	1721	0644	1645	0714	1636
16	0445	1927	0513	1855	0542	1808	0611	1720	0645	1644	0714	1637
17	0446	1926	0513	1854	0542	1806	0612	1718	0647	1643	0715	1637
18	0446	1926	0514	1853	0543	1804	0613	1717	0648	1642	0716	1637
19	0447	1925	0515	1851	0544	1803	0614	1715	0649	1642	0716	1638
20	0448	1924	0516	1850	0545	1801	0615	1714	0650	1642	0716	1638
21	0449	1923	1517	1848	0546	1759	0615	1713	0651	1640	0717	1639
22	0450	1923	0518	1847	0547	1758	0617	1711	0652	1640	0718	1639
23	0451	1922	0519	1845	0548	1756	0618	1710	0653	1639	0719	1640
24	0451	1921	0520	1844	0549	1754	0619	1709	0654	1639	0719	1640
25	0452	1920	0521	1842	0550	1753	0620	1707	0655	1638	0719	1641
26	0453	1919	0522	1841	0551	1751	0622	1706	0656	1638	0720	1641
27	0454	1918	0523	1839	0552	1750	0623	1705	0658	1637	0720	1642
28	0455	1917	0524	1838	0553	1748	0624	1703	0659	1637	0720	1643
29	0456	1916	0525	1836	0554	1746	0625	1702	0700	1637	0721	1644
30	0457	1915	0526	1835	0555	1745	0626	1701	0701	1636	0721	1644
31	0458	1914	0527	1833			0627	1700			0721	1645

Sunrise / Sunset Variations
for Colorado cities relative to Denver. In minutes.

City	Dec. 20	March 20	June 20	Sept. 20
Aspen	+6 / +8	+8 / +8	+9 / +7	+8 / +8
Durango	+5 / +18	+12 / +12	+19 / +5	+12 / +12
Grand Junction	+14 / +16	+15 / +15	+16 / +14	+15 / +15
Lamar	-13 / -5	-9 / -9	-4 / -13	-9 / -9
Sterling	-3 / -9	-6 / -6	-9 / -3	-6 / -6

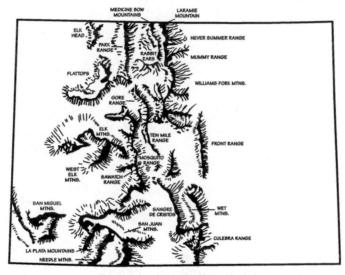

Figure 1.1 – Colorado Mountain Ranges

Mountain Ranges

Culebra Range
Elk Mountains
· West Elk Range
· Ruby Range
· Anthracite Range
· Williams Mts.
Elkhead Mountains
· Yampa
Flattops
Front Range
· Vasquez Mountains
· Tarryall Range
· Platte River Mountains
· Indian Peaks
· Rampart Range

· Kenosha Range
· Laramie Mountains
· Chicago Mountains
Gore Range
Mosquito Range
Mummy Range
Never Summer Range
Park Range
Rabbit Ears Range
Rawahs
Sangre de Cristo Range
· Sierra Blanca Range
San Juans
· La Garita Mountains
· La Plata Mountains

· Sneffels Range
· Needle Mountains
· Grenadiers
· Pico Mountains
· West Needle Mnts.
· Piedra Mountains
San Miguel Range
Sawatch Range
· New York Mountains
· Collegiate Peaks
Spanish Peaks
Wet Mountains
Williams Fork Mountains

Summits 14,000 feet or higher

There are many lists of Colorado 14ers. At issue is not in the height of the points, but in what constitutes a separate peak. A separate peak is defined by the drop of the saddle between the two high points, and the distance between the two high points. The generally accepted definition was first proposed in 1968 by William Graves in *Trail and Timberline* magazine, the official publication of the Colorado Mountain Club. To be considered a separate summit under the Graves proposal, a high point must rise at least 300 feet above any saddle connecting it to other peaks. His proposal has been generally adopted, but never formally adopted by any group. Let the academic debate rage as the mountains smirk.

Following is the USGS list of 54 recognized 14ers. Two of the peaks, El Diente and North Maroon Peak may or may not belong on the list, if one is to adhere strictly to the 300-foot saddle rule. Following the list of 14ers is a list of seven points higher than 14,000 feet that, like El Diente and North Maroon, don't qualify under the 300-foot rule. If El Diente and North Maroon made it on the official list, these points deserve at least separate mention. The seven auxiliary high points and saddle/distance data were compiled by Walter Borneman and Lyndon Lampert in their book, *A Climbing Guide to Colorado's 14ers.*

Rank	Peak Name	Feet	Meters	USGS 7.5 map
1	Mount Elbert	14,433	4,399	Mt Elbert
2	Mount Massive	14,421	4,395	Mt. Massive
3	Mount Harvard	14,420	4,395	Mt. Harvard
4	Blanca Peak	14,345	4,372	Blanca Peak
5	La Plata Peak	14,336	4,369	Mt. Elbert
6	Uncompahgre	14,309	4,361	Uncompahgre
7	Crestone Peak	14,294	4,357	Crestone Peak
8	Mount Lincoln	14,286	4,354	Alma
9	Grays Peak	14,270	4,349	Grays Peak
10	Mount Antero	14,269	4,349	Mt. Antero
11	Torreys Peak	14,267	4,348	Grays Peak
12	Castle Peak	14,265	4,348	Hayden Peak
13	Quandry Peak	14,265	4,348	Breckenridge
14	Mount Evans	14,264	4,347	Mt. Evans
15	Longs Peak	14,255	4,345	Longs Peak
16	Mount Wilson	14,246	4,342	Mt. Wilson
17	Mount Shavano	14,229	4,337	Maysville
18	Mount Princeton	14,197	4,327	Mt. Antero
19	Crestone Needle	14,197	4,327	Crestone Peak
20	Mount Belford	14,196	4,327	Mt. Harvard
21	Mount Yale	14,196	4,327	Mt. Yale

Summits 14,000 feet or higher *continued*

Rank	Peak Name	Feet	Meters	USGS 7.5 map
22	Mount Bross	14,172	4,319	Alma
23	Kit Carson Peak	14,165	4,317	Crestone Peak
24	El Diente Peak	14,159	4,315	Dolores Peak
25	Maroon Peak	14,156	4,315	Maroon Bells
26	Tabeguache Mtn	14,155	4,314	St. Elmo
27	Mount Oxford	14,153	4,314	Mt. Harvard
28	Mount Sneffels	14,150	4,313	Mt. Sneffels
29	Mount Democrat	14,148	4,312	Climax
30	Capitol Peak	14,130	4,307	Capitol Peak
31	Pikes Peak	14,110	4,300	Pike Peak
32	Snowmass Mountain	14,092	4,295	Snowmass Mtn.
33	Mount Eolus	14,083	4,292	Columbine Pass
34	Windom Peak	14,082	4,292	Columbine Pass
35	Mount Columbia	14,073	4,289	Mt. Harvard
36	Missouri Mountain	14,067	4,289	Winfield
37	Humbolt Peak	14,064	4,286	Crestone Peak
38	Mount Bierstadt	14,060	4,285	Mt. Evans
39	Sunlight Peak	14,059	4,285	Storm King Peak
40	Handies Peak	14,048	4,282	Handies Peak
41	Culebra Peak	14,047	4,281	Culebra Peak
42	Mount Lindsey	14,042	4,280	Blanca Peak
43	Ellingwood Peak	14,042	4,280	Blanca Peak
44	Little Bear Peak	14,037	4,278	Blanca Peak
45	Mount Sherman	14,036	4,278	Mt. Sherman
46	Redcloud Peak	14,034	4,277	Redcloud Peak
47	Pyramid Peak	14,018	4,272	Maroon Bells
48	Wilson Peak	14,017	4,272	Mt. Wilson
49	Wetterhorn Peak	14,015	4,272	Wetterhorn Peak
50	North Maroon Peak	14,014	4,271	Maroon Bells
51	San Luis Peak	14,014	4,271	San Luis Peak
52	Mt. of the Holy Cross	14,005	4,269	Mt. of Holy Cross
53	Huron Peak	14,003	4,268	Winfield
54	Sunshine Peak	14,001	4,267	Redcloud Peak

Other points 14,000 feet and higher

Peak Name	Altitude (ft./m)	Main Peak	Drop to Saddle	Distance
North Massive	14,320 / 4,365	Mt. Massive	259 / 79	.8 miles
Cameron	14,238 / 4,340	Mt Lincoln	138 / 42	.5 miles
South Massive	14,132 / 4,307	Mt. Massive	232 / 71	.7 miles
Challenger Pointe	14,081 / 4,292	Kit Carson Peak	301 / 92	.2 miles
North Eolus	14,039 / 4,279	Mt. Eolus	179 / 55	.25 miles
Conundrum	14,022 / 4,274	Castle Peak	240 / 73	.4 miles
North Maroon	14,014 / 4,271	Maroon	234 / 71	.4 miles

What's in a name?

Many of Colorado's place names are duplicated in other areas of the state. It is easy to see that Colorado's pioneers named geographical features for what they found. Thus, major themes develop and place names are repeated over and over across the state. Below are place names followed by the number of times they occur in Colorado, as counted by William Bright in his book, *Colorado Place Names*.

Apache Creek 4	Cottonwood Creek . .28	Horseshoe Creek 3
Alkali Creek 7	Cottonwood Gulch . .13	Horseshoe Mountain . .3
Antelope Creek 14	Cow Creek 12	Mosquito Creek 6
Bald Mountain 15	Cow Canyon 6	Oak Creek 7
Battle Mountain 3	Cow Gulch 4	Owl Creek 5
Bear Creek 30	Cow Lake 2	Pine Creek 13
Bear Gulch 16	Coyote Creek 5	Ptarmigan Peak 3
Bear Canyon 11	Crystal Creek 10	Rabbit Creek 3
Bear Lake 8	Crystal Peak 4	Rainbow Lake 16
Bear Mountain 11	Deadman Creek 6	Rainbow Creek 2
Bear Peak 2	Deadman Gulch 14	Rattlesnake Creek . . .3
Beaver Creek 27	Deer Creek 19	Red Creek 8
Beaver Lakes 10	Dear Mountain 5	Red Hill 8
Beaver Mountain 4	Echo Canyon 7	Red Mountain 14
Black Canyon 9	Elk Creek 18	Red Rocks 20
Black Lakes 7	Elk Mountain 7	Rock Creek 22
Black Mountain 17	Elkhorn Creek 2	Round Mountain 11
Brush Creek 16	Elkhorn Gulch 4	Sand Creek 23
Buck Creek 9	Emerald Lake 6	Sheep Creek 15
Buck Mountain 5	Fall Creek 13	Sheep Mountain 19
Buffalo Creek 8	Flattop Mountain 6	Silver Creek 18
Buffalo Mountain 2	Flatiron Mountain 3	Silver Mountain 6
Buffalo Peak 2	Fox Creek 5	Skull Creek 3
Bull Creek 6	French Creek 6	Skunk Creek 7
Bull Gulch 8	Gold Creek 4	Spring Creek 33
Bull Mountain 3	Green Mountain 15	Sugarloaf Mountain .11
Cache Creek 3	Grizzly Gulch 7	Sugarloaf Peak 6
Castle Rock 15	Grizzly Creek 3	Tenderfoot Mountain . .9
Cherry Creek 12	Grizzly Lake 4	Texas Creek 7
Chimney Rock 8	Grizzly Peak 5	Twin Lakes 11
Clear Creek 14	Groundhog Creek 3	Twin Peaks 7
Coal Creek 18	Horse Creek 18	West Creek 6
Coal Mountain 3	Horse Gulch 8	Willow Creek 35
Columbine Creek 3	Horse Mountain 6	Wolf Creek 12
Copper Mountain 5	Horseshoe Lake 5	

13

How to name a mountain

Many of Colorado's peaks are un-named. For information on naming an un-named point:

United States Board on Geographic Names

Manager, GNIS   **Phone:** 703-648-4544

U.S. Geological Survey   **Fax:** 703-648-4165

523 National Center   **e-mail:** gnis_manager@usgs.gov

Reston, VA 20192-0523

http://mapping.usgs.gov/www/gnis/pppdgn.html

Meteorites

84 meteorites are known to have fallen to earth in Colorado. The latest, somewhere near Cochepeta Pass, entered the atmosphere and broke into small pieces before hitting ground August 17, 2001. A search for pieces was not initiated, but Museum of Science and History officials in Denver hope hikers or ranchers eventually will find pieces for study.

2 Land Use, Land Management

Total Area: 104,247 miles²   270,000 km²   66,485,760 acres

Federal ownership: 37,866 miles²   98,073 km²   24,233,955 acres

Portion of state owned by federal government: 36%.

Federal Land managed by:

	Acres	% of State Total
U.S. Forest Service:	14,508,108	21.8%
Bureau of Land Management:	8,364,945	12.6%
U.S. Park Service:	712,248	1.0%
Fish & Wildlife Service:	72,486	0.11%
U.S. Military:	477,457	0.72%

Managed by federal agencies for conservation: 5,792,946 acres, which represents 24.7% of all federal lands and 8.71% of all land in Colorado.

Land held in trust for Indian Tribes: 1,076,890 acres.

Non-federal land:

	Acres
Total Non-Federal:	42,261,805
Developed:	1,694,000
Crops:	8,940,000
Pasture:	1,256,000
Range:	23,537,000
Forest:	3,755,000
Minor cover:	3,059,000

Colorado State Trust Lands: 3.2 million acres of State Trust Lands were given to the state by the federal government to be held in trust to generate revenue for state schools and education.

Number of Colorado State Parks: 41
Total land acres of Colorado State Parks: 172,089
Total water acres of Colorado State Parks: 46,845
Total area managed by Colorado State Parks: 218,934

Bureau of Land Management in Colorado
Source: BLM Colorado, October 2002

8,364,945 acres, 12.6% of state total.
27.3 million subsurface acres under management.
50 developed recreation sites.
346,000 acres recommened for wilderness designation.
52,000 acres designated as wilderness.
2.6 million acres of woodlands.
600 wildlife species.
7.9 million acres of small-game habitat.
7 million acres of big-game habitat.
39,000 acres of waterfowl habitat.
50,000 acres of riparian habitat.
1,500 miles of fishable streams.
4 wild horse herd management areas.
7.7 million acres grazed by livestock.
6 Colorado Scenic and Historical byways.
97,000 acres of alpine habitat.

Colorado BLM receipts by source, 1999

Mineral leases and permits:	$5,687,142
Timber sales:	$46,645
Sale of land and materials:	$408,695
Grazing leases, licenses, permits:	$650,576
Fees and commissions:	$71,295
Rights-of-way rents:	$290,522
Rent of land:	$33,330
Recreation fees:	$392,709
Other sources	$69,933
Total:	**$7,650,847**

Estimated Recreational use of BLM land
Source: BLM Recreation Management Information System Report #22

Visitor Use	# of participants (Thousands)	Hours (Thousands)	Days (Thousands)
Camping	11,424	355,728	29,644
Driving for pleasure	19,895	77,516	6,460
Educational Opp.	20,115	51,516	4,305
Fishing and Hunting	11,951	93,225	7,769
Other	616	692	58
Picnicking	4,759	9,928	827
Specialized Sports	1,248	7,759	647
Trail Activities	23,226	131,497	10,958
Water Sports	11,313	52,366	4,364
Winter Sports	1,499	7,496	625
Total Recreational Visits:	**62,154,497**		

United States Forest Service land in Colorado
Source: United States Forest Service

Unit	Headquarters	Acres
Arapaho National Forest	Fort Collins	1,027,659
Grand Mesa National Forest	Delta	346,543
Gunnison National Forest	Delta	1,665,485
Manti-La Sal National Forest	Price, UT	27,105
Pike National Forest	Pueblo	1,110,443
Rio Grande National Forest	Monte Vista	1,859,444
Roosevelt National Forest	Fort Collins	810,931
Routt National Forest	Steamboat Springs	1,125,568
San Isabel National Forest	Pueblo	1,117,878
San Juan National Forest	Durango	1,877,650
Uncompahgre National Forest	Delta	944,867
White River National Forest	Glenwood Springs	1,966,155
National Forest Total		**13,879,728**
Comanche National Grasslands	Pueblo	435,320
Pawnee National Grasslands	Fort Collins	193,060
National Grass Lands Total		**628,380**
USFS Colorado Total		**14,508,108***

21.76% of total Colorado land area

*Another 1,543,758 acres are within National Forest or National Grassland boundaries but are not owned by the Forest Service.

Colorado Wilderness Areas

Managed by U.S. Forest Service and Bureau of Land Management. Does not include National Parks, Monuments or Historical Sites managed by the U.S. Park Service. See Chapter 7 for details on National Parks, Monuments and Historical Sites. Another 513,904 acres of designated wilderness area lies within National Park boundaries.

Name	Acres
Black Ridge Canyons	75,500*
Buffalo Peaks	43,410
Byers Creek	8,095
Cache la Poudre	9,238
Collegiate Peaks	167,994
Comanche Peak	66,791
Eagles Nest	133,688
Flat Tops	235,035
Fossil Ridge	33,060
Greenhorn Mountains	22,040
Gunnison Gorge	17,700**
Holy Cross	121,883
Hunter-Frying Pan	82,729
Indian Peaks	73,391
La Garita	129,626
Lizard Head	41,496
Lost Creek	120,700
Maroon Bells-Snowmass	180,962
Mount Evans	74,401
Mount Massive	30,540
Mount Sneffels	16,505
Mount Zirkel	160,568
Neota	9,924
Never Summer	20,692
Platte River	743***
Powderhorn	60,100
Ptarmigan Peak	13,175
Raggeds	65,019
Rawah	73,899
Sangre de Cristo	226,455
Sarvis Creek	47,140
South San Juan	158,790
Uncompahgre	102,668
Vasquez Peak	12,300
Weminuche	492,418
West Elk	176,092
TOTAL	**3,304,767**

* Included in the 122,300-acre Colorado Canyons National Conservation Area.

** Included in the 57,725-acre Gunnison Gorge National Conservation Area.

*** Wyoming is home to 22,749 acres of the Platte River Wilderness; Colorado has only 743 acres.

Wilderness Study or Conservation Areas

Name	Acres	Status
Black Ridge Canyons	70,249	Study Area
Bull Canyon	13,187	Study Area
Colorado Canyons National Conservation Area	122,300*	
Diamond Breaks	32,680	Study Area
Dolores River Canyon	29,415	Study Area
Gunnison Gorge Conservation Area	63,425**	
Irish Canyon	11,680	Critical Environment Concern
Piedra	62,550	
Roubideau	19,650	
Spanish Peaks	18,540	
Tabeguache	17,240	
Total	**460,916**	

* Includes 75,500-acre Black Ridge Canyon Wilderness
** Includes 17,700-acres Gunnison Gorge Wilderness

Designated Wilderness within National Parks: 513,904 acres

National Park Service National Parks

Name	Gross Acres	2003 Budget	2002 Visits
Black Canyon of the Gunnison	32,770	$1,026,000	174,346
Great Sand Dunes Park and Preserve	83,958	$1,455,000	235,535
Mesa Verde	52,122	$4,806,000	411,399
Rocky Mountain	265,723	$10,082,000	3,005,524
TOTALS	**434,573**	**$17,369,000**	**3,826,804**

National Park Service National Monuments

Colorado	20,534	$954,000	292,750
Dinosaur	210,278	$2,780,000	299,622
Florissant Fossil Beds	5,998	$630,000	63,944
Hovenweep	785	$280,000	32,817
Yucca House	34	$100,000	unknown
TOTALS	**237,629**	**$4,744,000**	**689,133**

National Park Service National Recreation Area

Curecanti	41,972	$2,971,000	892,408

National Park Service National Historic Site

Bent's Old Fort	799	$1,000,000	29,709
NPS GRAND TOTALS	**714,973**	**$26,084,000**	**5,438,054**

19

Colorado State Parks

	Campsites	Picnic Sites	Boat Ramps	Trails (miles)	Annual Visits	Total Acres
Arkansas Headwaters	100	100	0	0	692,182	5,804
Barbour Ponds	60	15	0	0.5	124,416	123
Barr Lake	0	32	1	9.0	82,092	3,773
Boyd Lake	148	90	2	2.5	544,140	2,085
Castlewood Canyon	0	55	0	11.0	172,498	1,950
Chatfield	163	139	3	18.0	959,763	5,318
Cherry Creek	102	106	2	9.0	1,156,163	4,198
Colorado River	80	94	2	9.0	412,888	745
Crawford	0	40	2	1.5	110,821	734
Eldorado Canyon	0	42	0	12.0	218,628	1,320
Eleven Mile	358	20	3	1.5	220,675	7,480
Golden Gate Canyon	168	125	0	35.0	559,210	14,363
Harvey Gap	0	30	1	0	34,301	320
Highline Lake	25	64	2	3.0	238,304	670
Jackson Lake	262	60	1	0.5	237,144	3,055
Lake Pueblo	401	348	2	18.0	1,161,422	13,610
Lathrop	98	40	3	2.0	127,136	1,594
Lory	6	17	0	25.0	89,344	2,419
Mancos	33	12	1	5.0	37,378	550
Mueller	132	41	0	80.0	157,959	12,103
Navajo	71	6	1	1.0	209,748	5,045
North Sterling	141	38	3	5.5	230,407	5,646
Paonia	15	3	1	0	16,879	1,857
Pearl Lake	38	7	1	0	42,023	272
Picnic Rock	0	20	0	0	49,751	13
Ridgway	283	87	1	17.0	255,857	3,200
Rifle Gap	47	14	1	0	147,524	1,970
Rifle Falls	20	11	0	2.0	63,298	48
Roxborough	0	0	0	12.0	85,792	3,305
San Luis	51	27	1	4.0	22,184	817
Spinney Mountain	0	20	2	0	41,712	6,080
Stagecoach	92	50	2	5.0	184,052	1,646
State Forest	152	7	2	50.0	196,117	70,838
Staunton	0	0	0	0	not reported	3,535
Sweltzer Lake	0	32	1	0.5	37,869	210
Steamboat Lake	198	26	3	1.0	301,180	2,636
Sylvan lake	46	15	1	1.0	40,562	1,428
Trinidad Lake	62	46	1	10.0	174,319	2,522
Vega	0	25	3	2.0	85,591	1,798
Yampa River Legacy	110	47	0	10.8	36,450	437
Totals	3,652	5,049	54	364	9,659,892	202,417

New Parks

	Total Acres
Lone Mesa	11,679
Brush Creek	1,273
Elk Falls/Davis Ranch	1,885
Cheyenne Mountain	1,680

Source: Colorado State Parks Horizons 2000 Report

CHAPTER

3 Water

One-half of 1% of Colorado is covered with water. It is the state's most precious commodity, and most of it is on its way out, flowing ever downhill. As the Highest State, Colorado is the Headwaters State.

Only three rivers, the Green, Little Snake and Cimarron, flow in to Colorado, and that for only short distances. Discounting the short stints of the Green, Little Snake and Cimarron, Colorado receives not one drop of water from another state. Every raindrop, every snowflake that falls on the state is collected in one of our 94 watersheds and sent to the Pacific or the Atlantic Oceans via one of 10 major river drainages.

If only it were that simple.

The people have settled where the water isn't. Colorado's Western Slope, the area west of the Continental Divide, accounts for three-quarters of the state's precipitation, but only two-fifths of the state's land area, and one-fifth of the population. East of the Continental Divide, the arid Front Range, is home to nearly 80% of the state's population, but only 25% of the water.

The answer has been to move it and store it. More than 40 diversion projects move water from one drainage to another – 24 move water across the Continental Divide west to east. Nearly 2,000 reservoirs collect what they can – about 8.9 million acre-feet.

In all, approximately 10 million acre-feet of water leaves the state annually via the 10 major drainages. Approximately 8.5 million acre-feet are promised to downstream users via one of 18 interstate water compacts. Even with 1,900 reservoirs, roughly 1.5 million acre-feet of water belonging to Colorado is not captured and flows to other states – a fact some use to argue for more water projects.

87% of the water leaving Colorado does so via the Colorado River and its tributaries. Seven states and Mexico share the cherished moisture. On the Front Range, only ambitious water projects make farming practical and large cities possible.

Flow of Colorado Rivers at State Line

19 major rivers leave Colorado with an annual average of 10,434,830 acre-feet of water. 87%, or 9,097,470 acre-feet, flow west, eventually to the Colorado River and the Pacific Ocean. Only 1,337,360 acre-feet escape to make it to the Gulf of Mexico – 25% of that in the Rio Grande, the rest in the Platte and Arkansas River systems.

Most of Colorado's water is stored in the form of snow. While reservoirs today mitigate raging spring floods, it is estimated that 50% of the state's river volume runs in only two months of each year. About 4.5 million acre-feet are used annually to replenish the 1,900 reservoirs across the state. Agricultural irrigation uses a whopping 11 million acre-feet each year. Another 2 million acre-feet are used for municipalities, industrial uses and fisheries. Colorado residents use roughly one-half of the state's surface water, leaving the other half for downstream users. Approximately 29% of the water used by state residents is groundwater.

Eastward Flow: Historic Average Annual Stream Flows at State Line	
River	Flow (Acre-feet)
North Platte	313,600
Laramie	122,400
South Platte	387,100
North Fork Republican	33,080
South Fork Republican	13,980
Arkansas	142,200
Rio Grande	325,000
East Total	**1,337,360**

Westward Flow: Historic Average Annual Stream Flows at State Line	
River	Flow (Acre-feet)
Navajo	61,610
San Juan	469,900
Piedra	299,800
Los Pinos	175,700
Animas & Florida	712,600
La Plata	26,290
Mancos	37,950
McElmo	36,420
Dolores	568,100
Colorado	4,491,000
White	595,100
Yampa	1,623,000
West Total	**9,097,470**
Total Flow All Rivers at State Line	**10,434,830**

Source: Colorado State University, Colorado Water Knowledge

Major River and Stream Lengths
Source: Colorado State University, Colorado Water Knowledge

River	Drainage	Miles in Colo.	Km in Colo.	Total Miles	Total Km
Alamosa	Rio Grande	45	72	45	72
Animas	Colorado	85	137	110	177
Apishapa	Arkansas	100	161	100	161
Arikaree	Republican	120	193	129	208
Arkansas	Arkansas	315	507	1450	2333
Big Thompson	South Platte	65	105	65	105
Blue	Colorado	65	105	65	105
Cache La Poudre	South Platte	75	121	75	121
Canadian	North Platte	32	51	32	51
Canadian	Arkansas	1	2	768	1236
Cimarron	Colorado	28	45	28	45
Cimarron	Arkansas	45	72	538	866
Colorado	Colorado	225	362	1440	2317
Conejos	Rio Grande	100	161	100	161
Crystal	Colorado	45	72	45	72
Cuchara	Arkansas	58	93	58	93
Dolores	Colorado	180	290	230	370*
Eagle	Colorado	70	113	70	113
East	Colorado	40	64	40	64
Elk	Colorado	40	64	40	64
Elkhead	Colorado	37	60	37	60
Encampment	North Platte	15	24	35	56
Fall (Big Thompson)	South Platte	13	21	13	21
Fall (Clear Creek)	South Platte	15	24	15	24
Florida	Colorado	52	84	52	84
Fraser	Colorado	53	85	53	85
Frenchman	Republican	55	89	130	209
Fryingpan	Colorado	40	64	40	64
Green	Colorado	39	63	741	1192
Greenhorn	Arkansas	34	55	34	55
Gunnison	Colorado	140	225	140	225
Hidden	South Platte	10	16	10	16

* Various river guide books gauge the length of the Dolores River from the Colorado-Utah state line to its confluence with the Colorado River as 22 miles, not 50 as indicated in this report.

Major River and Stream Lengths *continued*

River	Drainage	Miles in Colo.	Km in Colo.	Total Miles	Total Km
Huerfano	Arkansas	.90	.145	.90	.145
Illinois	North Platte	.25	.40	.25	.40
La Plata	Colorado	.40	.64	.65	.105
Laramie	North Platte	.40	.64	.183	.294
Little Cimarron	Colorado	.25	.40	.25	.40
Little Dolores	Colorado	.25	.40	.35	.56
Little Navajo	Colorado	.16	.26	.16	.26
Little Snake	Colorado	.120	.193	.135	.217
Little Thompson	South Platte	.32	.51	.32	.51
Los Pinos	Colorado	.65	.105	.70	.113
Mancos	Colorado	.75	.121	.80	.129
Michigan	North Platte	.21	.34	.21	.34
Navajo	Colorado	.27	.43	.45	.72
North Platte	North Platte	.25	.40	.618	.995
Piedra	Colorado	.60	.97	.60	.97
Piney	Colorado	.26	.42	.26	.42
Purgatoire	Arkansas	.157	.253	.157	.253
Republican	Republican	.100	.161	.420	.676
Rio Blanco	Colorado	.32	.51	.32	.51
Rio Chama	Rio Grande	.11	.18	.95	.153
Rio Chamita	Rio Grande	.4	.6	.15	.24
Rio de Los Pinos	Rio Grande	.18	.29	.37	.60
Rio Grande	Rio Grande	.180	.290	.1887	.3037
Rio San Antonio	Rio Grande	.25	.40	.40	.64
Roaring	South Platte	.10	.16	.10	.16
Roaring Fork	Colorado	.57	.92	.57	.92
St. Charles	Arkansas	.45	.72	.45	.72
St. Vrain	South Platte	.48	.77	.48	.77
Saguache	Rio Grande	.72	.116	.72	.116
San Juan	Colorado	.86	.138	.366	.589
San Miguel	Colorado	.83	.134	.83	.134
Slate	Colorado	.20	.32	.20	.32

Major River and Stream Lengths *continued*

River	Drainage	Miles in Colo.	Km in Colo.	Total Miles	Total Km
Smoky Hill	Republican	94	151	550	885
Snake	Colorado	20	32	20	32
South	Rio Grande	11	18	11	18
South Platte	South Platte	360	579	450	724
Swan	Colorado	21	34	21	34
Taylor	Colorado	42	68	42	68
Uncompahgre	Colorado	63	101	63	404
Vermejo	Arkansas	10	16	60	97
West Dolores	Colorado	30	48	30	48
White	Colorado	110	177	183	294
Wind	South Platte	15	24	15	24
Williams Fork	Colorado	45	72	45	72
Williams Fork (Yampa)	Colorado	40	64	40	64
Yampa	Colorado	175	282	175	282

The acre-foot

An acre-foot is the amount of water it takes to cover one acre of land with one foot of water, or:
- 325,851 gallons.
- Enough water to flood the infield at Coors Field to a depth of 5.4 feet.
- A year's supply of water for one or two households.

Cubic feet per second

Moving water is measured in cubic feet per second, or:
- 7.5 gallons per second passing a fixed point.
- 450 gallons a minute passing a fixed point.
- A flow of 100 cubic feet/second will fill an acre-foot in 8 minutes.

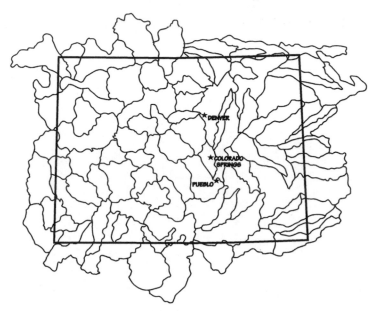

Figure 3.1 – Colorado Watersheds

Watersheds

A watershed can be defined as an area of land that drains water to a single point. They come in all shapes and sizes from a few acres to millions of square miles. Just as creeks drain into rivers, a watershed is almost always part of a larger watershed. Conversely, almost every watershed is comprised of smaller watersheds.

The USGS uses a national system based on surface hydrologic features to divide the country into 21 regions, 222 subregions, 352 accounting units, and 2,262 cataloguing units. Of the 2,262 cataloguing units, 94 are wholly or partially in Colorado.

Watershed boundaries ignore politcal boundaries. They are critical in studying, controlling and monitoring water quality – a basic building block to human and environmental health. The Environmental Protection Agency has adopted a "watershed approach" strategy for protecting and restoring aquatic ecosystems. Watersheds in italics in the following list include portions of neighboring states.

To learn more about your watershed, or find which watershed you live in, visit the Environmental Protection Agency's *Surf Your Watershed* Website at www.epa.gov/surf3/.

Colorado Watersheds

Source: U.S. Environmental Protection Agency

Watershed Name	Lakes	Lake acres	Rivers / Streams	Perennial River Miles	Total River Miles
Alamosa-Trinchera	.98	.4,240.0	.13	.881.6	.2,330.4
Animas	.96	.2,680.4	.24	.744.1	.1,323.9
Apishapa	.4	.37.4	.4	.32.6	.1,006.3
Arikaree	n/a	n/a	.5	.79.6	.1,233.4
Arkansas H.waters	.137	.5,955.6	.28	.1,538.3	.3,640.0
Bear	.29	.397.4	.12	.89.8	.985.7
Beaver	.8	.47.8	.7	.29.7	.1,412.6
Big Sandy	.20	.283.0	.4	.55.7	.1,409.7
Big Thompson	.173	.7,212.3	.11	.530.9	.974.1
Bijou	.22	.266.4	.14	.181.7	.1,346.6
Blue	.79	.6,357.6	.10	.564.2	.822.6
Cache La Poudre	.270	.14,189.1	.22	.877.7	.2,827.2
Canadian H.waters	.35	.2,913.1	.7	.250.8	.1,309.3
Chico	.17	.131.5	.4	.10.1	.665.2
Cimarron Headwaters	.3	.16.3	.5	.104.6	.966.1
Clear	.137	.2,066.8	.14	.364.2	.546.3
Colorado H.waters	.249	.14,377.3	.31	.2,113.8	.3,690.8
Colorado Headwaters-Plateau	.145	.3,386.7	.51	.1,077.7	.3,732.9
Crow	.47	.1,308.9	.15	.155.3	.960.9
Eagle	.64	.1,177.4	.13	.570.6	.1,084.0
East Taylor	.57	.2,526.8	.9	.543.4	.748.6
Fountain	.82	.2,594.8	.6	.298.1	.1,306.1
Frenchman	.25	.1,952.7	.7	.143.6	.1,023.6
Horse	.16	.3,389.2	.6	.134.3	.983.5
Huerfano	.43	.1,824.2	.8	.506.6	.1,841.5
Kiowa	.7	.97.4	.9	.29.9	.574.9
Ladder	.3	.89.4	.5	.26.2	.1,046.1
Little Beaver	.10	.95.1	.4	.45.0	.467.2
Little Snake	.35	.348.8	.29	.689.8	.3,518.0
Lone Tree-Owl	.25	.378.7	.8	.88.2	.581.3
Lower Dolores	.7	.79.7	.11	.324.4	.1,017.2
L. Green-Diamond	.63	.1,788.1	.11	.281.7	.2,080.7

Colorado Watersheds *continued*

Watershed Name	Lakes	Lake acres	Rivers / Streams	Perennial River Miles	Total River Miles
Lower Gunnison	74	1,396.1	20	757.4	2,130.1
Lower Lodgepole	18	394.4	5	170.1	1,363.3
Lower San Juan-Four Corners	24	165.3	12	214.2	1,249.8
Lower South Platte	89	3,892.8	5	286.5	1,361.8
Lower White	18	78.0	25	386.4	4,563.6
Lower Yampa	7	105.3	14	297.0	2,153.1
Mancos	18	700.9	15	216.3	1,010.3
McElmo	27	1,385.5	11	162.9	799.5
Middle Arkansas-Lake Mckinney	49	1,232.4	4	185.2	1,321.8
Middle San Juan	98	1,996.6	21	318.3	2,348.8
Middle South Platte-Cherry Creek	344	18,030.2	42	314.4	2,655.1
Middle South Platte-Sterling	109	5,507.5	7	495.8	2,840.4
Montezuma	9	116.0	15	71.8	952.0
North Fork Cimarron	6	74.5	2	22.2	409.2
North Fork Gunnison	26	690.0	13	475.6	1,033.3
N. Fork Republican	22	198.5	8	178.0	1,523.8
N. Fork Smoky Hill	13	150.9	2	20.3	804.9
N. Platte Headwaters	152	4,427.5	35	1,016.0	2,443.0
Parachute-Roan	0	0.0	14	336.4	769.3
Pawnee	5	87.5	10	45.8	634.0
Piceance-Yellow	6	30.3	20	232.6	1,217.3
Piedra	23	1,212.8	10	335.3	528.3
Purgatoire	23	2,094.5	29	448.6	3,198.1
Rio Chama	94	19,221.3	20	890.1	3,389.6
Rio Grande H.waters	76	2,356.8	22	868.8	1,097.1
Roaring Fork	95	2,627.2	17	813.7	1,274.3
Rush	4	27.6	5	106.7	697.2
Saguache	27	585.9	13	470.0	1,146.0
San Luis	54	513.9	5	418.7	1,365.0

Colorado Watersheds *continued*

Watershed Name	Lakes	Lake acres	Rivers / Streams	Perennial River Miles	Total River Miles
San Miguel	39	1,221.9	18	554.9	1,723.2
Sand Arroyo	3	36.8	3	17.5	454.2
Sidney Draw	1	3.8	2	15.0	547.7
Smoky Hill H.waters	7	49.1	6	72.6	1,256.6
South Fork Beaver	20	137.4	5	53.7	719.8
S. Fork Republican	33	4,543.8	15	138.8	2,482.0
S. Platte Headwaters	38	6,284.8	20	643.5	1,563.1
Saint Vrain	281	8,787.2	14	572.3	1,248.9
Stinking Water	5	74.7	4	112.7	713.2
Tomichi	23	313.5	13	604.8	964.9
Two Butte	4	2,010.5	6	34.3	623.2
Uncompahgre	21	401.8	12	531.6	1,212.3
Upper Arkansas	67	3,670.9	18	634.8	2,976.4
Upper Arkansas-John Martin	61	11,303.3	9	828.6	2,408.5
Upper Arkansas-Lake Meredith	32	7,653.3	10	193.6	1,480.4
Upper Cimarron	7	289.9	3	213.2	1,583.3
Upper Colorado-Kane Springs	51	942.4	13	444.3	2,135.7
Upper Dolores	43	1,702.6	24	684.6	2,218.5
Upper Green-Flaming Gorge Res.	138	40,010.9	20	1,175.1	3,034.7
Upper Gunnison	59	11,808.6	35	1,386.3	2,131.4
Upper Laramie	184	10,730.1	22	899.9	2,616.8
Upper Lodgepole	13	91.2	4	157.9	1,056.5
Upper North Platte	128	4,245.9	36	1,617.0	3,190.5
Upper Republican	28	258.7	17	223.0	2,532.9
Upper Rio Grande	41	1,051.5	21	860.1	3,253.4
Upper San Juan	151	21,064.0	25	1,062.9	3,368.0
Upper South Platte	119	7,513.1	40	1,045.3	1,696.6
Upper White	123	1,759.6	24	519.1	1,825.3
Upper Yampa	184	3,863.8	27	1,443.5	3,493.7

Colorado Watersheds *continued*

Watershed Name	Lakes	Lake acres	Rivers / Streams	Perennial River Miles	Total River Miles
Vermilion	3	118.8	8	138.7	1,196.6
Westwater Canyon	24	384.7	11	212.9	1,599.9
Whitewoman	5	23.2	2	12.8	557.6
Totals / Avg.	**5,447**	**303,839**	**1,313**	**41,012**	**151,045**

Major River Basins

Watersheds roll up into river basins. It is a matter of definition as to counting watersheds, drainages and basins. We already have identified 10 major river drainages in the state, but also identified 19 rivers that flow past state boundaries. All the rivers already mentioned will roll in to Colorado State University's definition of 4 major river basins: Missouri, Arkansas, Rio Grande and Colorado.

In Colorado, the Missouri basin is comprised of three sub-basins: North Platte, South Platte and Republican River basins.

Colorado River Basin Source: Colorado State University, Colorado Water Knowledge
Area: 22,200 square miles (57,498 km²).
Major Reservoirs: Lake Granby, Williams Fork, Green Mountain, Lake Dillon, Ruedi, Taylor Park, Blue Mesa, McPhee, Vallecito and Navajo.
Major Rivers: Gunnison, White, Yampa, Eagle, Animas, Dolores, San Juan, Roaring Fork, La Plata, Williams Fork, Blue, San Miguel.
Total Basin Inflow Native Water: 10,738,000 acre-feet.
Total Basin Outflow 1993: 9,097,000 acre-feet.
Export to other basins: 412,000 acre-feet.
Irrigation, reservoir and conveyance loss: 1,277,000 acre-feet.
Irrigated acres: 958,000.
Outflow as percent of Inflow: 85%.

Arkansas River Basin
Area: 24,904 square miles (64,501 km²).
Major Reservoirs: Pueblo, John Martin, Great Plains, Twin Lakes, Turquoise Lake.
Major Tributaries: Fountain, Purgatoire.

Total Basin Inflow Native Water: 875,000 acre-feet.
Imported Water: 101,000.
Total Basin Outflow 1993: 142,000 acre-feet.
Irrigation, reservoir and conveyance loss: 704,000 acre-feet.
Irrigated acres: 440,200.
Outflow as percent of Inflow: 14.5%.

Rio Grande River Basin

Area: 7,700 square miles (19,943 km²).
Major Reservoirs: Rio Grande, La Jara, Platoro, Continental, San Luis Lake.
Major Tributaries: Conejos, Alamosa.
Total Basin Inflow Native Water: 1,576,000 acre-feet.
Imported Water: 4,000.
Total Basin Outflow 1993: 325,000 acre-feet.
Irrigation, reservoir and conveyance loss: 617,000 acre-feet.
Irrigated acres: 452,700.
Outflow as percent of Inflow: 20%.

North Platte River Basin

Area: 1,431 square miles (3,706 km²).
Major Reservoirs: Walden, McFarlane, Lake John.
Major Tributaries: Canadian, Michigan, Illinois Rivers.
Total Basin Inflow Native Water: 600,000 acre-feet.
Total Basin Outflow 1993: 436,000 acre-feet.
Irrigation, reservoir and conveyance loss: 108,000 acre-feet.
Irrigated acres: 114,000.
Outflow as percent of Inflow: 73%.

South Platte River Basin

Area: 19,020 square miles (49,261 km²).
Major Reservoirs: Lake Granby, Grand Lake (Big Thompson Project), Carter Lake, Horsetooth, Chatfield, Cherry Creek, Barr Lake, Riverside, Empire, Sterling, Julesburg.
Major Tributaries: Poudre, Big Thompson, St. Vrain, Boulder Creek, Clear Creek,Cherry Creek.
Total Basin Inflow Native Water: 1,440,000 acre-feet.
Imported Water: 336,000 acre-feet.
Total Basin Outflow 1993: 387,000 acre-feet.
Irrigation, reservoir and conveyance loss: 1,251,000 acre-feet.
Irrigated acres: 730,700.
Outflow as percent of Inflow: 22%.

Republican River Basin

Total Basin Inflow Native Water: 353,000 acre-feet.
Total Basin Outflow 1993: 47,000 acre-feet.
Irrigation, reservoir and conveyance loss: 1,251,000 acre-feet.
Outflow as percent of Inflow: 13.3%.

31

Figure 3.2 – At 265 feet, Grand Lake is Colorado's deepest natural lake, a popular summer and winter resort and an important part of the Colorado–Big Thompson water project. (Photo courtesy Grand County Newspapers.)

Lakes

Colorado can boast 2,286 naturally occuring lakes. 89% of the lakes are above 9,000 feet, pools in the upper reaches of high mountain valleys. The total surface area of Colorado's lakes is a mere 20,333 acres The deepest lake is Grand Lake in Grand County at 265 feet. Grand Lake also serves as the headwaters for the Colorado River, and as an important link in the state's largest transbasin diversion project, the Colorado-Big Thompson.

Following are the number of lakes in the 10 major river drainages.

River Drainage	# of Lakes	Surface Area	Average
Yampa	104	775 acres	7.45 acres
North Platte	141	2,089 acres	14.82 acres
South Platte	297	2,254 acres	7.59 acres
Republican	0	0	0
Arkansas	219	1,354 acres	6.18 acres
Rio Grande	247	2,652 acres	10.73 acres
San Juan	220	1,994 acres	9.06 acres
Dolores	28	275 acres	9.82 acres
Colorado	805	6,843 acres	8.50 acres
White	121	1,322 acres	10.92 acres
Yampa	104	775 acres	7.45 acres

The San Luis Ditch: 1st Irrigation System, Oldest Water Right

Colorado's first irrigation system is the San Luis People's Ditch. It has been in continuous operation since 1852.

The ditch, at 8,000 feet, is fed by Culebra Creek. It travels four miles and irrigates 1,600 acres. When built, the land along the ditch was divided into strips roughly 100 yards wide and 16 to 20 miles long so settlers had access to irrigated land and timber. The District Court of Costilla County in 1890 awarded it "Priority 1" – the first recognized water right in Colorado.

Hot Springs

Along Colorado's tertiary lava flows and near fault zones are found a variety of natural hot springs. Temperatures range from lukewarm to 180 degrees F. The largest is Big Spring in Glenwood Springs, which has a maximum discharge of 2,200 gallons per minute. The hottest is Hortense Hot Springs in Chaffee County at 180 degrees F. Many of the springs are developed, some, as in Glenwood Springs and Ouray, famously so.

Water Storage – Reservoirs

With 1,900 reservoirs collecting and storing approximately 8.9 million acre feet of water, Colorado is ill prepared to withstand a prolonged drought. The recent drought and devastating dry year of 2002 made this point abundantly clear. The four-year drought reduced even mighty rivers to a trickle and left many reservoirs empty. Without reservoirs, Colorado can not support its cities or agriculture base.

With an estimated one-half of the state's water flowing during a two-month Spring runoff period, reservoirs are vitally important in capturing and holding the spring swell of water. The water is carefully measured, even as it sits as snow on the mountains. Colorado snow, fresh and uncompacted, is generally 90% to 95% trapped air. Still, it is the primary source of Colorado water and without reservoirs, much of our water would flow out of the state unused.

More than 90% of Colorado's water is used to irrigate crops. Less than 1% of the water treated by public water systems is used for drinking and cooking. Approximately 10% of water stored in reservoirs is lost to evaporation or conveyance loss.

Blue Mesa is the largest reservoir, Lake Granby is second. Of the 104 reservoirs exceeding 10,000 acre-feet of storage, 65 are dedicated to irrigation, 17 to municipal uses, six to hydro-electric power generation, eight to recreation, five to flood control and one each to domestic and industrial uses.

South Platte River Basin Reservoirs
Exceeding 10,000 acre-feet capacity

Reservoir	Capacity (acre-feet)	Owned by	Use
Antero	85,564	Denver Water	Mun
Aurora	51,680	City of Aurora	Mun
Barker Meadow	11,500	Public Service Company	Hyd
Barr Lake	32,100	Farmers Reservoir and Irrig. Co.	Irr
Bear Creek	55,290	U.S. Army Corps of Engineers	Fld
Bonny	348,390	U.S. Bureau of Reclamation	Rec
Boulder	13,300	City of Boulder	Mun
Boyd Lake	52,438	Greeley-Loveland Irrigation Co.	Dom
Button Rock	16,080	City of Longmont	Mun
Cache La Poudre	10,070	Cache La Poudre Reservoir Co.	Irr
Carter Lake	112,200	U.S. Bureau of Reclamation	Irr
Chatfield	235,000	U.S. Army Corps of Engineers	Fld

Cheesman	79,064	Denver Water	Mun
Cherry Creek	79,960	U.S. Army Corps of Engineers	Fld
Cobb Lake	22,300	Windsor Reservoir and Canal Co.	Irr
Eleven Mile	97,800	Denver Water	Mun
Empire	37,700	Bijou Irrigation Co.	Irr
Fossil Creek	11,100	North Poudre Irrigation Co.	Irr
Gross	41,811	Denver Water	Mun
Horse Creek	18,747	Henrylyn Irrigation District	Irr
Horsetooth	152,000	U.S. Bureau of Reclamation	Irr
Hudson	11,878	Henrylyn Irrigation District	Irr
Jack Pot	14,608	N. Fort Morgan Reservoir Co.	Irr
Jackson Lake	35,629	Jackson Lake Reservoir Co.	Irr
Julesberg	31,800	Julesberg Irrigation District	Irr
Lake Loveland	12,736	Greeley-Loveland Irrigation Co.	Irr
Long Draw	10,900	Water Supply & Storage Co.	Irr
Lost Park	45,900	Denver Water	Irr
Marshall Lake	11,518	Farmers Reservoir & Irrigation Co.	Irr
Marston Lake	19,795	Denver Water	Mun
Milton Lake	29,732	Farmers Reservoir & Irrigation Co.	Irr
North Sterling	74,010	North Sterling Irrigation Dist.	Irr
Prewitt	28,840	Logan Irrigation District	Irr
Ralston	11,272	Denver Water	Mun
Rawhide	15,400	Platte River Power Authority	Ind
Riverside	65,000	Riverside Irrigation District	Irr
Spinney Mtn.	53,873	City of Aurora	Mun
Standley Lake	42,380	Frisco & City of Westminster	Irr
Union	12,739	Union Ditch Company	Irr
Wildcat	64,000	Riverside Irrigation District	Irr
Windsor	17,538	Windsor Reservoir & Canal Co.	Irr

Use Codes: Dom – domestic; Fld – flood control; Fsh – fishery; hyd – hydroelectric power generation; Ind – industrial; Irr – irrigation; Mun – municipal; Rec – recreation.
Source: Office of the State Engineer, Denver, Colorado.

Arkansas River Basin Reservoirs
Exceeding 10,000 acre-feet capacity

Reservoir	Capacity (acre-feet)	Owned by	Use
Adobe	71,000	Fort Lyon Canal Co.	Irr
Bent County	34,602	Bent County Reservoir Co.	Irr
Bradford Lake	34,822	Pueblo-Rocky Ford Irr. Co.	Irr
Clear Creek	11,500	Pueblo Board of Water Works	Mun
Cucharas	40,960	Huerfano-Cucharas Irr. Co.	Irr
Horse Creek	28,000	Fort Lyon Canal Co.	Irr
John Martin	232,942	U.S. Army Corp of Engineers	Irr
Kit Carson	34,435	Robert E. Lisco	Irr

Lake Meridith . . . . .39,804 . . . . .Lake Meredith Reservoir Co. . . . . .Irr
Model . . . . .20,359 . . . . .John T. Oxley .Irr
Mount Elbert . . . . .11,530 . . . . .U.S. Bureau of Reclamation . . . . .Hyd
Muddy Creek . . . . .31,866 . . . . .Colorado Division of Wildlife . . . . .Rec
Nee-Granda . . . . .23,040 . . . . .Amity Mutual Irr. Co. . . . . .Irr
Nee-Noshe . . . . .60,618 . . . . .Amity Mutual Irr. Co. . . . . .Irr
Ne-So-Pah . . . . .23,458 . . . . .Mity Mutual Irr. Co. . . . . .Irr
N. Catamount . . . . . . .12,300 . . . . .City of Colorado Springs . . . . .Mun
Pueblo . . . . .357,000 . . . . .U.S. Bureau of Reclamation . . . . .Irr
Queen . . . . .23,040 . . . . .Amity Mutual Irr. Co. . . . . .Irr
Rampart . . . . .38,783 . . . . .City of Colorado Springs . . . . .Mun
Sugarloaf . . . . .129,432 . . . . .U.S. Bureau of Reclamation . . . . .Irr
Trinidad . . . . .119,877 . . . . .U.S. Army Corp of Engineers . . . . .Fld
Twin Lakes . . . . .141,000 . . . . .U.S. Bureau of Reclamation . . . . .Irr
Two Buttes . . . . .37,464 . . . . .Colorado Division of Wildlife . . . . .Rec

Rio Grande River Basin Reservoirs
Exceeding 10,000 acre-feet capacity

Reservoir	Capacity (acre-feet)	Owned by	Use
Continental	22,679	Santa Maria Reservoir Co.	Irr
La Jara	14,052	Colorado Division of Wildlife	Rec
Mountain Home	17,374	Trinchera Irrigation Co.	Irr
Platoro	59,571	U.S. Bureau of Reclamation	Fld
Rio Grande	52,192	San Luis Valley Irr. Dist.	Irr
Sanchez	103,114	Sanchez Ditch and Reservoir Co.	Irr
Santa Maria	43,826	Santa Maria Reservoir Co.	Irr
Terrace	15,182	Terrace Irrication Co.	Rec

Gunnison River Basin Reservoirs
Exceeding 10,000 acre-feet capacity

Reservoir	Capacity (acre-feet)	Owned by	Use
Blue Mesa	940,800	U.S. Bureau of Reclamation	Hyd
Crawford	14,395	U.S. Bureau of Reclamation	Irr
Crystal	26,000	U.S. Bureau of Reclamation	Hyd
Morrow Point	117,190	Farmers Water Development Co.	Irr
Paonia	20,950	U.S. Bureau of Reclamation	Irr
Ridgeway	125,000	U.S. Bureau of Reclamation	Irr
Silver Jack	13,520	U.S. Bureau of Reclamation	Irr
Taylor Park	106,200	U.S. Bureau of Reclamation	Irr

Use Codes: Dom – domestic; Fld – flood control; Fsh – fishery; hyd – hydroelectric power generation; Ind – industrial; Irr – irrigation; Mun – municipal; Rec – recreation.
Source: Office of the State Engineer, Denver, Colorado.

Colorado River Basin Reservoirs
Exceeding 10,000 acre-feet capacity

Reservoir	Capacity (acre-feet)	Owned by	Use
Dillon	254,036	Denver Water	Mun
Granby	539,800	U.S. Bureau of Reclamation	Irr
Green Mountain	154,600	U.S. Bureau of Reclamation	Irr
Homestake Project	43,600	Aurora and Colorado Springs	Mun
*Navajo Reservoir	747,000	U.S. Bureau of Reclamation	Irr
Rifle Gap	13,602	U.S. Bureau of Reclamation	Irr
Ruedi	102,369	U.S. Bureau of Reclamation	Irr
Shadow Mountain	18,400	U.S. Bureau of Reclamation	Irr
Vega	33,800	U.S. Bureau of Reclamation	Irr
Williams Fork	96,822	Denver Water	Mun
Willow Creek	10,600	U.S. Bureau of Reclamation	Irr
Wolford Mountain	56,000	Colo. River Water Cons. Dist.	Mun

* Navajo Dam is in New Mexico, but lake water backs up into southwest Colorado.

Yampa, White and North Platte River Basin Reservoirs
Exceeding 10,000 acre-feet capacity

Reservoir	Capacity (acre-feet)	Owned by	Use
Elkhead Creek	13,500	Colo. Division of Wildlife	Fsh
Lake John	11,232	Colo. Division of Wildlife	Rec
Stagecoach	33,700	Upper Yampa Water Cons. Dist.	Rec
Taylor Draw	13,800	Water Users Assoc. No. 1	Irr
Willow Creek	10,600	U.S. Bureau of Reclamation	Irr

San Miguel, Dolores, Animas and San Juan River Basin Reservoirs
Exceeding 10,000 acre-feet capacity

Reservoir	Capacity (acre-feet)	Owned by	Use
Groundhog	21,000	Montezuma Valley Irrigation Co.	Irr
Lemon	40,146	U.S. Bureau of Reclamation	Irr
McPhee	381,100	U.S. Bureau of Reclamation	Irr
Narraguinnep	18,960	Montezuma Valley Irrigation Co.	Irr
Terminal	23,385	Colo. Ute Electric Association	Hyd
Vallecito	129,700	U.S. Bureau of Reclamation	Irr
Williams Creek	10,084	Colorado Division of Wildlife	Rec

Use Codes: Dom – domestic; Fld – flood control; Fsh – fishery; hyd – hydroelectric power generation; Ind – industrial; Irr – irrigation; Mun – municipal; Rec – recreation.
Source: Office of the State Engineer, Denver, Colorado.

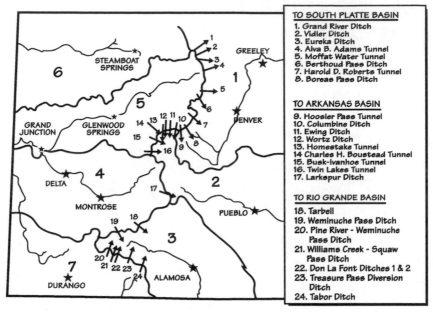

Figure 3.3 – 24 diversion projects move water west to east across the Continental Divide.

Water Diversions

Water, as the Colorado saying goes, flows uphill toward money. There isn't much water on the arid Front Range, but there are a lot of people. People equal money and political clout, enough clout to reverse the flow of Western Slope streams. Instead of the streams running west to the Colorado River, they've been halted, gathered and piped across the Continental Divide to the cities and farms of the Front Range.

This isn't to say all diversions benefit the lawns and farms of eastern Colorado. Of the 40 significant trans-basin diversion projects, 24 transport water across the Continental Divide west to east. Seventeen of those send water to the Front Range, the other seven transport water to the San Luis Valley

The 24 diversions shunting water from the upper Colorado River Basin to the Rio Grande, Arkansas and South Platte Basins account for more than 500,000 acre-feet a year. The amount of water sent east instead of west would equal the annual flow of the White River. Some of the diversion projects are among America's greatest engineering achievements (see Man-Made Marvels chapter).

Water Diversion Projects

Structure	Diverted (acre-feet)
Wilson Supply Ditch	1,412
Laramie-Poudre Tunnel	13,789
Skyline Ditch	0
Michigan Ditch	322
Cameron Pass Ditch	0
Sarvis Ditch	980
Grand River Ditch	20,831
Eureka Ditch	0
Alva B. Adams Tunnel	285,200
Stillwater Ditch	3,430
Dome Creek Ditch	370
Moffat Water Tunnel	77,545
Berthoud Pass Ditch	567
Vidler Tunnel	369
Harold D. Roberts Tunnel	299
Boreas Pass Ditch	0
Hoosier Pass Ditch	7,400
Columbine Ditch	1,809
Ewing Ditch	1,359
Wurtz Ditch	3,832
Charles H. Boustead Tunnel	71,797
Homestake Tunnel	10,180
Busk-Ivanhoe Tunnel	6,268
Twin Lakes Tunnel	8,016
Divide Creek Highline Fdr. Ditch	2,483
Aurora-Homestake Pipeline	3,892
Larkspur Ditch	329
Tarbell Ditch	172
Tabor Ditch	1,435
Weminuche Pass Ditch	2,088
Pine River-Weminuche Pass Ditch	873
Williams Creek Squaw Pass Ditch	253
Don La Font Ditches 1 and 2	447
Treasure Pass Diversion Ditch	613
Main Canal 1	54,000
Main Canal 2	68,000
Summit Reservoir Outlet Canal	8,644
Mendano Ditch	385
Hudson Branch Ditch	100
Azotea Tunnel	91,790
TOTAL	751,279

Source: Colorado State University. Water Knowledge.
VASQUEZ . . . . .See paragraph below.
GUNNISON TUNNEL . . . . .See Chapter 10

Vasquez Tunnel story

A major collection basin for the Denver Water Department is the Williams Fork Valley. Water there is gathered and piped under Jones Pass and the Continental Divide. Not where Denver wants it, the water then is piped through Vasquez Tunnel and the Continental Divide again to the upper Fraser River Basin. Denver gathers it up again and sends it on its third journey under the Contintal Divide through the 6.2-mile Moffat Tunnel where it eventually finds South Boulder Creek and Gross Reservoir, ready to serve the thirsty Front Range.

Keeping Track

Colorado water flow is monitored from 82 positions by electronic sensors that report, via satellite, data including flow, depth, velocity and salinity. The sensors report every 15 minutes every day to the State Water Engineer in Denver before being distributed to the seven district water offices across the state.

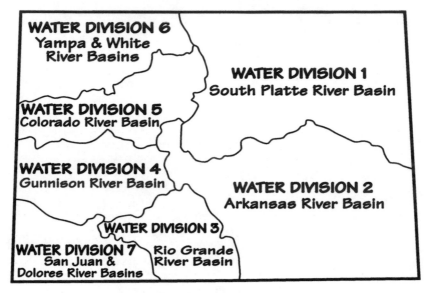

Figure 3.4 — Colorado water divisions.

Water Use

Colorado water is used to irrigate crops. The billions of dollars spent on trans-basin water tunnels, canals, ditches and reservoirs primarily benefit the state's agriculture industry. Colorado Division of Water Resources reports from 1996 to 2001 show 64% of Colorado's surface water going to irrigation. More than 20% is used to replenish reservoirs, which eventually are drawn down, primarily by irrigation.

Municipal use accounts for about 4% of the state's water. Fisheries use another 2%. All other uses combined – commercial, domestic, stock, industrial and recreation – consume only 4%.

More than 3 million acres of Colorado cropland is irrigated, about one third of the nearly 11 million acres of crops in the state. According to the 1992 United States Department of Agriculture census, the market value of Colorado agricultural products sold was $4.1 billion.

About 4% of the total land in Colorado is under irrrigation. Only California and Texas irrigate more acreage. Each acre of that land artificially receives an average of 3.5 feet of water each year.

Water Deliveries by Use
Oct. 1, 1996 to Sept. 30, 1997
In acre-feet. Source: Colorado Division of Water Resources

	Div. 1	Div. 2	Div. 3	Div. 4	Div. 5	Div. 6	Div. 7	Total	% of Total
Irrigation	1,982,346	1,935,335	1,400,945	2,032,594	2,046,695	1,039,637	708,811	11,146,363	60.99%
Storage	1,512,348	1,147,941	99,605	1,587,282	575,777	7,052	388,375	5,318,380	29.10%
Municipal	468,107	145,977	10,041	17,868	54,816	7,274	14,606	718,689	3.93%
Commercial	9,494	251	189	22,713	201	86	1,702	34,636	0.19%
Domestic	10,937	175	6,172	1,450	5,621	2,265	744	27,364	0.15%
Stock	598	643	228	22,865	44,871	32,052	46,365	147,622	0.81%
Industrial	73,341	145,526	0	1,004	6,119	23,993	422	250,405	1.37%
Recreation	3,648	17	0	12,487	3,895	2,545	1,105	23,697	0.13%
Fishery	4,491	21,891	1,075	201,851	95,701	37,389	32,712	395,110	2.16%
Augmentation	51,563	18,374	3,409	30	5,842	0	373	79,591	0.44%
Recharge	104,672	2,128	27,587	376	0	0	38	134,801	0.74%
Total	4,221,545	3,418,258	1,549,251	3,900,520	2,839,538	1,152,293	1,195,253	18,276,658	
Irr. acres	975,995	777,437	568,345	309,138	298,301	228,440	194,314	2,851,970	
Acre ft./irr. acre	2.04	6.98	2.47	6.58	6.87	4.56	3.65	3.91	

Water Deliveries by Use
Oct. 1, 2000 to Sept. 30, 2001
In acre-feet. Source: Colorado Division of Water Resources

	Div. 1	Div. 2	Div. 3	Div. 4	Div. 5	Div. 6	Div. 7	Total	%of Total
Irrigation	1,805,815	1,393,999	1,237,385	2,057,978	1,590,084	1,026,317	816,995	9,928,573	64.59%
Storage	1,233,347	538,150	75,820	940,246	462,018	11,399	316,151	3,577,131	23.27%
Municipal	622,265	167,751	11,255	21,205	48,879	8,929	17,268	897,552	5.84%
Commercial	1,572	2,691	1,719	0	690	303	2,416	9,391	0.06%
Domestic	85	25,138	3,372	1,216	6,953	1,804	995	39,563	0.26%
Stock	1,077	1,157	413	24,212	30,938	40,234	19,249	117,280	0.76%
Industrial	72,955	92,978	384	2,514	4,485	19,521	581	193,418	1.26%
Recreation	3,639	403	0	7,630	17,881	2,152	472	32,177	0.21%
Fishery	6,945	3,397	80	130,716	81,124	38,199	24,519	284,980	1.85%
Augmentation	101,769	7,274	9,706	515	5,395	29	450	125,138	0.81%
Recharge	151,821	3,094	11,053	312	0	0	39	166,319	1.08%
Total	4,001,290	2,236,032	1,351,187	3,186,544	2,248,447	1,148,887	1,199,135	15,371,522	
Irrigated acres	993,815	420,000	620,873	318,439	266,911	225,195	200,689	3,045,922	
Acre ft./irr. acre	1.82	3.32	1.99	6.46	5.96	4.56	4.07	3.26	

First-In-Time, First-In-Right

Colorado Water Law is based on two primary tenets:

• First-in-time, First-in-right. Also known as the Doctrine of Prior Appropriation, as set forth in the Colorado Constitution in 1876. Simply stated, those who use the water first have rights over those who arrive later and wish to use the water.

• Water rights are similar to property rights, but do not necessarily follow property rights. That is, a water right is a property right to a certain amount of water. It can be bought, sold or traded, inherited or changed to another use. Water rights not used for the beneficial use for which it was acquired are lost to the owner.

The basic rules of Colorado water law originated in California during the Gold Rush of 1849. Colorado incorporated the same guidelines and in 1876 adopted them as part of the state constitution.

To obtain a water right, water must be put to a beneficial use. Historical beneficial uses have been domestic, agricultural and industrial. Recently, mandated instream flows to protect wildlife and the environment have become recognized as beneficial uses.

The law recognizes priority uses. Domestic has the highest priority, then agriculture and industrial.

Interstate Water Compacts

As has been noted, roughly 10 million acre-feet of water leaves Colorado by way of its many streams and rivers. 8.5 million acre feet of that is already promised to downstream users in accordance with 18 different insterstate water compacts. Even Mexico looks to Colorado for water and has interests in both the Colorado and the Rio Grande Rivers.

The Colorado River carries most of Colorado's water, and also is burdened with a full one-half of the state's interstate water compacts. Following are interstate water compacts or laws affecting Colorado rivers.

Colorado River Basin Agreements
· Colorado River Compact – 1922
· Boulder Canyon Project Act – 1928
· Mexican Treaty – 1944
· Upper Colorado River Compact – 1948
· Colo. River Storage Project Act – 1956
· Arizona vs. Calif. 373 U.S. 546 – 1963
· Colo. River Basin Project Act – 1968
· Coordinated Long Range Operating Criteria -- Colo. River Reservoir – 1970
· Colo. River Basin Salinity Act – 1974

Other Rivers
· Animas-La Plata River Compact – 1963
· Arkansas River Compact – 1948
· Costilla Creek compact – 1963
· La Plata River Compact – 1922
· Laramie River Litigation – 1957
· North Platte River Litigation – 1954
· Republican River Compact – 1942
· Rio Grande River Compact – 1938
· South Platte River Compact –1923

4 Weather

Colorado weather is influenced by its latitude, topography, elevation, distance from large bodies of water and the jet streams. Lower elevations are generally mild, but given to vast extremes of hot and cold. Violent weather, even deadly weather, can strike anywhere in the state at virtually any time. Global trends and factors have their influence, but local factors can rapidly change conditions. Even a short drive across the Rocky Mountains from the plains to the canyons might render a variety of different weather conditions, sometimes only a few miles, or minutes, apart.

Latitude affects the sun's position in the sky and therefore hours of daylight and the angle and intensity of the rays as they strike earth. Between 37 and 41 degrees north latitude, Colorado receives between 9 and 15 hours of daylight. Predominant winds also are influenced by latitude. Colorado weather is greatly affected by westerly winds that bring storms from the Pacific Ocean inward. Jet streams to the north and south can shift position, affecting storm paths and weather conditions.

At nearly 1,000 miles from the Pacific Ocean, Colorado weather is not heavily influenced by any adjacent large body of water, nor does the atmosphere carry much humidity. Storms moving in from the Pacific often lose much of their moisture to mountain ranges encountered along the way. The state's average humidty is 38%.

Temperatures and atmospheric pressures decrease with increasing altitude. Temperatures drop between 3.3 and 3.6 degrees F for every 1,000 feet in altitude gained. Atmospheric pressures will range from 24 inches of mercury to under 20 inches of mercury. Air masses moving west to east must rise over the mountains or significant upthrusts such as the Colorado Plateau. As the air rises, it cools. The cooler the air, the less moisture it can carry. The result is significantly more snow and rain on the Western Slope of the Rocky Mountains compared to the eastern plains. Precipitation can vary by more than 300% from protected leeside valleys to windward mountain peaks.

Any area 9,000 feet or higher will experience a very short growing season. Frost can occur any day of the year at 9,000 feet. Fraser, in the upper reaches of Middle Park, is credited with having the shortest growing season in the state with an average of 48 frost-free days a year. Fruita, near the Utah border in the Grand Valley, enjoys one of the state's longest growing seasons.

Dense cold air often will settle in the low points of high mountain valleys causing extreme low overnight temperatures.

A winter phenomenon known as chinook winds can blow down off the mountains to the eastern plains to warm winter days. Rapid temperature increases of 25 to 30 degrees are not uncommon.

Higher elevations are analagous to northern latitudes. In a 20-mile drive from the Great Plains to the summit of Pikes Peak, one passes through four separate ecosystems – Grassland, Montane Forest, Subalpine Forest and Alpine Tundra. To pass through similar life zones without gaining altitude, one would have to drive as far north as Northern Alaska. Many of the plants and animals living in Colorado between 9,000 and 11,500 feet, in the spruce-fir forest life-zones, thrive at 1,000 feet in northern Canada. The low tundra vegetation above timberline in Colorado (approx. 11,000 feet) is similar to plant life found in the Arctic tundra. The 35-degree difference in annual mean temperature between the summit of Pikes Peak and Las Animas, 90 miles southeast, is comparable to the difference between south Florida and Iceland.

Highly varied topography results in highly varied micro-climates. Differences in slope, elevation and aspect impact the amount of solar heating from one point to the next. Steep slopes create shaded valleys, while any slope with a northern aspect gets only minimal sun all winter. Conversely, south-facing slopes soak up the sun's heat. They are warmer and drier than other areas and therefore will feature different vegetation.

Because of the varied terrain and altitude of the state, it is impossible to summarize Colorado's weather. Instead, we have included weather summaries from various points across the state. The points were selected from the more than 130 weather stations across the state to represent major geographical regions, various elevations and population centers.

Colorado Extreme Weather Records
Source: Western Regional Climate Center

Record high temperature:
118°F on July 11, 1888 in Bennett, Colo.

Record low temperature:
-61°F on Feb. 1, 1985 in Maybell, Colo.

Highest average annual temperature:
56.4°F at Eversoll Ranch in Baca County.

Lowest average annual temperature:
29.2°F at the summit of Berthoud Pass.

Most consecutive days with high temperature of 90°F or greater:
76 days from June through September 1983 in Las Animas, Colo.

Most consecscutive days with low temperature of 32°F or lower:
310 days from Aug. 1985 to June 1986 in Taylor Park near Gunnison, Colo.

Record maximum annual precipitation:
92.84 inches in 1897 in Ruby, Colo.

Record minimum annual precipitation:
1.69 inches in 1939 in Buena Vista, Colo.

Record maximum 24-hour precipitation:
11.08 inches on June 17, 1965 in Holly, Colo.

Highest average annual precipitation:
45.35 inches at the summit of Wolf Creek Pass.

Lowest average annual precipitation:
7.05 in Center, Colo. in the San Luis Valley.

Most consecutive days with measurable precipitation:
45 days from November 1983 to January 1984 at the summit of Berthoud Pass.

Most consecutive days with no measurable precipitation:
156 days from October 1936 through March 1937 in Haswell.

Record maximum winter snowfall:
807 inches in 1978-1979 at the summit of Wolf Creek Pass.

Record maximum 1-day snowfall:
75.8 inches April 14-15, 1921 at Silver Lake, Colo.

Highest average annual snowfall:
434.8 inches at the summit of Wolf Creek Pass.

Aspen, Colorado

Monthly Temperature and Precipitation Averages; Daily and Monthly Extremes.
Data: 1980 to 2003 — Station 050372. Table updated May 20, 2003.
All temperatures F; Precipitation in inches; Boldface indicates record for period.
Latitude: 39.11; Longitude: 106.50; Elevation: 8,161 ft.
Source: Western Regional Climate Center

TEMPS.	JAN.	FEB.	MARCH	APRIL	MAY	JUNE	JULY	AUG.	SEPT.	OCT.	NOV.	DEC.	ANNUAL
Monthly Avg.													
Max	35.1	39.4	45.2	52.1	62.3	72.5	77.5	75.7	68.7	57.3	43.2	34.9	55.3
Min	8.6	11.7	19.2	26.0	34.4	41.3	46.6	46.3	39.0	29.1	18.5	9.4	27.5
Mean	21.9	25.5	32.2	39.1	48.4	56.9	62.1	61.0	53.9	43.2	30.9	22.1	41.4
Daily Extremes													
High	58	60	68	73	84	87	**92**	89	86	77	70	62	
Date dd-yy	17-2000	25-1986	06-1987	29-1992	30-2000	30-1990	**01-1983**	01-2002	05-1995	06-1997	15-1999	01-1999	
Low	-20	**-25**	-14	0	15	20	29	29	18	6	-5	-23	
Date dd-yy	08-1982	**07-1989**	03-2002	05-1983	12-1983	04-1993	05-1993	25-1992	27-1996	21-1996	03-1991	18-1996	
Monthly Extremes													
High Mean	28.6	32.2	37.8	44.1	52.6	62.3	66.6	63.7	58.8	47.0	39.8	32.3	43.5
Year	2003	1995	1999	2002	2000	2002	2002	2002	1998	1988	1999	1980	2000
Low Mean	17.3	18.7	28.4	33.0	42.5	52.7	56.8	57.4	49.9	37.1	22.6	17.5	39.0
Year	1984	1985	1988	1983	1983	1993	1992	1992	1985	1984	1992	1992	1982
No. of Days													
Max Temp													
>= 90	0	0	0	0	0	0	0.2	0	0	0	0	0	0.2
<= 32	11.7	5.6	2.2	0.5	0	0	0	0	0	0.6	5.0	11.9	37.6
Min Temp													
<= 32	31.0	28.1	30.3	24.3	11.2	2.5	0.2	0.3	4.6	20.8	29.5	31.0	213.9
<= 0	5.7	3.1	1.0	0	0	0	0	0	0	0	1.2	5.3	16.4
PRECIPITATION													
Mean	1.57	2.16	2.81	2.55	2.17	1.40	1.83	1.62	1.98	2.01	2.55	1.78	24.44
High	3.40	4.73	5.53	3.87	5.41	4.35	4.26	3.45	5.08	5.47	5.05	4.87	33.27
Year	1997	1996	1995	1999	1995	1984	1998	1984	1985	1984	1983	1983	1984
Low	0.32	0.89	1.30	1.00	0.21	0	0.32	0.55	0.61	0.22	0.42	0.56	18.51
Year	1985	1981	1986	1987	2002	2002	1994	1996	1983	1988	1999	1991	2002
1-day Max	0.79	1.92	1.56	1.05	1.30	**2.35**	0.80	1.00	1.05	0.96	1.80	0.83	
Date dd-yy	04-1997	21-1996	03-1995	08-1981	17-1983	**07-1984**	29-1982	01-1984	29-1985	20-1996	09-1988	22-1981	
No. of Days													
>= 0.01	11	11	13	13	11	8	11	12	11	9	11	11	131
>= 0.1	6	6	8	8	7	4	6	6	7	6	8	6	78
>= 0.5	0	1	2	1	1	1	1	0	1	1	1	1	10
>= 1	0	0	0	0	0	0	0	0	0	0	0	0	0
SNOWFALL													
Mean	23.6	28.0	29.3	20.4	7.7	1.1	0	0	1.1	11.8	27.6	24.5	175.1
High	49.0	50.0	52.0	35.0	44.3	15.5	0	0	7.5	39.8	52.0	71.0	288.6
Year	1982	1993	1984	1991	1983	1984	--	--	1996	1984	1983	1983	1983

Alamosa, Colorado

Monthly Temperature and Precipitation Averages; Daily and Monthly Extremes.
Data: 1948 to 2003 — Station 050130. Table updated May 20, 2003.
All temperatures F; Precipitation in inches; Boldface indicates record for period.
Latitude: 37.27; Longitude: 105.52, Elevation: 7,540 ft.
Source: Western Regional Climate Center

TEMPS.	JAN.	FEB.	MARCH	APRIL	MAY	JUNE	JULY	AUG.	SEPT.	OCT.	NOV.	DEC.	ANNUAL
Monthly Avg.													
Max	34.5	40.6	49.0	58.6	68.1	78.2	82.0	79.4	73.5	62.6	47.0	36.2	59.1
Min	-2.0	5.6	15.8	23.7	33.2	41.2	47.5	45.6	36.6	24.4	11.5	0.3	23.6
Mean	16.3	23.1	32.4	41.2	50.6	59.7	64.7	62.5	55.0	43.5	29.3	18.2	41.4
Daily Extremes													
High	62	66	73	80	90	95	**96**	991	87	81	71	61	
Date dd-yy	20-1971	25-1986	26-1971	20-1989	31 2002	20-1994	**05-1989**	17-2002	03-1960	07-1979	09-1980	08-1958	
Low	-41	-30	20	-6	11	24	30	29	15	-9	-30	**-42**	
Date dd-yy	13-1963	01-1951	04-1964	08-1973	01-1967	02-1990	02-1997	21-1964	30-1985	31-1991	27-1952	**14-1964**	
Monthly Extremes													
Highest Mean	26.4	33.2	37.7	47.0	55.2	63.1	67.5	65.9	58.3	49.5	34.8	28.1	44.2
Year	2003	1995	1974	1992	1984	1956	1966	1969	1990	1950	1965	1980	1954
Low Mean	1.4	10.6	25.0	36.2	46.7	56.5	62.1	59.3	52.2	38.5	18.6	5.1	38.6
Year	1992	1979	1964	1970	1953	1983	1995	1974	1985	1969	1972	1991	1979
No. of Days													
Max Temp													
>= 90	0	0	0	0	0	0.4	0.8	0.1	0	0	0	0	1.3
<= 32	12.5	5.9	1.4	0.1	0	0	0	0	0	0.2	3.2	10.6	33.8
Min Temp													
<= 32	30.9	28.1	30.6	26.9	13.5	1.9	0.0	0.2	7.9	26.6	29.6	30.9	227.1
<= 0	17.7	8.9	1.4	0	0	0	0	0	0	0.1	3.9	15.3	47.2
PRECIPITATION													
Mean	0.24	0.25	0.41	0.50	0.67	0.56	1.08	1.23	0.80	0.64	0.38	0.32	7.08
High	0.75	1.42	1.62	1.72	1.85	2.58	3.50	5.40	1.94	2.37	1.23	1.52	11.55
Year	1979	1963	1992	1990	1973	1969	1968	1993	1959	1969	1991	1964	1969
Low	0	0	0	0	0.01	0	0.02	0.21	0	0	0	0	3.40
Year	1981	1954	1955	1972	1975	1980	1994	1980	1953	1964	1949	1949	1956
1-day Max	0.33	0.88	1.15	1.22	0.86	1.02	1.56	1.31	**1.77**	0.89	0.71	0.91	
Date dd-yy	18-1952	10-1963	04-1992	20-1952	26-1967	16-1969	18-1971	27-1993	**30-1959**	11-1969	07-1981	03-1964	
No. of Days													
>= 0.01	4	4	5	5	6	5	9	10	6	4	4	4	66
>= 0.1	1	1	1	2	2	2	3	4	2	2	1	1	21
>= 0.5	0	0	0	0	0	0	0	0	0	0	0	0	2
>= 1	0	0	0	0	0	0	0	0	0	0	0	0	0
SNOWFALL													
Mean	4.2	3.9	5.7	4.1	1.6	0	0	0	0.2	2.9	4.0	5.3	32.0
High	13.8	16.0	29.2	14.2	13.5	1.2	0.2	0	4.2	20.3	19.8	27.7	69.1
Year	1979	1963	1973	1957	1978	1950	1952	--	1961	1969	1972	1967	1973

Berthoud Pass Summit, Colorado

Monthly Temperature and Precipitation Averages; Daily and Monthly Extremes.
Data: 1950 to 1985 — Station 050674.
All temperatures F; Precipitation in inches; Boldface indicates record for period.
Latitude: 39.48; Longitude: 105.47; Elevation: 11,310 ft.
Source: Western Regional Climate Center

TEMPS.	JAN.	FEB.	MARCH	APRIL	MAY	JUNE	JULY	AUG.	SEPT.	OCT.	NOV.	DEC.	ANNUAL
Monthly Avg.													
Max	21.2	24.2	28.7	36.2	45.0	54.2	61.9	59.9	53.0	42.4	30.4	23.2	40.0
Min	1.4	2.0	6.2	13.6	23.1	32.0	39.2	38.0	31.0	20.9	9.8	3.2	18.4
Mean	11.3	13.1	17.4	24.9	34.1	43.1	50.5	48.9	42.0	31.7	20.1	13.2	29.2
Daily Extremes													
High	42	47	50	57	62	70	**76**	75	73	63	54	47	
Date dd-yy	17-1974	14-1979	27-1971	27-1981	28-1969	28-1970	**07-1973**	06-1979	07-1978	08-1980	06-1975	07-1965	
Low	-33	**-34**	-24	-12	-3	11	26	21	4	-5	-28	-30	
Date dd-yy	02-1979	01-1985	03-1965	08-1973	01-1972	01-1979	01-1968	15-1978	19-1971	25-1975	28-1976	08-1978	
Monthly Extremes													
High Mean	19.1	18.0	22.8	31.1	39.3	48.4	53.8	52.5	46.2	39.7	25.5	23.0	31.7
Year	1981	1976	1978	1981	1969	1977	1966	1969	1963	1963	1981	1980	1981
Low Mean	4.7	5.7	11.3	19.1	30.0	39.2	44.0	44.5	37.5	24.4	13.2	7.9	28.2
Year	1979	1964	1965	1973	1983	1975	1965	1968	1965	1969	1979	1978	1975
No. of Days													
Max Temp													
>= 90	0	0	0	0	0	0	0	0	0	0	0	0	0
<= 32	27.1	22.3	19.4	9.5	2.4	0.1	0	0	0.7	5.3	16.5	25.0	128.4
Min Temp													
<= 32	31.0	28.1	31.0	30.0	28.9	15.7	1.1	2.8	16.4	30.0	30.0	31.0	275.9
<= 0	13.4	11.3	7.3	2.4	0.1	0	0	0	0	0.6	4.9	12.4	52.4
PRECIPITATION													
Mean	3.49	2.90	4.11	4.43	3.85	2.23	2.45	2.63	2.05	2.36	3.36	3.63	37.48
High	7.37	5.12	6.72	7.42	6.88	5.16	5.98	6.68	3.93	6.84	7.67	8.45	58.47
Year	1980	1968	1983	1983	1983	1969	1965	1983	1970	1969	1983	1983	1983
Low	1.24	1.50	1.62	2.15	0.59	0	0.98	0.36	0.40	0.74	1.27	1.18	27.37
Year	1968	1982	1966	1981	1974	1980	1978	1978	1979	1964	1980	1980	1966
1-day Max	1.24	0.85	1.66	1.48	**3.06**	1.76	1.19	0.88	1.45	1.20	1.37	1.50	
Date dd-yy	25-1975	15-1984	11-1977	28-1973	**07-1969**	08-1979	23-1965	02-1976	22-1970	04-1969	14-1983	05-1977	
No. of Days													
>= 0.01	19	16	20	17	16	11	14	14	11	10	15	18	180
>= 0.1	12	10	12	12	10	6	8	8	6	7	10	11	111
>= 0.5	1	1	2	3	2	1	1	1	1	1	2	2	17
>= 1	0	0	0	0	0	0	0	0	0	0	0	0	2
SNOWFALL													
Mean	49.8	42.4	57.9	54.6	37.2	11.8	0	0.3	8.7	28.0	49.1	51.4	391.2
High	99.0	76.5	92.8	93.0	69.6	44.0	0	3.0	34.5	90.0	91.5	123.0	591.1
Year	1980	1968	1965	1983	1983	1974	--	1972	1970	1969	1983	1983	1983

Boulder, Colorado

Monthly Temperature and Precipitation Averages; Daily and Monthly Extremes.
Data: 1948 to 2003 — Station 050848. Table updated May 20, 2003.
All temperatures F; Precipitation in inches; Boldface indicates record for period.
Latitude: 40.01; Longitude: 105.16; Elevation: 5,400 ft.
Source: Western Regional Climate Center

TEMPS.	JAN.	FEB.	MARCH	APRIL	MAY	JUNE	JULY	AUG.	SEPT.	OCT.	NOV.	DEC.	ANNUAL
Monthly Avg.													
Max	45.3	48.4	53.8	62.7	71.8	82.0	87.5	85.7	77.7	67.1	53.4	47.1	65.2
Min	20.3	23.6	27.8	35.6	44.5	53.0	58.7	57.4	49.0	39.0	28.5	22.9	38.4
Mean	32.8	36.0	40.8	49.2	58.1	67.5	73.1	71.5	63.3	53.0	40.9	35.0	51.8
Daily Extremes													
High	72	79	80	88	95	**104**	**104**	101	100	90	79	76	
Date dd-yy	09-1953	08-1954	20-1997	21-1989	28-1900	**23-1954**	**11-1954**	08-1969	02-1983	01-1953	04-1952	17-1980	
Low	-22	**-24**	-6	3	22	30	42	42	15	5	-8	**-24**	
Date dd-yy	12-1963	**05-1989**	02-2002	02-1975	02-1954	02-1951	05-1972	27-1992	30-1985	31-1991	25-1993	**22-1990**	
Monthly Extremes													
High Mean	43.5	47.6	48.7	56.7	64.3	74.9	78.3	75.0	69.8	61.9	53.1	44.1	56.0
Year	1953	1954	1986	1981	1958	1956	1954	1948	1948	1950	1949	1957	1954
Low Mean	21.9	24.1	30.8	42.8	50.9	62.2	68.3	66.3	55.9	41.8	31.1	20.7	49.6
Year	1949	1989	1965	1997	1995	1967	1992	1992	1965	1969	1985	1983	1985
No. of Days													
Max Temp													
>= 90	0	0	0	0	0.4	6.7	13.1	9.0	2.5	0	0	0	31.7
<= 32	5.4	2.8	1.8	0.2	0	0	0	0	0	0.2	1.9	3.4	15.5
Min Temp													
<= 32	26.7	22.9	21.5	10.8	1.2	0	0	0	0.8	6.8	19.3	25.7	135.7
<= 0	2.3	0.9	0.3	0	0	0	0	0	0	0	0.2	1.0	4.7
PRECIPITATION													
Mean	0.68	0.76	1.7	2.36	3.10	2.11	1.84	1.59	1.65	1.27	1.22	0.68	18.96
High	2.19	2.44	5.17	6.85	9.59	7.40	5.20	7.49	4.89	5.39	3.46	2.16	29.43
Year	1996	1987	1992	1957	1995	1949	1965	1951	1961	1969	1983	1988	1995
Low	0.01	0	0.31	0.15	0	0.32	0.09	0.03	0.01	0.03	0	0.01	10.91
Year	1952	1992	1966	1963	1974	1980	1902	1985	1953	1988	1949	1991	1954
1-day Max	1.04	1.03	2.02	**3.56**	3.51	3.40	2.18	3.06	1.64	1.90	1.19	1.14	
Date dd-yy	06-1998	28-1957	18-1998	**03-1986**	17-1995	04-1949	21-1977	03-1951	17-1971	22-1978	14-1994	24-1982	
No. of Days													
>= 0.01	5	5	8	8	11	10	11	10	8	6	6	5	93
>= 0.1	2	3	4	5	6	5	5	4	4	3	3	2	46
>= 0.5	0	0	1	1	2	1	1	1	1	1	1	0	10
>= 1	0	0	0	0	1	0	0	0	0	0	0	0	3
SNOWFALL													
Mean	10.7	10.7	17.7	11.6	1.5	0	0	0	1.5	5.2	13.5	10.8	82.9
High	29.1	28.8	56.7	44.0	23.0	2.2	0	0	21.0	49.3	44.7	31.55	125.4
Year	1996	1997	1970	1957	1978	1951	--	--	1971	1969	1992	1988	1987

Craig, Colorado

Monthly Temperature and Precipitation Averages; Daily and Monthly Extremes.
Data: 1977 to 2003 —— Station 051932. Table updated May 20, 2003.
All temperatures F; Precipitation in inches; Boldface indicates record for period.
Latitude: 40.27; Longitude: 107.36; Elevation: 6,440 ft.
Source: Western Regional Climate Center

TEMPS.	JAN.	FEB.	MARCH	APRIL	MAY	JUNE	JULY	AUG.	SEPT.	OCT.	NOV.	DEC.	ANNUAL
Monthly Avg.													
Max	30.2	33.8	45.5	56.8	65.7	78.2	84.2	83.0	74.1	60.9	43.3	32.3	57.3
Min	6.2	9.8	21.1	29.2	36.7	44.2	50.1	48.8	40.2	29.4	19.4	8.7	28.7
Mean	18.2	21.8	32.9	43.0	51.1	61.2	67.1	65.7	57.2	45.2	31.3	20.6	42.9
Daily Extremes													
High	57	59	71	80	88	95	**99**	96	97	85	73	60	
Date dd-yy	24-1981	20-1981	21-1997	21-1989	31-2002	30-1990	**08-1989**	06-1979	06-1978	01-2001	08-1999	04-1980	
Low	-36	**-41**	-22	3	19	23	34	31	16	1	-15	-31	
Date dd-yy	19-1984	**06-1989**	03-2002	14-1997	08-1978	25-1978	13-1987	18-1978	30-1985	31-1991	30-1979	08-1978	
Monthly Extremes													
High Mean	29.6	28.1	39.6	48.2	56.0	66.7	71.6	69.0	62.3	50.5	37.0	31.4	45.4
Year	1981	1986	1986	1992	1992	1977	1902	1983	1990	1988	1901	1980	1981
Low Mean	9.0	12.5	26.3	35.3	46.7	57.1	63.3	63.1	53.5	39.3	24.9	12.9	39.4
Year	1984	1985	1984	1984	1983	1984	1993	1987	1986	1984	1979	1978	1984
No. of Days													
Max Temp													
>= 90	0	0	0	0	0	1.4	5.4	3.8	0.5	0	0	0	11.1
<= 32	17.3	11.1	2.7	0.2	0	0	0	0	0	0.3	6.4	15.2	53.1
Min Temp													
<= 32	30.6	27.8	29.4	19.2	8.2	0.5	0	0.2	4.1	20.4	28.4	30.6	199.4
<= 0	9.0	6.6	0.7	0	0	0	0	0	0	0	1.1	6.7	24.1
PRECIPITATION													
Mean	1.02	1.13	1.48	1.56	1.50	1.09	1.33	1.26	1.53	1.74	1.40	0.94	15.96
High	2.34	2.25	2.69	3.43	3.95	2.98	3.00	2.43	5.19	4.52	2.94	3.35	24.97
Year	1980	1990	1980	1993	1981	1983	1986	1984	1997	1981	1985	1983	1983
Low	0.28	0.24	0.14	0.35	0.06	0.11	0.01	0.19	0.12	0.22	0.38	0.47	11.16
Year	1981	1902	1997	1989	1994	1977	1994	1981	1979	1988	1980	1979	1988
1-day Max	0.65	1.22	0.78	1.07	1.31	1.00	1.04	1.24	**2.18**	1.19	0.99	0.70	
Date dd-yy	28-1980	20-1986	18-1998	06-1993	03-1979	12-1983	24-1992	05-1983	**19-1997**	09-1985	09-1985	23-1987	
No. of Days													
>= 0.01	10	8	10	9	10	7	8	8	8	8	9	8	102
>= 0.1	3	4	5	5	5	3	4	4	4	5	4	3	49
>= 0.5	0	0	0	1	1	1	1	0	1	1	1	0	6
>= 1	0	0	0	0	0	0	0	0	0	0	0	0	1
SNOWFALL													
Mean	15.4	14.2	11.2	5.8	1.3	0.1	0	0	0.4	3.7	11.8	12.7	76.5
High	45.5	37.5	27.0	16.0	7.0	2.0	0	0	5.0	20.0	25.0	42.0	121.8
Year	1996	1990	1980	1984	1979	1990	--	--	1984	1985	1985	1983	1985

Weather

Colorado Springs, Colorado

Monthly Temperature and Precipitation Averages; Daily and Monthly Extremes.
Data: 1948 to 2003 — Station 051778. Table updated May 20, 2003.
All temperatures F; Precipitation in inches; Boldface indicates record for period.
Latitude: 38.49; Longitude: 104 42; Elevation: 6,170 ft.
Source: Western Regional Climate Center

TEMPS.	JAN.	FEB.	MARCH	APRIL	MAY	JUNE	JULY	AUG.	SEPT.	OCT.	NOV.	DEC.	ANNUAL
Monthly Avg.													
Max	42.4	45.4	50.1	59.4	68.7	79.4	84.7	82.1	74.7	63.9	50.6	43.7	62.1
Min	16.4	19.4	24.2	32.7	42.3	51.4	56.9	55.4	47.3	36.3	24.7	18.0	35.4
Mean	29.4	32.4	37.2	46.1	55.5	65.4	70.8	68.8	61.0	50.1	37.7	30.8	48.8
Daily Extremes													
High	73	76	81	87	93	**100**	**100**	99	94	86	78	77	
Date dd-yy	02-1997	05-1963	26-1971	30-1992	24-1984	**23-1954**	**13-1954**	03-1954	08-1959	01-1964	17-1981	23-1955	
Low	-26	**-27**	-11	-3	21	32	42	39	22	5	-8	-24	
Date dd-yy	31-1951	**01-1951**	12-1956	10-1959	02-1954	03-1951	08-1952	27-1992	29-1985	13-1969	02-1951	22-1990	
Monthly Extremes													
High Mean	38.2	41.1	44.3	53.8	60.2	70.8	75.5	71.9	65.3	58.2	47.4	39.7	51.7
Year	1986	1954	1986	1981	1963	2002	1963	1995	1963	1963	1949	1980	1954
Low Mean	16.9	21.7	25.6	39.3	49.4	59.0	66.0	65.7	54.3	41.5	29.8	18.4	46.6
Year	1979	1960	1965	1957	1995	1951	1950	1968	1961	1969	1972	1983	1961
No. of Days													
Max Temp													
>= 90	0	0	0	0	0.1	3.9	8.4	3.6	0.8	0	0	0	17.0
<= 32	6.9	4.9	3.6	0.8	0	0	0	0	0	0.4	3.2	5.8	25.4
Min Temp													
<= 32	29.9	26.6	26.1	14.1	2.2	0	0	0	0.9	8.9	24.4	29.6	162.6
<= 0	2.6	1.4	0.4	0	0	0	0	0	0	0	0.4	1.5	6.3
PRECIPITATION													
Mean	0.29	0.32	0.92	1.37	2.26	2.29	2.92	2.92	1.24	0.83	0.48	0.33	16.17
High	1.17	2.45	2.42	7.50	5.67	8.00	5.27	7.04	4.28	5.01	2.21	1.05	27.58
Year	1987	1987	1998	1999	1957	1965	1968	1999	1976	1984	1957	1988	1999
Low	0	0	0.01	0.01	0.33	0.13	0.67	0.15	0	0.01	0	0	7.85
Year	1953	1991	1966	1964	1970	1990	1987	1962	1953	1955	1949	1970	2002
1-day Max	0.77	1.49	1.63	2.63	2.23	2.65	3.63	**3.98**	1.38	1.54	0.81	0.66	
Date dd-yy	15-1987	26-1987	18-1998	30-1999	18-1955	20-1970	29-1997	**04-1999**	29-1959	18-1960	19-1979	21-1981	
No. of Days													
>= 0.01	4	4	7	8	10	10	13	12	7	5	4	4	90
>= 0.1	1	1	3	3	5	5	7	6	3	2	1	1	38
>= 0.5	0	0	0	1	1	1	2	2	1	0	0	0	8
>= 1	0	0	0	0	0	0	0	0	0	0	0	0	2
SNOWFALL													
Mean	5.0	4.8	9.0	6.6	1.4	0	0	0	1.0	3.3	5.3	5.3	41.5
High	28.7	23.2	23.2	42.7	19.4	1.1	0	0.2	27.9	25.9	26.3	26.3	87.8
Year	1987	1987	1984	1957	1978	1975	--	1952	1959	1984	1991	1991	1979

Colorado by the Numbers

Cortez, Colorado

Monthly Temperature and Precipitation Averages; Daily and Monthly Extremes.
Data: 1929 to 2003 — Station 051886. Table updated May 20, 2003.
All temperatures F; Precipitation in inches; Boldface indicates record for period.
Latitude: 37.22; Longitude: 108.33; Elevation: 6,180 ft.
Source: Western Regional Climate Center

TEMPS.	JAN.	FEB.	MARCH	APRIL	MAY	JUNE	JULY	AUG.	SEPT.	OCT.	NOV.	DEC.	ANNUAL
Monthly Avg.													
Max	41.0	45.7	53.2	63.0	72.7	83.4	88.6	86.2	79.0	67.2	52.1	42.7	64.6
Min	13.0	18.3	24.2	30.6	38.5	46.1	54.1	52.9	44.5	33.7	22.5	15.1	32.8
Mean	27.0	32.0	38.7	46.8	55.6	64.7	71.4	69.6	61.7	50.4	37.3	28.9	48.7
Daily Extremes													
High	63	78	76	88	95	100	**101**	99	96	86	72	65	
Date dd-yy	21-1994	17-1943	31-1966	18-1932	17-1932	22-1954	**13-1971**	15-1962	02-1995	07-1943	09-1934	01-1999	
Low	-27	**-31**	-15	6	17	27	37	36	23	12	-14	-22	
Date dd-yy	22-1937	**08-1933**	06-1935	04-1945	01-1967	07-1934	04-1995	21-1964	26-1930	29-1929	24-1931	08-1978	
Monthly Extremes													
High Mean	36.3	39.9	45.2	53.7	60.4	70.4	75.7	74.0	66.8	57.2	42.9	36.3	51.7
Year	2003	1995	1999	1943	2000	2002	2002	2000	1998	1950	1965	1980	2000
Low Mean	15.3	18.2	33.4	40.5	49.7	60.6	67.6	65.2	56.6	43.2	30.9	19.1	46.7
Year	1937	1933	1948	1970	1933	1965	1992	1968	1985	1984	1979	1931	1932
No. of Days													
Max Temp													
>= 90	0	0	0	0	0.1	5.6	14.2	8.4	1.0	0	0	0	29.5
<= 32	4.2	1.8	0.3	0	0	0	0	0	0	0	0.6	3.7	10.5
Min Temp													
<= 32	30.4	27.2	27.5	18.4	5.8	0.5	0	0	1.3	13.7	27.0	30.0	181.6
<= 0	4.2	1.8	0.1	0	0	0	0	0	0	0	0.2	2.3	8.6
PRECIPITATION													
Mean	1.00	0.98	1.20	0.95	0.89	0.47	1.20	1.55	1.37	1.45	0.96	1.02	13.01
High	3.51	3.22	4.60	3.40	3.82	1.94	4.06	3.80	4.72	6.56	2.78	3.60	26.34
Year	57	80	95	57	57	49	57	57	41	72	85	51	57
Low	0	0	0	0	0	0	0	0.11	0	0	0	0	5.23
Year	1934	1967	1934	1991	1974	1930	1993	1950	1953	1950	1932	1930	1989
1-day Max	1.02	0.93	1.50	1.26	1.19	1.33	1.36	1.82	**1.96**	1.65	1.62	1.17	
Date dd-yy	18-1943	14-1937	06-1995	28-1952	08-1957	18-1949	26-1957	14-1955	**22-1941**	13-1941	16-1964	11-1954	
No. of Days													
>= 0.01	6	6	7	5	5	3	7	8	6	6	5	6	71
>= 0.1	4	3	4	3	3	1	4	4	4	3	3	3	39
>= 0.5	0	0	0	0	0	0	1	1	1	1	0	0	6
>= 1	0	0	0	0	0	0	0	0	0	0	0	0	1
SNOWFALL													
Mean	9.4	6.1	5.1	1.8	0.1	0	0	0	0	0.3	2.9	7.8	33.6
High	34.3	20.5	25.8	16.0	2.0	0	0	0	2.0	6.3	15.3	38.5	71.8
Year	1949	1969	1961	1932	1961	--	--	--	1965	1949	1931	1967	1949

Denver, Colorado

Monthly Temperature and Precipitation Averages; Daily and Monthly Extremes.
Data: 1948 to 2003 — Station 052220. Table updated May 20, 2003.
All temperatures F; Precipitation in inches; Boldface indicates record for period.
Latitude: 39.46; Longitude: 104.53; Elevation: 5,290 ft.
Source: Western Regional Climate Center

TEMPS.	JAN.	FEB.	MARCH	APRIL	MAY	JUNE	JULY	AUG.	SEPT.	OCT.	NOV.	DEC.	ANNUAL
Monthly Avg.													
Max	43.7	47.1	52.4	61.3	70.8	81.9	88.0	85.9	77.5	66.2	52.4	45.3	64.3
Min	16.9	20.7	25.9	34.4	44.1	53.0	59.0	57.4	48.2	36.8	25.4	18.5	36.7
Mean	30.3	33.9	39.1	47.8	57.4	67.4	73.5	71.7	62.8	51.5	38.9	31.9	50.5
Daily Extremes													
High	74	76	84	90	95	**104**	103	102	97	89	79	75	
Date dd-yy	02-1997	05-1963	28-19/1	30-1992	16-1996	26-1994	06-1973	01-2002	04-1960	16-1991	19-1989	27-1980	
Low	-25	-25	-8	-2	22	30	43	41	17	3	-8	-25	
Date dd-yy	11-1963	01-1951	03-1960	02-1975	02-1954	02-1951	07-1952	23-1964	29-1985	13-1969	09-1950	22-1990	
Monthly Extremes													
High Mean	40.3	43.7	47.1	56.3	63.2	73.5	77.3	75.3	68.2	59.9	48.6	41.2	54.0
Year	1986	1954	1986	1981	1994	1994	2002	1995	1981	1950	1949	1980	1981
Low Mean	16.3	22.3	29.0	41.0	50.0	60.6	68.9	68.1	55.6	38.9	29.7	17.4	48.3
Year	1949	1989	1965	1983	1995	1967	1950	1968	1965	1969	1985	1983	1951
No. of Days													
Max Temp													
>= 90	0	0	0	0	0.4	7.0	14.8	9.9	2.8	0	0	0	35.0
<= 32	6.3	4.2	2.9	0.5	0	0	0	0	0	0.3	2.5	4.7	21.5
Min Temp													
<= 32	29.5	25.9	24.3	12.0	1.5	0	0	0	0.8	8.4	23.9	29.2	155.4
<= 0	3.1	1.6	0.5	0	0	0	0	0	0	0	0.4	2.1	7.7
PRECIPITATION													
Mean	0.51	0.59	1.24	1.77	2.48	1.67	2.04	1.58	1.17	0.97	0.86	0.55	15.58
High	1.33	1.66	4.56	5.35	7.31	4.69	6.99	5.85	4.67	4.17	2.67	2.84	23.84
Year	1962	1960	1983	1999	1957	1967	1998	1979	1961	1969	1991	1973	1997
Low	0.00	0.01	0.18	0.03	0.06	0.09	0.50	0.06	0.01	0.05	0.01	0.00	7.51
Year	2003	1970	1982	1963	1974	1980	1994	1960	1956	1962	1949	2002	1954
1-day Max	0.92	1.01	2.68	3.25	3.27	3.16	**3.83**	1.98	1.44	1.58	0.95	2.00	
Date dd-yy	08-1962	19-1953	05-1983	13-1967	06-1973	11-1970	19-1997	24-1992	28-1973	18-1960	20-1979	24-1982	
No. of Days													
>= 0.01	6	6	8	9	11	9	9	9	7	5	6	5	88
>= 0.1	1	2	4	4	5	4	4	3	3	3	3	2	38
>= 0.5	0	0	0	1	1	1	1	1	1	1	0	0	7
>= 1	0	0	0	0	1	0	1	0	0	0	0	0	2
SNOWFALL													
Mean	7.6	7.4	12.6	8.8	1.6	0	0	0	1.7	4.1	9.1	7.4	60.3
High	24.3	18.3	35.2	25.5	13.7	0.8	0.0	1.3	17.2	31.2	29.6	30.8	112.0
Year	1992	1960	2003	1957	1950	1951	--	1951	1971	1969	1991	1973	1959

Durango, Colorado

Monthly Temperature and Precipitation Averages; Daily and Monthly Extremes.
Data: 1900 to 1991 — Station 052432.
All temperatures F; Precipitation in inches; Boldface indicates record for period.
Latitude: 37.17; Longitude: 107.53; Elevation: 6,550 ft.
Source: Western Regional Climate Center

TEMPS.	JAN.	FEB.	MARCH	APRIL	MAY	JUNE	JULY	AUG.	SEPT.	OCT.	NOV.	DEC.	ANNUAL
Monthly Avg.													
Max	39.6	44.8	51.7	61.3	70.3	80.7	85.1	83.1	76.7	65.7	52.1	41.4	62.7
Min	10.2	15.9	22.3	29.1	35.2	41.7	49.9	48.9	40.6	30.9	21.3	12.9	29.9
Mean	24.9	30.3	37.0	45.2	52.8	61.2	67.5	66.0	58.6	48.3	36.8	27.2	46.3
Daily Extremes													
High	65	71	78	82	92	98	**102**	99	93	87	74	64	
Date dd-yy	11-1956	25-1986	31-1966	30-1943	27-1974	24-1990	**05-1989**	02-1902	13-1990	01-1980	02-1924	06-1969	
Low	**-30**	-27	-9	0	15	16	33	31	15	5	-14	-21	
Date dd-yy	**13-1963**	08-1933	06-1939	05-1901	05-1901	12-1901	02-1928	24-1900	07-1983	31-1900	24-1931	24-1990	
Monthly Extremes													
High Mean	33.9	38.7	44.2	51.4	58.3	67.2	71.0	69.8	62.3	53.5	41.8	35.3	48.9
Year	1956	1907	1934	1989	1984	1918	1989	1901	1910	1950	1901	1980	1954
Low Mean	14.9	16.6	29.7	39.7	47.0	53.1	61.2	60.6	53.9	42.3	29.4	16.7	43.8
Year	1937	1939	1917	1920	1917	1901	1926	1927	1912	1984	1938	1909	1935
No. of Days													
Max Temp													
>= 90	0	0	0	0	0	2.7	6.6	3.2	0.5	0	0	0	13
<= 32	5.8	2.0	0.3	0	0	0	0	0	0	0	0.6	4.9	13.6
Min Temp													
<= 32	30.6	27.8	28.8	21.1	9.5	1.8	0	0	3.5	19.3	28.0	30.5	201.1
<= 0	5.6	2.2	0.2	0	0	0	0	0	0	0	0.2	3.2	11.5
PRECIPITATION													
Mean	1.64	1.47	1.71	1.41	1.09	0.80	1.93	2.32	1.75	1.87	1.34	1.78	19.09
High	6.94	7.02	4.87	5.54	3.72	5.53	5.36	5.97	5.10	11.79	4.55	7.37	33.64
Year	1916	1911	1938	1926	1947	1927	1981	1947	1990	1972	1982	1921	1941
Low	0.08	0	0	0	0	0	0.02	0.24	0	0	0	0	8.9
Year	1936	1972	1934	1989	1918	1916	1900	1985	1953	1915	1901	1900	1901
1-day Max	2.02	1.60	1.74	1.44	1.88	2.68	2.30	2.30	2.62	**3.65**	1.90	2.12	
Date dd-yy	28-1916	19-1911	17-1922	28-1952	08-1955	28-1927	21-1930	30-1936	05-1970	**19-1972**	01-1986	06-1966	
No. of Days													
>= 0.01	7	7	8	7	6	4	10	11	7	6	5	7	87
>= 0.1	4	4	5	4	3	2	5	6	4	4	3	4	49
>= 0.5	1	1	1	1	1	0	1	1	1	1	1	1	11
>= 1	0	0	0	0	0	0	0	0	0	0	0	0	2
SNOWFALL													
Mean	17.6	15.0	10.5	3.5	0.5	0	0	0	0	1.0	5.3	15.4	68.8
High	74.0	100.0	33.5	18.1	11.0	0	0	0	1.2	17.0	27.0	46.0	130.6
Year	1916	1915	1961	1920	1978	--	--	--	1950	1984	1900	1967	1980

Weather

Fort Collins, Colorado

Monthly Temperature and Precipitation Averages; Daily and Monthly Extremes.
Data: 1900 to 2003 — Station 053005. Table updated May 20, 2003.
All temperatures F; Precipitation in inches; Boldface indicates record for period.
Latitude: 40.35; Longitude: 105.05; Elevation: 5,000 ft.
Source: Western Regional Climate Center

TEMPS.	JAN.	FEB.	MARCH	APRIL	MAY	JUNE	JULY	AUG.	SEPT.	OCT.	NOV.	DEC.	ANNUAL
Monthly Avg.													
Max	41.1	44.2	50.8	60.2	68.8	79.1	85.0	83.3	75.1	64.2	50.9	42.6	62.1
Min	13.4	17.1	23.8	32.9	42.0	50.3	55.8	54.1	45.1	34.1	22.9	15.5	33.9
Mean	27.2	30.7	37.3	46.6	55.4	64.7	70.4	68.7	60.1	49.1	36.9	29.1	48.0
Daily Extreme6													
High	73	76	81	89	97	**102**	**102**	100	97	88	79	76	
Date dd-yy	13-1996	25-1986	18-1921	30-1992	29-2000	23-1954	15-1925	01-1902	13-1990	17-1926	06-1934	11-1939	
Low	-38	-41	-31	-10	12	29	36	32	18	-8	-21	-35	
Date dd-yy	17 1930	01-1951	06-1943	04-1945	08-1917	13-1947	04-1903	25-1910	30-1985	31-1905	13-1916	09-1919	
Monthly Extremes													
High Mean	37.2	41.2	47.1	54.2	61.5	71.3	76.1	73.8	66.4	54.7	45.8	38.8	51.4
Year	2003	1954	1910	1981	2000	2002	2002	1983	1998	1963	1949	1980	1999
Low Mean	9.0	14.1	22.5	36.6	46.9	57.3	64.7	62.8	51.2	40.1	27.5	15.5	43.4
Year	1930	1903	1912	1920	1917	1928	1915	1915	1912	1969	1929	1932	1012
No. of Days													
Max Temp													
>= 90	0	0	0	0	0.1	3.7	8.2	5.1	0.9	0	0	0	18.0
<= 32	7.4	5.0	3.0	0.5	0	0	0	0	0	0.3	2.4	6.0	24.5
Min Temp													
<= 32	30.1	26.8	26.0	13.6	2.4	0.1	0	0	1.4	12.6	26.4	30.1	169.7
<= 0	4.3	2.8	0.9	0.1	0	0	0	0	0	0	0.7	3.0	11.8
PRECIPITATION													
Mean	0.37	0.48	1.16	1.99	2.80	1.81	1.58	1.39	1.31	1.10	0.61	0.46	15.06
High	1.29	1.65	5.63	10.56	7.47	6.31	6.71	7.39	7.34	6.70	2.29	4.08	27.57
Year	1940	1912	1990	1900	1901	1949	1997	1951	1938	1942	1973	1913	1923
Low	0	0	0.01	0.05	0.01	0.03	0	0.03	0.01	0	0	0	7.34
Year	1919	1992	1966	1908	1974	1917	1939	1960	1932	1933	1904	1905	1966
1-day Max	0.86	1.02	3.48	2.41	3.21	3.54	**4.63**	3.06	4.34	2.19	1.26	1.71	
Date dd-yy	08-1962	27-1918	06-1990	30-1999	13-1961	04-1949	29-1997	03-1951	21-1902	16-1942	20-1979	02-1913	
No. of Days													
>= 0.01	4	5	7	8	11	9	8	8	6	5	4	4	81
>= 0.1	1	1	3	4	6	4	4	3	3	3	2	1	36
>= 0.5	0	0	1	1	2	1	1	1	1	1	0	0	8
>= 1	0	0	0	0	1	0	0	0	0	0	0	0	2
SNOWFALL													
Mean	6.1	6.8	10.2	6.5	1.1	0	0	0	0.5	3.0	6.7	6.1	47.1
High	20.5	25.7	39.6	34.1	27.8	0.5	0	0	15.0	17.5	29.1	20.7	105.8
Year	1940	1911	1988	1945	1978	1947	--	--	1971	1997	1979	1979	1979

Fraser, Colorado

Monthly Temperature and Precipitation Averages; Daily and Monthly Extremes.

Data: 1909 to 1974 — Station 053113.

All temperatures F; Precipitation in inches; Boldface indicates record for period.

Latitude: 39.57; Longitude: 105.50; Elevation: 8,560 ft.

Source: Western Regional Climate Center. Fraser did not report 1975-1988.

TEMPS.	JAN.	FEB.	MARCH	APRIL	MAY	JUNE	JULY	AUG.	SEPT.	OCT.	NOV.	DEC.	ANNUAL
Monthly Avg.													
Max	28.5	31.8	36.8	46.4	57.9	67.9	73.4	71.6	65.3	54.0	39.2	30.0	50.2
Min	-5.4	-2.4	4.1	16.0	24.1	29.4	34.4	32.6	24.9	16.9	5.9	-3.5	14.8
Mean	11.6	14.7	20.5	31.2	41.0	48.6	53.9	52.1	45.1	35.5	22.6	13.3	32.5
Daily Extremes													
High	50	55	63	72	81	87	94	**98**	82	75	65	58	
Date dd-yy	30-1931	03-1934	30-1946	30-1943	26-1942	23-1954	10-1939	01-1969	02-1947	09-1910	02-1947	11-1939	
Low	**-53**	-49	-39	-30	-1	12	18	15	-2	-18	-37	-50	
Date dd-yy	10-1962	01-1951	14-1962	04-1970	04-1944	25-1914	01-1968	26-1910	30-1959	30-1923	16-1955	25-1924	
Monthly Extremes													
High Mean	21.0	24.4	29.1	39.8	46.6	52.5	58.0	55.7	50.0	41.2	31.2	21.9	36.6
Year	1953	1934	1946	1943	1934	1936	1946	1969	1940	1950	1949	1921	1934
Low Mean	3.5	4.8	11.6	22.8	34.9	42.8	50.9	48.5	38.3	26.7	14.1	4.0	28.7
Year	1937	1939	1964	1970	1914	1914	1912	1927	1912	1969	1968	1912	1912
No. of Days													
Max Temp													
>= 90	0	0	0	0	0	0	0	0	0	0	0	0	0
<= 32	19.9	14.2	9.1	2.7	0.2	0	0	0	0	1.0	7.4	17.9	72.5
Min Temp													
<= 32	30.8	28.1	30.9	29.8	29.3	22.5	12.0	16.1	26.0	30.4	29.9	30.8	316.6
<= 0	20.2	15.7	11.6	2.2	0	0	0	0	0	0.9	9.2	18.7	78.6
PRECIPITATION													
Mean	1.61	1.55	1.67	1.99	1.72	1.49	1.95	1.71	1.50	1.27	1.21	1.46	19.12
High	4.06	6.77	4.39	6.33	5.02	4.76	4.76	5.70	7.69	5.12	3.64	5.14	30.33
Year	1957	1936	1932	1933	1957	1969	1929	1963	1961	1969	1927	1951	1957
Low	0.15	0.36	0.35	0.23	0.14	0.01	0.09	0.21	0.03	0.05	0.15	0.23	11.04
Year	1931	1935	1914	1937	1974	1916	1915	1942	1944	1952	1914	1946	1944
1-day Max	1.14	1.22	1.00	3.03	2.5	1.61	1.31	0.97	3.20	2.30	1.06	**3.30**	
Date dd-yy	24-1921	23-1936	18-1922	15-1921	09-1957	09-1923	12-1962	09-1971	27-1959	15-1916	29-1927	05-1913	
No. of Days													
>= 0.01	13	12	13	12	11	9	12	12	9	8	9	12	130
>= 0.1	6	5	6	6	5	5	6	6	4	4	4	5	62
>= 0.5	0	0	0	1	1	1	1	1	1	0	0	0	6
>= 1	0	0	0	0	0	0	0	0	0	0	0	0	1
SNOWFALL													
Mean	23.4	22.9	21.6	20.6	5.6	0.7	0.0	0.0	1.5	9.3	16.8	20.0	142.5
High	55.5	82.4	49.4	68.5	25.0	10.0	0	0	14.0	55.0	55.5	595	275.5
Year	1936	1936	1932	1921	1927	1947	1910	1910	1970	1969	1927	1922	1927

Weather

Glenwood Springs, Colorado

Monthly Temperature and Precipitation Averages; Daily and Monthly Extremes.
Data: 1900 to 2003 — Station 053359. Table updated Sept., 2003.
All temperatures F; Precipitation in inches; Boldface indicates record for period.
Latitude: 39.31; Longitude: 107.19; Elevation: 5,910 ft.
Source: Western Regional Climate Center

TEMPS.	JAN.	FEB.	MARCH	APRIL	MAY	JUNE	JULY	AUG.	SEPT.	OCT.	NOV.	DEC.	ANNUAL
Monthly Avg.													
Max	36.9	42.7	51.3	61.6	72.1	82.4	88.4	86.1	78.4	66.4	49.8	38.1	62.9
Min	11.6	16.6	24.2	31.1	38.2	44.0	50.6	49.4	41.8	31.8	22.2	13.4	31.2
Mean	24.3	29.6	37.8	46.3	55.1	63.2	69.5	67.7	60.0	49.1	35.9	25.7	47.0
Daily Extremes													
High	68	67	79	88	95	**102**	**102**	100	100	88	80	65	102
Date dd-yy	20-1923	25-1981	29-1943	25-1946	31-2002	**23-1954**	**07-1989**	08-1958	04-1924	08-1910	01-1975	01-1999	
Low	**-38**	-30	-14	2	17	27	30	28	20	10	-9	-22	
Date dd-yy	**07-1913**	13-1905	01-1917	05-1966	16-1916	08-1906	04-1903	31-1903	28-1907	10-1905	28-1911	27-1904	
Monthly Extremes													
High Mean	32.0	39.6	45.6	53.7	61.5	68.9	74.9	72.7	65.8	55.0	41.9	36.5	49.6
Year	1981	1934	1934	1946	1934	1977	2002	1983	1998	1950	1962	1980	1954
Low Mean	14.4	17.2	27.0	39.6	46.8	56.2	62.8	61.7	54.2	40.8	29.0	14.7	43.3
Year	1973	1903	1948	1973	1917	1908	1902	1916	1961	1969	1992	1909	1909
No. of Days													
Max Temp													
>= 90	0	0	0	0	0.1	5.6	14.4	9.1	1.5	0	0	0	30.8
<= 32	8.4	3.0	0.6	0	0	0	0	0	0	0	1.3	7.5	20.9
Min Temp													
<= 32	30.6	27.1	26.8	17.5	4.9	0.6	0	0	2.1	16.3	27.5	30.4	183.9
<= 0	5.2	2.3	0.3	0	0	0	0	0	0	0	0.4	3.8	12.0
PRECIPITATION													
Mean	1.46	1.29	1.43	1.63	1.42	1.12	1.27	1.50	1.58	1.47	1.15	1.30	16.62
High	6.01	5.17	4.13	5.75	5.83	4.92	4.51	3.93	5.38	4.21	2.89	4.45	26.48
Year	52	36	12	78	95	69	37	27	61	84	86	51	95
Low	0	0.06	0.04	0.08	0	0	0	0.26	0	0	0	0.17	8.28
Year	2003	1917	1966	1992	1911	1906	1908	1975	1901	1952	1904	1976	1966
1-day Max	1.30	1.30	1.35	1.78	1.75	**3.20**	1.80	1.45	1.93	2.00	1.13	1.47	3.20
Date dd-yy	19-1952	07-1967	11-1940	01-1978	09-2003	**24-1969**	28-1937	21-1970	04-1982	08-1924	10-2002	30-1951	
No. of Days													
>= 0.01	8	7	8	8	7	5	7	9	7	6	6	8	86
>= 0.1	5	4	5	5	4	3	4	5	5	4	4	4	53
>= 0.5	0	1	1	1	1	1	1	1	1	1	0	0	7
>= 1	0	0	0	0	0	0	0	0	0	0	0	0	1
SNOWFALL													
Mean	18.4	11.7	6.7	1.9	0.3	0	0	0	0	1.2	5.4	15.3	60.9
High	58.5	43.3	34.0	12.3	6.0	1.0	0	0	3.0	19.0	28.0	61.0	119.5
Year	1996	1939	1929	1945	1922	1976	--	--	1920	1908	1919	1983	1951

Colorado by the Numbers

Grand Junction, Colorado

Monthly Temperature and Precipitation Averages; Daily and Monthly Extremes.
Data: 1900 to 2003 — Station 053488. Table updated May 20, 2003.
All temperatures F; Precipitation in inches; Boldface indicates record for period.
Latitude: 39.07; Longitude: 108.32; Elevation: 4,850 ft.
Source: Western Regional Climate Center

TEMPS.	JAN.	FEB	MARCH	APRIL	MAY	JUNE	JULY	AUG.	SEPT.	OCT.	NOV.	DEC.	ANNUAL
Monthly Avg.													
Max	36.6	44.6	55.0	65.1	75.4	86.8	92.6	89.4	80.6	67.3	51.2	39.9	65.3
Min	15.9	23.3	31.2	39.3	48.3	57.2	64.1	62.0	53.1	41.1	28.3	18.7	40.2
Mean	26.2	34.0	43.1	52.2	61.9	72	78.3	75.7	66.9	54.2	39.7	28.8	52.8
Daily Extremes													
High	62	70	81	89	100	**105**	**105**	103	100	88	75	66	
Date dd-yy	31-1911	24-1904	19-1907	29-1992	31-2002	**27-1990**	**15-1925**	02-1902	04-1995	01-1963	05-1977	06-1901	
Low	**-23**	-21	5	11	26	34	44	43	28	16	-2	-21	
Date dd-yy	**13-1963**	08-1933	05-1939	02-1975	02-1970	14-1976	05-1993	23-1968	27-1908	29-1917	28-1976	26-1924	
Monthly Extremes													
High Mean	36.8	43.5	51.2	60.3	68.9	79.1	82.5	80.3	72	61.3	48.3	40.1	57.4
Year	1981	1907	1910	1943	1934	1977	1934	1983	1979	1963	1965	1980	1934
Low Mean	11.5	15.3	35.5	45.7	55.1	66.6	74.7	70.3	58.9	47.3	32.5	15.6	49.9
Year	1973	1903	1948	1920	1917	1947	1912	1968	1961	1969	1948	1919	1912
No. of Days													
Max Temp													
>= 90	0	0	0	0	1.0	13.1	23.3	17.3	3.3	0	0	0	57.8
<= 32	9.8	2.7	0.2	0	0	0	0	0	0	0	0.7	6.8	20.3
Min Temp													
<= 32	30.3	24.8	17.6	5.5	0.3	0	0	0	0.1	3.7	22.1	29.8	134.2
<= 0	2.8	1.0	0	0	0	0	0	0	0	0	0	1.1	4.9
PRECIPITATION													
Mean	0.59	0.57	0.83	0.78	0.79	0.44	0.62	1.01	0.93	0.91	0.63	0.57	8.68
High	2.46	1.56	2.36	2.15	2.74	2.07	2.72	3.65	3.29	3.45	2.0	1.89	15.69
Year	1957	1948	1912	1997	1906	1969	1929	1921	1927	1972	1983	1951	1957
Low	0	0	0.02	0.05	0	0	0.01	0.02	0	0	0	0	3.56
Year	1961	1972	1909	1939	1940	1916	1994	1903	1901	1917	1904	1900	1900
1-day Max	0.64	0.58	1.02	0.86	1.83	1.12	1.39	1.43	**1.87**	1.35	1.08	1.16	
Date dd-yy	16-1956	19-1934	16-1918	27-1965	24-1906	08-1912	18-1974	24-1921	**22-1941**	18-1908	26-1919	30-1951	
No. of Days													
>= 0.01	7	7	7	7	6	4	6	7	6	6	5	6	74
>= 0.1	2	2	3	3	3	1	2	3	3	3	2	2	28
>= 0.5	0	0	0	0	0	0	0	0	0	0	0	0	2
>= 1	0	0	0	0	0	0	0	0	0	0	0	0	0
SNOWFALL													
Mean	6.0	3.8	3.1	0.9	0.1	0	0	0	0	0.4	2.4	5.0	21.6
High	33.7	18.4	14.9	14.3	5	0	0	0	3.1	6.1	23.6	19.0	55.7
Year	1957	1948	1948	1975	1979	--	--	--	1965	1975	1919	1983	1948

58

Gunnison, Colorado

Monthly Temperature and Precipitation Averages; Daily and Monthly Extremes.
Data: 1900 to 2003 — Station 053662. Table updated May 20, 2003.
All temperatures F; Precipitation in inches; Boldface indicates record for period.
Latitude: 38.33; Longitude: 106.55; Elevation: 7,630 ft.
Source: Western Regional Climate Center

TEMPS.	JAN.	FEB.	MARCH	APRIL	MAY	JUNE	JULY	AUG.	SEPT.	OCT.	NOV.	DEC.	ANNUAL
Monthly Avg.													
Max	26.0	31.1	41.8	55.9	66.4	76.2	80.8	78.7	72.6	61.7	45.4	30.0	55.5
Min	-7.1	-1.6	11.5	22.3	29.3	35.7	42.5	40.7	32.2	21.5	10.6	-2.3	19.6
Mean	9.5	14.7	26.6	39.1	47.9	56.0	61.7	59.7	52.4	41.6	28.0	13.9	37.9
Daily Extremes													
High	63	61	75	78	87	95	95	**98**	91	82	69	62	
Date dd-yy	31-1954	25-1904	27-1928	10-1930	30-1936	15-1932	07-1932	**15-1931**	03-1930	01-1938	01-1906	10-1939	
Low	-45	-43	-29	-14	-7	15	23	24	9	-6	-26	**-47**	
Date dd-yy	22-1906	01-1916	02-1903	08-1973	07-1968	01-1919	01-1968	25-1962	21-1978	25-1932	27-1952	**25-1924**	
Monthly Extremes													
High Mean	21.7	31.4	38.1	43.8	53.3	60.9	65.0	63.7	57.2	46.6	35.1	27.4	41.9
Year	1981	1934	1934	1915	1934	1918	1919	1934	1940	1963	1913	1980	1981
Low Mean	-4.8	-0.4	15.0	31.5	42.2	50.8	57.6	49.4	46.1	34.6	16.0	1.5	32.8
Year	1984	1974	1914	1929	1907	1908	1929	1927	1912	1969	1930	1909	1975
No. of Days													
Max Temp													
>= 90	0	0	0	0	0	0.3	0.7	0.3	0	0	0	0	1.3
<= 32	22.0	14.6	5.0	0.2	0	0	0	0	0	0.1	3.4	17.9	63.2
Min Temp													
<= 32	30.9	28.1	30.8	28.3	21.8	8.8	0.7	2.7	16.0	28.1	29.7	30.9	257.8
<= 0	22.1	15.2	5.5	0.2	0	0	0	0	0	0	4.2	18.4	65.6
PRECIPITATION													
Mean	0.82	0.76	0.68	0.69	0.79	0.69	1.46	1.48	0.97	0.73	0.55	0.77	10.40
High	3.52	2.61	3.31	2.29	2.72	2.95	4.21	3.61	3.32	4.13	1.87	3.10	17.75
Year	1956	1936	1961	1996	1914	1949	1911	1971	1970	1969	1965	1997	1959
Low	0	0	0	0	0	0	0	0.14	0	0	0	0	6.01
Year	1931	1931	1915	1901	1932	1916	1900	1985	1932	1934	1904	1976	2002
1-day Max	1.54	1.03	1.50	1.90	1.04	1.10	1.42	1.24	1.16	1.33	1.25	**2.80**	
Date dd-yy	07-1952	19-1955	01-1948	13-1996	29-1937	17-1912	21-1935	02-1994	10-1918	14-1947	04-1959	**08-1997**	
No. of Days													
>= 0.01	6	6	6	6	6	5	10	11	7	5	5	6	77
>= 0.1	3	3	2	2	3	2	5	5	3	2	2	3	34
>= 0.5	0	0	0	0	0	0	1	0	0	0	0	0	3
>= 1	0	0	0	0	0	0	0	0	0	0	0	0	0
SNOWFALL													
Mean	12.0	10.3	7.0	3.5	0.8	0.1	0	0	0.2	1.3	5.3	10.3	50.8
High	50.2	34.8	26.0	16.0	7.0	5.5	0	0	7.0	24.0	21.0	37.8	97.5
Year	1957	1936	1943	1933	1915	1928	--	--	1912	1969	1975	1983	1916

Leadville, Colorado

Monthly Temperature and Precipitation Averages; Daily and Monthly Extremes.
Data: 1976 to 2003 — Station 054885. Table updated May 20, 2003.
All temperatures F; Precipitation in inches; Boldface indicates record for period.
Latitude: 39.14; Longitude: 106.18; Elevation: 10,050 ft.
Source: Western Regional Climate Center

TEMPS.	JAN.	FEB.	MARCH	APRIL	MAY	JUNE	JULY	AUG.	SEPT.	OCT.	NOV.	DEC.	ANNUAL
Monthly Avg.													
Max	31.0	33.8	38.6	45.3	56.3	67.4	71.6	69.4	62.5	51.3	38.0	31.1	49.7
Min	2.7	4.2	10.2	18.2	26.5	32.7	37.4	36.9	30.7	22.2	11.2	3.1	19.7
Mean	16.9	19.0	24.4	31.7	41.4	50.1	54.4	53.2	46.6	36.7	24.6	17.1	34.7
Daily Extremes													
High	56	54	61	65	80	82	**84**	83	80	71	66	53	
Date dd-yy	12-1987	21-1995	06-1987	29-1992	31-2002	29-1990	**06-2000**	19-2002	06-1978	05-1997	16-1999	04-1987	
Low	-27	**-38**	-30	-17	7	19	26	25	8	-7	-24	-31	
Date dd-yy	12-1989	**01-1985**	05-2002	12-1980	06-1999	16-1981	08-1994	19-1978	27-1996	30-1993	28-1976	23-1990	
Monthly Extremes													
High Mean	24.3	24.2	29.3	38.5	46.8	53.7	58.3	56.0	50.8	40.4	32.0	21.7	36.3
Year	2003	1995	1999	2002	2000	2002	2002	1995	1998	1988	1999	1998	1999
Low Mean	9.7	14.1	17.9	24.2	36.1	46.5	51.4	48.7	42.5	30.5	18.1	12.3	33.0
Year	1979	1985	1977	1983	1983	1995	1976	1976	1985	1984	1992	1978	1984
No. of Days													
Max Temp													
>= 90	0	0	0	0	0	0	0	0	0	0	0	0	0
<= 32	17.5	11.6	6.7	2.4	0.1	0	0	0	0	1.1	9.4	16.6	65.4
Min Temp													
<= 32	30.6	28.1	30.8	29.9	27.5	16.0	3.8	5.5	18.9	39.8	29.7	30.6	281.1
<= 0	12.6	9.7	5.3	1.0	0	0	0	0	0	0.2	4.0	11.9	44.8
PRECIPITATION													
Mean	0.71	0.87	1.01	1.04	0.68	0.85	1.79	1.96	1.02	0.72	0.86	0.78	12.29
High	4.83	3.19	2.13	2.93	2.42	2.17	4.17	4.25	1.99	2.19	2.29	4.37	20.20
Year	1996	1986	2001	1997	1995	1992	1992	1984	202	1996	1977	1977	1996
Low	0	0.12	0.06	0	0.04	0	0.41	0.50	0.20	0.04	0.10	0.01	8.81
Year	1981	1985	1999	1981	1998	1999	1994	2002	1998	1976	1980	1998	1994
1-day Max	1.60	1.70	1.30	0.92	1.0	0.98	1.30	1.27	0.56	1.30	0.74	**2.10**	
Date dd-yy	30-1996	13-1986	05-1996	11-1997	26-1996	08-1979	12-1992	24-1992	18-2002	29-1996	01-1986	**24-1983**	
No. of Days													
>= 0.01	9	8	11	10	7	6	12	14	9	6	9	8	110
>= 0.1	2	2	3	4	2	3	5	6	4	2	2	2	38
>= 0.5	0	0	0	0	0	0	1	1	0	0	0	0	3
>= 1	0	0	0	0	0	0	0	0	0	0	0	0	1
SNOWFALL													
Mean	17.7	18.6	22.5	25.4	8.3	2.1	0.1	0	2.5	10.1	20.6	17.7	145.5
High	55.8	63.2	47.5	64.1	19.9	15.0	3.4	0.0	16.2	34.5	39.9	49.0	247.9
Year	1996	1995	1991	1995	1990	1979	1995	1976	1985	1990	1992	1996	1996

Weather

Lamar, Colorado
Monthly Temperature and Precipitation Averages; Daily and Monthly Extremes.
Data: 1918 to 2003 — Station 054770. Table updated May 20, 2003.
All temperatures F; Precipitation in inches; Boldface indicates record for period.
Latitude: 38.04; Longitude: 102.37; Elevation: 3,640 ft.
Source: Western Regional Climate Center

TEMPS.	JAN.	FEB.	MARCH	APRIL	MAY	JUNE	JULY	AUG.	SEPT.	OCT.	NOV.	DEC.	ANNUAL
Monthly Avg.													
Max	44.9	51.3	58.9	69.6	78.4	88.8	94.2	92.0	84.2	72.3	56.3	46.5	69.8
Min	13.9	19.3	26.2	36.8	47.4	57.5	62.9	61.0	51.3	37.4	23.9	16.1	37.8
Mean	29.4	35.3	42.5	53.2	62.9	73.1	78.5	76.5	67.7	54.9	40.1	31.3	53.8
Daily Extremes													
High	82	84	92	98	103	108	**111**	110	105	99	89	82	
Date dd-yy	14-1928	20-1981	28-1963	22-1989	20-1925	24-1927	13-1934	01-1938	06-1931	04-1922	10-1927	24-1955	
Low	**-29**	-21	-26	8	20	34	43	40	23	8	-18	-23	
Date dd-yy	30-1949	08-1933	11-1948	04-1920	13-1920	02-1919	08-1952	27-1992	30-1985	29-1991	03-1991	12-1932	
Monthly Extremes													
High Mean	40.5	44.7	52.3	60.0	70.2	79.7	85.2	83.6	75.3	62.7	47.6	40.8	57.0
Year	1986	1930	1918	1981	1934	1918	1934	1934	1931	1963	1949	1933	1933
Low Mean	15.8	21.8	31.4	46.4	56.6	65.0	71.2	68.2	61.3	48.5	30.5	18.1	50.4
Year	1940	1960	1924	1944	1995	1992	1992	1992	1965	1969	1946	1924	1993
No. of Days													
Max Temp													
>= 90	0	0	0.1	0.8	5.1	15.7	23.5	21.1	11.0	1.5	0	0	78.9
<= 32	5.8	3.1	1.3	0.1	0	0	0	0	0	0.1	1.3	4.4	16.2
Min Temp													
<= 32	30.6	26.9	23.5	9.1	0.8	0	0	0	0.4	8.8	26.3	30.6	157
<= 0	3.5	1.3	0.4	0	0	0	0	0	0	0	0.2	2.0	7.4
PRECIPITATION													
Mean	0.43	0.42	0.90	1.25	2.45	2.22	2.27	2.14	1.17	0.88	0.59	0.41	15.15
High	1.43	2.07	4.67	5.71	7.38	7.54	9.00	7.51	4.42	5.22	5.31	2.24	24.51
Year	1960	1960	1973	1944	1944	1949	1927	1997	1941	1930	1946	1918	1946
Low	0	0	0	0	0	0.09	0.13	0.06	0	0	0	0	7.67
Year	1922	1926	1930	1935	1966	1952	1931	1974	1934	1922	1921	1928	1937
1-day Max	1.25	1.25	1.67	2.19	**5.64**	4.70	2.83	2.72	2.65	2.51	1.58	1.70	
Date dd-yy	23-1921	11-1934	16-1924	16-1969	29-1964	04-1949	25-1957	11-1992	22-1941	11-1930	02-1946	03-1921	
No. of Days													
>= 0.01	3	3	5	5	8	7	8	7	5	3	3	3	59
>= 0.1	1	1	2	3	5	4	5	4	3	2	1	1	33
>= 0.5	0	0	0	1	1	1	1	1	1	0	0	0	9
>= 1	0	0	0	0	1	0	1	1	0	0	0	0	3
SNOWFALL													
Mean	5.1	4.5	5.5	1.8	0.1	0	0	0	0	1.0	4.0	4.6	26.7
High	31.5	30.4	25.5	16.0	3.5	0	0	0	2.0	30.0	38.1	19.5	74.0
Year	2001	1960	1948	1919	1954	--	--	--	1985	1997	1946	1918	1997

Pueblo, Colorado

Monthly Temperature and Precipitation Averages; Daily and Monthly Extremes.
Data: 1954 to 2003 — Station 056740. Table updated May 20, 2003.
All temperatures F; Precipitation in inches; Boldface indicates recordfor period.
Latitude: 38.17; Longitude: 104.31; Elevation: 4,650 ft.
Source: Western Regional Climate Center

TEMPS.	JAN.	FEB.	MARCH	APRIL	MAY	JUNE	JULY	AUG.	SEPT.	OCT.	NOV.	DEC.	ANNUAL
Monthly Avg.													
Max	45.8	50.7	57.3	67.1	76.6	87.5	92.6	89.7	81.7	70.2	55.9	47.5	68.5
Min	13.8	18.7	25.5	35.0	45.3	54.0	60.3	58.6	49.3	36.1	23.6	15.9	36.3
Mean	29.8	34.8	41.4	51.0	60.9	70.7	76.4	74.1	65.5	53.1	39.7	31.7	52.4
Daily Extremes													
High	81	81	86	93	102	**108**	106	104	101	94	84	82	
Date dd-yy	02-1997	27-1980	10-1989	21-1989	19-2000	29-1990	29-1980	06-1969	05-1995	16-1991	07-1980	17-1980	
Low	**-28**	-26	-10	2	26	36	44	40	27	4	-17	**-28**	
Date dd-yy	04-1959	03-1996	09-1964	08-1957	01-1972	10-1998	08-1994	24-1968	29-1983	26-1997	03-1991	12-1961	
Monthly Extremes													
High Mean	39.4	41.8	47.8	59.6	65.5	76.2	80.3	79.8	70.0	61.0	46.3	41.2	56.5
Year	1986	1970	1986	1981	1974	1956	1970	1970	1963	1963	1981	1980	1981
Low Mean	16.1	24.0	31.5	43.7	54.0	65.1	71.8	70.5	59.9	48.3	31.1	20.8	49.7
Year	1979	1989	1965	1997	1995	1995	1995	1992	1961	2002	1985	1983	1993
No. of Days													
Max Temp													
>= 90	0	0	0	0.1	2.6	14.0	22.3	18.3	67.1	0.3	0	0	64.8
<= 32	6.0	3.1	1.3	0.1	0	0	0	0	0	0.1	1.7	4.5	16.8
Min Temp													
<= 32	30.3	26.8	24.7	10.6	0.8	0	0	0	0.6	10.0	25.8	30.1	159.8
<= 0	3.8	1.6	0.3	0	0	0	0	0	0	0	0.3	2.4	8.5
PRECIPITATION													
Mean	0.31	0.28	0.82	1.11	1.49	1.29	1.96	2.07	0.84	0.75	0.52	0.34	11.79
High	0.94	1.39	2.94	5.30	5.43	4.26	5.14	5.85	2.73	4.91	2.48	0.97	23.09
Year	1988	1987	2000	1999	1957	1961	1990	1955	1976	1957	1991	1979	1957
Low	0.01	0	0.04	0	0.22	0	0.09	0.08	0	0	0	0	3.94
Year	1995	1970	2002	1963	2002	1990	1987	1960	1956	1977	1966	1959	2002
1-day Max	0.55	0.60	1.26	2.00	2.67	2.24	1.96	**2.95**	1.57	2.77	0.78	0.61	
Date dd-yy	19-1990	14-1987	18-1998	30-1999	17-1995	24-1979	25-1977	29-1955	13-1982	08-1957	16-1991	27-1979	
No. of Days													
>= 0.01	4	4	6	6	8	7	9	9	5	4	4	4	70
>= 0.1	1	1	3	3	4	3	5	4	2	2	2	1	30
>= 0.5	0	0	0	1	1	1	1	1	0	0	0	0	6
>= 1	0	0	0	0	0	0	0	0	0	0	0	0	1
SNOWFALL													
Mean	5.4	3.9	6.1	3.8	0.4	0	0	0	0.6	1.5	4.0	4.8	30.5
High	18.3	14.4	15.7	21.2	10.6	0	0	0	14.0	16.3	25.6	15.3	72.4
Year	1988	1965	1964	1957	1990	--	--	--	1959	1991	1991	1967	1990

Silverton, Colorado

Monthly Temperature and Precipitation Averages; Daily and Monthly Extremes.
Data: 1906 to 2003 — Station 057656. Table updated May 20, 2003.
All temperatures F; Precipitation in inches; Boldface indicates record for period
Latitude: 37.48; Longitude: 107.40; Elevation: 9,420 ft.
Source: Western Regional Climate Center

TEMPS.	JAN.	FEB.	MARCH	APRIL	MAY	JUNE	JULY	AUG.	SEPT.	OCT.	NOV.	DEC.	ANNUAL
Monthly Avg.													
Max	34	36.7	40.5	47.3	57.5	67.9	73.0	70.5	64.8	55.0	43.2	35.1	52.1
Min	-1.9	1.1	8.1	18.5	26.4	31.8	37.9	37.1	30.3	21.9	9.4	0.2	18.4
Mean	16.1	18.9	24.3	32.9	41.9	49.9	55.5	53.8	47.5	38.5	26.3	17.6	35.3
Daily Extremes													
High	64	61	68	72	79	**96**	93	92	88	78	68	65	
Date dd-yy	10-1953	27-1932	22-1925	25-1927	31-2002	**26-1929**	14-1922	02-1924	28-1981	08-1960	24-1917	19-1931	
Low	-38	**-39**	-25	-18	2	10	20	13	5	-12	-24	-35	
Date dd-yy	18-1984	**01-1985**	14-1962	01-1980	05-1912	20-1911	10-1931	13-1907	27-1908	28-1919	24-1931	23-1990	
Monthly Extremes													
High Mean	23.0	27.3	32.7	39.7	46.5	54.5	60.1	57.6	52.1	44.2	33.9	26.9	38.1
Year	1911	1930	1999	1943	1925	1918	2002	1995	1963	1963	1965	1980	1934
Low Mean	7.3	9.8	17.2	20.7	31.7	43.3	52.1	49.0	41.7	30.6	16.3	10.0	31.5
Year	1937	1939	1952	1912	1912	1907	1906	1908	1912	1984	2000	1909	1912
No. of Days													
Max Temp													
>= 90	0	0	0	0	0	0	0.1	0	0	0	0	0	0.1
<= 32	13.2	8.5	5.1	1.6	0.2	0	0	0	0	0.4	3.8	11.6	44.5
Min Tem9													
<= 32	30.9	28.2	30.8	29.1	26.9	17.3	4.1	6.2	19.7	29.0	29.8	30.9	283.5
<= 0	19.0	14.0	8.1	1.1	0	0	0	0	0	0.3	6.1	17.1	65.6
PRECIPITATION													
Mean	1.62	1.71	2.32	1.68	1.49	1.39	2.75	3.10	2.76	2.36	1.46	1.74	24.38
High	6.50	5.20	6.83	5.87	5.34	5.85	5.74	6.44	8.83	8.50	5.32	6.40	44.78
Year	1916	1989	1912	1999	1981	1927	1926	1923	1927	1941	1985	1981	1911
Low	0.03	0.1	0.4	0	0	0	0.46	0.84	0.18	0	0	0.05	16.63
Year	1919	1972	1997	1913	1974	1916	1980	1974	1956	1952	1914	1930	1939
1-day Max	1.90	2.10	2.15	1.26	1.71	2.00	1.68	2.20	2.05	**4.05**	2.10	2.20	
Date dd-yy	17-1913	04-1989	28-1985	28-1944	02-1999	28-1927	02-1990	27-1932	06-1970	**05-1911**	27-1919	31-1981	
No. of Days													
>= 0.01	8	9	10	9	8	7	14	15	11	8	7	8	114
>= 0.1	5	5	7	6	5	4	9	10	7	6	5	5	73
>= 0.5	1	1	1	1	1	1	1	1	2	1	1	1	11
>= 1	0	0	0	0	0	0	0	0	0	0	0	0	2
SNOWFALL													
Mean	25.2	25.2	28.7	17.1	4.3	0.4	0	0	0.9	8.7	19.9	24.0	154.3
High	81.5	88.0	81.0	48.5	31.5	8.0	0	0	17.0	42.0	69.5	90.8	231.0
Year	1957	1993	1912	1917	1999	1947	--	--	1906	1920	1985	1983	1952

Steamboat Springs, Colorado

Monthly Temperature and Precipitation Averages; Daily and Monthly Extremes.
Data: 1908 to 2003 — Station 057936. Table updated May 20, 2003.
All temperatures F; Precipitation in inches; Boldface indicates record for period.
Latitude: 40.30; Longitude: 106.50; Elevation: 6,770 ft.
Source: Western Regional Climate Center

TEMPS.	JAN.	FEB.	MARCH	APRIL	MAY	JUNE	JULY	AUG.	SEPT.	OCT.	NOV.	DEC.	ANNUAL
Monthly Avg.													
Max	28.8	34.0	42.0	53.4	65.1	75.2	82.3	80.3	72.3	60.1	43.0	30.6	55.6
Min	0.9	4.1	13.4	24.2	31.3	35.7	41.4	40.1	32.5	23.9	14.1	3.3	22.1
Mean	14.8	19.1	27.7	38.8	48.2	55.5	61.8	60.2	52.5	42.0	28.5	16.9	38.8
Daily Extremes													
High	57	59	67	79	88	96	97	**98**	93	89	72	64	
Date dd-yy	24-1910	13-1947	30-1986	30-1943	31-2000	30-1990	25-1931	**26-1948**	07-1908	10-1910	03-1909	10-1939	
Low	**-54**	-48	-34	-15	8	19	25	20	6	-16	-28	-44	
Date dd-yy	**07-1913**	10-1933	11-1948	04-1945	29-1927	02-1918	01-1968	26-1910	24-1926	27-1919	28 1976	18-1909	
Monthly Extremes													
High Mean	27.4	29.5	37.0	45.4	54.1	62.7	67.9	65.8	58.6	47.5	36.2	29.2	43.2
Year	1981	1934	1992	1989	1914	1988	2002	2001	1998	1963	1949	1980	1934
Low Mean	5.6	7.4	17.3	31.1	43.2	50.8	58.3	55.2	45.9	35.8	17.1	6.4	34.4
Year	1924	1923	1923	1920	1917	1945	1992	1927	1961	1919	2000	1919	1924
No. of Days													
Max Temp													
>= 90	0	0	0	0	0	0.3	2.3	1.2	0.1	0	0	0	4.0
<= 32	20.4	11.4	3.8	0.4	0	0	0	0	0	0.2	5.2	17.8	59.2
Min Temp													
<= 32	30.9	28.2	30.6	26.8	18.8	8.7	1.6	3.3	15.4	27.1	29.4	30.8	251.5
<= 0	15.1	11.3	4.7	0.2	0	0	0	0	0	0.1	3.5	13.4	48.2
PRECIPITATION													
Mean	2.50	2.24	2.11	2.26	2.08	1.49	1.54	1.60	1.77	1.91	1.96	2.39	23.81
High	5.86	5.13	5.73	5.13	5.66	4.31	4.98	5.36	8.15	5.97	5.59	7.26	35.14
Year	1996	1936	1929	1920	1995	1945	1912	1914	1961	1908	1985	1951	1957
Low	0.23	0.30	0.49	0.60	0.07	0	0.14	0.17	0.07	0	0.14	0.63	15.84
Year	1919	1935	1910	1966	1948	1919	1971	1944	1953	1933	1914	1979	1934
1-day Max	1.48	1.93	**2.71**	1.50	1.70	2.57	1.39	1.15	2.55	1.75	1.57	1.42	
Date dd-yy	29-1965	19-1986	**02-1929**	20-1971	18-1944	14-1921	13-1937	03-1965	22-1961	05-1911	26-1919	30-1951	
No. of Days													
>= 0.01	13	11	11	10	10	8	9	10	8	7	9	12	120
>= 0.1	8	7	7	7	6	4	5	5	5	5	6	8	74
>= 0.5	1	1	1	1	1	1	1	1	1	1	1	1	10
>= 1	0	0	0	0	0	0	0	0	0	0	0	0	1
SNOWFALL													
Mean	35.6	29.5	23.9	13.2	2.8	0.1	0	0	0.9	76.9	19.9	32.8	165.6
High	111.6	65.8	73.4	52.4	20.5	5.6	0	0	19.6	32.3	57.0	92.6	301.6
Year	1996	1936	1929	1920	1944	1976	--	--	1961	1996	1983	1983	1996

Sterling, Colorado

Monthly Temperature and Precipitation Averages; Daily and Monthly Extremes.
Data: 1948 to 2003 — Station 057950. Table updated May 20, 2003.
All temperatures F; Precipitation in inches; Boldface indicates record for period.
Latitude: 40.37; Longitude: 103.12; Elevation: 3,940 ft.
Source: Western Regional Climate Center

TEMPS.	JAN.	FEB.	MARCH	APRIL	MAY	JUNE	JULY	AUG.	SEPT.	OCT.	NOV.	DEC.	ANNUAL
Monthly Avg.													
Max	39.0	45.2	521.9	62.4	72.2	83.3	89.9	88.0	78.7	66.7	50.9	41.2	64.1
Min	11.2	16.8	23.4	33.2	44.1	53.7	59.1	56.9	46.3	33.8	22.0	13.7	34.5
Mean	25.1	31.0	37.7	47.8	58.1	68.5	74.5	72.5	62.5	50.2	36.4	27.4	49.3
Daily Extremes													
High	71	77	86	92	98	**110**	108	105	103	93	86	74	
Date dd-yy	22-1950	09-1954	29-1963	18-1987	29-1974	**28-1990**	02-1990	06-1960	10-19/9	12-1996	01-1950	05-1980	
Low	-26	-30	-21	-3	23	30	37	35	14	3	-10	**-35**	
Date dd-yy	18-1984	05-1982	03-1960	02-1975	02-1954	03-1954	13-1951	28-1964	30-1985	26-1997	27-1952	22-1989	
Monthly Extremes													
High Mean	34.5	41.1	45.6	53.1	63.9	75.0	79.2	78.0	69.8	56.2	44.4	34.9	52.5
Year	2003	1954	1986	1992	1994	1988	2002	1995	1998	1963	1999	1957	1994
Low Mean	10.5	22.1	25.6	41.5	51.7	61.5	69.2	68.1	52.2	41.1	26.0	12.2	46.6
Year	1949	1989	1965	1984	1950	1951	1951	1956	1965	1969	1985	1983	1951
No. of Days													
Max Temp													
>= 90	0	0	0	0.1	1.3	9.1	17.1	14.7	5.3	0.3	0	0	47.9
<= 32	8.9	5.2	3.2	0.5	0	0	0	0	0	0.3	3.3	7.1	28.6
Min Temp													
<= 32	30.9	27.7	26.7	13.6	1.8	0.1	0	0	1.2	12.9	27.7	30.7	173.2
<= 0	65.7	2.6	0.6	0	0	0	0	0	0	0	0.7	3.4	13.0
PRECIPITATION													
Mean	0.31	0.28	0.85	1.19	2.82	2.73	2.57	1.74	1.12	0.89	0.50	0.29	15.27
High	1.28	1.24	3.52	3.51	6.44	8.26	10.52	5.90	3.88	4.21	2.13	1.19	21.60
Year	1978	1993	1984	1977	1987	1992	1998	1968	1973	1969	1972	1973	1979
Low	0	0	0	0.10	0.29	0.15	0.13	0.02	0	0	0	0	7.27
Year	1964	1949	1966	2002	1974	2001	1952	1970	1956	19/7	1949	1959	1954
1-day Max	0.90	0.70	1.75	1.52	3.07	3.11	2.56	**4.88**	1.94	1.75	0.93	0.54	
Date dd-yy	20-1990	10-1998	19-1984	20-1981	29-1975	04-1985	27-1963	**15-1968**	01-1992	23-1995	03-1956	13-1952	
No. of Days													
>= 0.01	3	3	5	5	9	8	8	6	5	4	3	2	62
>= 0.1	1	1	2	3	6	5	5	4	3	2	1	1	35
>= 0.5	0	0	0	1	2	2	2	1	1	0	0	0	9
>= 1	0	0	0	0	1	1	1	0	0	0	0	0	3
SNOWFALL													
Mean	4.1	3.0	4.4	2.1	0.2	0	0	0	0.2	0.2	3.3	3.3	20.8
High	15.3	19.0	18.8	11.0	5.0	0	0	0	7.0	3.3	23.9	18.1	49.4
Year	1992	1987	1958	1975	1954	--	--	--	1985	1991	1983	1985	1987

Trinidad, Colorado

Monthly Temperature and Precipitation Averages; Daily and Monthly Extremes.
Data: 1948 to 2003 — Station 058434. Table updated May 20, 2003.
All temperatures F; Precipitation in inches; Boldface indicates record.
Latitude: 37.15; Longitude: 104.20; Elevation: 5,750 ft.
Source: Western Regional Climate Center

TEMPS.	JAN.	FEB.	MARCH	APRIL	MAY	JUNE	JULY	AUG.	SEPT.	OCT.	NOV.	DEC.	ANNUAL
Monthly Avg.													
Max	46.9	50.8	56.5	65.2	74.3	84.6	88.8	86.6	79.8	69.3	55.8	47.9	67.2
Min	16.6	19.8	25.2	34.1	43.8	53.1	58.6	57.0	49.1	37.3	25.4	17.9	36.5
Mean	31.8	35.3	40.9	49.7	59.0	68.8	73.7	71.8	64.5	53.3	40.6	32.9	51.8
Daily Extremes													
High	80	82	85	91	97	**103**	**103**	100	100	89	81	81	
Date dd-yy	01-1997	13-1979	26-1971	21-1989	16-1996	21-1981	01-1973	07-1980	05-1995	01-1954	09-1980	17-1980	
Low	**-32**	-24	-13	3	22	35	43	43	23	1	-17	-19	
Date dd-yy	11-1963	05-1982	02-2002	12-1997	01-1991	02-1949	08-1952	28-1964	29-1984	30-1993	27-1976	23-1990	
Monthly Extremes													
High Mean	40.6	43.2	47.6	57.0	64.7	74.2	77.2	74.9	69.4	61.6	48.2	41.8	54.5
Year	1986	2000	1986	1981	1996	1956	1980	1983	1998	1950	1999	1980	1954
Low Mean	21.0	21.1	30.8	42.6	54.1	63.4	69.2	68.5	60.2	45.9	31.7	20.8	50.2
Year	1979	1964	1965	1973	1995	1969	1950	1950	1965	1969	1992	1983	1997
No. of Days													
Max Temp													
>= 90	0	0	0	0.1	0.9	9.4	15.8	10.7	3.2	0	0	0	40.1
<= 32	4.5	2.9	1.7	0.2	0	0	0	0	0	0.2	1.6	4.0	15.1
Min Temp													
<= 32	29.5	26.3	24.7	12.5	2.0	0	0	0	0.6	8.0	24.1	29.5	157.3
<= 0	2.7	1.6	0.3	0	0	0	0	0	0	0	0.5	1.8	6.9
PRECIPITATION													
Mean	0.37	0.43	0.80	1.03	1.76	1.4	2.10	2.00	1.07	0.83	0.69	0.50	12.97
High	1.30	1.27	2.58	4.21	6.40	6.39	6.55	4.95	2.97	2.83	2.37	1.81	20.76
Year	1966	1990	2000	1999	1955	1965	1981	1997	1982	1998	1992	1973	1979
Low	0.01	0	0.05	0	0.12	0.11	0.35	0.20	0	0	0	0	7.23
Year	1950	1957	2002	1963	2002	1954	1987	1973	1956	1952	1965	1970	2002
1-day Max	0.60	0.63	0.95	1.67	2.69	1.76	**4.52**	2.56	1.77	1.44	0.98	0.77	
Date dd-yy	02-1966	25-1977	18-1984	26-1998	18-1955	18-1982	03-1981	05-1997	09-1980	31-1972	02-1990	09-1961	
No. of Days													
>= 0.01	5	4	6	6	8	7	9	9	6	4	5	5	74
>= 0.1	1	1	2	2	4	4	5	5	3	2	2	2	35
>= 0.5	0	0	0	0	1	1	1	1	1	0	0	0	6
>= 1	0	0	0	0	0	0	0	0	0	0	0	0	0
SNOWFALL													
Mean	4.7	5.4	7.2	4.9	1.3	0	0	0	0.4	3.3	6.5	6.3	40.2
High	13.2	18.9	23.4	20.6	12.4	0	0	0	6.6	18.9	23.9	20.0	74.2
Year	1990	1964	2000	1980	1978	--	--	--	1985	1972	1992	1967	1990

Vail, Colorado

Monthly Temperature and Precipitation Averages; Daily and Monthly Extremes.
Data: 1985 to 2003 — Station 058575. Table updated May 20, 2003.
All temperatures F; Precipitation in inches; Boldface indicates record for period.
Latitude: 39.38; Longitude: 106.22; Elevation: 8,225 ft.
Source: Western Regional Climate Center

TEMPS.	JAN.	FEB.	MARCH	APRIL	MAY	JUNE	JULY	AUG.	SEPT.	OCT.	NOV.	DEC.	ANNUAL
Monthly Avg.													
Max	39.9	34.0	42.6	50.2	61.5	72.8	77.7	76.0	67.8	54.8	37.3	28.1	52.8
Min	5.8	8.4	16.8	23.9	31.0	35.2	40.5	40.0	32.8	23.9	14.3	5.9	23.2
Mean	17.8	21.2	29.7	37.1	46.3	54.0	59.1	58.0	50.3	39.4	25.8	17.0	38.0
Daily Extremes													
High	51	55	66	74	82	91	**95**	92	86	79	66	51	
Date dd-yy	30-1986	25-1986	10-1980	21-1989	31-2002	27-1990	**07-1989**	18-1986	16-1990	12-1991	02-1988	04-1987	
Low	-21	**-32**	-16	4	14	19	28	22	14	1	-13	-22	
Date dd-yy	21-1988	**02-1985**	02-2002	17-1999	11-1999	02-1990	03-1992	27-1992	30-1985	22-1996	04-1991	11-1986	
Monthly Extremes													
High Mean	23.3	26.4	33.5	41.7	49.8	57.8	62.3	60.5	54.9	42.6	30.5	18.9	39.1
Year	2003	1986	1986	1992	1992	1988	2002	2000	1990	1991	1999	1998	2000
Low Mean	12.9	13.3	25.0	31.7	41.4	50.2	55.4	55.7	46.8	35.4	18.2	14.7	36.1
Year	1989	1985	1996	1997	1995	1998	1995	1997	1996	1995	2000	1988	1997
No. of Days													
Max Temp													
>= 90	0	0	0	0	0	0.2	0.6	0.1	0	0	0	0	0.9
<= 32	19.0	11.5	4.1	1.2	0.1	0	0	0	0	0.8	9.8	21.9	68.3
Min Temp													
<= 32	30.9	28.0	30.7	28.3	19.5	8.3	1.5	1.7	14.4	28.5	29.9	31.0	252.7
<= 0	9.9	6.5	1.6	0	0	0	0	0	0	0	2.3	10.3	30.6
PRECIPITATION													
Mean	1.87	2.03	1.78	2.21	1.80	1.37	2.06	1.71	1.95	1.57	2.00	1.39	21.23
High	4.17	5.19	3.05	4.25	4.86	2.12	3.77	2.62	3.33	3.46	3.56	3.03	29.60
Year	1996	1993	1993	2001	1995	2000	1985	1999	1990	2002	2001	2001	1995
Low	0.81	0.65	0.64	0.77	0.64	0.29	0.45	0.40	0.70	0.15	0.96	0.19	15.84
Year	1992	1987	1997	2002	1998	2002	1994	1996	1998	1988	1999	1991	1994
1-day Max	1.8	1.45	1.20	**2.67**	1.34	1.50	1.01	0.94	1.20	1.10	0.85	1.20	
Date dd-yy	16-2003	21-1996	28-1993	**11-2001**	25-1999	02-1990	28-1987	03-2002	06-1990	22-1986	26-2001	07-2001	
No. of Days													
>= 0.01	12	12	10	10	10	8	11	12	11	7	11	10	125
>= 0.1	6	7	6	6	5	4	6	6	6	4	6	5	69
>= 0.5	1	1	0	1	1	1	1	0	1	1	1	0	8
>= 1	0	0	0	0	0	0	0	0	0	0	0	0	1
SNOWFALL													
Mean	33.9	33.8	25.1	20.7	3.7	0.4	0	0	1.2	8.2	31.0	26.8	184.8
High	92.5	76.0	42.8	53.6	19.3	4.0	0.5	0	8.0	17.0	55.3	75.3	331.7
Year	1996	1993	1993	1993	1995	1993	1993	--	1996	1996	1985	1996	1996

Severe Weather
Tornados

Colorado tornados have been recorded in nine different months in 49 of the state's 63 counties. Peak tornado season is mid-May through the summer months. The Front Range and grassland plains see the vast majority of the tornados – 1,223 of the 1,282 tornados recorded 1950 through 2000. Weld County has one of the highest tornado frequency rates in the nation with 213 recorded 1950-2000. Adams county, with 120, is second. Washington (110), Arapahoe (72), Yuma (68) and Kit Carson (76) Counties round out the top six to

Figure 4.1 – A May 18, 1975 tornado near Stapleton International Airport in Denver. (NOAA Central Library, Historic National Weather Service Collection. Ms. Carol A. Silberg, photographer.)

create what can be considered Colorado's tornado alley.

Colorado tornados have occurred day and night, but more than half develop between 3 and 6 p.m. 88% develop between 1 and 9 p.m.

Only two tornado-caused deaths have been recorded since 1950, the last on June 27, 1960 in Sedgwick County. Injuries total 157. Total damages are estimated at more than $68 million. The deadliest tornado on record caused 10 deaths in the town of Thurman on Aug. 10, 1924.

Compared to other states, Colorado ranks 9th in tornado frequency, 38th in fatalities, 31st for injuries and 30th in damage costs, according to DisasterCenter.com, an independent tracking source.

Tornados by year 1950-1995
Source: DisasterCenter.com

Year	# Tornados	Deaths	Injuries	Cost
1950	2	0	1	$65,607
1951	8	0	2	$68,840
1952	3	0	6	$715,986
1953	14	0	0	$137,565
1954	9	0	0	$25,862
1955	18	0	1	$739,358
1956	10	0	0	$1,802
1957	24	0	1	$35,674
1958	18	0	5	$98,862
1959	1	0	0	$54,335
1960	14	2	3	$658,201
1961	13	0	2	$169,747
1962	25	0	0	$19,581
1963	3	0	0	$10,334
1964	2	0	0	$5,100
1965	32	0	5	$377,565
1966	11	0	0	$4,880
1967	21	0	8	$1,051,456
1968	6	0	2	$100,411
1969	10	0	0	$95,213
1970	5	0	0	$44,826
1971	16	0	9	$4,303,028
1972	11	0	3	$45,770
1973	11	0	5	$391,723
1974	12	0	0	$352,789
1975	20	0	0	$449,654
1976	42	0	1	$397,368
1977	32	0	3	$1,046,264
1978	18	0	3	$281,549
1979	37	0	1	$2,422,901
1980	25	0	0	$27,440
1981	25	0	44	$20,893,936
1982	58	0	0	$25,462
1983	32	0	0	$181,529
1984	41	0	0	$243,638
1985	26	0	5	$370,303
1986	20	0	6	$1,602,774
1987	40	0	0	$44,539
1988	47	0	7	$15,307,604
1989	22	0	0	$295,826
1990	55	0	16	$12,646,658
1991	76	0	0	$626,883
1992	81	0	4	$172,426
1993	71	0	14	$1,248,494
1994	46	0	0	$21,338
1995	48	0	0	$230,323
Total	**1161**	**2**	**157**	**$68,111,424**

Tornados by county 1950-2000
Source: National Weather Service / NOAA

County	1950-2000	1996	1997	1998	1999	2000
Adams	120	17	2	2	0	1
Alamosa	9	0	1	1	0	0
Arapahoe	72	8	1	9	1	1
Archuleta	1	0	0	0	1	0
Baca	52	7	0	0	3	2
Bent	25	0	3	1	0	2
Boulder	10	2	1	0	0	0
Chaffee	1	0	0	0	0	0
Cheyenne	33	1	2	0	0	0
Clear Creek	0	0	0	0	0	0
Conejos	2	0	0	0	0	0
Costilla	5	0	0	0	0	0
Crowley	10	0	1	0	0	0
Custer	6	0	1	0	0	0
Delta	1	0	0	0	0	0
Denver	13	1	0	0	0	0
Dolores	0	0	0	0	0	0
Douglas	49	0	2	0	0	0
Eagle	1	0	0	0	0	0
El Paso	67	0	0	1	0	2
Elbert	52	1	3	1	0	0
Fremont	5	0	1	0	0	0
Garfield	0	0	0	0	0	0
Gilpin	0	0	0	0	0	0
Grand	1	0	0	0	0	0
Gunnison	0	0	0	0	0	0
Hinsdale	0	0	0	0	0	0
Huerfano	6	0	0	0	0	0
Jackson	1	0	0	0	0	0
Jefferson	13	1	0	0	0	0
Kiowa	42	6	2	1	0	3
Kit Carson	76	2	4	3	2	0
La Plata	3	0	2	0	1	0
Lake	0	0	0	0	0	0
Larimer	28	0	0	0	0	0
Las Animas	17	0	0	1	0	1
Lincoln	66	7	1	0	6	0
Logan	64	1	4	0	9	11
Mesa	4	0	0	1	0	3
Mineral	1	0	1	0	0	0
Moffat	3	0	2	0	1	0

Tornados by county *continued*

County	1950-2000	1996	1997	1998	1999	2000
Montezuma	2	0	0	0	0	0
Montrose	0	0	0	0	0	0
Morgan	54	7	4	2	1	5
Otera	22	0	2	2	0	0
Ouray	0	0	0	0	0	0
Park	0	0	0	0	0	0
Phillips	30	3	1	0	0	3
Pitkin	1	0	0	0	0	0
Prowers	48	3	0	2	1	2
Pueblo	12	1	0	1	1	0
Rio Blanco	1	0	0	0	0	0
Rio Grande	2	0	0	0	0	0
Routt	2	0	0	0	0	0
Saguache	4	0	0	0	0	1
San Juan	0	0	0	0	0	0
San Miguel	0	0	0	0	0	0
Sedgwick	29	0	3	1	5	0
Summit	0	0	0	0	0	0
Teller	4	1	0	0	0	0
Washington	110	13	0	1	2	14
Weld	213	13	6	7	7	7
Yuma	68	4	2	1	2	3
TOTALS	1461	99	52	38	43	61

Lightning

Convection-caused thunderstorms are an almost daily event in Colorado through the spring and summer months. Thunderstorms can range from light and brief afternoon showers to violent storms from towering thunderheads. Since it is lightning that causes the thunder, Colorado's summer weather could just as easily be marked by lightning storms. Florida far exceeds all states in number of lightning strikes, but Colorado consistently ranks near the top in both lightning strikes and lightning fatalities.

Year	Colo. Lightning Deaths	National Total	State Ranking
1995	4	85	5th
1996	3	52	3rd
1997	5	42	2nd
1998	3	44	2nd
1999	2	46	4th
2000	2	51	5th

Figure 4.2 – Lightning strikes in the Grand Valley near Grand Junction. (Photo courtesy Grand Junction Daily Sentinel. Chris Tomlinson photographer.)

Colorado Lightning Injuries 1982-2002

Source: Colorado Lightning Resource Center

Year	April	May	June	July	Aug.	Sept.	Oct.	Total
2002	0	0	1	0	1	0	0	2
2001	1	5	5	1	5	0	0	17
2000	0	0	0	13	0	0	2	15
1999	0	4	2	6	10	0	0	22
1998	1	1	0	3	9	4	0	18
1997	0	0	8	2	1	0	0	11
1996	0	0	2	3	5	2	3	15
1995	0	7	8	5	5	5	0	30
1994	2	1	1	1	12	3	0	20
1993	0	0	0	0	1	0	0	1
1992	2	3	9	4	4	0	0	22
1991	2	4	14	0	2	1	0	23
1990	0	0	0	8	4	1	0	13
1989	0	1	1	4	3	1	0	10
1988	1	0	7	15	0	1	0	24
1987	0	2	5	4	3	2	0	16
1986	0	0	5	0	0	0	0	5
1985	0	1	0	1	0	0	0	2
1984	0	0	0	1	1	0	0	2
1983	0	0	2	2	1	1	0	6
1982	0	2	5	0	3	0	0	10
Total	**9**	**31**	**75**	**73**	**70**	**21**	**5**	**284**

Colorado Lightning Deaths 1982-2002

Source: Colorado Lightning Resource Center

Year	April	May	June	July	Aug.	Sept.	Total
2002	0	0	0	0	0	0	0
2001	0	2	0	0	1	0	3
2000	0	0	0	2	0	0	2
1999	0	0	0	1	1	0	2
1998	0	0	0	0	2	1	3
1997	0	0	1	3	1	0	5
1996	0	0	1	1	0	1	3
1995	0	0	0	2	0	2	4
1994	1	0	0	1	0	1	3
1993	0	0	0	0	0	1	1
1992	1	0	1	0	1	0	3
1991	0	0	1	1	0	0	2
1990	0	0	0	1	0	1	2
1989	0	0	0	3	1	0	4
1988	1	0	3	2	0	0	6
1987	0	0	1	2	0	0	3
1986	0	0	1	0	0	0	1
1985	0	1	0	0	0	0	1
1984	0	0	2	1	1	0	4
1983	1	0	0	0	0	0	1
1982	0	2	3	0	0	1	6
Total	**4**	**5**	**14**	**20**	**9**	**7**	**59**

Floods

While infrequent, Colorado does experience flooding on a massive and tragic scale. By mid-summer, upper atmosphere winds are at their weakest, which allows thunderstorms to stall or hover over one area for relatively long periods of time. The combination of slow-moving storms dropping considerable moisture over steep mountain valleys often results in flash flooding. Some are deadly.

Big Thompson Flood of 1976

July 31, 1976 marks one of Colorado's worst natural disasters. As afternoon thunderstorms built over the steep mountain valleys of the eastern rampart of the Rockies between Estes Park and Loveland, low level easterly winds funneled moisture to the storms. Upper atmosphere winds that typically push the afternoon storms east over the plains were nearly non-existent. The storm remained stationary for hours pouring an estimated 12 to 14 inches of rain into the steep, rock-walled, narrow canyon. While most measuring devices were destroyed in the resulting flood, some estimates claim seven to eight inches of rain fell in the area in just two hours.

Big Thompson Creek, a mountain stream typically running at about 140 cubic feet per second that time of year, became a wall of water. Gauges at the mouth of the canyon recorded flows of 31,200 cubic feet per second during the height of the storm.

With the canyon crowded with weekend campers, the storm proved deadly. At least 139 deaths are attributed to the storm. Seven bodies were never recovered. The flood destroyed 316 homes, 45 mobile homes and 52 businesses. Another 73 mobile homes were seriously damaged. Total dollar figure for the damage is estimated at $35 million.

Fort Collins Flood of July 1997

A similar condition of weak upper atmosphere winds and a resulting stationary storm hit the southwest side of Fort Collins on the evening of July 28, 1997. With 14 inches of rain recorded in one day, a small drainage dammed by a railroad bed swelled with water. The culvert under the railroad bed eventually gave way under the pressure, which sent a wall of water into a nearby mobile home park. Five died in the flood.

Water from the same storm damaged the Colorado State University library. Water poured into a basement and damaged thousands of books.

The following night, an even bigger storm dropped 13 inches of rain on Pawnee Creek near Sterling. The resulting flood destroyed crops and damaged homes.

Denver Flood of 1965

Denver was the flood victim June 14-18, 1965. Several days of huge thunderstorms caused widespread flooding along the Front Range of Colorado. Bridges over Interstate 25 were washed out and water poured into the lower sections of downtown. Property damage was estimated at $600 million. Twenty deaths were blamed on the storm that affected not only Denver, but most of eastern Colorado. Two people were killed when a dam failed in Prowers County, causing $18 million in damage in Holly, Granada and Lamar.

Colorado Flood Fatalities 1995-2000

Year	In vehicle	In water	Mobile home	Other	Total
1995	0	0	0	0	0
1996	2	0	1	0	3
1997	1	3	4	1	9
1998	0	0	0	0	0
1999	0	0	0	0	0
2000	0	1	0	0	1
Totals	3	4	5	1	13

Thunderstorm phenomena

On July 11, 1990, moist easterly surface winds once again started feeding moisture in to building thunderstorms over the mountains west of Front Range cities. This time, cool air aloft allowed for the creation of large hailstones. Prevailing winds pushed the hailstorm in a slow path along the Front Range corridor – the state's most heavily populated area. The one-two punch of the storm damaged almost any car left outside, and hammered home roofs. At more than $600 million dollars in damage, the storm ranks as the second most expensive hailstorm in U.S. history. Such hailstorms have forced many auto insurance companies to leave the state, while homeowner's insurance premiums are higher to cover expected losses. No fatalities were recorded, but many were cut and bruised by the barrage.

Routt County Blowdown

Weather damage isn't confined to population centers. An Oct. 25, 1997 storm in an unpopulated area of Routt County created a massive downdraft. Winds of 120 miles per hour howled down from the east near the Continental Divide blowing down more than 4 million trees. A United States Forest Service report summarized the following. "The path of wind was almost 30 miles wide and five miles long and affected approximately 13,000 acres, with 8,000 of those acres within the Mount Zirkel Wilderness. Although numerous individual trees were blown down, most of the impact occurred in patches ranging from 50 to 4,000 acres." The depth of downed timber in some places exceeded 30 feet. After extensive study, the Forest Service agreed to salvage an estimated 43.3 million board feet of timber from the downed areas, which is enough wood to construct more than 4,000 homes. Controversy over the salvage project has resulted in nothing being done to date.

Avalanche

The Colorado Avalanche Information Center estimates more than 20,000 avalanches occur in Colorado's mountains yearly. Roughly 60 people are caught in avalanches each year. On average, six are killed. While all mountain areas are prone to avalanches, Colorado conditions – shallower and colder snowpack – creates a higher incidence of avalanches than in other mountainous areas. Some avalanches are rather small and slow – maybe 30 miles per hour. Others encompass entire mountainsides or steep chutes and may reach speeds exceeding 100 miles per hour.

105 people died in Colorado avalanches in the 17 winters from 1985-86 to 2001-2002, representing 29% of all avalanche fatalities in the United States. Direct property damage from avalanches averages $100,000 per year.

Avalanche Fatalites by state 1985-86 to 2001-02

Source: Colorado Avalanch Information Center

Year	CO	AK	UT	MT	CA	WA	WY	ID	OR	NV	NH	NY	TOTAL
85-86	.4	.0	.5	.2	.2	.2	.0	.0	.0	.0	.0	.0	.17
86-87	.11	.6	.2	.1	.0	.1	.0	.0	.0	.0	.0	.0	.21
87-88	.5	.2	.0	.0	.0	.1	.0	.0	.0	.0	.0	.0	.8
88-89	.4	.0	.0	.0	.0	.0	.0	.0	.1	.1	.0	.0	.6
89-90	.4	.1	.1	.1	.1	.0	.0	.0	.0	.0	.0	.0	.8
90-91	.6	.1	.0	.0	.0	.0	.0	.0	.0	.0	.1	.0	.8
91-92	.9	.2	.5	.1	.2	.2	.2	.0	.0	.1	.0	.0	.24
92-93	.12	.7	.3	.1	.1	.0	.1	.2	.1	.0	.0	.1	.29
93-94	.1	.2	.1	.6	.0	.0	.1	.0	.2	.0	.0	.0	.13
94-95	.9	.6	.5	.3	.0	.0	.2	.1	.1	.0	.0	.0	.28*
95-96	.7	.8	.2	.3	.0	.0	.3	.3	.0	.0	.3	.0	.30*
96-97	.1	.4	.6	.1	.0	.5	.2	.3	.0	.0	.0	.0	.22
97-98	.6	.3	.2	.7	.1	.2	.1	.3	.1	.0	.0	.0	.26
98-99	.6	.12	.5	.2	.1	.4	.2	.0	.0	.0	.0	.0	.32
99-00	.8	.5	.2	.2	.0	.1	.0	.2	.0	.0	.1	.1	.22
00-01	.4	.4	.6	.7	.2	.3	.7	.0	.0	.0	.0	.0	.33
01-02	.8	.11	.3	.10	.1	.0	.1	.1	.0	.0	.0	.0	.35
Total	.105	.74	.48	.37	.13	.21	.23	.15	.5	.2	.5	.2	.362*

* 1 fatalaity in Arizona (94-95) and 1 fatality in New Mexico (95-96) reflected in total.

Avalanche Fatalites by activity – all U.S. 1985-86 to 2001-02
Source: Colorado Avalanch Information Center

	17-Year Total	%of total
Climbers	55	16%
Backcountry skiers	73	21%
Ski area	3	1%
Out of Bounds skiers	39	11%
Backcountry snowboard	19	6%
Out of Bounds snowboard	12	4%
Snowmobile	101	28%
Misc. recreation	37	11%
Non-Recreation activities		
Patrollers	6	2%
Motorist / highway worker	4	1%
Residents	6	2%
Other at work	7	2%
Total	362	

Colorado Total Severe Weather Fatalities, Injuries, Property Damage
1995-2000

Year	Fatalities		Injuries		Damage ($Millions)	
	CO	U.S.	CO	U.S.	CO	U.S.
1995	5	1,362	28	3,864	7.6	11,383
1996	11	540	62	2,711	164.4	7,975
1997	30	600	67	3,799	380.5	10,786
1998	10	687	45	11,171	96.6	16,111
1999	9	908	44	5,148	141.6	12,254
2000	6	430	34	2,547	40.8	7,687
Total	71	4,527	280	239,240	831.5	66,196

Landslides

Ragged Mountain near Paonia is the site of one of the largest landslides in U.S. history. Heavy rains and snow in 1983 and 1984 are blamed for the slide that started on the lower reaches of Ragged Mountain and eventually closed McClure Pass, the auto route between Paonia and Carbondale. The slide started in May of 1986 when 140 million cubic yards of earth covering more than 1,060 acres started moving at about one foot per hour down the slope. The width of the slide was estimated at 3,500 feet, while the depth reached 150 feet at points. By July, the slide slowed to roughly ten feet a day. Construction crews kept the slide from damming Muddy Creek, creating a new lake and eventually re-built the highway. When a new highway was built, it was 40 feet above the original when reopened.

Drought

A series of bright sunny days can add up to a vague, yet frequent weather hazard in Colorado – drought. Most often, drought is associated with lower than normal precipitation, but according to the Colorado Office of Emergency Management, drought can also be induced by humans. It occurs when the demand for water exceeds available water and typically affects agriculture, wildfire management, municipal usage, tourism, recreation and widllife preservation.

Colorado's diverse weather patterns and ecosystems experience droughts differently. At any given time, one area of the state can be experiencing drought, while another luxuriates in a wet year. Colorado also depends on only a few big storms a year to meet its average or normal precipitation levels. More than half of the state's annual precipitation falls during only one-fifth of the days it rains or snows.

The Colorado Climate Center at Colorado State University has analyzed historical drought patterns and discovered the following:

• Single season droughts with 75% of average precipitation lasting one to three consecutive months occur nearly every year somewhere in Colorado. A moderate precipitation shortage over three months has occurred somewhere in Colorado in 90 of the past 100 years.

• 93% of the time, at least 5% of the state is experiencing drought at either a three-, six-, 12-, or 24-month level.

• Only 5% of the time does moderate or greater drought encompass at least half the state at the same time.

• A moderate drought has never covered the entire state at the same time since records have been kept.

• Short-term droughts of three months have covered as much as 80 percent of the state. Long-term droughts of two to four years have reached to about 70% of the state.

• Most droughts are of six months or fewer. They may be localized or widespread. Geographic region of a drought has no relation to severity.

• Periods of three consecutive years with less than 80% of average precipitation is very rare. In some areas, such as the northern half of the state, it has never happened.

• Only three examples exist of four-year spans of 80% or lower average precipitation: 1899-1902 in southwestern Colorado; 1933-1937 in southeastern Colorado – the Dust Bowl years; and 1952-1956 in eastern Colorado.

• Drought episodes have lasted up to 10 years, but these spans have experienced intermittent periods of wet weather. Three of the state's wettest months – April 1900, May 1935 and September 1938 – were part of larger-scope, long-term drought periods.

• Many areas of Colorado have experienced stretches of up to 60 days with no measurable precipitation.

• Six-month winter snow accumulation of 25 - 40% of average represents an extremely dry winter. Twelve months of 50 - 60% of average consitutes an extreme drought. Two to four consecutive months with below average precipitation is common. Five or more months is very rare.

• Drought cycles are not apparent. Despite widespread belief in three-year cycles, seven-year cycles or 11-year double sunspot cycles, data indicate no reliable pattern. There is some evidence of a two- to three-year cycle in some areas of southern and eastern Colorado.

Drought Periods

1890-1894 – Severe but brief drought in 1890, particularly east of mountains, followed by a very wet 1891. Dry 1893 with severe drought 1894; again most pronounced over eastern Colorado.

1898-1904 – Sustained and very severe drought over southwestern Colorado. Worst drought on record in Durango area. Some dry years elsewhere in Colorado, but not as severe or sustained. Very wet 1900 in northeast Colorado.

1930-1940 – Most widespread and longest-lasting drought in Colorado recorded history. Responsible for the Dust Bowl. Severe drought developed in 1931 and peaked in 1934 and early 1935. Interrupted by heavy spring rains in 1935 and more widespread heavy rains in 1938. Culminated with one more extremely dry year in 1939 when several stations along the Front Range recorded their driest years in history.

1950-1956 – Extremely dry period statewide except for one heavy snow winter 1951-52. Most of state affected and drought worse than the 1930s in some areas such as Front Range.

1959-1973 – Alternating very wet and fairly dry periods and large spatial variations. Local drought was prevalent in 1959, 1960, 1962, 1963, 1964, 1966 and 1972. Very wet weather was reported in 1961, 1965, 1969, 1970 and 1973 with episodes of flooding.

1974-1978 – Colorado's most recent period of sustained multi-year drought culminating in the record-breaking winter drought of 1976-1977, the driest winter in recorded history for much of Colorado's mountain areas.

1981 – An extreme but brief drought over the winter of 1980-81 in the mountains. This drought devastated the ski industry and prompted most areas to invest in snowmaking equipment.

1999-present -- Following Colorado's second-longest sustained wet period, the state entered into a multi-year dry spell with 2002 ranking as one of the driest years on record. 2001-2002 winter snowpack levels fell to 53% of historic averages. While the winter of 2002-2003 saw snowpack levels return to near normal averages in most areas of the state, it was not enough to end statewide water availability concerns. Drought conditions in the Durango area continued through 2003.

Wet Periods

1905-1929 – Longest recorded wet period in Colorado history with greatest areal extent in 1905-1906, 1914-15, 1921, 1923 and 1927. Significant but brief droughts did occur during this period, most notably 1910-11 and 1924-25.

1931-1949 – Widespread wet weather, especially 1941, 1947 and 1949. Wet period interrupted with dry mountain winter 1944-45 and 1945-46.

1957-1958 – 1957 featured persistent widespread drought-breaking precipitation across nearly all of Colorado. It was the wettest year in recorded history.

1979-1980 – Brief but pronounced wet period with heavy winter snows helped replenish reservoirs following dry years from 1974-1978.

1982-1999 – Colorado's second longest sustained wet period and the most drought-free period since 1890. Extremely abundant snowpack and surface water supplies 1982-87 with the largest annual streamflow volumes this century on several rivers. 1987 to 1994 experienced modest snow pack accumulations and consistently below-average streamflow, but low elevation precipitation reduced demand for surface water. The state experienced a significant but brief drought in 1989 to early 1990 in southwest Colorado. Northeast Colorado experienced a brief growing-season drought in 1994 while southwest Colorado experienced a localized drought from late 1995 into 1996. Very wet statewide in 1995, 1997 and 1999. The decade of the 1990s was the wettest in recorded history over much of southeastern Colorado.

Source: A History of Drought in Colorado by Thomas B. McKee, Nolan J. Doesken and John Kleist, Colorado Climate Center, Atmospheric Science Department Colorado State University, and Catherine Shrier, Colorado Water Resources Research Institute in collaboration with William P. Stanton, Colorado Water

CHAPTER

5 People and Demographics

Despite a history of economic booms and busts, steady – even explosive
population growth has been a Colorado constant since the mid-1850s.
Colorado lost population in the mid-1860s when the gold rush ended, in
the mid-1890s when the silver boom ended and again in the mid-1980s
when the oil industry collapsed, but never has it lost population over a 10-
year census period.

Colorado experienced 30% growth from 1990 to 2000, which ranks it
the third-fastest growing state by percentage. With just more than 1 million new residents between 1990 and 2000, Colorado ranks eighth in population growth. Overall, Colorado is the 24th most populous state.

The growth prompted unprecedented economic prosperity, but at a
price. For many residents, the beauty and splendor of the state has been
compromised by growth and development.

Of Colorado's 4.3 million residents in 2000, 3.3 million, or 77%, live
in nine Front Range counties which contain the cities and suburbs of Fort
Collins, Greeley, Boulder, Longmont, Denver, Colorado Springs and
Pueblo. The only other metropolitan area is Grand Junction, in far western Colorado, with 116,255 Mesa County residents.

Population trends show slow or no growth on the eastern plains of the
state, explosive growth in most resort mountainous counties and steady,
but relatively controlled growth in the far west. Only six counties lost population between 1990 and 2000: Baca, Cheyenne, Jackson, Kiowa, Rio
Blanco and San Juan.

Eleven Colorado counties have population densities below two people
per square mile: Baca, Cheyenne, Jackson, Kiowa, Rio Blanco, San Juan,
Dolores, Hinsdale, Mineral, Saguache and Washington. Hinsdale County
has the fewest people of all Colorado counties with 790, and a density of
0.7 people per square mile. That contrasts to Denver County's 554,446
people and a density of 3,617 people per square mile.

Colorado 2000 Census - 2001 Estimated Population
Source: United States Census Bureau

	Colorado	USA	% Colo. of USA
Population 2001 estimate	4,417,714	284,796,887	1.55%
% change, April 1, 2000-July 1, 2001	2.70%	1.20%	
Population, 2000	4,301,261	281,421,906	1.53%
Population, % change, 1990 to 2000	30.60%	13.10%	
Under 5 years old, %	6.90%	6.80%	
Under 18 years old, %	25.60%	25.70%	
65 years and over, %	9.70%	12.40%	
Female, %	49.60%	50.90%	
White, % (a)	82.80%	75.10%	
Black /African American, % (a)	3.80%	12.30%	
American Indian/Alaska Native, % (a)	1.00%	0.90%	
Asian, % (a)	2.20%	3.60%	
Native Hawaiian/Pacific Islander (a)	0.10%	0.10%	
Reporting some other race, % (a)	7.20%	5.50%	
Reporting two or more races, %	2.80%	2.40%	
Hispanic or Latino origin, % (b)	17.10%	12.50%	
White persons, not of Hispanic/Latino origin, %	74.50%	69.10%	
Living in same house 1995 -2000, % age 5+	44.10%	54.10%	
Foreign born persons, %	8.60%	11.10%	
Language other than English at home, % age 5+	15.10%	17.90%	
High school graduates, %, age 25+	86.90%	80.40%	
Bachelor's degree or higher, %, age 25+	32.70%	24.40%	
With a disability, age 5+	638,654	49,746,248	1.28%
Mean travel time to work, age 16+ (minutes)	24.3	25.5	
Housing unit	1,808,037	115,904,641	1.56%
Homeownership rate	67.30%	66.20%	
Housing units in multi-unit structures, %	25.70%	26.40%	
Median value of owner-occupied housing units	$166,600	$119,600	
Households	1,658,238	105,480,101	1.57%
Persons per household	2.53	2.59	
Median household money income, 1999	$47,203	$41,994	
Per capita money income, 1999	$24,049	$21,587	
Persons below poverty, %, 1999	9.30%	12.40%	

Geography

Land area, 2000 (square miles)	104,247	3,537,438	2.93%
Persons per square mile, 2000	41.5	79.6	

(a) Includes persons reporting only one race.
(b) Hispanics may be of any race, so also are included in applicable race categories.

Adams County, Colorado, 2000-2001 Census

Organized April 15, 1901 from Arapahoe County. Annexed a portion of Denver County in 1909. Named for Alva Adams, statesman and governor. County seat Brighton.

	County	Colorado	% of Colo.
Population 2001 estimate	374,891	4,417,714	8.49%
% change, April 1, 2000-July 1, 2001	3.00%	2.70%	
Population, 2000	363,857	4,301,261	8.46%
Population, % change, 1990 to 2000	37.30%	30.60%	
Under 5 years old, %	8.40%	6.90%	
Under 18 years old, %	28.60%	25.60%	
65 years and over, %	7.80%	9.70%	
Female, %	49.30%	49.60%	
White, % (a)	77.30%	82.80%	
Black /African American, % (a)	3.00%	3.80%	
American Indian/Alaska Native, % (a)	1.20%	1.00%	
Asian, % (a)	3.20%	2.20%	
Native Hawaiian/Pacific Islander (a)	0.10%	0.10%	
Reporting some other race, % (a)	11.70%	7.20%	
Reporting two or more races, %	3.50%	2.80%	
Hispanic or Latino origin, % (b)	28.20%	17.10%	
White persons, not of Hispanic/Latino origin, %	63.30%	74.50%	
Living in same house 1995 -2000, % age 5+	43.80%	44.10%	
Foreign born persons, %	12.50%	8.60%	
Language other than English at home, % age 5+	21.60%	15.10%	
High school graduates, %, age 25+	78.80%	86.90%	
Bachelor's degree or higher, %, age 25+	17.40%	32.70%	
With a disability, age 5+	61,512	638,654	9.63%
Mean travel time to work, age 16+ (minutes)	27.60	24.3	
Housing unit	132,594	1,808,037	7.33%
Homeownership rate	70.60%	67.30%	
Housing units in multi-unit structures, %	23.20%	25.70%	
Median value of owner-occupied housing units	$149,800	$166,600	
Households	128,156	1,658,238	7.73%
Persons per household	2.81	2.53	
Median household money income, 1999	$47,323	$47,203	
Per capita money income, 1999	$19,944	$24,049	
Persons below poverty, %, 1999	8.90%	9.30%	

Geography

	County	Colorado	% of Colo.
Land area, 2000 (square miles)	1,192	104,247	1.15%
Persons per square mile, 2000	305.3	41.5	
Metropolitan Area	Denver, CO PMSA		

(a) Includes persons reporting only one race.
(b) Hispanics may be of any race, so also are included in applicable race categories.
Source: United States Census Bureau

Alamosa County, Colorado, 2000-2001 Census

Organized March 8, 1913 from Costilla County. Name from Spanish meaning cotton-wood trees or many cottonwood trees. County seat Alamosa.

	County	Colorado	% of Colo.
Population 2001 estimate	14,884	4,417,714	0.34%
% change, April 1, 2000-July 1, 2001	-0.50%	2.70%	
Population, 2000	14,966	4,301,261	0.35%
Population, % change, 1990 to 2000	9.90%	30.60%	
Under 5 years old, %	6.90%	6.90%	
Under 18 years old, %	27.20%	25.60%	
65 years and over, %	9.60%	9.70%	
Female, %	50.20%	49.60%	
White, % (a)	71.20%	82.80%	
Black /African American, % (a)	1.00%	3.80%	
American Indian/Alaska Native, % (a)	2.30%	1.00%	
Asian, % (a)	0.80%	2.20%	
Native Hawaiian/Pacific Islander (a)	0.20%	0.10%	
Reporting some other race, % (a)	20.30%	7.20%	
Reporting two or more races, %	4.20%	2.80%	
Hispanic or Latino origin, % (b)	41.40%	17.10%	
White persons, not of Hispanic/Latino origin, %	54.00%	74.50%	
Living in same house 1995 -2000, % age 5+	51.80%	44.10%	
Foreign born persons, %	4.70%	8.60%	
Language other than English at home, % age 5+	28.30%	15.10%	
High school graduates, %, age 25+	82.60%	86.90%	
Bachelor's degree or higher, %, age 25+	27.00%	32.70%	
With a disability, age 5+	2,474	638,654	0.39%
Mean travel time to work, age 16+ (minutes)	13.50	24.3	
Housing unit	6,088	1,808,037	0.34%
Homeownership rate	64.00%	67.30%	
Housing units in multi-unit structures, %	16.10%	25.70%	
Median value of owner-occupied housing units	$87,900	$166,600	
Households	5,467	1,658,238	0.33%
Persons per household	2.56	2.53	
Median household money income, 1999	$29,447	$47,203	
Per capita money income, 1999	$15,037	$24,049	
Persons below poverty, %, 1999	21.30%	9.30%	

Geography

	County	Colorado	% of Colo.
Land area, 2000 (square miles)	723	104,247	0.70%
Persons per square mile, 2000	20.7	41.5	
Metropolitan Area	None		

(a) Includes persons reporting only one race.
(b) Hispanics may be of any race, so also are included in applicable race categories.
Source: United States Census Bureau

84

Arapahoe County, Colorado, 2000-2001 Census

An original county, organized Nov. 1, 1861 prior to statehood. Named for the Arapahoe Indians. County seat Littleton.

	County	Colorado	% of Colo.
Population 2001 estimate	500,785	4,417,714	11.34%
% change, April 1, 2000-July 1, 2001	2.60%	2.70%	
Population, 2000	487,967	4,301,261	11.34%
Population, % change, 1990 to 2000	24.60%	30.60%	
Under 5 years old, %	6.90%	6.90%	
Under 18 years old, %	26.70%	25.6	
65 years and over, %	8.60%	9.70%	
Female, %	50.70%	49.60%	
White, % (a)	79.90%	82.80%	
Black /African American, % (a)	7.70%	3.80%	
American Indian/Alaska Native, % (a)	0.70%	1.00%	
Asian, % (a)	3.90%	2.20%	
Native Hawaiian/Pacific Islander (a)	0.10%	0.10%	
Reporting some other race, % (a)	4.50%	7.20%	
Reporting two or more races, %	3.20%	2.80%	
Hispanic or Latino origin, % (b)	11.80%	17.10%	
White persons, not of Hispanic/Latino origin, %	73.90%	74.50%	
Living in same house 1995-2000, % age 5+	44.30%	44.10%	
Foreign born persons, %	11.00%	8.60%	
Language other than English at home, % age 5+	15.50%	15.10%	
High school graduates, %, age 25+	90.70%	86.90%	
Bachelor's degree or higher, %, age 25+	37.00%	32.70%	
With a disability, age 5+	66,507	638,654	10.41%
Mean travel time to work, age 16+ (minutes)	26.1	24.3	
Housing unit	196,835	1,808,037	10.89%
Homeownership rate	68.00%	67.30%	
Housing units in multi-unit structures, %	31.20%	25.70%	
Median value of owner-occupied housing units	$171,700	$166,600	
Households	190,909	1,658,238	11.51%
Persons per household	2.53	2.53	
Median household money income, 1999	$53,570	$47,203	
Per capita money income, 1999	$28,147	$24,049	
Persons below poverty, %, 1999	5.80%	9.30%	

Geography

Land area, 2000 (square miles)	803	104,247	0.77%
Persons per square mile, 2000	607.6	41.5	
Metropolitan Area	Denver, CO PMSA		

(a) Includes persons reporting only one race.
(b) Hispanics may be of any race, so also are included in applicable race categories.
Source: United States Census Bureau

Archuleta County, Colorado, 2000-2001 Census

Organized April 14, 1885 from Conejos County. Named for Antonio D. Archuleta, Colorado legislator. County seat Pagosa Springs.

	County	Colorado	% of Colo.
Population 2001 estimate	10,659	4,417,714	0.24%
% change, April 1, 2000-July 1, 2001	7.70%	2.70%	
Population, 2000	9,898	4,301,261	0.23%
Population, % change, 1990 to 2000	85.20%	30.60%	
Under 5 years old, %	5.40%	6.90%	
Under 18 years old, %	25.30%	25.60%	
65 years and over, %	11.90%	9.70%	
Female, %	49.30%	49.60%	
White, % (a)	88.30%	82.80%	
Black /African American, % (a)	0.40%	3.80%	
American Indian/Alaska Native, % (a)	1.40%	1.00%	
Asian, % (a)	0.30%	2.20%	
Native Hawaiian/Pacific Islander (a)	--	--	
Reporting some other race, % (a)	7.00%	7.20%	
Reporting two or more races, %	2.60%	2.80%	
Hispanic or Latino origin, % (b)	16.80%	17.10%	
White persons, not of Hispanic/Latino origin, %	80.10%	74.50%	
Living in same house 1995 -2000, % age 5+	42.00%	44.10%	
Foreign born persons, %	2.90%	8.60%	
Language other than English at home, % age 5+	11.90%	15.10%	
High school graduates, %, age 25+	87.30	86.90%	
Bachelor's degree or higher, %, age 25+	29.00%	32.70%	
With a disability, age 5+	1,939	638,654	0.30%
Mean travel time to work, age 16+ (minutes)	19.2	24.3	
Housing unit	6,212	1,808,037	0.34%
Homeownership rate	76.80%	67.30%	
Housing units in multi-unit structures, %	17.40%	25.70%	
Median value of owner-occupied housing units	$167,400	$166,600	
Households	3,980	1,658,238	0.24%
Persons per household	2.47	2.53	
Median household money income, 1999	$37,901	$47,203	
Per capita money income, 1999	$21,683	$24,049	
Persons below poverty, %, 1999	11.70%	9.30%	

Geography

	County	Colorado	% of Colo.
Land area, 2000 (square miles)	1,350	104,287	1.29%
Persons per square mile, 2000	7.3	41.5	
Metropolitan Area	None		

(a) Includes persons reporting only one race.

(b) Hispanics may be of any race, so also are included in applicable race categories.

Source: United States Census Bureau

Baca County, Colorado, 2000-2001 Census

Organized April 16 1889 from Las Animas County. Named for the Baca family, pioneers from Trinidad. County seat Springfield.

	County	Colorado	% of Colo.
Population 2001 estimate	4,495	4,417,714	0.10%
% change, April 1, 2000-July 1, 2001	-0.50%	2.70%	
Population, 2000	4,517	4,301,261	0.11%
Population, % change, 1990 to 2000	-0.90%	30.60%	
Under 5 years old, %	5.90%	6.90%	
Under 18 years old, %	24.50%	25.60%	
65 years and over, %	22.40%	9.70%	
Female, %	50.30%	49.60%	
White, % (a)	93.70%	82.80%	
Black /African American, % (a)	--	-	
American Indian/Alaska Native, % (a)	1.20%	1.00%	
Asian, % (a)	0.20%	2.20%	
Native Hawaiian/Pacific Islander (a)	0.10%	0.10%	
Reporting some other race, % (a)	3.00%	7.20%	
Reporting two or more races, %	1.80%	2.80%	
Hispanic or Latino origin, % (b)	7.00%	17.10%	
White persons, not of Hispanic/Latino origin, %	90.40%	74.50%	
Living in same house 1995 -2000, % age 5+	63.10%	44.10%	
Foreign born persons, %	2.50%	8.60%	
Language other than English at home, % age 5+	5.80%	15.10%	
High school graduates, %, age 25+	78.50%	86.90%	
Bachelor's degree or higher, %, age 25+	14.00%	32.70%	
With a disability, age 5+	905	638,654	0.14%
Mean travel time to work, age 16+ (minutes)	15.2	24.3	
Housing unit	2,364	1,808,037	0.13%
Homeownership rate	76.10%	67.30%	
Housing units in multi-unit structures, %	5.20%	25.70%	
Median value of owner-occupied housing units	$47,300	$166,600	
Households	1,905	1,658,238	0.11%
Persons per household	2.33	2.53	
Median household money income, 1999	$28,099	$47,203	
Per capita money income, 1999	$15,068	$24,049	
Persons below poverty, %, 1999	16.90%	9.30%	

Geography

	County	Colorado	% of Colo.
Land area, 2000 (square miles)	2,556	104,247	2.46%
Persons per square mile, 2000	1.8	41.5	
Metropolitan Area	None		

(a) Includes persons reporting only one race.
(b) Hispanics may be of any race, so also are included in applicable race categories.
Source: United States Census Bureau

Bent County, Colorado, 2000-2001 Census

Organized Feb. 11, 1870 from Greenwood County. Greenwood County organized in 1874, but abolished to become Bent and Elbert Counties. Named for William Bent, settler, fur trader, Indian agent and builder of Bent's Fort. County seat Las Animas.

	County	Colorado	% of Colo.
Population 2001 estimate	5,883	4,417,714	0.13%
% change, April 1, 2000-July 1, 2001	-1.90%	2.70%	
Population, 2000	5,998	4,301,261	0.14%
Population, % change, 1990 to 2000	18.80%	30.60%	
Under 5 years old, %	5.90%	6.90%	
Under 18 years old, %	23.80%	25.60%	
65 years and over, %	15.90%	9.70%	
Female, %	43.70%	49.60%	
White, % (a)	79.50%	82.80%	
Black /African American, % (a)	3.70%	3.80%	
American Indian/Alaska Native, % (a)	2.20%	1.00%	
Asian, % (a)	0.60%	2.20%	
Native Hawaiian/Pacific Islander (a)	0.00%	0.10%	
Reporting some other race, % (a)	10.30%	7.20%	
Reporting two or more races, %	3.80%	2.80%	
Hispanic or Latino origin, % (b)	30.20%	17.10%	
White persons, not of Hispanic/Latino origin, %	63.30%	74.50%	
Living in same house 1995 -2000, % age 5+	49.70%	44.10%	
Foreign born persons, %	4.40%	8.60%	
Language other than English at home, % age 5+	16.80%	15.10%	
High school graduates, %, age 25+	77.20%	86.90%	
Bachelor's degree or higher, %, age 25+	11.50%	32.70%	
With a disability, age 5+	1,186	638,654	0.19%
Mean travel time to work, age 16+ (minutes)	18.6	24.3	
Housing unit	2,366	1,808,037	0.13%
Homeownership rate	68.00%	67.30%	
Housing units in multi-unit structures, %	8.40%	25.70%	
Median value of owner-occupied housing units	$57,200	$166,600	
Households	2,003	1,658,238	0.12%
Persons per household	2.53	2.53	
Median household money income, 1999	$28,125	$47,203	
Per capita money income, 1999	$13,567	$24,049	
Persons below poverty, %, 1999	19.50%	9.30%	

Geography

	County	Colorado	% of Colo.
Land area, 2000 (square miles)	1,514	104,247	1.46%
Persons per square mile, 2000	4	41.5	
Metropolitan Area	None		

(a) Includes persons reporting only one race.
(b) Hispanics may be of any race, so also are included in applicable race categories.
Source: United States Census Bureau

Boulder County, Colorado, 2000-2001 Census

Original county organized prior to statehood Nov. 1, 1861. Named for Boulder City and Boulder Creek, named for geologic formations in the area. County Seat Boulder.

	County	Colorado	% of Colo.
Population 2001 estimate	297,686	4,417,714	6.74%
% change, April 1, 2000-July 1, 2001	2.20%	2.70%	
Population, 2000	291,288	4,301,261	6.77%
Population, % change, 1990 to 2000	29.30%	30.60%	
Under 5 years old, %	6.00%	6.90%	
Under 18 years old, %	22.90%	25.60%	
65 years and over, %	7.80%	9.70%	
Female, %	49.40%	49.60%	
White, % (a)	88.50%	82.80%	
Black / African American, % (a)	0.90%	3.80%	
American Indian/Alaska Native, % (a)	0.60%	1.00%	
Asian, % (a)	3.10%	2.20%	
Native Hawaiian/Pacific Islander (a)	0.10%	0.10%	
Reporting some other race, % (a)	4.70%	7.20%	
Reporting two or more races, %	2.20%	2.80%	
Hispanic or Latino origin, % (b)	10.50%	17.10%	
White persons, not of Hispanic/Latino origin, %	83.60%	74.50%	
Living in same house 1995 -2000, % age 5+	40.80%	44.10%	
Foreign born persons, %	9.40%	8.60%	
Language other than English at home, % age 5+	13.60%	15.10%	
High school graduates, %, age 25+	92.80%	86.90%	
Bachelor's degree or higher, %, age 25+	52.40%	32.70%	
With a disability, age 5+	32,214	638,654	5.04%
Mean travel time to work, age 16+ (minutes)	22.4	24.3	
Housing unit	119,900	1,808,037	6.63%
Homeownership rate	64.70%	67.30%	
Housing units in multi-unit structures, %	28.60%	25.70%	
Median value of owner-occupied housing units	$241,900	$166,600	
Households	114,680	1,658,238	6.92%
Persons per household	2.47	2.53	
Median household money income, 1999	$55,861	$47,203	
Per capita money income, 1999	$28,976	$24,049	
Persons below poverty, %, 1999	9.50%	9.30%	

Geography

	County	Colorado	% of Colo.
Land area, 2000 (square miles)	742	104,247	0.72%
Persons per square mile, 2000	392.3	41.5	
Metropolitan Area	Boulder-Longmont, CO PMSA		

(a) Includes persons reporting only one race.
(b) Hispanics may be of any race, so also are included in applicable race categories.
Source: United States Census Bureau

Chaffee County, Colorado, 2000-2001 Census

Organized prior to statehood as Lake County Nov. 1, 1861; name changed Feb. 10, 1879. Named for Jerome Bounty Chaffee, territorial legislator and U.S. senator. County seat Salida.

	County	Colorado	% of Colo.
Population 2001 estimate	16,520	4,417,714	0.37%
% change, April 1, 2000-July 1, 2001	1.70%	2.70%	
Population, 2000	16,242	4,301,261	0.38%
Population, % change, 1990 to 2000	28.10%	30.60	
Under 5 years old, %	4.40%	6.90	
Under 18 years old, %	19.70%	25.60%	
65 years and over, %	17.00%	9.70%	
Female, %	46.80%	49.60%	
White, % (a)	90.90%	82.80%	
Black /African American, % (a)	1.60%	3.80%	
American Indian/Alaska Native, % (a)	1.10%	1.00%	
Asian, % (a)	0.40%	2.20%	
Native Hawaiian/Pacific Islander (a)	--	--	
Reporting some other race, % (a)	4.20%	7.20%	
Reporting two or more races, %	1.70%	2.80%	
Hispanic or Latino origin, % (b)	8.60%	17.10%	
White persons, not of Hispanic/Latino origin, %	87.30%	74.50%	
Living in same house 1995 -2000, % age 5+	48.20%	44.10%	
Foreign born persons, %	2.00%	8.60%	
Language other than English at home, % age 5+	8.70%	15.10%	
High school graduates, %, age 25+	88.50%	86.90%	
Bachelor's degree or higher, %, age 25+	24.30%	32.70%	
With a disability, age 5+	2,624	638,654	0.41%
Mean travel time to work, age 16+ (minutes)	14.8	24.3	
Housing unit	8,392	1,808,037	0.46%
Homeownership rate	73.40%	67.30%	
Housing units in multi-unit structures, %	8.60%	25.70%	
Median value of owner-occupied housing units	$152,800	$166,600	
Households	6,584	1,658,238	0.40%
Persons per household	2.26	2.53	
Median household money income, 1999	$34,368	$47,203	
Per capita money income, 1999	$19,430	$24,049	
Persons below poverty, %, 1999	11.70%	9.30%	

Geography

Land area, 2000 (square miles)	1,013	104,247	0.98%
Persons per square mile, 2000	16	41.5	
Metropolitan Area	None		

(a) Includes persons reporting only one race.
(b) Hispanics may be of any race, so also are included in applicable race categories.
Source: United States Census Bureau

Cheyenne County, Colorado, 2000-2001 Census

Organized March 25, 1889 from Bent and Elbert Counties. Named for Cheyenne Indians. County seat Cheyenne Wells.

	County	Colorado	% of Colo.
Population 2001 estimate	2,204	4,417,714	0.05%
% change, April 1, 2000-July 1, 2001	-1.20%	2.70%	
Population, 2000	2,231	4,301,261	0.05%
Population, % change, 1990 to 2000	-6.90%	30.60%	
Under 5 years old, %	6.40%	6.90%	
Under 18 years old, %	28.80%	25.60%	
65 years and over, %	16.60%	9.70%	
Female, %	49.80%	49.60%	
White, % (a)	92.90%	82.80%	
Black /African American, % (a)	0.50%	3.80%	
American Indian/Alaska Native, % (a)	0.80%	1.00%	
Asian, % (a)	0.10%	2.20%	
Native Hawaiian/Pacific Islander (a)	0.00%	0.10%	
Reporting some other race, % (a)	5.10%	7.20%	
Reporting two or more races, %	0.60%	2.80%	
Hispanic or Latino origin, % (b)	8.10%	17.10%	
White persons, not of Hispanic/Latino origin, %	90.50%	74.50%	
Living in same house 1995 -2000, % age 5+	62.30%	44.10%	
Foreign born persons, %	4.10%	8.60%	
Language other than English at home, % age 5+	7.60%	15.10%	
High school graduates, %, age 25+	84.10%	86.90%	
Bachelor's degree or higher, %, age 25+	14.20%	32.70%	
With a disability, age 5+	332	638,654	0.05%
Mean travel time to work, age 16+ (minutes)	13.5	24.3	
Housing unit	1,105	1,808,037	0.06%
Homeownership rate	74.30%	67.30%	
Housing units in multi-unit structures, %	4.00%	25.70%	
Median value of owner-occupied housing units	$62,400	$166,600	
Households	880	1,658,238	0.05%
Persons per household	2.5	2.53	
Median household money income, 1999	$37,054	$47,203	
Per capita money income, 1999	$17,850	$24,049	
Persons below poverty, %, 1999	11.10%	9.30%	

Geography

Land area, 2000 (square miles)	1,781	104,247	1.72%
Persons per square mile, 2000	1.3	41.5	
Metropolitan Area	None		

(a) Includes persons reporting only one race.
(b) Hispanics may be of any race, so also are included in applicable race categories.
Source: United States Census Bureau

Clear Creek County, Colorado, 2000-2001 Census

Original county organized Nov. 1, 1861. Name from Clear Creek, which runs through the county. The waterway's name originally was Vasquez Fork. The new name was adopted in 1860. County seat Georgetown.

	County	Colorado	% of Colo.
Population 2001 estimate	9,440	4,417,714	0.21%
% change, April 1, 2000-July 1, 2001	1.30%	2.70%	
Population, 2000	9,322	4,301,261	0.22%
Population, % change, 1990 to 2000	22.40%	30.60%	
Under 5 years old, %	5.70%	6.90%	
Under 18 years old, %	22.60%	25.60%	
65 years and over, %	7.10%	9.70%	
Female, %	47.90%	49.60%	
White, % (a)	96.40%	82.80%	
Black /African American, % (a)	0.30%	3.80%	
American Indian/Alaska Native, % (a)	0.70%	1.00%	
Asian, % (a)	0.40%	2.20%	
Native Hawaiian/Pacific Islander (a)	--	--	
Reporting some other race, % (a)	1.00%	7.20%	
Reporting two or more races, %	1.20%	2.80%	
Hispanic or Latino origin, % (b)	3.90%	17.10%	
White persons, not of Hispanic/Latino origin, %	94.00%	74.50%	
Living in same house 1995 -2000, % age 5+	52.70%	44.10%	
Foreign born persons, %	1.90%	8.60%	
Language other than English at home, % age 5+	3.50%	15.10%	
High school graduates, %, age 25+	93.40%	86.90%	
Bachelor's degree or higher, %, age 25+	38.80%	32.70%	
With a disability, age 5+	1,363	638,654	0.21%
Mean travel time to work, age 16+ (minutes)	32.6	24.3	
Housing unit	5,128	1,808,037	0.28%
Homeownership rate	76.10%	67.30%	
Housing units in multi-unit structures, %	10.50%	25.70%	
Median value of owner-occupied housing units	$200,400	$166,600	
Households	4,019	1,658,238	0.24%
Persons per household	2.31	2.53	
Median household money income, 1999	$50,997	$47,203	
Per capita money income, 1999	$28,160	$24,049	
Persons below poverty, %, 1999	5.40%	9.30%	

Geography

Land area, 2000 (square miles)	395	104,247	0.38%
Persons per square mile, 2000	23.6	41.5	
Metropolitan Area	None		

(a) Includes persons reporting only one race.

(b) Hispanics may be of any race, so also are included in applicable race categories.

Source: United States Census Bureau

Conejos County, Colorado, 2000-2001 Census

Original county organized as Guadalupe County Nov. 1, 1861. Name changed one week later to Conejos on Nov. 7, 1861. Named for the river which runs through the county. Conejos is Spanish for rabbit. County seat Conejos.

	County	Colorado	% of Colo.
Population 2001 estimate	8,355	4,417,714	0.19%
% change, April 1, 2000-July 1, 2001	-0.50%	2.70%	
Population, 2000	8,400	4,301,261	0.20%
Population, % change, 1990 to 2000	12.70%	30.60%	
Under 5 years old, %	7.90%	6.90%	
Under 18 years old, %	32.10%	25.60%	
65 years and over, %	15.00%	9.70%	
Female, %	50.40%	49.60%	
White, % (a)	72.80%	82.80%	
Black /African American, % (a)	0.20%	3.80%	
American Indian/Alaska Native, % (a)	1.70%	1.00%	
Asian, % (a)	0.20%	2.20%	
Native Hawaiian/Pacific Islander (a)	0.10%	0.10%	
Reporting some other race, % (a)	21.50%	7.20%	
Reporting two or more races, %	3.60%	2.80%	
Hispanic or Latino origin, % (b)	58.90%	17.10%	
White persons, not of Hispanic/Latino origin, %	39.30%	74.50%	
Living in same house 1995 -2000, % age 5+	68.80%	44.10%	
Foreign born persons, %	3.00%	8.60%	
Language other than English at home, % age 5+	42.10%	15.10%	
High school graduates, %, age 25+	72.10%	86.90%	
Bachelor's degree or higher, %, age 25+	14.40%	32.70%	
With a disability, age 5+	1,754	638,654	0.27%
Mean travel time to work, age 16+ (minutes)	22.4	24.3	
Housing unit	3,886	1,808,037	0.21%
Homeownership rate	78.80%	67.30%	
Housing units in multi-unit structures, %	5.30%	25.70%	
Median value of owner-occupied housing units	$57,000	$166,600	
Households	2,980	1,658,238	0.18%
Persons per household	2.8	2.53	
Median household money income, 1999	$24,744	$47,203	
Per capita money income, 1999	$12,050	$24,049	
Persons below poverty, %, 1999	23.00%	9.30%	

Geography

	County	Colorado	% of Colo.
Land area, 2000 (square miles)	1,287	104,247	1.24%
Persons per square mile, 2000	6.5	41.5	
Metropolitan Area	None		

(a) Includes persons reporting only one race.
(b) Hispanics may be of any race, so also are included in applicable race categories.
Source: United States Census Bureau

93

Costilla County, Colorado, 2000-2001 Census

Original county organized Nov. 1, 1861. Name from Costilla Creek, from Spanish meaning rib or framing timber. County seat San Luis.

	County	Colorado	% of Colo.
Population 2001 estimate	3,647	4,417,714	0.08%
% change, April 1, 2000-July 1, 2001	-0.40%	2.70%	
Population, 2000	3,663	4,301,261	0.09%
Population, % change, 1990 to 2000	14.80%	30.60%	
Under 5 years old, %	5.70%	6.90%	
Under 18 years old, %	25.00%	25.60%	
65 years and over, %	16.80%	9.70%	
Female, %	50.00%	49.60%	
White, % (a)	60.90%	82.80%	
Black /African American, % (a)	0.80%	3.80%	
American Indian/Alaska Native, % (a)	2.50%	1.00%	
Asian, % (a)	1.00%	2.20%	
Native Hawaiian/Pacific Islander (a)	0.10%	0.10%	
Reporting some other race, % (a)	29.50%	7.20%	
Reporting two or more races, %	5.20%	2.80%	
Hispanic or Latino origin, % (b)	67.60%	17.10%	
White persons, not of Hispanic/Latino origin, %	28.20%	74.50%	
Living in same house 1995 -2000, % age 5+	65.40%	44.10%	
Foreign born persons, %	6.90%	8.60%	
Language other than English at home, % age 5+	59.50%	15.10%	
High school graduates, %, age 25+	68.20%	86.90%	
Bachelor's degree or higher, %, age 25+	12.80%	32.70%	
With a disability, age 5+	1,057	638,654	0.17%
Mean travel time to work, age 16+ (minutes)	23.3	24.3	
Housing unit	2,202	1,808,037	0.12%
Homeownership rate	78.20%	67.30%	
Housing units in multi-unit structures, %	4.50%	25.70%	
Median value of owner-occupied housing units	$61,200	$166,600	
Households	1,503	1,658,238	0.09%
Persons per household	2.44	2.53	
Median household money income, 1999	$19,531	$47,203	
Per capita money income, 1999	$10,748	$24,049	
Persons below poverty, %, 1999	26.80%	9.30%	

Geography

	County	Colorado	% of Colo.
Land area, 2000 (square miles)	1,227	104,247	1.18%
Persons per square mile, 2000	3	41.5	
Metropolitan Area	None		

(a) Includes persons reporting only one race.
(b) Hispanics may be of any race, so also are included in applicable race categories.
Source: United States Census Bureau

Crowley County, Colorado, 2000-2001 Census

Organized May 29, 1911 from Otero County. Named for Otero County state senator John Crowley. County seat Ordway.

	County	Colorado	% of Colo.
Population 2001 estimate	5,434	4,417,714	0.12%
% change, April 1, 2000-July 1, 2001	-1.50%	2.70%	
Population, 2000	5,518	4,301,261	0.13%
Population, % change, 1990 to 2000	39.80%	30.60%	
Under 5 years old, %	4.40%	6.90%	
Under 18 years old, %	18.80%	25.60%	
65 years and over, %	10.80%	9.70%	
Female, %	32.70%	49.60%	
White, % (a)	82.90%	82.80%	
Black /African American, % (a)	7.00%	3.80%	
American Indian/Alaska Native, % (a)	2.60%	1.00%	
Asian, % (a)	0.80%	2.20%	
Native Hawaiian/Pacific Islander (a)	--	--	
Reporting some other race, % (a)	4.80%	7.20%	
Reporting two or more races, %	1.80%	2.80%	
Hispanic or Latino origin, % (b)	22.50%	17.10%	
White persons, not of Hispanic/Latino origin, %	66.50%	74.50%	
Living in same house 1995 -2000, % age 5+	42.20%	44.10%	
Foreign born persons, %	1.10%	8.60%	
Language other than English at home, % age 5+	14.70%	15.10%	
High school graduates, %, age 25+	77.50%	86.90%	
Bachelor's degree or higher, %, age 25+	11.90%	32.70%	
With a disability, age 5+	864	638654	0.14%
Mean travel time to work, age 16+ (minutes)	22	24	
Housing unit	1,542.00	1,808,037	0.09%
Homeownership rate	72.50%	67.30%	
Housing units in multi-unit structures, %	4.70%	25.70%	
Median value of owner-occupied housing units	$57,200	$166,600	
Households	1,358	1,658,238	0.08%
Persons per household	2.59	2.53	
Median household money income, 1999	$26,803	$47,203	
Per capita money income, 1999	$12,836	$24,049	
Persons below poverty, %, 1999	18.50%	9.30%	

Geography

Land area, 2000 (square miles)	789	104,247	0.76%
Persons per square mile, 2000	7.00	41.50	
Metropolitan Area	None		

(a) Includes persons reporting only one race.
(b) Hispanics may be of any race, so also are included in applicable race categories.
Source: United States Census Bureau

Custer County, Colorado, 2000-2001 Census

Organized March 9, 1877 from Fremont County. Named for General George Armstrong Custer. County seat Westcliffe.

	County	Colorado	% of Colo.
Population 2001 estimate	3,693	4,417,714	0.08%
% change, April 1, 2000-July 1, 2001	5.40%	2.70%	
Population, 2000	3,503	4,301,261	0.08%
Population, % change, 1990 to 2000	81.90%	30.60%	
Under 5 years old, %	5.50%	6.90%	
Under 18 years old, %	22.50%	25.60%	
65 years and over, %	14.80%	9.70%	
Female, %	49.00%	49.60%	
White, % (a)	95.90%	82.80%	
Black /African American, % (a)	0.40%	3.80%	
American Indian/Alaska Native, % (a)	1.10%	1.00%	
Asian, % (a)	0.30%	2.20%	
Native Hawaiian/Pacific Islander (a)	0.00%	0.10%	
Reporting some other race, % (a)	0.70%	7.20%	
Reporting two or more races, %	1.60%	2.80%	
Hispanic or Latino origin, % (b)	2.50%	17.10%	
White persons, not of Hispanic/Latino origin, %	94.20%	74.50%	
Living in same house 1995 -2000, % age 5+	45.40%	44.10%	
Foreign born persons, %	1.70%	8.60%	
Language other than English at home, % age 5+	3.60%	15.10%	
High school graduates, %, age 25+	90.30%	86.90%	
Bachelor's degree or higher, %, age 25+	26.70%	32.70%	
With a disability, age 5+	625	638,654	0.10%
Mean travel time to work, age 16+ (minutes)	26	24	
Housing unit	2,989.00	1,808,037	0.17%
Homeownership rate	79.20%	67.30%	
Housing units in multi-unit structures, %	2.90%	25.70%	
Median value of owner-occupied housing units	$134,100	$166,600	
Households	1,480	1,658,238	0.09%
Persons per household	2.36	2.53	
Median household money income, 1999	$34,731	$47,203	
Per capita money income, 1999	$19,817	$24,049	
Persons below poverty, %, 1999	13.30%	9.30%	

Geography

	County	Colorado	% of Colo.
Land area, 2000 (square miles)	739	104,247	0.71%
Persons per square mile, 2000	4.70	41.50	
Metropolitan Area	None		

(a) Includes persons reporting only one race.
(b) Hispanics may be of any race, so also are included in applicable race categories.
Source: United States Census Bureau

Delta County, Colorado, 2000-2001 Census

Organized Feb. 11, 1883 from Gunnison County. Named for the Uncompahgre River delta. County seat Delta.

	County	Colorado	% of Colo.
Population 2001 estimate	28,421	4,417,714	0.64%
% change, April 1, 2000-July 1, 2001	2.10%	2.70%	
Population, 2000	27,834	4,301,261	0.65%
Population, % change, 1990 to 2000	32.70%	30.60%	
Under 5 years old, %	5.80%	6.90%	
Under 18 years old, %	24.00%	25.60%	
65 years and over, %	19.70%	9.70%	
Female, %	49.80%	49.60%	
White, % (a)	92.30%	82.80%	
Black /African American, % (a)	0.50%	3.80%	
American Indian/Alaska Native, % (a)	0.80%	1.00%	
Asian, % (a)	0.30%	2.20%	
Native Hawaiian/Pacific Islander (a)	--	--	
Reporting some other race, % (a)	4.30%	7.20%	
Reporting two or more races, %	1.80%	2.80%	
Hispanic or Latino origin, % (b)	11.40%	17.10%	
White persons, not of Hispanic/Latino origin, %	86.00%	74.50%	
Living in same house 1995-2000, % age 5+	52.00%	44.10%	
Foreign born persons, %	4.20%	8.60%	
Language other than English at home, % age 5+	10.30%	15.10%	
High school graduates, %, age 25+	80.10%	86.90%	
Bachelor's degree or higher, %, age 25+	17.60%	32.70%	
With a disability, age 5+	5,494	638,654	0.86%
Mean travel time to work, age 16+ (minutes)	24	24	
Housing unit	12,374	1,808,037	0.68%
Homeownership rate	77.50%	67.30%	
Housing units in multi-unit structures, %	5.50%	25.70%	
Median value of owner-occupied housing units	$115,500	$166,600	
Households	11,058	1,658,238	0.67%
Persons per household	2.43	2.53	
Median household money income, 1999	$32,785	$47,203	
Per capita money income, 1999	$17,152	$24,049	
Persons below poverty, %, 1999	12.10%	9.30%	

Geography

Land area, 2000 (square miles)	1,142	104,247	1.10%
Persons per square mile, 2000	24.40	41.50	
Metropolitan Area	None		

(a) Includes persons reporting only one race.
(b) Hispanics may be of any race, so also are included in applicable race categories.
Source: United States Census Bureau

Denver County, Colorado, 2000-2001 Census

Organized March 18, 1901 from Adams County. Named for General James William Denver, governor of Kansas Territory. Organized as city and county of Denver.

	County	Colorado	% of Colo.
Population 2001 estimate	554,446	4,417,714	12.55%
% change, April 1, 2000-July 1, 2001	0.00%	2.70%	
Population, 2000	554,636	4,301,261	12.89%
Population, % change, 1990 to 2000	18.60%	30.60%	
Under 5 years old, %	6.80%	6.90%	
Under 18 years old, %	22.00%	25.60%	
65 years and over, %	11.30%	9.70%	
Female, %	49.50%	49.60%	
White, % (a)	65.30%	82.80%	
Black /African American, % (a)	11.10%	3.80%	
American Indian/Alaska Native, % (a)	1.30%	1.00%	
Asian, % (a)	2.80%	2.20%	
Native Hawaiian/Pacific Islander (a)	0.10%	0.10%	
Reporting some other race, % (a)	15.60%	7.20%	
Reporting two or more races, %	3.70%	2.80%	
Hispanic or Latino origin, % (b)	31.70%	17.10%	
White persons, not of Hispanic/Latino origin, %	51.90%	74.50%	
Living in same house 1995 -2000, % age 5+	42.70%	44.10%	
Foreign born persons, %	17.40%	8.60%	
Language other than English at home, % age 5+	27.00%	15.10%	
High school graduates, %, age 25+	78.90%	86.90%	
Bachelor's degree or higher, %, age 25+	34.50%	32.70%	
With a disability, age 5+	105,943	638,654	16.59%
Mean travel time to work, age 16+ (minutes)	24.5	24.3	
Housing unit	251,435	1,808,037	13.91%
Homeownership rate	52.50%	67.30%	
Housing units in multi-unit structures, %	44.80%	25.70%	
Median value of owner-occupied housing units	$165,800	$166,600	
Households	239,235	1,658,238	14.43%
Persons per household	2.27	2.53	
Median household money income, 1999	$39,500	$47,203	
Per capita money income, 1999	$24,101	$24,049	
Persons below poverty, %, 1999	14.30%	9.30%	

Geography

Land area, 2000 (square miles)	153	104,247	0.15%
Persons per square mile, 2000	3,616.80	41.50	
Metropolitan Area	Denver, CO PMSA		

(a) Includes persons reporting only one race.
(b) Hispanics may be of any race, so also are included in applicable race categories.
Source: United States Census Bureau

Dolores County, Colorado, 2000-2001 Census

Organized Feb. 19, 1891 from Ouray County. Named for the Dolores River. Dolores from Spanish Rio de Nuestra Senora de los Dolores, River of Our Lady of Sorrows. County seat Dove Creek.

	County	Colorado	% of Colo.
Population 2001 estimate	1,837	4,417,714	0.04%
% change, April 1, 2000-July 1, 2001	-0.40%	2.70%	
Population, 2000	1,844	4,301,261	0.04%
Population, % change, 1990 to 2000	22.60%	30.60%	
Under 5 years old, %	5.00%	6.90%	
Under 18 years old, %	21.90%	25.60%	
65 years and over, %	17.10%	9.70%	
Female, %	48.30%	49.60%	
White, % (a)	95.30%	82.80%	
Black /African American, % (a)	0.10%	3.80%	
American Indian/Alaska Native, % (a)	2.00%	1.00%	
Asian, % (a)	0.40%	2.20%	
Native Hawaiian/Pacific Islander (a)	0.10%	0.10%	
Reporting some other race, % (a)	0.60%	7.20%	
Reporting two or more races, %	1.70%	2.80%	
Hispanic or Latino origin, % (b)	3.90%	17.10%	
White persons, not of Hispanic/Latino origin, %	92.80%	74.50%	
Living in same house 1995 -2000, % age 5+	55.70%	44.10%	
Foreign born persons, %	0.90%	8.60%	
Language other than English at home, % age 5+	5.70%	15.10%	
High school graduates, %, age 25+	76.00%	86.90%	
Bachelor's degree or higher, %, age 25+	13.50%	32.70%	
With a disability, age 5+	387	638,654	0.06%
Mean travel time to work, age 16+ (minutes)	25.6	24.3	
Housing unit	1,193	1,808,037	0.07%
Homeownership rate	76.80%	67.30%	
Housing units in multi-unit structures, %	1.20%	25.70%	
Median value of owner-occupied housing units	$76,800	$166,600	
Households	785	1,658,238	0.05%
Persons per household	2.35	2.53	
Median household money income, 1999	$32,196	$47,203	
Per capita money income, 1999	$17,106	$24,049	
Persons below poverty, %, 1999	13.10%	9.30%	

Geography

	County	Colorado	% of Colo.
Land area, 2000 (square miles)	1,067	104,247	1.03%
Persons per square mile, 2000	1.70	41.50	
Metropolitan Area	None		

(a) Includes persons reporting only one race.
(b) Hispanics may be of any race, so also are included in applicable race categories.
Source: United States Census Bureau

Douglas County, Colorado, 2000-2001 Census

One of 17original counties organized Nov. 1, 1861. Named for Stephen Arnold Douglas, orator and statesman. County seat Castle Rock.

	County	Colorado	% of Colo.
Population 2001 estimate	199,753	4,417,714	4.52%
% change, April 1, 2000-July 1, 2001	13.60%	2.70%	
Population, 2000	175,766	4,301,261	4.09%
Population, % change, 1990 to 2000	191.00%	30.60%	
Under 5 years old, %	9.60%	6.90%	
Under 18 years old, %	31.60%	25.60%	
65 years and over, %	4.20%	9.70%	
Female, %	50.10%	49.60%	
White, % (a)	92.80%	82.80%	
Black /African American, % (a)	1.00%	3.80%	
American Indian/Alaska Native, % (a)	0.40%	1.00%	
Asian, % (a)	2.50%	2.20%	
Native Hawaiian/Pacific Islander (a)	0.10%	0.10%	
Reporting some other race, % (a)	1.40%	7.20%	
Reporting two or more races, %	1.90%	2.80%	
Hispanic or Latino origin, % (b)	5.10%	17.10%	
White persons, not of Hispanic/Latino origin, %	89.70%	74.50%	
Living in same house 1995 -2000, % age 5+	34.30%	44.10%	
Foreign born persons, %	5.20%	8.60%	
Language other than English at home, % age 5+	7.20%	15.10%	
High school graduates, %, age 25+	97.00%	86.90%	
Bachelor's degree or higher, %, age 25+	51.90%	32.70%	
With a disability, age 5+	13,069	638,654	2.05%
Mean travel time to work, age 16+ (minutes)	29.3	24.3	
Housing unit	63,333	1,808,037	3.50%
Homeownership rate	87.90%	67.30%	
Housing units in multi-unit structures, %	9.60%	25.70%	
Median value of owner-occupied housing units	$236,000	$166,600	
Households	60,924	1,658,238	3.67%
Persons per household	2.88	2.53	
Median household money income, 1999	$82,929	$47,203	
Per capita money income, 1999	$34,848	$24,049	
Persons below poverty, %, 1999	2.10%	9.30%	

Geography

Land area, 2000 (square miles)	840	104,247	0.81%
Persons per square mile, 2000	209.20	41.50	
Metropolitan Area	Denver, CO PMSA		

(a) Includes persons reporting only one race.
(b) Hispanics may be of any race, so also are included in applicable race categories.
Source: United States Census Bureau

Eagle County, Colorado, 2000-2001 Census

Organized Feb. 11, 1883 from Summit County. Named for the Eagle River, which flows through the county. County seat Eagle.

	County	Colorado	% of Colo.
Population 2001 estimate	43,027	4,417,714	0.97%
% change, April 1, 2000-July 1, 2001	3.30%	2.70%	
Population, 2000	41,659	4,301,261	0.97%
Population, % change, 1990 to 2000	90.00%	30.60%	
Under 5 years old, %	7.10%	6.90%	
Under 18 years old, %	23.50%	25.60%	
65 years and over, %	3.00%	9.70%	
Female, %	45.20%	49.60%	
White, % (a)	85.40%	82.80%	
Black /African American, % (a)	0.30%	3.80%	
American Indian/Alaska Native, % (a)	0.70%	1.00%	
Asian, % (a)	0.80%	2.20%	
Native Hawaiian/Pacific Islander (a)	0.10%	0.10%	
Reporting some other race, % (a)	10.80%	7.20%	
Reporting two or more races, %	1.90%	2.80%	
Hispanic or Latino origin, % (b)	23.20%	17.10%	
White persons, not of Hispanic/Latino origin, %	74.20%	74.50%	
Living in same house 1995 -2000, % age 5+	35.00%	44.10%	
Foreign born persons, %	18.20%	8.60%	
Language other than English at home, % age 5+	24.70%	15.10%	
High school graduates, %, age 25	86.60%	86.90%	
Bachelor's degree or higher, %, age 25+	42.60%	32.70%	
With a disability, age 5+	4,007	638,654	0.63%
Mean travel time to work, age 16+ (minutes)	21.3	24.3	
Housing unit	22,111	1,808,037	1.22%
Homeownership rate	63.70%	67.30%	
Housing units in multi-unit structures, %	42.20%	25.70%	
Median value of owner-occupied housing units	$369,100	$166,600	
Households	15,148	1,658,238	0.91%
Persons per household	2.73	2.53	
Median household money income, 1999	$62,682	$47,203	
Per capita money income, 1999	$32,011	$24,049	
Persons below poverty, %, 1999	7.80%	9.30%	

Geography

	County	Colorado	% of Colo.
Land area, 2000 (square miles)	1,688	104,247	1.63%
Persons per square mile, 2000	24.70	41.50	
Metropolitan Area	None		

(a) Includes persons reporting only one race.
(b) Hispanics may be of any race, so also are included in applicable race categories.
Source: United States Census Bureau

El Paso County, Colorado, 2000-2001 Census

Original county organized Nov. 1, 1861 prior to statehood. Spanish for "the pas," referring to Ute Pass. County seat Colorado Springs.

	County	Colorado	% of Colo.
Population 2001 estimate	533,428	4,417,714	12.07%
% change, April 1, 2000-July 1, 2001	3.20%	2.70%	
Population, 2000	516,929	4,301,261	12.02%
Population, % change, 1990 to 2000	30.20%	30.60%	
Under 5 years old, %	7.60%	6.90%	
Under 18 years old, %	27.60%	25.60%	
65 years and over, %	8.70%	9.70%	
Female, %	49.80%	49.60%	
White, % (a)	81.20%	82.80%	
Black /African American, % (a)	6.50%	3.80%	
American Indian/Alaska Native, % (a)	0.90%	1.00%	
Asian, % (a)	2.50%	2.20%	
Native Hawaiian/Pacific Islander (a)	0.20%	0.10%	
Reporting some other race, % (a)	4.70%	7.20%	
Reporting two or more races, %	3.90%	2.80%	
Hispanic or Latino origin, % (b)	11.30%	17.10%	
White persons, not of Hispanic/Latino origin, %	76.20%	74.50%	
Living in same house 1995 -2000, % age 5+	40.40%	44.10%	
Foreign born persons, %	6.40%	8.60%	
Language other than English at home, % age 5+	11.40%	15.10%	
High school graduates, %, age 25+	91.30%	86.90%	
Bachelor's degree or higher, %, age 25+	31.80%	32.70%	
With a disability, age 5+	70,710	638,654	11.07%
Mean travel time to work, age 16+ (minutes)	22.3	24.3	
Housing unit	202,428	1,808,037	11.20%
Homeownership rate	64.70%	67.30%	
Housing units in multi-unit structures, %	25.50%	25.70%	
Median value of owner-occupied housing units	$147,100	$166,600	
Households	192,409	1,658,238	11.60%
Persons per household	2.61	2.53	
Median household money income, 1999	$46,844	$47,203	
Per capita money income, 1999	$22,005	$24,049	
Persons below poverty, %, 1999	8.00%	9.30%	

Geography

Land area, 2000 (square miles)	2,126	104,247	2.05%
Persons per square mile, 2000	243.10	41.50	
Metropolitan Area	Colorado Springs, CO MSA		

(a) Includes persons reporting only one race.

(b) Hispanics may be of any race, so also are included in applicable race categories.

Source: United States Census Bureau

Elbert County, Colorado, 2000-2001 Census

Organized Feb. 2, 1874 from Douglas and Greenwood Counties. Greenwood County abolished when divided to form Bent and Elbert Counties. Named for Samuel Elbert, territorial governor and Colorado Supreme Court chief justice. County seat Kiowa.

	County	Colorado	% of Colo.
Population 2001 estimate	21,445	4,417,714	0.49%
% change, April 1, 2000-July 1, 2001	7.90%	2.70%	
Population, 2000	19,872	4,301,261	0.46%
Population, % change, 1990 to 2000	106.00%	30.60%	
Under 5 years old, %	6.60%	6.90%	
Under 18 years old, %	30.20%	25.60%	
65 years and over, %	6.00%	9.70%	
Female, %	49.80%	49.60%	
White, % (a)	95.20%	82.80%	
Black /African American, % (a)	0.60%	3.80%	
American Indian/Alaska Native, % (a)	0.60%	1.00%	
Asian, % (a)	0.40%	2.20%	
Native Hawaiian/Pacific Islander (a)	0.10%	0.10%	
Reporting some other race, % (a)	1.30%	7.20%	
Reporting two or more races, %	1.80%	2.80%	
Hispanic or Latino origin, % (b)	3.90%	17.10%	
White persons, not of Hispanic/Latino origin, %	93.20%	74.50%	
Living in same house 1995 -2000, % age 5+	44.10%	44.10%	
Foreign born persons, %	1.90%	8.60%	
Language other than English at home, % age 5+	4.80%	15.10%	
High school graduates, %, age 25+	92.50%	86.90%	
Bachelor's degree or higher, %, age 25+	26.60%	32.70%	
With a disability, age 5+	2,184	638,654	0.34%
Mean travel time to work, age 16+ (minutes)	41.1	24.3	
Housing unit	7,113	1,808,037	0.39%
Homeownership rate	89.60%	67.30%	
Housing units in multi-unit structures, %	1.70%	25.70%	
Median value of owner-occupied housing units	$221,700	$166,600	
Households	6,770	1,658,238	0.41%
Persons per household	2.93	2.53	
Median household money income, 1999	$62,480	$47,203	
Per capita money income, 1999	$24,960	$24,049	
Persons below poverty, %, 1999	4.00%	9.30%	

Geography

	County	Colorado	% of Colo.
Land area, 2000 (square miles)	1,851	104,247	1.78%
Persons per square mile, 2000	10.70	41.50	
Metropolitan Area	None		

(a) Includes persons reporting only one race.

(b) Hispanics may be of any race, so also are included in applicable race categories.

Source: United States Census Bureau

Fremont County, Colorado, 2000-2001 Census

Original county organized Nov. 1, 1861 prior to statehood. Named for John Charles Fremont, soldier, explorer, California senator and governor of the Arizona Territory. County seat Canon City.

	County	Colorado	% of Colo.
Population 2001 estimate	47,209	4,417,714	1.07%
% change, April 1, 2000-July 1, 2001	2.30%	2.70%	
Population, 2000	46,145	4,301,261	1.07%
Population, % change, 1990 to 2000	43.00%	30.60%	
Under 5 years old, %	4.80%	6.90%	
Under 18 years old, %	20.60%	25.60%	
65 years and over, %	14.60%	9.70%	
Female, %	42.80%	49.60%	
White, % (a)	89.50%	82.80%	
Black /African American, % (a)	5.30%	3.80%	
American Indian/Alaska Native, % (a)	1.50%	1.00%	
Asian, % (a)	0.50%	2.20%	
Native Hawaiian/Pacific Islander (a)	0.10%	0.10%	
Reporting some other race, % (a)	1.20%	7.20%	
Reporting two or more races, %	1.80%	2.80%	
Hispanic or Latino origin, % (b)	10.30%	17.10%	
White persons, not of Hispanic/Latino origin, %	81.10%	74.50%	
Living in same house 1995 -2000, % age 5+	41.10%	44.10%	
Foreign born persons, %	1.50%	8.60%	
Language other than English at home, % age 5+	7.40%	15.10%	
High school graduates, %, age 25+	80.50%	86.90%	
Bachelor's degree or higher, %, age 25+	13.50%	32.70%	
With a disability, age 5+	7,652	638,654	1.20%
Mean travel time to work, age 16+ (minutes)	23.9	24.3	
Housing unit	17,145	1,808,037	0.95%
Homeownership rate	75.90%	67.30%	
Housing units in multi-unit structures, %	9.90%	25.70%	
Median value of owner-occupied housing units	$104,900	$166,600	
Households	15,232	1,658,238	0.92%
Persons per household	2.43	2.53	
Median household money income, 1999	$34,150	$47,203	
Per capita money income, 1999	$17,420	$24,049	
Persons below poverty, %, 1999	11.70%	9.30%	

Geography

Land area, 2000 (square miles)	1,533	104,247	1.48%
Persons per square mile, 2000	30.10	41.50	
Metropolitan Area	None		

(a) Includes persons reporting only one race.
(b) Hispanics may be of any race, so also are included in applicable race categories.
Source: United States Census Bureau

Garfield County, Colorado, 2000-2001 Census

Organized Feb. 10, 1883 from Summit County. Named for James A. Garfield, 20th U.S. president. County seat Glenwood Springs.

	County	Colorado	% of Colo.
Population 2001 estimate	45,521	4,417,714	1.03%
% change, April 1, 2000-July 1, 2001	4.00%	2.70%	
Population, 2000	43,791	4,301,261	1.02%
Population, % change, 1990 to 2000	46.10%	30.60%	
Under 5 years old, %	7.50%	6.90%	
Under 18 years old, %	27.10%	25.60%	
65 years and over, %	8.80%	9.70%	
Female, %	48.60%	49.60%	
White, % (a)	90.00%	82.80%	
Black /African American, % (a)	0.40%	3.80%	
American Indian/Alaska Native, % (a)	0.70%	1.00%	
Asian, % (a)	0.40%	2.20%	
Native Hawaiian/Pacific Islander (a)	0.10%	0.10%	
Reporting some other race, % (a)	6.50%	7.20%	
Reporting two or more races, %	1.80%	2.80%	
Hispanic or Latino origin, % (b)	16.70%	17.10%	
White persons, not of Hispanic/Latino origin, %	81.00%	74.50%	
Living in same house 1995 -2000, % age 5+	39.90%	44.10%	
Foreign born persons, %	10.40%	8.60%	
Language other than English at home, % age 5+	15.50%	15.10%	
High school graduates, %, age 25+	85.40%	86.90%	
Bachelor's degree or higher, %, age 25+	23.80%	32.70%	
With a disability, age 5+	5,688	638,654	0.89%
Mean travel time to work, age 16+ (minutes)	30.6	24.3	
Housing unit	17,336	1,808,037	0.96%
Homeownership rate	65.20%	67.30%	
Housing units in multi-unit structures, %	21.10%	25.70%	
Median value of owner-occupied housing units	$200,700	$166,600	
Households	16,229	1,658,238	0.98%
Persons per household	2.65	2.53	
Median household money income, 1999	$47,016	$47,203	
Per capita money income, 1999	$21,341	$24,049	
Persons below poverty, %, 1999	7.50%	9.30%	

Geography

Land area, 2000 (square miles)	2,947	104,247	2.84%
Persons per square mile, 2000	14.90	41.50	
Metropolitan Area	None		

(a) Includes persons reporting only one race.
(b) Hispanics may be of any race, so also are included in applicable race categories.
Source: United States Census Bureau

Gilpin County, Colorado, 2000-2001 Census

Original county organized Nov. 1, 1861 prior to statehood. Named for Colonel William Gilpin, first territorial governor of Colorado. County seat Central City.

	County	Colorado	% of Colo.
Population 2001 estimate	4,823	4,417,714	0.11%
% change, April 1, 2000-July 1, 2001	1.40%	2.70%	
Population, 2000	4,757	4,301,261	0.11%
Population, % change, 1990 to 2000	55.00%	30.60%	
Under 5 years old, %	5.70%	6.90%	
Under 18 years old, %	21.10%	25.60%	
65 years and over, %	5.70%	9.70%	
Female, %	47.00%	49.60%	
White, % (a)	94.40%	82.80%	
Black /African American, % (a)	0.50%	3.80%	
American Indian/Alaska Native, % (a)	0.80%	1.00%	
Asian, % (a)	0.70%	2.20%	
Native Hawaiian/Pacific Islander (a)	0.20%	0.10%	
Reporting some other race, % (a)	1.50%	7.20%	
Reporting two or more races, %	1.90%	2.80%	
Hispanic or Latino origin, % (b)	4.20%	17.10%	
White persons, not of Hispanic/Latino origin, %	92.00%	74.50%	
Living in same house 1995 -2000, % age 5+	43.40%	44.10%	
Foreign born persons, %	3.40%	8.60%	
Language other than English at home, % age 5+	4.70%	15.10%	
High school graduates, %, age 25+	94.10%	86.90%	
Bachelor's degree or higher, %, age 25+	31.20%	32.70%	
With a disability, age 5+	526	638,654	0.08%
Mean travel time to work, age 16+ (minutes)	34.7	24.3	
Housing unit	2,929	1,808,037	0.16%
Homeownership rate	78.40%	67.30%	
Housing units in multi-unit structures, %	6.90%	25.70%	
Median value of owner-occupied housing units	$180,600	$166,600	
Households	2,043	1,658,238	0.12%
Persons per household	2.32	2.53	
Median household money income, 1999	$51,942	$47,203	
Per capita money income, 1999	$26,148	$24,049	
Persons below poverty, %, 1999	4.00%	9.30%	

Geography

Land area, 2000 (square miles)	150	104,247	0.14%
Persons per square mile, 2000	31.7	41.5	
Metropolitan Area	None		

(a) Includes persons reporting only one race.
(b) Hispanics may be of any race, so also are included in applicable race categories.
Source: United States Census Bureau

Grand County, Colorado, 2000-2001 Census

Organized Feb. 2, 1874 from Summit County. Named for the Grand River, now known as the Colorado River. County seat Hot Sulphur Springs.

	County	Colorado	% of Colo.
Population 2001 estimate	12,711	4,417,714	0.29%
% change, April 1, 2000-July 1, 2001	2.20%	2.70%	
Population, 2000	12,442	4,301,261	0.29%
Population, % change, 1990 to 2000	56.20%	30.60%	
Under 5 years old, %	5.80%	6.90%	
Under 18 years old, %	21.80%	25.60%	
65 years and over, %	7.80%	9.70%	
Female, %	47.00%	49.60%	
White, % (a)	95.20%	82.80%	
Black /African American, % (a)	0.50%	3.80%	
American Indian/Alaska Native, % (a)	0.40%	1.00%	
Asian, % (a)	0.70%	2.20%	
Native Hawaiian/Pacific Islander (a)	0.10%	0.10%	
Reporting some other race, % (a)	2.00%	7.20%	
Reporting two or more races, %	1.10%	2.80%	
Hispanic or Latino origin, % (b)	4.40%	17.10%	
White persons, not of Hispanic/Latino origin, %	93.00%	74.50%	
Living in same house 1995 -2000, % age 5+	42.20%	44.10%	
Foreign born persons, %	3.40%	8.60%	
Language other than English at home, % age 5+	6.10%	15.10%	
High school graduates, %, age 25+	92.30%	86.90%	
Bachelor's degree or higher, %, age 25+	34.50%	32.70%	
With a disability, age 5+	1,535	638,654	0.24%
Mean travel time to work, age 16+ (minutes)	22.7	24.3	
Housing unit	10,894	1,808,037	0.60%
Homeownership rate	68.20%	67.30%	
Housing units in multi-unit structures, %	30.80%	25.70%	
Median value of owner-occupied housing units	$205,500	$166,600	
Households	5,075	1,658,238	0.31%
Persons per household	2.37	2.53	
Median household money income, 1999	$47,759	$47,203	
Per capita money income, 1999	$25,198	$24,049	
Persons below poverty, %, 1999	7.30%	9.30%	

Geography

Land area, 2000 (square miles)	1,847	104,247	1.78%
Persons per square mile, 2000	6.7	41.5	
Metropolitan Area	None		

(a) Includes persons reporting only one race.
(b) Hispanics may be of any race, so also are included in applicable race categories.
Source: United States Census Bureau

Gunnison County, Colorado, 2000-2001 Census

Organized March 9, 1877 from Lake County. Named for John William Gunnison, noted early surveyor. County seat Gunnison.

	County	Colorado	% of Colo.
Population 2001 estimate	13,947	4,417,714	0.32%
% change, April 1, 2000-July 1, 2001	-0.10%	2.70%	
Population, 2000	$13,956	$4,301,261	0.32%
Population, % change, 1990 to 2000	35.90%	30.60%	
Under 5 years old, %	4.60%	6.90%	
Under 18 years old, %	17.90%	25.60%	
65 years and over, %	6.90%	9.70%	
Female, %	45.80%	49.60%	
White, % (a)	95.10%	82.80%	
Black /African American, % (a)	0.50%	3.80%	
American Indian/Alaska Native, % (a)	0.70%	1.00%	
Asian, % (a)	0.50%	2.20%	
Native Hawaiian/Pacific Islander (a)	--	--	
Reporting some other race, % (a)	1.40%	7.20%	
Reporting two or more races, %	1.70%	2.80%	
Hispanic or Latino origin, % (b)	5.00%	17.10%	
White persons, not of Hispanic/Latino origin, %	92.30%	74.50%	
Living in same house 1995 -2000, % age 5+	36.80%	44.10%	
Foreign born persons, %	2.90%	8.60%	
Language other than English at home, % age 5+	6.60%	15.10%	
High school graduates, %, age 25+	94.10%	86.90%	
Bachelor's degree or higher, %, age 25+	43.60%	32.70%	
With a disability, age 5+	1,297	638,654	0.20%
Mean travel time to work, age 16+ (minutes)	15.9	24.3	
Housing unit	9,135	1,808,037	0.51%
Homeownership rate	58.30%	67.30%	
Housing units in multi-unit structures, %	26.60%	25.70%	
Median value of owner-occupied housing units	$189,400	$166,600	
Households	5,649	1,658,238	0.34%
Persons per household	2.3	2.53	
Median household money income, 1999	$36,916	$47,203	
Per capita money income, 1999	$21,407	$24,049	
Persons below poverty, %, 1999	15.00%	9.30%	

Geography

	County	Colorado	% of Colo.
Land area, 2000 (square miles)	3,239	104,247	3.12%
Persons per square mile, 2000	4.3	41.5	
Metropolitan Area	None		

(a) Includes persons reporting only one race.
(b) Hispanics may be of any race, so also are included in applicable race categories.
Source: United States Census Bureau

Hinsdale County, Colorado, 2000-2001 Census

Organized Feb. 10, 1874 from Conejos and Summit Counties. Named for George A. Hinsdale, a lieutenant governor of the state. County seat Lake City.

	County	Colorado	% of Colo.
Population 2001 estimate	800	4,417,714	0.02%
% change, April 1, 2000-July 1, 2001	1.30%	2.70%	
Population, 2000	790	4,301,261	0.02%
Population, % change, 1990 to 2000	69.20%	30.60%	
Under 5 years old, %	6.10%	6.90%	
Under 18 years old, %	19.50%	25.60%	
65 years and over, %	11.60%	9.70%	
Female, %	48.60%	49.60%	
White, % (a)	97.30%	82.80%	
Black /African American, % (a)	0.00%	3.80%	
American Indian/Alaska Native, % (a)	1.50%	1.00%	
Asian, % (a)	0.30%	2.20%	
Native Hawaiian/Pacific Islander (a)	0.00%	0.10%	
Reporting some other race, % (a)	0.40%	7.20%	
Reporting two or more races, %	0.50%	2.80%	
Hispanic or Latino origin, % (b)	1.50%	17.10%	
White persons, not of Hispanic/Latino origin, %	96.60%	74.50%	
Living in same house 1995 -2000, % age 5+	50.00%	44.10%	
Foreign born persons, %	2.00%	8.60%	
Language other than English at home, % age 5+	4.90%	15.10%	
High school graduates, %, age 25+	93.10%	86.90%	
Bachelor's degree or higher, %, age 25+	34.90%	32.70%	
With a disability, age 5+	81	638,654	0.01%
Mean travel time to work, age 16+ (minutes)	16	24.3	
Housing unit	1,304	1,808,037	0.07%
Homeownership rate	64.90%	67.30%	
Housing units in multi-unit structures, %	3.20%	25.70%	
Median value of owner-occupied housing units	$213,300	$166,600	
Households	359	1,658,238	0.02%
Persons per household	2.2	2.53	
Median household money income, 1999	$37,279	$47,203	
Per capita money income, 1999	$22,360	$24,049	
Persons below poverty, %, 1999	7.20%	9.30%	

Geography

	County	Colorado	% of Colo.
Land area, 2000 (square miles)	1,118	104,247	1.08%
Persons per square mile, 2000	0.7	41.5	
Metropolitan Area	None		

(a) Includes persons reporting only one race.
(b) Hispanics may be of any race, so also are included in applicable race categories.
Source: United States Census Bureau

Huerfano County, Colorado, 2000-2001 Census

Original county organized Nov. 1, 1861 prior to statehood. Named for the Huerfano River. The name is Spanish for orphan, referring to an isolated butte. County seat Walsenburg.

	County	Colorado	% of Colo.
Population 2001 estimate	7,845	4,417,714	0.18%
% change, April 1, 2000-July 1, 2001	-0.20%	2.70%	
Population, 2000	7,862	4,301,261	0.18%
Population, % change, 1990 to 2000	30.80%	30.60%	
Under 5 years old, %	4.40%	6.90%	
Under 18 years old, %	20.90%	25.60%	
65 years and over, %	17.00%	9.70%	
Female, %	45.70%	49.60%	
White, % (a)	81.00%	82.80%	
Black /African American, % (a)	2.70%	3.80%	
American Indian/Alaska Native, % (a)	2.70%	1.00%	
Asian, % (a)	0.40%	2.20%	
Native Hawaiian/Pacific Islander (a)	0.10%	0.10%	
Reporting some other race, % (a)	9.40%	7.20%	
Reporting two or more races, %	3.70%	2.80%	
Hispanic or Latino origin, % (b)	35.10%	17.10%	
White persons, not of Hispanic/Latino origin, %	58.40%	74.50%	
Living in same house 1995 -2000, % age 5+	51.10%	44.10%	
Foreign born persons, %	1.60%	8.60%	
Language other than English at home, % age 5+	18.20%	15.10%	
High school graduates, %, age 25+	77.80%	86.90%	
Bachelor's degree or higher, %, age 25+	16.10%	32.70%	
With a disability, age 5+	1,494	638,654	0.23%
Mean travel time to work, age 16+ (minutes)	25	24	
Housing unit	4,599.00	1,808,037	0.25%
Homeownership rate	70.70%	67.30%	
Housing units in multi-unit structures, %	9.60%	25.70%	
Median value of owner-occupied housing units	$75,200	$166,600	
Households	3,082	1,658,238	0.19%
Persons per household	2.25	2.53	
Median household money income, 1999	$25,775	$47,203	
Per capita money income, 1999	$15,242	$24,049	
Persons below poverty, %, 1999	18.00%	9.30%	

Geography

Land area, 2000 (square miles)	1,591	104,247	1.53%
Persons per square mile, 2000	4.90	41.50	
Metropolitan Area	None		

(a) Includes persons reporting only one race.
(b) Hispanics may be of any race, so also are included in applicable race categories.
Source: United States Census Bureau

Jackson County, Colorado, 2000-2001 Census

Organized May 5, 1909 from Larimer County. Named for Andrew Jackson, seventh U.S. president. County seat Walden.

	County	Colorado	% of Colo.
Population 2001 estimate	1,589	4,417,714	0.04%
% change, April 1, 2000-July 1, 2001	0.80%	2.70%	
Population, 2000	1,577	4,301,261	0.04%
Population, % change, 1990 to 2000	-1.70%	30.60%	
Under 5 years old, %	5.60%	6.90%	
Under 18 years old, %	25.60%	25.60%	
65 years and over, %	13.10%	9.70%	
Female, %	49.70%	49.60%	
White, % (a)	96.20%	82.80%	
Black /African American, % (a)	0.30%	3.80%	
American Indian/Alaska Native, % (a)	0.80%	1.00%	
Asian, % (a)	0.10%	2.20%	
Native Hawaiian/Pacific Islander (a)	0.00%	0.10%	
Reporting some other race, % (a)	1.50%	7.20%	
Reporting two or more races, %	1.30%	2.80%	
Hispanic or Latino origin, % (b)	6.50%	17.10%	
White persons, not of Hispanic/Latino origin, %	92.10%	74.50%	
Living in same house 1995 -2000, % age 5+	57.70%	44.10%	
Foreign born persons, %	1.90%	8.60%	
Language other than English at home, % age 5+	3.80%	15.10%	
High school graduates, %, age 25+	86.20%	86.90%	
Bachelor's degree or higher, %, age 25+	19.90%	32.70%	
With a disability, age 5+	206	638,654	0.03%
Mean travel time to work, age 16+ (minutes)	14	24	
Housing unit	1,145.00	1,808,037	0.06%
Homeownership rate	67.60%	67.30%	
Housing units in multi-unit structures, %	3.80%	25.70%	
Median value of owner-occupied housing units	$86,000	$166,600	
Households	661	1,658,238	0.04%
Persons per household	2.37	2.53	
Median household money income, 1999	$31,821	$47,203	
Per capita money income, 1999	$17,826	$24,049	
Persons below poverty, %, 1999	14.00%	9.30%	

Geography

	County	Colorado	% of Colo.
Land area, 2000 (square miles)	1,613	104,247	1.56%
Persons per square mile, 2000	1.00	41.50	
Metropolitan Area	None		

(a) Includes persons reporting only one race.
(b) Hispanics may be of any race, so also are included in applicable race categories.
Source: United States Census Bureau

Jefferson County, Colorado, 2000-2001 Census

Original county organized Nov. 1, 1861 prior to statehood. Named for Thomas Jefferson, third U.S. president, and for the Jefferson Territory, which preceded the Colorado Territory. County seat Golden.

	County	Colorado	% of Colo.
Population 2001 estimate	530,966	4,417,714	12.02%
% change, April 1, 2000-July 1, 2001	0.70%	2.70%	
Population, 2000	527,056	4,301,261	12.25%
Population, % change, 1990 to 2000	20.20%	30.60%	
Under 5 years old, %	6.30%	6.90%	
Under 18 years old, %	25.30%	25.60%	
65 years and over, %	9.60%	9.70%	
Female, %	50.20%	49.60%	
White, % (a)	90.60%	82.80%	
Black /African American, % (a)	0.90%	3.80%	
American Indian/Alaska Native, % (a)	0.80%	1.00%	
Asian, % (a)	2.30%	2.20%	
Native Hawaiian/Pacific Islander (a)	0.10%	0.10%	
Reporting some other race, % (a)	3.20%	7.20%	
Reporting two or more races, %	2.20%	2.80%	
Hispanic or Latino origin, % (b)	10.00%	17.10%	
White persons, not of Hispanic/Latino origin, %	84.90%	74.50%	
Living in same house 1995 -2000, % age 5+	50.90%	44.10%	
Foreign born persons, %	5.40%	8.60%	
Language other than English at home, % age 5+	9.20%	15.10%	
High school graduates, %, age 25+	91.80%	86.90%	
Bachelor's degree or higher, %, age 25+	36.50%	32.70%	
With a disability, age 5+	68,851	638,654	10.78%
Mean travel time to work, age 16+ (minutes)	.27	.24	
Housing unit	212,488	1,808,037	11.75%
Homeownership rate	72.50%	67.30%	
Housing units in multi-unit structures, %	23.80%	25.70%	
Median value of owner-occupied housing units	$187,900	$166,600	
Households	206,067	1,658,238	12.43%
Persons per household	2.52	2.53	
Median household money income, 1999	$57,339	$47,203	
Per capita money income, 1999	$28,066	$24,049	
Persons below poverty, %, 1999	5.20%	9.30%	

Geography

Land area, 2000 (square miles)	772	104,247	0.74%
Persons per square mile, 2000	682.60	41.50	
Metropolitan Area	Denver, CO PMSA		

(a) Includes persons reporting only one race.
(b) Hispanics may be of any race, so also are included in applicable race categories.
Source: United States Census Bureau

Kiowa County, Colorado, 2000-2001 Census

Organized April 11, 1889 from Bent County. Named for the Kiowa Indian tribe. County seat Eads.

	County	Colorado	% of Colo.
Population 2001 estimate	1,537	4,417,714	0.03%
% change, April 1, 2000-July 1, 2001	-5.20%	2.70%	
Population, 2000	1,622	4,301,261	0.04%
Population, % change, 1990 to 2000	-3.90%	30.60%	
Under 5 years old, %	6.00%	6.90%	
Under 18 years old, %	25.90%	25.60%	
65 years and over, %	17.60%	9.70%	
Female, %	50.00%	49.60%	
White, % (a)	96.10%	82.80%	
Black /African American, % (a)	0.50%	3.80%	
American Indian/Alaska Native, % (a)	1.10%	1.00%	
Asian, % (a)	0.00%	2.20%	
Native Hawaiian/Pacific Islander (a)	0.10%	0.10%	
Reporting some other race, % (a)	1.40%	7.20%	
Reporting two or more races, %	0.80%	2.80%	
Hispanic or Latino origin, % (b)	3.10%	17.10%	
White persons, not of Hispanic/Latino origin, %	94.30%	74.50%	
Living in same house 1995 -2000, % age 5+	64.40%	44.10%	
Foreign born persons, %	1.40%	8.60%	
Language other than English at home, % age 5+	3.50%	15.10%	
High school graduates, %, age 25+	86.30%	86.90%	
Bachelor's degree or higher, %, age 25+	16.10%	32.70%	
With a disability, age 5+	321	638,654	0.05%
Mean travel time to work, age 16+ (minutes)	18.3	24.3	
Housing unit	817	1,808,037	0.05%
Homeownership rate	71.30%	67.30%	
Housing units in multi-unit structures, %	5.60%	25.70%	
Median value of owner-occupied housing units	$46,100	$166,600	
Households	665	1,658,238	0.04%
Persons per household	2.4	2.53	
Median household money income, 1999	$30,494	$47,203	
Per capita money income, 1999	$16,382	$24,049	
Persons below poverty, %, 1999	12.20%	9.30%	

Geography

Land area, 2000 (square miles)	1,771	104,247	1.71%
Persons per square mile, 2000	0.90	41.50	
Metropolitan Area	None		

(a) Includes persons reporting only one race.
(b) Hispanics may be of any race, so also are included in applicable race categories.
Source: United States Census Bureau

Kit Carson County, Colorado, 2000-2001 Census

Organized April 11, 1889 from Elbert County. Named for Kit Carson, guide and Indian agent. County seat Burlington.

	County	Colorado	% of Colo.
Population 2001 estimate	7,813	4,417,714	0.18%
% change, April 1, 2000-July 1, 2001	-2.50%	2.70%	
Population, 2000	8,011	4,301,261	0.19%
Population, % change, 1990 to 2000	12.20%	30.60%	
Under 5 years old, %	6.10%	6.90%	
Under 18 years old, %	26.70%	25.60%	
65 years and over, %	14.60%	9.70%	
Female, %	47.10%	49.60%	
White, % (a)	87.30%	82.80%	
Black /African American, % (a)	1.70%	3.80%	
American Indian/Alaska Native, % (a)	0.50%	1.00%	
Asian, % (a)	0.30%	2.20%	
Native Hawaiian/Pacific Islander (a)	--	--	
Reporting some other race, % (a)	9.20%	7.20%	
Reporting two or more races, %	0.90%	2.80%	
Hispanic or Latino origin, % (b)	13.70%	17.10%	
White persons, not of Hispanic/Latino origin, %	83.40%	74.50%	
Living in same house 1995 -2000, % age 5+	57.40%	44.10%	
Foreign born persons, %	5.80%	8.60%	
Language other than English at home, % age 5+	13.20%	15.10%	
High school graduates, %, age 25+	77.00%	86.90%	
Bachelor's degree or higher, %, age 25+	15.40%	32.70%	
With a disability, age 5+	1,280	638,654	0.20%
Mean travel time to work, age 16+ (minutes)	14.6	24.3	
Housing unit	3,430	1,808,037	0.19%
Homeownership rate	71.90%	67.30%	
Housing units in multi-unit structures, %	8.10%	25.70%	
Median value of owner-occupied housing units	$80,400	$166,600	
Households	2,990	1,658,238	0.18%
Persons per household	2.5	2.53	
Median household money income, 1999	$33,152	$47,203	
Per capita money income, 1999	$16,964	$24,049	
Persons below poverty, %, 1999	12.10%	9.30%	

Geography

Land area, 2000 (square miles)	2,161	104,247	2.08%
Persons per square mile, 2000	3.70	41.50	
Metropolitan Area	None		

(a) Includes persons reporting only one race.
(b) Hispanics may be of any race, so also are included in applicable race categories.
Source: United States Census Bureau

114

Lake County, Colorado, 2000-2001 Census

Original county organized Nov. 1, 1861. Name changed from Carbonate Feb. 10, 1879. Named for Twin Lakes. County seat Leadville.

	County	Colorado	% of Colo.
Population 2001 estimate	7,679	4,417,714	0.17%
% change, April 1, 2000-July 1, 2001	-1.70%	2.70%	
Population, 2000	7,812	4,301,261	0.18%
Population, % change, 1990 to 2000	30.00%	30.60%	
Under 5 years old, %	7.80%	6.90%	
Under 18 years old, %	26.90%	25.60%	
65 years and over, %	6.60%	9.70%	
Female, %	46.30%	49.60%	
White, % (a)	77.60%	82.80%	
Black /African American, % (a)	0.20%	3.80%	
American Indian/Alaska Native, % (a)	1.30%	1.00%	
Asian, % (a)	0.30%	2.20%	
Native Hawaiian/Pacific Islander (a)	0.10%	0.10%	
Reporting some other race, % (a)	18.00%	7.20%	
Reporting two or more races, %	2.60%	2.80%	
Hispanic or Latino origin, % (b)	36.10%	17.10%	
White persons, not of Hispanic/Latino origin, %	61.60%	74.50%	
Living in same house 1995 -2000, % age 5+	44.60%	44.10%	
Foreign born persons, %	15.60%	8.60%	
Language other than English at home, % age 5+	26.40%	15.10%	
High school graduates, %, age 25+	79.50%	86.90%	
Bachelor's degree or higher, %, age 25+	19.50%	32.70%	
With a disability, age 5+	1,187	638,654	0.19%
Mean travel time to work, age 16+ (minutes)	35.8	24.3	
Housing unit	3,913	1,808,037	0.22%
Homeownership rate	68.20%	67.30%	
Housing units in multi-unit structures, %	14.20%	25.70%	
Median value of owner-occupied housing units	$115,400	$166,600	
Households	2,977	1,658,238	0.18%
Persons per household	2.59	2.53	
Median household money income, 1999	$37,691	$47,203	
Per capita money income, 1999	$18,524	$24,049	
Persons below poverty, %, 1999	12.90%	9.30%	

Geography

Land area, 2000 (square miles)	377	104,247	0.36%
Persons per square mile, 2000	20.70	41.50	
Metropolitan Area	None		

(a) Includes persons reporting only one race.
(b) Hispanics may be of any race, so also are included in applicable race categories.
Source: United States Census Bureau

La Plata County, Colorado, 2000-2001 Census

Organized Feb. 10, 1874 prior to statehood from Conejos and Lake Counties. Named for the La Plata River meaning silver in Spanish. County seat Durango.

	County	Colorado	% of Colo.
Population 2001 estimate	45,157	4,417,714	1.02%
% change, April 1, 2000-July 1, 2001	2.80%	2.70%	
Population, 2000	43,941	4,301,261	1.02%
Population, % change, 1990 to 2000	36.10%	30.60%	
Under 5 years old, %	5.10%	6.90%	
Under 18 years old, %	22.70%	25.60%	
65 years and over, %	9.40%	9.70%	
Female, %	49.10%	49.60%	
White, % (a)	87.30%	82.80%	
Black /African American, % (a)	0.30%	3.80%	
American Indian/Alaska Native, % (a)	5.80%	1.00%	
Asian, % (a)	0.40%	2.20%	
Native Hawaiian/Pacific Islander (a)	0.10%	0.10%	
Reporting some other race, % (a)	3.90%	7.20%	
Reporting two or more races, %	2.30%	2.80%	
Hispanic or Latino origin, % (b)	10.40%	17.10%	
White persons, not of Hispanic/Latino origin, %	82.30%	74.50%	
Living in same house 1995 -2000, % age 5+	45.40%	44.10%	
Foreign born persons, %	2.70%	8.60%	
Language other than English at home, % age 5+	9.40%	15.10%	
High school graduates, %, age 25+	91.40%	86.90%	
Bachelor's degree or higher, %, age 25+	36.40%	32.70%	
With a disability, age 5+	5,509	638,654	0.86%
Mean travel time to work, age 16+ (minutes)	20.7	24.3	
Housing unit	20,765	1,808,037	1.15%
Homeownership rate	68.40%	67.30%	
Housing units in multi-unit structures, %	14.00%	25.70%	
Median value of owner-occupied housing units	$183,900	$166,600	
Households	17,342	1,658,238	1.05%
Persons per household	2.43	2.53	
Median household money income, 1999	$40,159	$47,203	
Per capita money income, 1999	$21,534	$24,049	
Persons below poverty, %, 1999	11.70%	9.30%	

Geography

	County	Colorado	% of Colo.
Land area, 2000 (square miles)	1,692	104,247	1.63%
Persons per square mile, 2000	26.00	41.50	
Metropolitan Area	None		

(a) Includes persons reporting only one race.
(b) Hispanics may be of any race, so also are included in applicable race categories.
Source: United States Census Bureau

Larimer County, Colorado, 2000-2001 Census

Original county organized Nov. 1, 1861. Named for General William Larimer, a founder of Denver. County seat Fort Collins.

	County	Colorado	% of Colo.
Population 2001 estimate	259,472	4,417,714	5.87%
% change, April 1, 2000-July 1, 2001	3.20%	2.70%	
Population, 2000	251,494	4,301,261	5.85%
Population, % change, 1990 to 2000	35.10%	30.60%	
Under 5 years old, %	6.10%	6.90%	
Under 18 years old, %	23.80%	25.60%	
65 years and over, %	9.60%	9.70%	
Female, %	50.00%	49.60%	
White, % (a)	91.40%	82.80%	
Black /African American, % (a)	0.70%	3.80%	
American Indian/Alaska Native, % (a)	0.70%	1.00%	
Asian, % (a)	1.60%	2.20%	
Native Hawaiian/Pacific Islander (a)	0.10%	0.10%	
Reporting some other race, % (a)	3.40%	7.20%	
Reporting two or more races, %	2.20%	2.80%	
Hispanic or Latino origin, % (b)	8.30%	17.10%	
White persons, not of Hispanic/Latino origin, %	87.50%	74.50%	
Living in same house 1995 -2000, % age 5+	41.50%	44.10%	
Foreign born persons, %	4.30%	8.60%	
Language other than English at home, % age 5+	8.50%	15.10%	
High school graduates, %, age 25+	92.30%	86.90%	
Bachelor's degree or higher, %, age 25+	39.50%	32.70%	
With a disability, age 5+	31,107	638,654	4.87%
Mean travel time to work, age 16+ (minutes)	21.4	24.3	
Housing unit	105,392	1,808,037	5.83%
Homeownership rate	67.70%	67.30%	
Housing units in multi-unit structures, %	21.50%	25.70%	
Median value of owner-occupied housing units	$172,000	$166,600	
Households	97,164	1,658,238	5.86%
Persons per household	2.52	2.53	
Median household money income, 1999	$48,655	$47,203	
Per capita money income, 1999	$23,689	$24,049	
Persons below poverty, %, 1999	9.20%	9.30%	

Geography

Land area, 2000 (square miles)	2,601	104,247	2.51%
Persons per square mile, 2000	96.70	41.50	
Metropolitan Area	Fort Collins-Loveland, CO MSA		

(a) Includes persons reporting only one race.
(b) Hispanics may be of any race, so also are included in applicable race categories.
Source: United States Census Bureau

117

Las Animas County, Colorado, 2000-2001 Census

Organized prior to statehood Feb. 9, 1866 from Huerfano County. Named for the river El Rio de las Animas Perdidas en Purgatorio - "river of souls lost in Purgatory." River name shortened to Purgatoire. County seat Trinidad.

	County	Colorado	% of Colo.
Population 2001 estimate	15,341	4,417,714	0.35%
% change, April 1, 2000-July 1, 2001	0.90%	2.70%	
Population, 2000	15,207	4,301,261	0.35%
Population, % change, 1990 to 2000	10.50%	30.60%	
Under 5 years old, %	5.60%	6.90%	
Under 18 years old, %	24.20%	25.60%	
65 years and over, %	18.00%	9.70%	
Female, %	51.10%	49.60%	
White, % (a)	82.60%	82.80%	
Black /African American, % (a)	0.40%	3.80%	
American Indian/Alaska Native, % (a)	2.50%	1.00%	
Asian, % (a)	0.40%	2.20%	
Native Hawaiian/Pacific Islander (a)	0.20%	0.10%	
Reporting some other race, % (a)	10.00%	7.20%	
Reporting two or more races, %	3.80%	2.80%	
Hispanic or Latino origin, % (b)	41.50%	17.10%	
White persons, not of Hispanic/Latino origin, %	55.20%	74.50%	
Living in same house 1995 -2000, % age 5+	58.30%	44.10%	
Foreign born persons, %	2.30%	8.60%	
Language other than English at home, % age 5+	20.80%	15.10%	
High school graduates, %, age 25+	76.90%	86.90%	
Bachelor's degree or higher, %, age 25+	16.20%	32.70%	
With a disability, age 5+	3,671	638,654	0.57%
Mean travel time to work, age 16+ (minutes)	20.6	24.3	
Housing unit	7,629	1,808,037	0.42%
Homeownership rate	70.60%	67.30%	
Housing units in multi-unit structures, %	11.10%	25.70%	
Median value of owner-occupied housing units	$84,500	$166,600	
Households	6,173	1,658,238	0.37%
Persons per household	2.4	2.53	
Median household money income, 1999	$28,273	$47,203	
Per capita money income, 1999	$16,829	$24,049	
Persons below poverty, %, 1999	17.30%	9.30%	

Geography

Land area, 2000 (square miles)	4,773	104,247	4.60%
Persons per square mile, 2000	3.20	41.50	
Metropolitan Area	None		

(a) Includes persons reporting only one race.
(b) Hispanics may be of any race, so also are included in applicable race categories.
Source: United States Census Bureau

118

Lincoln County, Colorado, 2000-2001 Census

Organized April 11, 1889 from Bent and Elbert Counties. Named for Abraham Lincoln, 16th U.S. president. County seat Hugo.

	County	Colorado	% of Colo.
Population 2001 estimate	5,927	4,417,714	0.13%
% change, April 1, 2000-July 1, 2001	-2.60%	2.70%	
Population, 2000	6,087	4,301,261	0.14%
Population, % change, 1990 to 2000	34.40%	30.60%	
Under 5 years old, %	5.00%	6.90%	
Under 18 years old, %	23.90%	25.60%	
65 years and over, %	14.30%	9.70%	
Female, %	43.30%	49.60%	
White, % (a)	86.30%	82.80%	
Black /African American, % (a)	5.00%	3.80%	
American Indian/Alaska Native, % (a)	0.90%	1.00%	
Asian, % (a)	0.60%	2.20%	
Native Hawaiian/Pacific Islander (a)	--	--	
Reporting some other race, % (a)	5.70%	7.20%	
Reporting two or more races, %	1.60%	2.80%	
Hispanic or Latino origin, % (b)	8.50%	17.10%	
White persons, not of Hispanic/Latino origin, %	84.20%	74.50%	
Living in same house 1995 -2000, % age 5+	43.90%	44.10%	
Foreign born persons, %	1.80%	8.60%	
Language other than English at home, % age 5+	6.90%	15.10%	
High school graduates, %, age 25+	81.80%	86.90%	
Bachelor's degree or higher, %, age 25+	13.20%	32.70%	
With a disability, age 5+	900	638,654	0.14%
Mean travel time to work, age 16+ (minutes)	19.2	24.3	
Housing unit	2,406	1,808,037	0.13%
Homeownership rate	69.00%	67.30%	
Housing units in multi-unit structures, %	7.60%	25.70%	
Median value of owner-occupied housing units	$77,800	$166,600	
Households	2,058	1,658,238	0.12%
Persons per household	2.44	2.53	
Median household money income, 1999	$31,914	$47,203	
Per capita money income, 1999	$15,510	$24,049	
Persons below poverty, %, 1999	11.70%	9.30%	

Geography

Land area, 2000 (square miles)	2,586	104,247	2.49%
Persons per square mile, 2000	2.40	41.50	
Metropolitan Area	None		

(a) Includes persons reporting only one race.
(b) Hispanics may be of any race, so also are included in applicable race categories.
Source: United States Census Bureau

Logan County, Colorado, 2000-2001 Census

Organized Feb. 25, 1887 from Weld County. Named for General John Alexander Logan, army officer and U.S. senator from Illinois. County seat Sterling.

	County	Colorado	% of Colo.
Population 2001 estimate	20,921	4,417,714	0.47%
% change, April 1, 2000-July 1, 2001	2.00%	2.70%	
Population, 2000	20,504	4,301,261	0.48%
Population, % change, 1990 to 2000	16.70%	30.60%	
Under 5 years old, %	6.30%	6.90%	
Under 18 years old, %	24.70%	25.60%	
65 years and over, %	14.50%	9.70%	
Female, %	47.20%	49.60%	
White, % (a)	91.70%	82.80%	
Black /African American, % (a)	2.00%	3.80%	
American Indian/Alaska Native, % (a)	0.60%	1.00%	
Asian, % (a)	0.40%	2.20%	
Native Hawaiian/Pacific Islander (a)	0.10%	0.10%	
Reporting some other race, % (a)	3.80%	7.20%	
Reporting two or more races, %	1.40%	2.80%	
Hispanic or Latino origin, % (b)	11.90%	17.10%	
White persons, not of Hispanic/Latino origin, %	84.40%	74.50%	
Living in same house 1995 -2000, % age 5+	53.10%	44.10%	
Foreign born persons, %	3.10%	8.60%	
Language other than English at home, % age 5+	8.20%	15.10%	
High school graduates, %, age 25+	82.30%	86.90%	
Bachelor's degree or higher, %, age 25+	14.60%	32.70%	
With a disability, age 5+	3,414	638,654	0.53%
Mean travel time to work, age 16+ (minutes)	15.2	24.3	
Housing unit	8,424	1,808,037	0.47%
Homeownership rate	69.90%	67.30%	
Housing units in multi-unit structures, %	12.50%	25.70%	
Median value of owner-occupied housing units	$87,700	$166,600	
Households	7,551	1,658,238	0.46%
Persons per household	2.45	2.53	
Median household money income, 1999	$32,724	$47,203	
Per capita money income, 1999	$16,721	$24,049	
Persons below poverty, %, 1999	12.20%	9.30%	

Geography

	County	Colorado	% of Colo.
Land area, 2000 (square miles)	1,839	104,247	1.77%
Persons per square mile, 2000	11.20	41.50	
Metropolitan Area	None		

(a) Includes persons reporting only one race.

(b) Hispanics may be of any race, so also are included in applicable race categories.

Source: United States Census Bureau

Mesa County, Colorado, 2000-2001 Census

Organized Feb. 14, 1883 from Gunnison County. Name is Spanish for table. Named for Grand Mesa. County seat Grand Junction.

	County	Colorado	% of Colo.
Population 2001 estimate	119,281	4,417,714	2.70%
% change, April 1, 2000-July 1, 2001	2.60%	2.70%	
Population, 2000	116,255	4,301,261	2.70%
Population, % change, 1990 to 2000	24.80%	30.60%	
Under 5 years old, %	6.30%	6.90%	
Under 18 years old, %	25.00%	25.60%	
65 years and over, %	15.20%	9.70%	
Female, %	51.00%	49.60%	
White, % (a)	92.30%	82.80%	
Black /African American, % (a)	0.50%	3.80%	
American Indian/Alaska Native, % (a)	0.90%	1.00%	
Asian, % (a)	0.50%	2.20%	
Native Hawaiian/Pacific Islander (a)	0.10%	0.10%	
Reporting some other race, % (a)	3.70%	7.20%	
Reporting two or more races, %	2.00%	2.80%	
Hispanic or Latino origin, % (b)	10.00%	17.10%	
White persons, not of Hispanic/Latino origin, %	87.00%	74.50%	
Living In same house 1995-2000, % age 5+	45.10%	44.10%	
Foreign born persons, %	3.00%	8.60%	
Language other than English at home, % age 5+	8.00%	15.10%	
High school graduates, %, age 25+	85.00%	86.90%	
Bachelor's degree or higher, %, age 25+	22.00%	32.70%	
With a disability, age 5+	22,750	638,654	3.56%
Mean travel time to work, age 16+ (minutes)	18.4	24.3	
Housing unit	48,427	1,808,037	2.68%
Homeownership rate	72.70%	67.30%	
Housing units in multi-unit structures, %	16.90%	25.70%	
Median value of owner-occupied housing units	$118,900	$166,600	
Households	45,823	1,658,238	2.76%
Persons per household	2.47	2.53	
Median household money income, 1999	$35,864	$47,203	
Per capita money income, 1999	$18,715	$24,049	
Persons below poverty, %, 1999	10.20%	9.30%	

Geography

	County	Colorado	% of Colo.
Land area, 2000 (square miles)	3,328	104,247	3.21%
Persons per square mile, 2000	34.90	41.50	
Metropolitan Area	Grand Junction, CO MSA		

(a) Includes persons reporting only one race.
(b) Hispanics may be of any race, so also are included in applicable race categories.
Source: United States Census Bureau

Mineral County, Colorado, 2000-2001 Census

Organized March 27, 1893 from Saguache and Rio Grande Counties. Named for the mineral resources in the area. County seat Creede.

	County	Colorado	% of Colo.
Population 2001 estimate	.809	4,417,714	0.02%
% change, April 1, 2000-July 1, 2001	-2.60%	2.70%	
Population, 2000	.831	4,301,261	0.02%
Population, % change, 1990 to 2000	48.90%	30.60%	
Under 5 years old, %	4.50%	6.90%	
Under 18 years old, %	20.50%	25.60%	
65 years and over, %	17.30%	9.70%	
Female, %	49.00%	49.60%	
White, % (a)	96.90%	82.80%	
Black /African American, % (a)	0.00%	3.80%	
American Indian/Alaska Native, % (a)	0.80%	1.00%	
Asian, % (a)	0.00%	2.20%	
Native Hawaiian/Pacific Islander (a)	0.00%	0.10%	
Reporting some other race, % (a)	0.10%	7.20%	
Reporting two or more races, %	2.20%	2.80%	
Hispanic or Latino origin, % (b)	2.00%	17.10%	
White persons, not of Hispanic/Latino origin, %	95.40%	74.50%	
Living in same house 1995 -2000, % age 5+	50.60%	44.10%	
Foreign born persons, %	0.70%	8.60%	
Language other than English at home, % age 5+	1.90%	15.10%	
High school graduates, %, age 25+	91.60%	86.90%	
Bachelor's degree or higher, %, age 25+	31.20%	32.70%	
With a disability, age 5+	134	638,654	0.02%
Mean travel time to work, age 16+ (minutes)	15.9	24.3	
Housing unit	1,119	1,808,037	0.06%
Homeownership rate	74.00%	67.30%	
Housing units in multi-unit structures, %	1.60%	25.70%	
Median value of owner-occupied housing units	$127,400	$166,600	
Households	377	1,658,238	0.02%
Persons per household	2.2	2.53	
Median household money income, 1999	$34,844	$47,203	
Per capita money income, 1999	$24,475	$24,049	
Persons below poverty, %, 1999	10.20%	9.30%	

Geography

Land area, 2000 (square miles)	.876	104,247	0.84%
Persons per square mile, 2000	0.90	41.50	
Metropolitan Area	None		

(a) Includes persons reporting only one race.

(b) Hispanics may be of any race, so also are included in applicable race categories.

Source: United States Census Bureau

Moffat County, Colorado, 2000-2001 Census

Organized Feb. 27, 1911 from Routt County. Named for David H. Moffat, builder of the Moffat Line railroad across Colorado's Rocky Mountains. County seat Craig.

	County	Colorado	% of Colo.
Population 2001 estimate	13,154	4,417,714	0.30%
% change, April 1, 2000-July 1, 2001	-0.20%	2.70%	
Population, 2000	$13,184	$4,301,261	0.31%
Population, % change, 1990 to 2000	16.10%	30.60%	
Under 5 years old, %	6.80%	6.90%	
Under 18 years old, %	28.50%	25.60%	
65 years and over, %	9.40%	9.70%	
Female, %	48.10%	49.60%	
White, % (a)	93.60%	82.80%	
Black /African American, % (a)	0.20%	3.80%	
American Indian/Alaska Native, % (a)	0.90%	1.00%	
Asian, % (a)	0.30%	2.20%	
Native Hawaiian/Pacific Islander (a)	--	--	
Reporting some other race, % (a)	3.20%	7.20%	
Reporting two or more races, %	1.80%	2.80%	
Hispanic or Latino origin, % (b)	9.50%	17.10%	
White persons, not of Hispanic/Latino origin, %	88.20%	74.50%	
Living in same house 1995 -2000, % age 5+	49.50%	44.10%	
Foreign born persons, %	4.10%	8.60%	
Language other than English at home, % age 5+	8.40%	15.10%	
High school graduates, %, age 25+	79.60%	86.90%	
Bachelor's degree or higher, %, age 25+	12.50%	32.70%	
With a disability, age 5+	2,105	638,654	0.33%
Mean travel time to work, age 16+ (minutes)	23.4	24.3	
Housing unit	5,635	1,808,037	0.31%
Homeownership rate	72.10%	67.30%	
Housing units in multi-unit structures, %	16.40%	25.70%	
Median value of owner-occupied housing units	$104,600	$166,600	
Households	4,983	1,658,238	0.30%
Persons per household	2.58	2.53	
Median household money income, 1999	$41,528	$47,203	
Per capita money income, 1999	$18,540	$24,049	
Persons below poverty, %, 1999	8.30%	9.30%	

Geography

	County	Colorado	% of Colo.
Land area, 2000 (square miles)	4,742	104,247	4.57%
Persons per square mile, 2000	2.80	41.50	
Metropolitan Area	None		

(a) Includes persons reporting only one race.
(b) Hispanics may be of any race, so also are included in applicable race categories.
Source: United States Census Bureau

123

Montezuma County, Colorado, 2000-2001 Census

Organized April 16, 1889 from La Plata County. Named for the Aztec emperor con-quered by Cortez. County seat Cortez.

	County	Colorado	% of Colo.
Population 2001 estimate	24,035	4,417,714	0.54%
% change, April 1, 2000-July 1, 2001	0.90%	2.70%	
Population, 2000	23,830	4,301,261	0.55%
Population, % change, 1990 to 2000	27.60%	30.60%	
Under 5 years old, %	6.90%	6.90%	
Under 18 years old, %	27.50%	25.60%	
65 years and over, %	13.80%	9.70%	
Female, %	50.80%	49.60%	
White, % (a)	81.70%	82.80%	
Black /African American, % (a)	0.10%	3.80%	
American Indian/Alaska Native, % (a)	11.20%	1.00%	
Asian, % (a)	0.20%	2.20%	
Native Hawaiian/Pacific Islander (a)	0.10%	0.10%	
Reporting some other race, % (a)	4.30%	7.20%	
Reporting two or more races, %	2.40%	2.80%	
Hispanic or Latino origin, % (b)	9.50%	17.10%	
White persons, not of Hispanic/Latino origin, %	77.50%	74.50%	
Living in same house 1995 -2000, % age 5+	52.50%	44.10%	
Foreign born persons, %	2.20%	8.60%	
Language other than English at home, % age 5+	13.30%	15.10%	
High school graduates, %, age 25+	81.10%	86.90%	
Bachelor's degree or higher, %, age 25+	21.00%	32.70%	
With a disability, age 5+	4,158	638,654	0.65%
Mean travel time to work, age 16+ (minutes)	21.8	24.3	
Housing unit	10,497	1,808,037	0.58%
Homeownership rate	74.80%	67.30%	
Housing units in multi-unit structures, %	7.10%	25.70%	
Median value of owner-occupied housing units	$109,100	$166,600	
Households	9,201	1,658,238	0.55%
Persons per household	2.54	2.53	
Median household money income, 1999	$32,083	$47,203	
Per capita money income, 1999	$17,003	$24,049	
Persons below poverty, %, 1999	16.40%	9.30%	

Geography

	County	Colorado	% of Colo.
Land area, 2000 (square miles)	2,037	104,247	1.96%
Persons per square mile, 2000	11.7	41.5	
Metropolitan Area	None		

(a) Includes persons reporting only one race.
(b) Hispanics may be of any race, so also are included in applicable race categories.
Source: United States Census Bureau

124

Montrose County, Colorado, 2000-2001 Census

Organized Feb. 11, 1883 from Gunnison County. Named from the "Legend of Montrose," by Sir Walter Scott. County seat Montrose.

	County	Colorado	% of Colo.
Population 2001 estimate	34,572	4,417,714	0.78%
% change, April 1, 2000-July 1, 2001	3.40%	2.70%	
Population, 2000	33,432	4,301,261	0.78%
Population, % change, 1990 to 2000	36.90%	30.60%	
Under 5 years old, %	6.80%	6.90%	
Under 18 years old, %	26.80%	25.60%	
65 years and over, %	15.20%	9.70%	
Female, %	50.80%	49.60%	
White, % (a)	90.00%	82.80%	
Black /African American, % (a)	0.30%	3.80%	
American Indian/Alaska Native, % (a)	1.00%	1.00%	
Asian, % (a)	0.40%	2.20%	
Native Hawaiian/Pacific Islander (a)	0.10%	0.10%	
Reporting some other race, % (a)	5.70%	7.20%	
Reporting two or more races, %	2.50%	2.80%	
Hispanic or Latino origin, % (b)	14.90%	17.10%	
White persons, not of Hispanic/Latino origin, %	82.40%	74.50%	
Living in same house 1995 -2000, % age 5+	48.60%	44.10%	
Foreign born persons, %	5.60%	8.60%	
Language other than English at home, % age 5+	11.60%	15.10%	
High school graduates, %, age 25+	80.70%	86.90%	
Bachelor's degree or higher, %, age 25+	18.70%	32.70%	
With a disability, age 5+	6,186	638,654	0.97%
Mean travel time to work, age 16+ (minutes)	21.5	24.3	
Housing unit	14,202	1,808,037	0.79%
Homeownership rate	74.90%	67.30%	
Housing units in multi-unit structures, %	9.10%	25.70%	
Median value of owner-occupied housing units	$121,200	$166,600	
Households	13,043	1,658,238	0.79%
Persons per household	2.52	2.53	
Median household money income, 1999	$35,234	$47,203	
Per capita money income, 1999	$17,158	$24,049	
Persons below poverty, %, 1999	12.60%	9.30%	

Geography

Land area, 2000 (square miles)	2,241	104,247	2.16%
Persons per square mile, 2000	14.9	41.5	
Metropolitan Area	None		

(a) Includes persons reporting only one race.
(b) Hispanics may be of any race, so also are included in applicable race categories.
Source: United States Census Bureau

Morgan County, Colorado, 2000-2001 Census

Organized Feb. 19, 1889 from Weld County. Named for Fort Morgan and Col. Christopher Morgan, army officer and inspector general of the Department of Missouri. County seat Fort Morgan.

	County	Colorado	% of Colo.
Population 2001 estimate	27,543	4,417,714	0.78%
% change, April 1, 2000-July 1, 2001	1.40%	2.70%	
Population, 2000	27,171	4,301,261	0.78%
Population, % change, 1990 to 2000	23.80%	30.60%	
Under 5 years old, %	8.50%	6.90%	
Under 18 years old, %	30.40%	25.60%	
65 years and over, %	13.00%	9.70%	
Female, %	49.90%	49.60%	
White, % (a)	79.70%	82.80%	
Black /African American, % (a)	0.30%	3.80%	
American Indian/Alaska Native, % (a)	0.80%	1.00%	
Asian, % (a)	0.20%	2.20%	
Native Hawaiian/Pacific Islander (a)	0.20%	0.10%	
Reporting some other race, % (a)	16.40%	7.20%	
Reporting two or more races, %	2.50%	2.80%	
Hispanic or Latino origin, % (b)	31.20%	17.10%	
White persons, not of Hispanic/Latino origin, %	67.00%	74.50%	
Living in same house 1995 -2000, % age 5+	50.00%	44.10%	
Foreign born persons, %	14.60%	8.60%	
Language other than English at home, % age 5+	25.60%	15.10%	
High school graduates, %, age 25+	71.40%	86.90%	
Bachelor's degree or higher, %, age 25+	13.50%	32.70%	
With a disability, age 5+	4,214	638,654	0.97%
Mean travel time to work, age 16+ (minutes)	18.50	24	
Housing unit	10,410	1,808,037	0.79%
Homeownership rate	68.40%	67.30%	
Housing units in multi-unit structures, %	12.90%	25.70%	
Median value of owner-occupied housing units	$95,900	$166,600	
Households	9,539.00	1,658,238.00	0.79%
Persons per household	2.80	2.53	
Median household money income, 1999	$34,568	$47,203	
Per capita money income, 1999	$15,492	$24,049	
Persons below poverty, %, 1999	12.40%	9.30%	

Geography

	County	Colorado	% of Colo.
Land area, 2000 (square miles)	1,285	104,247	2.16%
Persons per square mile, 2000	21.10	41.50	
Metropolitan Area	None		

(a) Includes persons reporting only one race.

(b) Hispanics may be of any race, so also are included in applicable race categories.

Source: United States Census Bureau

Otero County, Colorado, 2000-2001 Census

Organized March 25, 1889 from Bent County. Named for Miguel A. Otero, New Mexico territorial governor. County seat La Junta.

	County	Colorado	% of Colo.
Population 2001 estimate	19,972	4,417,714	0.78%
% change, April 1, 2000-July 1, 2001	-1.70%	2.70%	
Population, 2000	20,311	4,301,261	0.78%
Population, % change, 1990 to 2000	0.60%	30.60%	
Under 5 years old, %	6.50%	6.90%	
Under 18 years old, %	26.90%	25.60%	
65 years and over, %	16.50%	9.70%	
Female, %	51.10%	49.60%	
White, % (a)	79.00%	82.80%	
Black /African American, % (a)	0.80%	3.80%	
American Indian/Alaska Native, % (a)	1.40%	1.00%	
Asian, % (a)	0.70%	2.20%	
Native Hawaiian/Pacific Islander (a)	0.10%	0.10%	
Reporting some other race, % (a)	15.10%	7.20%	
Reporting two or more races, %	3.00%	2.80%	
Hispanic or Latino origin, % (b)	37.60%	17.10%	
White persons, not of Hispanic/Latino origin, %	59.20%	74.50%	
Living in same house 1995 -2000, % age 5+	56.20%	44.10%	
Foreign born persons, %	4.90%	8.60%	
Language other than English at home, % age 5+	21.90%	15.10%	
High school graduates, %, age 25+	75.70%	86.90%	
Bachelor's degree or higher, %, age 25+	15.40%	32.70%	
With a disability, age 5+	4,637	638,654	0.97%
Mean travel time to work, age 16+ (minutes)	18	24.3	
Housing unit	8,813	1,808,037	0.79%
Homeownership rate	69.10%	67.30%	
Housing units in multi-unit structures, %	11.90%	25.70%	
Median value of owner-occupied housing units	$66,300	$166,600	
Households	7,920	1,658,238	0.79%
Persons per household	2.49	2.53	
Median household money income, 1999	$29,738	$47,203	
Per capita money income, 1999	$15,113	$24,049	
Persons below poverty, %, 1999	18.80%	9.30%	

Geography

	County	Colorado	% of Colo.
Land area, 2000 (square miles)	1,263	104,247	2.16%
Persons per square mile, 2000	16.1	41.5	
Metropolitan Area	None		

(a) Includes persons reporting only one race.
(b) Hispanics may be of any race, so also are included in applicable race categories.
Source: United States Census Bureau

Ouray County, Colorado, 2000-2001 Census

Organized as Uncompahgre County Jan. 18, 1877. Name was changed to Ouray March 2, 1889. Named for the leader of the Uncompahgre Ute Indians. County seat Ouray.

	County	Colorado	% of Colo.
Population 2001 estimate	3,882	4,417,714	0.78%
% change, April 1, 2000-July 1, 2001	3.70%	2.70%	
Population, 2000	3,742	4,301,261	0.78%
Population, % change, 1990 to 2000	63.10%	30.60%	
Under 5 years old, %	4.80%	6.90%	
Under 18 years old, %	22.50%	25.60%	
65 years and over, %	12.20%	9.70%	
Female, %	49.50%	49.60%	
White, % (a)	96.30%	82.80%	
Black /African American, % (a)	0.10%	3.80%	
American Indian/Alaska Native, % (a)	0.90%	1.00%	
Asian, % (a)	0.30%	2.20%	
Native Hawaiian/Pacific Islander (a)	0.10%	0.10%	
Reporting some other race, % (a)	0.50%	7.20%	
Reporting two or more races, %	1.70%	2.80%	
Hispanic or Latino origin, % (b)	4.10%	17.10%	
White persons, not of Hispanic/Latino origin, %	93.20%	74.50%	
Living in same house 1995 -2000, % age 5+	46.10%	44.10%	
Foreign born persons, %	3.20%	8.60%	
Language other than English at home, % age 5+	5.70%	15.10%	
High school graduates, %, age 25+	93.40%	86.90%	
Bachelor's degree or higher, %, age 25+	36.80%	32.70%	
With a disability, age 5+	462	638,654	0.97%
Mean travel time to work, age 16+ (minutes)	23.60	24	
Housing unit	2,146	1,808,037	0.79%
Homeownership rate	73.40%	67.30%	
Housing units in multi-unit structures, %	9.50%	25.70%	
Median value of owner-occupied housing units	$244,700	$166,600	
Households	1,576.00	1,658,238.00	0.79%
Persons per household	2.36	2.53	
Median household money income, 1999	$42,019	$47,203	
Per capita money income, 1999	$24,335	$24,049	
Persons below poverty, %, 1999	7.20%	9.30%	

Geography

	County	Colorado	% of Colo.
Land area, 2000 (square miles)	540	104,247	2.16%
Persons per square mile, 2000	6.90	41.50	
Metropolitan Area	None		

(a) Includes persons reporting only one race.
(b) Hispanics may be of any race, so also are included in applicable race categories.
Source: United States Census Bureau

Park County, Colorado, 2000-2001 Census

Original county organized prior to statehood. Named for the geographic feature known as South Park. County seat Fairplay.

	County	Colorado	% of Colo.
Population 2001 estimate	15,580	4,417,714	0.78%
% change, April 1, 2000-July 1, 2001	7.30%	2.70%	
Population, 2000	14,523	4,301,261	0.78%
Population, % change, 1990 to 2000	102.40%	30.60%	
Under 5 years old, %	5.70%	6.90%	
Under 18 years old, %	23.50%	25.60%	
65 years and over, %	7.30%	9.70%	
Female, %	48.30%	49.60%	
White, % (a)	95.10%	82.80%	
Black /African American, % (a)	0.50%	3.80%	
American Indian/Alaska Native, % (a)	0.90%	1.00%	
Asian, % (a)	0.40%	2.20%	
Native Hawaiian/Pacific Islander (a)	--	--	
Reporting some other race, % (a)	1.20%	7.20%	
Reporting two or more races, %	1.80%	2.80%	
Hispanic or Latino origin, % (b)	4.30%	17.10%	
White persons, not of Hispanic/Latino origin, %	92.50%	74.50%	
Living in same house 1995 -2000, % age 5+	41.50%	44.10%	
Foreign born persons, %	2.20%	8.60%	
Language other than English at home, % age 5+	4.20%	15.10%	
High school graduates, %, age 25+	93.30%	86.90%	
Bachelor's degree or higher, %, age 25+	30.30%	32.70%	
With a disability, age 5+	1,920	638,654	0.97%
Mean travel time to work, age 16+ (minutes)	45	24	
Housing unit	10,697	1,808,037	0.79%
Homeownership rate	87.60%	67.30%	
Housing units in multi-unit structures, %	1.30%	25.70%	
Median value of owner-occupied housing units	$172,100	$166,600	
Households	5,894.00	1,658,238.00	0.79%
Persons per household	2.45	2.53	
Median household money income, 1999	$51,899	$47,203	
Per capita money income, 1999	$25,019	$24,049	
Persons below poverty, %, 1999	5.60%	9.30%	

Geography

	County	Colorado	% of Colo.
Land area, 2000 (square miles)	2,201	104,247	2.16%
Persons per square mile, 2000	6.60	41.50	
Metropolitan Area	None		

(a) Includes persons reporting only one race.
(b) Hispanics may be of any race, so also are included in applicable race categories.
Source: United States Census Bureau

Phillips County, Colorado, 2000 Census

Organized March 27, 1889 from Logan County. Named for R.O. Phillips, an offical in the Lincoln Land Co. that organized many eastern Colorado towns. County seat Holyoke.

	County	Colorado	% of Colo.
Population 2001 estimate	4,472	4,417,714	0.78%
% change, April 1, 2000-July 1, 2001	-0.20%	2.70%	
Population, 2000	4,480	4,301,261	0.78%
Population, % change, 1990 to 2000	6.90%	30.60%	
Under 5 years old, %	6.90%	6.90%	
Under 18 years old, %	26.90%	25.60%	
65 years and over, %	19.40%	9.70%	
Female, %	51.70%	49.60%	
White, % (a)	93.00%	82.80%	
Black /African American, % (a)	0.20%	3.80%	
American Indian/Alaska Native, % (a)	0.30%	1.00%	
Asian, % (a)	0.40%	2.20%	
Native Hawaiian/Pacific Islander (a)	--	--	
Reporting some other race, % (a)	4.70%	7.20%	
Reporting two or more races, %	1.30%	2.80%	
Hispanic or Latino origin, % (b)	11.80%	17.10%	
White persons, not of Hispanic/Latino origin, %	86.30%	74.50%	
Living in same house 1995 -2000, % age 5+	54.70%	44.10%	
Foreign born persons, %	8.10%	8.60%	
Language other than English at home, % age 5+	10.90%	15.10%	
High school graduates, %, age 25+	81.60%	86.90%	
Bachelor's degree or higher, %, age 25+	19.90%	32.70%	
With a disability, age 5+	698	638,654	0.97%
Mean travel time to work, age 16+ (minutes)	15	24	
Housing unit	2,014	1,808,037	0.79%
Homeownership rate	75.60%	67.30%	
Housing units in multi-unit structures, %	5.50%	25.70%	
Median value of owner-occupied housing units	$79,800	$166,600	
Households	1,781	1,658,238	0.79%
Persons per household	2.47	2.53	
Median household money income, 1999	$32,177	$47,203	
Per capita money income, 1999	$16,394	$24,049	
Persons below poverty, %, 1999	11.60%	9.30%	

Geography

Land area, 2000 (square miles)	688	104,247	2.16%
Persons per square mile, 2000	6.50	41.50	
Metropolitan Area	None		

(a) Includes persons reporting only one race.
(b) Hispanics may be of any race, so also are included in applicable race categories.
Source: United States Census Bureau

Pitkin County, Colorado, 2000-2001 Census

Organized Feb. 23, 1881 from Gunnison County. Named for Frederick Walker Pitkin, governor of Colorado. County seat Aspen.

	County	Colorado	% of Colo.
Population 2001 estimate	14,810	4,417,714	0.78%
% change, April 1, 2000-July 1, 2001	-0.40%	2.70%	
Population, 2000	14,872	4,301,261	0.78%
Population, % change, 1990 to 2000	17.50%	30.60%	
Under 5 years old, %	4.10%	6.90%	
Under 18 years old, %	16.70%	25.60%	
65 years and over, %	6.80%	9.70%	
Female, %	46.50%	49.60%	
White, % (a)	94.30%	82.80%	
Black /African American, % (a)	0.50%	3.80%	
American Indian/Alaska Native, % (a)	0.30%	1.00%	
Asian, % (a)	1.10%	2.20%	
Native Hawaiian/Pacific Islander (a)	--	--	
Reporting some other race, % (a)	2.40%	7.20%	
Reporting two or more races, %	1.30%	2.80%	
Hispanic or Latino origin, % (b)	6.50%	17.10%	
White persons, not of Hispanic/Latino origin, %	90.60%	74.50%	
Living in same house 1995 -2000, % age 5+	44.00%	44.10%	
Foreign born persons, %	10.90%	8.60%	
Language other than English at home, % age 5+	12.10%	15.10%	
High school graduates, %, age 25+	96.30%	86.90%	
Bachelor's degree or higher, %, age 25+	57.10%	32.70%	
With a disability, age 5+	2,048	638,654	0.97%
Mean travel time to work, age 16+ (minutes)	17	24	
Housing unit	10,096	1,808,037	0.79%
Homeownership rate	59.20%	67.30%	
Housing units in multi-unit structures, %	40.90%	25.70%	
Median value of owner-occupied housing units	$750,000	$166,600	
Households	6,807	1,658,238	0.79%
Persons per household	2.14	2.53	
Median household money income, 1999	$59,375	$47,203	
Per capita money income, 1999	$40,811	$24,049	
Persons below poverty, %, 1999	6.20%	9.30%	

Geography

	County	Colorado	% of Colo.
Land area, 2000 (square miles)	970	104,247	2.16%
Persons per square mile, 2000	15.30	41.50	
Metropolitan Area	None		

(a) Includes persons reporting only one race.
(b) Hispanics may be of any race, so also are included in applicable race categories.
Source: United States Census Bureau

Prowers County, Colorado, 2000-2001 Census

Organized April 11, 1889 from Bent County. Named for John Wesley Prowers, a Colorado statesman who worked with Col. William Bent. County seat Lamar.

	County	Colorado	% of Colo.
Population 2001 estimate	14,206	4,417,714	0.78%
% change, April 1, 2000-July 1, 2001	-1.90%	2.70%	
Population, 2000	14,483	4,301,261	0.78%
Population, % change, 1990 to 2000	8.50%	30.60%	
Under 5 years old, %	7.90%	6.90%	
Under 18 years old, %	30.00%	25.60%	
65 years and over, %	12.60%	9.70%	
Female, %	49.70%	49.60%	
White, % (a)	78.60%	82.80%	
Black /African American, % (a)	0.30%	3.80%	
American Indian/Alaska Native, % (a)	1.20%	1.00%	
Asian, % (a)	0.40%	2.20%	
Native Hawaiian/Pacific Islander (a)	--	--	
Reporting some other race, % (a)	17.20%	7.20%	
Reporting two or more races, %	2.30%	2.80%	
Hispanic or Latino origin, % (b)	32.90%	17.10%	
White persons, not of Hispanic/Latino origin, %	65.10%	74.50%	
Living in same house 1995 -2000, % age 5+	51.70%	44.10%	
Foreign born persons, %	10.60%	8.60%	
Language other than English at home, % age 5+	24.40%	15.10%	
High school graduates, %, age 25+	72.00%	86.90%	
Bachelor's degree or higher, %, age 25+	11.90%	32.70%	
With a disability, age 5+	2,658	638,654	0.97%
Mean travel time to work, age 16+ (minutes)	16	24	
Housing unit	5,977	1,808,037	0.79%
Homeownership rate	66.20%	67.30%	
Housing units in multi-unit structures, %	11.20%	25.70%	
Median value of owner-occupied housing units	$67,900	$166,600	
Households	5,307	1,658,238	0.79%
Persons per household	2.67	2.53	
Median household money income, 1999	$29,935	$47,203	
Per capita money income, 1999	$14,150	$24,049	
Persons below poverty, %, 1999	19.50%	9.30%	

Geography

	County	Colorado	% of Colo.
Land area, 2000 (square miles)	1,640	104,247	2.16%
Persons per square mile, 2000	8.80	41.50	
Metropolitan Area	None		

(a) Includes persons reporting only one race.
(b) Hispanics may be of any race, so also are included in applicable race categories.
Source: United States Census Bureau

Pueblo County, Colorado, 2000-2001 Census

Original county organized Nov. 1, 1861. Named from the Spanish word for town.
County seat Pueblo.

	County	Colorado	% of Colo.
Population 2001 estimate	144,955	4,417,714	0.78%
% change, April 1, 2000-July 1, 2001	2.50%	2.70%	
Population, 2000	141,472	4,301,261	0.78%
Population, % change, 1990 to 2000	15.00%	30.60%	
Under 5 years old, %	6.70%	6.90%	
Under 18 years old, %	25.80%	25.60%	
65 years and over, %	15.20%	9.70%	
Female, %	51.10%	49.60%	
White, % (a)	79.50%	82.80%	
Black /African American, % (a)	1.90%	3.80%	
American Indian/Alaska Native, % (a)	1.60%	1.00%	
Asian, % (a)	0.70%	2.20%	
Native Hawaiian/Pacific Islander (a)	0.10%	0.10%	
Reporting some other race, % (a)	12.90%	7.20%	
Reporting two or more races, %	3.40%	2.80%	
Hispanic or Latino origin, % (b)	38.00%	17.10%	
White persons, not of Hispanic/Latino origin, %	57.70%	74.50%	
Living in same house 1995 -2000, % age 5+	51.50%	44.10%	
Foreign born persons, %	3.00%	8.60%	
Language other than English at home, % age 5+	16.10%	15.10%	
High school graduates, %, age 25+	81.30%	86.90%	
Bachelor's degree or higher, %, age 25+	18.30%	32.70%	
With a disability, age 5+	30,269	638,654	0.97%
Mean travel time to work, age 16+ (minutes)	21	24	
Housing unit	58,926	1,808,037	0.79%
Homeownership rate	70.40%	67.30%	
Housing units in multi-unit structures, %	16.70%	25.70%	
Median value of owner-occupied housing units	$95,200	$166,600	
Households	54,579	1,658,238	0.79%
Persons per household	2.52	2.53	
Median household money income, 1999	$32,775	$47,203	
Per capita money income, 1999	$17,163	$24,049	
Persons below poverty, %, 1999	14.90%	9.30%	

Geography

Land area, 2000 (square miles)	2,389	104,247	2.16%
Persons per square mile, 2000	59.20	41.50	
Metropolitan Area	Pueblo, CO MSA		

(a) Includes persons reporting only one race.
(b) Hispanics may be of any race, so also are included in applicable race categories.
Source: United States Census Bureau

133

Rio Blanco County, Colorado, 2000-2001 Census

Organized March 25, 1889 from Garfield County. Name is Spanish for "White River."
The White River flows through the county. County seat Meeker.

	County	Colorado	% of Colo.
Population 2001 estimate	5,945	4,417,714	0.78%
% change, April 1, 2000-July 1, 2001	-0.70%	2.70%	
Population, 2000	5,986	4,301,261	0.78%
Population, % change, 1990 to 2000	-1.10%	30.60%	
Under 5 years old, %	5.70%	6.90%	
Under 18 years old, %	26.50%	25.60%	
65 years and over, %	11.20%	9.70%	
Female, %	49.50%	49.60%	
White, % (a)	95.00%	82.80%	
Black /African American, % (a)	0.20%	3.80%	
American Indian/Alaska Native, % (a)	0.80%	1.00%	
Asian, % (a)	0.30%	2.20%	
Native Hawaiian/Pacific Islander (a)	0.00%	0.10%	
Reporting some other race, % (a)	2.00%	7.20%	
Reporting two or more races, %	1.70%	2.80%	
Hispanic or Latino origin, % (b)	4.90%	17.10%	
White persons, not of Hispanic/Latino origin, %	92.60%	74.50%	
Living in same house 1995 -2000, % age 5+	51.30%	44.10%	
Foreign born persons, %	3.20%	8.60%	
Language other than English at home, % age 5+	6.60%	15.10%	
High school graduates, %, age 25+	88.40%	86.90%	
Bachelor's degree or higher, %, age 25+	19.50%	32.70%	
With a disability, age 5+	801	638,654	0.97%
Mean travel time to work, age 16+ (minutes)	17	24	
Housing unit	2,855	1,808,037	0.79%
Homeownership rate	70.60%	67.30%	
Housing units in multi-unit structures, %	12.40%	25.70%	
Median value of owner-occupied housing units	$94,700	$166,600	
Households	2,306	1,658,238	0.79%
Persons per household	2.50	2.53	
Median household money income, 1999	$37,711	$47,203	
Per capita money income, 1999	$17,344	$24,049	
Persons below poverty, %, 1999	9.60%	9.30%	

Geography

Land area, 2000 (square miles)	3,221	104,247	2.16%
Persons per square mile, 2000	1.90	41.50	
Metropolitan Area	None		

(a) Includes persons reporting only one race.
(b) Hispanics may be of any race, so also are included in applicable race categories.
Source: United States Census Bureau

Rio Grande County, Colorado, 2000-2001 Census

Organized Feb. 10, 1874 from Conejos County. Named for the Rio Grande River. The river name has been shortened from Rio Grande Del Norte. County seat Del Norte.

	County	Colorado	% of Colo.
Population 2001 estimate	12,304	4,417,714	0.78%
% change, April 1, 2000-July 1, 2001	-0.90%	2.70%	
Population, 2000	12,413	4,301,261	0.78%
Population, % change, 1990 to 2000	15.30%	30.60%	
Under 5 years old, %	7.00%	6.90%	
Under 18 years old, %	28.10%	25.60%	
65 years and over, %	14.70%	9.70%	
Female, %	50.70%	49.60%	
White, % (a)	73.90%	82.80%	
Black /African American, % (a)	0.30%	3.80%	
American Indian/Alaska Native, % (a)	1.30%	1.00%	
Asian, % (a)	0.20%	2.20%	
Native Hawaiian/Pacific Islander (a)	--	--	
Reporting some other race, % (a)	21.40%	7.20%	
Reporting two or more races, %	2.80%	2.80%	
Hispanic or Latino origin, % (b)	41.70%	17.10%	
White persons, not of Hispanic/Latino origin, %	56.60%	74.50%	
Living in same house 1995 -2000, % age 5+	56.60%	44.10%	
Foreign born persons, %	6.00%	8.60%	
Language other than English at home, % age 5+	27.60%	15.10%	
High school graduates, %, age 25+	78.10%	86.90%	
Bachelor's degree or higher, %, age 25+	18.80%	32.70%	
With a disability, age 5+	2,364	638,654	0.97%
Mean travel time to work, age 16+ (minutes)	19	24	
Housing unit	6,003	1,808,037	0.79%
Homeownership rate	70.70%	67.30%	
Housing units in multi-unit structures, %	10.30%	25.70%	
Median value of owner-occupied housing units	$82,400	$166,600	
Households	4,701	1,658,238	0.79%
Persons per household	2.59	2.53	
Median household money income, 1999	$31,836	$47,203	
Per capita money income, 1999	$15,650	$24,049	
Persons below poverty, %, 1999	14.50%	9.30%	

Geography

Land area, 2000 (square miles)	912	104,247	2.16%
Persons per square mile, 2000	13.60	41.50	
Metropolitan Area	None		

(a) Includes persons reporting only one race.
(b) Hispanics may be of any race, so also are included in applicable race categories.
Source: United States Census Bureau

Routt County, Colorado, 2000-2001 Census

Organized Jan. 29, 1877 from Grand County. Named for John Long Routt, the last territorial governor and first state governor of Colorado. County seat Steamboat Springs.

	County	Colorado	% of Colo.
Population 2001 estimate	20,255	4,417,714	0.78%
% change, April 1, 2000-July 1, 2001	2.90%	2.70%	
Population, 2000	19,690	4,301,261	0.78%
Population, % change, 1990 to 2000	39.80%	30.60%	
Under 5 years old, %	5.50%	6.90%	
Under 18 years old, %	22.60%	25.60%	
65 years and over, %	5.00%	9.70%	
Female, %	46.20%	49.60%	
White, % (a)	96.90%	82.80%	
Black /African American, % (a)	0.10%	3.80%	
American Indian/Alaska Native, % (a)	0.50%	1.00%	
Asian, % (a)	0.40%	2.20%	
Native Hawaiian/Pacific Islander (a)	0.10%	0.10%	
Reporting some other race, % (a)	0.70%	7.20%	
Reporting two or more races, %	1.30%	2.80%	
Hispanic or Latino origin, % (b)	3.20%	17.10%	
White persons, not of Hispanic/Latino origin, %	94.80%	74.50%	
Living in same house 1995 -2000, % age 5+	41.10%	44.10%	
Foreign born persons, %	4.10%	8.60%	
Language other than English at home, % age 5+	6.10%	15.10%	
High school graduates, %, age 25+	95.30%	86.90%	
Bachelor's degree or higher, %, age 25+	42.50%	32.70%	
With a disability, age 5+	1,788	638,654	0.97%
Mean travel time to work, age 16+ (minutes)	19	24	
Housing unit	11,217	1,808,037	0.79%
Homeownership rate	69.20%	67.30%	
Housing units in multi-unit structures, %	32.80%	25.70%	
Median value of owner-occupied housing units	$268,500	$166,600	
Households	7,953	1,658,238	0.79%
Persons per household	2.44	2.53	
Median household money income, 1999	$53,612	$47,203	
Per capita money income, 1999	$28,792	$24,049	
Persons below poverty, %, 1999	6.10%	9.30%	

Geography

	County	Colorado	% of Colo.
Land area, 2000 (square miles)	2,362	104,247	2.16%
Persons per square mile, 2000	8.30	41.50	
Metropolitan Area	None		

(a) Includes persons reporting only one race.
(b) Hispanics may be of any race, so also are included in applicable race categories.
Source: United States Census Bureau

Saguache County, Colorado, 2000-2001 Census

Organized prior to statehood Dec. 29, 1866 from Costilla County. Named for Saguache Creek, an Indian word for blue earth. County seat Saguache.

	County	Colorado	% of Colo.
Population 2001 estimate	6,224	4,417,714	0.78%
% change, April 1, 2000-July 1, 2001	5.20%	2.70%	
Population, 2000	5,917	4,301,261	0.78%
Population, % change, 1990 to 2000	28.10%	30.60%	
Under 5 years old, %	6.80%	6.90%	
Under 18 years old, %	28.40%	25.60%	
65 years and over, %	10.80%	9.70%	
Female, %	49.60%	49.60%	
White, % (a)	71.30%	82.80%	
Black /African American, % (a)	0.10%	3.80%	
American Indian/Alaska Native, % (a)	2.10%	1.00%	
Asian, % (a)	0.50%	2.20%	
Native Hawaiian/Pacific Islander (a)	0.00%	0.10%	
Reporting some other race, % (a)	23.00%	7.20%	
Reporting two or more races, %	3.10%	2.80%	
Hispanic or Latino origin, % (b)	45.30%	17.10%	
White persons, not of Hispanic/Latino origin, %	51.60%	74.50%	
Living in same house 1995 2000, % age 5+	50.80%	44.10%	
Foreign born persons, %	14.50%	8.60%	
Language other than English at home, % age 5+	36.50%	15.10%	
High school graduates, %, age 25+	70.00%	86.90%	
Bachelor's degree or higher, %, age 25+	19.60%	32.70%	
With a disability, age 5+	1,158	638,654	0.97%
Mean travel time to work, age 16+ (minutes)	20	24	
Housing unit	3,087	1,808,037	0.79%
Homeownership rate	69.30%	67.30%	
Housing units in multi-unit structures, %	6.80%	25.70%	
Median value of owner-occupied housing units	$73,900	$166,600	
Households	2,300	1,658,238	0.79%
Persons per household	2.56	2.53	
Median household money income, 1999	$25,495	$47,203	
Per capita money income, 1999	$13,121	$24,049	
Persons below poverty, %, 1999	22.60%	9.30%	

Geography

	County	Colorado	% of Colo.
Land area, 2000 (square miles)	3,168	104,247	2.16%
Persons per square mile, 2000	1.90	41.50	
Metropolitan Area	None		

(a) Includes persons reporting only one race.
(b) Hispanics may be of any race, so also are included in applicable race categories.
Source: United States Census Bureau

San Juan County, Colorado, 2000-2001 Census

Organized 1876 from La Plata County. Named for St. John the Baptist. A prominent river and mountian range carry the same name. County seat Silverton.

	County	Colorado	% of Colo.
Population 2001 estimate	.586	.4,417,714	.0.78%
% change, April 1, 2000-July 1, 2001	.5.00%	.2.70%	
Population, 2000	.558	.4,301,261	.0.78%
Population, % change, 1990 to 2000	-25.10%	.30.60%	
Under 5 years old, %	.4.70%	.6.90%	
Under 18 years old, %	.20.10%	.25.60%	
65 years and over, %	.7.00%	.9.70%	
Female, %	.47.50%	.49.60%	
White, % (a)	.97.10%	.82.80%	
Black /African American, % (a)	.0.00%	.3.80%	
American Indian/Alaska Native, % (a)	.0.70%	.1.00%	
Asian, % (a)	.0.20%	.2.20%	
Native Hawaiian/Pacific Islander (a)	.0.40%	.0.10%	
Reporting some other race, % (a)	.0.70%	.7.20%	
Reporting two or more races, %	.0.90%	.2.80%	
Hispanic or Latino origin, % (b)	.7.30%	.17.10%	
White persons, not of Hispanic/Latino origin, %	.91.20%	.74.50%	
Living in same house 1995 -2000, % age 5+	.50.00%	.44.10%	
Foreign born persons, %	.2.50%	.8.60%	
Language other than English at home, % age 5+	.9.00%	.15.10%	
High school graduates, %, age 25+	.92.10%	.86.90%	
Bachelor's degree or higher, %, age 25+	.43.70%	.32.70%	
With a disability, age 5+	.64	.638,654	.0.97%
Mean travel time to work, age 16+ (minutes)	.16	.24	
Housing unit	.632	.1,808,037	.0.79%
Homeownership rate	.67.70%	.67.30%	
Housing units in multi-unit structures, %	.8.40%	.25.70%	
Median value of owner-occupied housing units	.$131,500	.$166,600	
Households	.269	.1,658,238	.0.79%
Persons per household	.2.06	.2.53	
Median household money income, 1999	.$30,764	.$47,203	
Per capita money income, 1999	.$17,584	.$24,049	
Persons below poverty, %, 1999	.20.90%	.9.30%	

Geography

Land area, 2000 (square miles)	.387	.104,247	.2.16%
Persons per square mile, 2000	.1.40	.41.50	
Metropolitan Area	.None		

(a) Includes persons reporting only one race.
(b) Hispanics may be of any race, so also are included in applicable race categories.
Source: United States Census Bureau

San Miguel County, Colorado, 2000-2001 Census

Organized prior to statehood Nov. 1, 1861 from Ouray County. Named for St. Michael the Archangel and for the river that flows through the county. County seat Telluride.

	County	Colorado	% of Colo.
Population 2001 estimate	6,951	4,417,714	0.78%
% change, April 1, 2000-July 1, 2001	5.40%	2.70%	
Population, 2000	6,594	4,301,261	0.78%
Population, % change, 1990 to 2000	80.50%	30.60%	
Under 5 years old, %	4.50%	6.90%	
Under 18 years old, %	17.60%	25.60%	
65 years and over, %	3.40%	9.70%	
Female, %	45.30%	49.60%	
White, % (a)	93.60%	82.80%	
Black /African American, % (a)	0.30%	3.80%	
American Indian/Alaska Native, % (a)	0.80%	1.00%	
Asian, % (a)	0.70%	2.20%	
Native Hawaiian/Pacific Islander (a)	0.10%	0.10%	
Reporting some other race, % (a)	3.40%	7.20%	
Reporting two or more races, %	1.10%	2.80%	
Hispanic or Latino origin, % (b)	6.70%	17.10%	
White persons, not of Hispanic/Latino origin, %	90.40%	74.50%	
Living in same house 1995 -2000, % age 5+	35.30%	44.10%	
Foreign born persons, %	7.30%	8.60%	
Language other than English at home, % age 5+	10.80%	15.10%	
High school graduates, %, age 25+	93.60%	86.90%	
Bachelor's degree or higher, %, age 25+	48.50%	32.70%	
With a disability, age 5+	501	638,654	0.97%
Mean travel time to work, age 16+ (minutes)	19	24	
Housing unit	5,197	1,808,037	0.79%
Homeownership rate	51.60%	67.30%	
Housing units in multi-unit structures, %	41.70%	25.70%	
Median value of owner-occupied housing units	$358,200	$166,600	
Households	3,015	1,658,238	0.79%
Persons per household	2.18	2.53	
Median household money income, 1999	$48,514	$47,203	
Per capita money income, 1999	$35,329	$24,049	
Persons below poverty, %, 1999	10.40%	9.30%	

Geography

	County	Colorado	% of Colo.
Land area, 2000 (square miles)	1,286	104,247	2.16%
Persons per square mile, 2000	5.10	41.50	
Metropolitan Area	None		

(a) Includes persons reporting only one race.
(b) Hispanics may be of any race, so also are included in applicable race categories.
Source: United States Census Bureau

Sedgewick County, Colorado, 2000-2001 Census

Organized April 9, 1889 from Logan County. Named for Fort Sedgwick and Maj. Gen. John Sedgewick, Indian fighter and Civil War officer. County seat Julesburg.

	County	Colorado	% of Colo.
Population 2001 estimate	2,668	4,417,714	0.78%
% change, April 1, 2000-July 1, 2001	-2.90%	2.70%	
Population, 2000	2,747	4,301,261	0.78%
Population, % change, 1990 to 2000	2.10%	30.60	
Under 5 years old, %	5.60%	6.90%	
Under 18 years old, %	22.80%	25.60%	
65 years and over, %	22.10%	9.70%	
Female, %	50.00%	49.60%	
White, % (a)	90.50%	82.80%	
Black /African American, % (a)	0.50%	3.80%	
American Indian/Alaska Native, % (a)	0.10%	1.00%	
Asian, % (a)	0.80%	2.20%	
Native Hawaiian/Pacific Islander (a)	0.10%	0.10%	
Reporting some other race, % (a)	6.00%	7.20%	
Reporting two or more races, %	2.00%	2.80%	
Hispanic or Latino origin, % (b)	11.40%	17.10%	
White persons, not of Hispanic/Latino origin, %	86.50%	74.50%	
Living in same house 1995 -2000, % age 5+	64.10%	44.10%	
Foreign born persons, %	2.70%	8.60%	
Language other than English at home, % age 5+	9.30%	15.10%	
High school graduates, %, age 25+	79.30%	86.90%	
Bachelor's degree or higher, %, age 25+	13.40%	32.70%	
With a disability, age 5+	518	638,654	0.97%
Mean travel time to work, age 16+ (minutes)	16	24	
Housing unit	1,387	1,808,037	0.79%
Homeownership rate	73.00%	67.30%	
Housing units in multi-unit structures, %	7.80%	25.70%	
Median value of owner-occupied housing units	$57,100	$166,600	
Households	1,165	1,658,238	0.79%
Persons per household	2.31	2.53	
Median household money income, 1999	$28,278	$47,203	
Per capita money income, 1999	$16,125	$24,049	
Persons below poverty, %, 1999	10.00%	9.30%	

Geography

Land area, 2000 (square miles)	548	104,247	2.16%
Persons per square mile, 2000	5.00	41.50	
Metropolitan Area	None		

(a) Includes persons reporting only one race.

(b) Hispanics may be of any race, so also are included in applicable race categories.

Source: United States Census Bureau

Summit County, Colorado, 2000-2001 Census

Original county organized prior to statehood Nov. 1, 1861. Named for mountainous terrain and headwaters status of the area. County seat Breckenridge.

	County	Colorado	% of Colo.
Population 2001 estimate	24,225	4,417,714	0.78%
% change, April 1, 2000-July 1, 2001	2.90%	2.70%	
Population, 2000	23,548	4,301,261	0.78%
Population, % change, 1990 to 2000	82.80%	30.60%	
Under 5 years old, %	5.30%	6.90%	
Under 18 years old, %	17.40%	25.60%	
65 years and over, %	3.30%	9.70%	
Female, %	41.80%	49.60%	
White, % (a)	91.80%	82.80%	
Black /African American, % (a)	0.70%	3.80%	
American Indian/Alaska Native, % (a)	0.50%	1.00%	
Asian, % (a)	0.90%	2.20%	
Native Hawaiian/Pacific Islander (a)	0.10%	0.10%	
Reporting some other race, % (a)	4.00%	7.20%	
Reporting two or more races, %	2.10%	2.80%	
Hispanic or Latino origin, % (b)	9.80%	17.10%	
White persons, not of Hispanic/Latino origin, %	86.70%	74.50%	
Living in same house 1995 -2000, % age 5+	29.10%	44.10%	
Foreign born persons, %	11.60%	8.60%	
Language other than English at home, % age 5+	13.60%	15.10%	
High school graduates, %, age 25+	93.30%	86.90%	
Bachelor's degree or higher, %, age 25+	48.30%	32.70%	
With a disability, age 5+	2,358	638,654	0.97%
Mean travel time to work, age 16+ (minutes)	17	24	
Housing unit	24,201	1,808,037	0.79%
Homeownership rate	58.90%	67.30%	
Housing units in multi-unit structures, %	58.80%	25.70%	
Median value of owner-occupied housing units	$317,500	$166,600	
Households	9,120	1,658,238	0.79%
Persons per household	2.48	2.53	
Median household money income, 1999	$56,587	$47,203	
Per capita money income, 1999	$28,676	$24,049	
Persons below poverty, %, 1999	9.00%	9.30%	

Geography

Land area, 2000 (square miles)	608	104,247	2.16%
Persons per square mile, 2000	38.70	41.50	
Metropolitan Area	None		

(a) Includes persons reporting only one race.
(b) Hispanics may be of any race, so also are included in applicable race categories.
Source: United States Census Bureau

141

Teller County, Colorado, 2000-2001 Census

Organized March 23, 1899 from El Paso and Fremont Counties. Named for Henry M. Teller, Colorado senator and U.S. secretary of the interior. County seat Cripple Creek.

	County	Colorado	% of Colo.
Population 2001 estimate	21,425	4,417,714	0.78%
% change, April 1, 2000-July 1, 2001	4.20%	2.70%	
Population, 2000	20,555	4,301,261	0.78%
Population, % change, 1990 to 2000	64.90%	30.60%	
Under 5 years old, %	5.70%	6.90%	
Under 18 years old, %	25.90%	25.60%	
65 years and over, %	7.50%	9.70%	
Female, %	49.30%	49.60%	
White, % (a)	94.90%	82.80%	
Black /African American, % (a)	0.50%	3.80%	
American Indian/Alaska Native, % (a)	1.00%	1.00%	
Asian, % (a)	0.60%	2.20%	
Native Hawaiian/Pacific Islander (a)	0.10%	0.10%	
Reporting some other race, % (a)	0.90%	7.20%	
Reporting two or more races, %	2.00%	2.80%	
Hispanic or Latino origin, % (b)	3.50%	17.10%	
White persons, not of Hispanic/Latino origin, %	92.90%	74.50%	
Living in same house 1995 -2000, % age 5+	41.40%	44.10%	
Foreign born persons, %	1.80%	8.60%	
Language other than English at home, % age 5+	4.00%	15.10%	
High school graduates, %, age 25+	94.00%	86.90%	
Bachelor's degree or higher, %, age 25+	31.70%	32.70%	
With a disability, age 5+	2,960	638,654	0.97%
Mean travel time to work, age 16+ (minutes)	30	24	
Housing unit	10,362	1,808,037	0.79%
Homeownership rate	80.90%	67.30%	
Housing units in multi-unit structures, %	6.40%	25.70%	
Median value of owner-occupied housing units	$162,000	$166,600	
Households	7,993	1,658,238	0.79%
Persons per household	2.56	2.53	
Median household money income, 1999	$50,165	$47,203	
Per capita money income, 1999	$23,412	$24,049	
Persons below poverty, %, 1999	5.40%	9.30%	

Geography

Land area, 2000 (square miles)	557	104,247	2.16%
Persons per square mile, 2000	36.9	41.5	
Metropolitan Area	None		

(a) Includes persons reporting only one race.

(b) Hispanics may be of any race, so also are included in applicable race categories.

Source: United States Census Bureau

Washington County, Colorado, 2000-2001 Census

Organized Feb. 9, 1887 from Weld County. Named for George Washington, first U.S. president. County seat Akron.

	County	Colorado	% of Colo.
Population 2001 estimate	4,861	4,417,714	0.78%
% change, April 1, 2000-July 1, 2001	-1.30%	2.70%	
Population, 2000	4,926	4,301,261	0.78%
Population, % change, 1990 to 2000	2.40%	30.60%	
Under 5 years old, %	6.20%	6.90%	
Under 18 years old, %	26.50%	25.60%	
65 years and over, %	18.20%	9.70%	
Female, %	49.20%	49.60%	
White, % (a)	96.40%	82.80%	
Black /African American, % (a)	--	--	
American Indian/Alaska Native, % (a)	0.60%	1.00%	
Asian, % (a)	0.10%	2.20%	
Native Hawaiian/Pacific Islander (a)	--	--	
Reporting some other race, % (a)	2.00%	7.20%	
Reporting two or more races, %	0.90%	2.80%	
Hispanic or Latino origin, % (b)	6.30%	17.10%	
White persons, not of Hispanic/Latino origin, %	92.70%	74.50%	
Living in same house 1995 -2000, % age 5+	64.20%	44.10%	
Foreign born persons, %	2.50%	8.60%	
Language other than English at home, % age 5+	5.20%	15.10%	
High school graduates, %, age 25+	81.70%	86.90%	
Bachelor's degree or higher, %, age 25+	14.30%	32.70%	
With a disability, age 5+	857	638,654	0.97%
Mean travel time to work, age 16+ (minutes)	21.00	24.30	
Housing unit	2,307	1,808,037	0.79%
Homeownership rate	73.60%	67.30%	
Housing units in multi-unit structures, %	6.00%	25.70%	
Median value of owner-occupied housing units	$70,800	$166,600	
Households	1,989	1,658,238	0.79%
Persons per household	2.46	2.53	
Median household money income, 1999	$32,431	$47,203	
Per capita money income, 1999	$17,788	$24,049	
Persons below poverty, %, 1999	11.40%	9.30%	

Geography

Land area, 2000 (square miles)	2,521	104,247	2.16%
Persons per square mile, 2000	2	41.5	
Metropolitan Area	None		

(a) Includes persons reporting only one race.
(b) Hispanics may be of any race, so also are included in applicable race categories.
Source: United States Census Bureau

143

Weld County, Colorado, 2000-2001 Census

Original county organized prior to statehood Nov. 1, 1861. Named for Lewis L. Weld, first secretary of the Colorado Territory. County seat Greeley.

	County	Colorado	% of Colo.
Population 2001 estimate	194,949	4,417,714	0.78%
% change, April 1, 2000-July 1, 2001	7.70%	2.70%	
Population, 2000	180,936	4,301,261	0.78%
Population, % change, 1990 to 2000	37.30%	30.60%	
Under 5 years old, %	7.80%	6.90%	
Under 18 years old, %	28.20%	25.60%	
65 years and over, %	9.00%	9.70%	
Female, %	49.90%	49.60%	
White, % (a)	81.70%	82.80%	
Black /African American, % (a)	0.60%	3.80%	
American Indian/Alaska Native, % (a)	0.90%	1.00%	
Asian, % (a)	0.80%	2.20%	
Native Hawaiian/Pacific Islander (a)	0.10%	0.10%	
Reporting some other race, % (a)	13.30%	7.20%	
Reporting two or more races, %	2.70%	2.80%	
Hispanic or Latino origin, % (b)	27.00%	17.10%	
White persons, not of Hispanic/Latino origin, %	70.00%	74.50%	
Living in same house 1995 -2000, % age 5+	42.50%	44.10%	
Foreign born persons, %	9.30%	8.60%	
Language other than English at home, % age 5+	20.30%	15.10%	
High school graduates, %, age 25+	79.60%	86.90%	
Bachelor's degree or higher, %, age 25+	21.60%	32.70%	
With a disability, age 5+	29,497	638,654	0.97%
Mean travel time to work, age 16+ (minutes)	23.7	24.3	
Housing unit	66,194	1,808,037	0.79%
Homeownership rate	68.60%	67.30%	
Housing units in multi-unit structures, %	18.40%	25.70%	
Median value of owner-occupied housing units	$140,400	$166,600	
Households	63,247	1,658,238	0.79%
Persons per household	2.78	2.53	
Median household money income, 1999	$42,321	$47,203	
Per capita money income, 1999	$18,957	$24,049	
Persons below poverty, %, 1999	12.50%	9.30%	

Geography

Land area, 2000 (square miles)	3,992	104,247	2.16%
Persons per square mile, 2000	45.3	41.5	
Metropolitan Area	Greeley, CO PMSA		

(a) Includes persons reporting only one race.
(b) Hispanics may be of any race, so also are included in applicable race categories.
Source: United States Census Bureau

144

Yuma County, Colorado, 2000-2001 Census

Organized March 15, 1889 from Washington County. Named for the Yuma Indian Tribe. County seat Wray.

	County	Colorado	% of Colo.
Population 2001 estimate	9,859	4,417,714	0.78%
% change, April 1, 2000-July 1, 2001	0.20%	2.70%	
Population, 2000	9,841	4,301,261	0.78%
Population, % change, 1990 to 2000	9.90%	30.60%	
Under 5 years old, %	6.60%	6.90%	
Under 18 years old, %	28.30%	25.60%	
65 years and over, %	16.30%	9.70%	
Female, %	50.80%	49.60%	
White, % (a)	94.20%	82.80%	
Black /African American, % (a)	0.10%	3.80%	
American Indian/Alaska Native, % (a)	0.30%	1.00%	
Asian, % (a)	0.10%	2.20%	
Native Hawaiian/Pacific Islander (a)	--	--	
Reporting some other race, % (a)	4.10%	7.20%	
Reporting two or more races, %	1.20%	2.80%	
Hispanic or Latino origin, % (b)	12.90%	17.10%	
White persons, not of Hispanic/Latino origin, %	86.10%	74.50%	
Living in same house 1995 -2000, % age 5+	57.30%	44.10%	
Foreign born persons, %	7.90%	8.60%	
Language other than English at home, % age 5+	11.50%	15.10%	
High school graduates, %, age 25+	79.50%	86.90%	
Bachelor's degree or higher, %, age 25+	15.50%	32.70%	
With a disability, age 5+	1,680	638,654	0.97%
Mean travel time to work, age 16+ (minutes)	15.4	24.3	
Housing unit	4,295	1,808,037	0.79%
Homeownership rate	70.80%	67.30%	
Housing units in multi-unit structures, %	7.90%	25.70%	
Median value of owner-occupied housing units	$77,100	$166,600	
Households	3,800	1,658,238	0.79%
Persons per household	2.55	2.53	
Median household money income, 1999	$33,169	$47,203	
Per capita money income, 1999	$16,005	$24,049	
Persons below poverty, %, 1999	12.90%	9.30%	

Geography

	County	Colorado	% of Colo.
Land area, 2000 (square miles)	2,366	104,247	2.16%
Persons per square mile, 2000	4.2	41.5	
Metropolitan Area	None		

(a) Includes persons reporting only one race.
(b) Hispanics may be of any race, so also are included in applicable race categories.
Source: United States Census Bureau

145

Vital Statistics – Births, Deaths, Net Migration

Source: Colorado Department of Local Affairs. Data estimated for years 2003, 2010, 2020.

COLORADO

Year	Population	Births	Deaths	Migration	Change
1970	2,224,610	40,348	17,274	35,636	58,710
1980	2,908,036	48,463	18,685	28,024	57,802
1990	3,303,377	53,107	21,303	-12,964	18,840
2000	4,327,191	63,917	26,998	74,288	111,207
2001	4,430,915	66,435	27,844	65,133	103,724
2002	4,512,300	66,484	28,444	43,364	81,385
2003	4,575,989	65,564	30,598	28,724	63,692
2010	5,131,092	68,897	33,805	50,784	85,881
2020	6,009,700	80,655	40,862	49,611	89,400

Archuleta County

Year	Population	Births	Deaths	Migration	Change
1970	2,698	57	19	-380	-342
1980	3,734	70	25	-168	-123
1990	5,378	85	33	130	182
2000	10,028	104	56	410	458
2001	10,548	113	59	466	520
2002	11,025	115	51	413	477
2003	11,341	104	80	292	316
2010	14,249	135	103	425	457
2020	18,933	183	146	423	461

Adams County

Year	Population	Births	Deaths	Migration	Change
1970	187,058	3,608	835	3,285	6,058
1980	247,377	4,681	1,251	-2,116	1,314
1990	266,205	4,792	1,495	-3,863	-566
2000	366,176	6,107	2,031	6,792	10,868
2001	375,450	6,182	2,102	5,194	9,274
2002	384,266	6,236	2,123	4,703	8,816
2003	391,880	6,173	2,101	3,542	7,614
2010	466,654	6,786	2,538	8,020	12,267
2020	581,635	8,562	3,363	5,543	10,742

Baca County

Year	Population	Births	Deaths	Migration	Change
1970	5,653	91	68	-190	-167
1980	5,407	82	55	-85	-58
1990	4,516	56	55	-114	-113
2000	4,516	54	74	13	-7
2001	4,514	28	64	34	-2
2002	4,507	34	58	18	-7
2003	4,501	34	65	24	-6
2010	4,562	51	58	25	19
2020	4,719	52	50	15	17

Alamosa County

Year	Population	Births	Deaths	Migration	Change
1970	11,484	218	76	342	484
1980	11,877	217	69	106	254
1990	13,597	250	97	-216	-63
2000	15,029	231	106	82	207
2001	15,282	250	112	115	253
2002	15,534	238	99	113	252
2003	15,759	230	106	102	226
2010	17,562	271	110	116	277
2020	20,478	303	127	117	294

Bent County

Year	Population	Births	Deaths	Migration	Change
1970	6,488	87	63	-286	-262
1980	5,944	93	48	-109	-64
1990	5,023	62	58	-191	-187
2000	5,971	67	65	-27	-25
2001	5,865	68	64	-110	-106
2002	5,913	69	99	78	48
2003	5,914	69	60	-7	1
2010	6,149	67	58	23	32
2020	6,509	70	55	21	37

Arapahoe County

Year	Population	Births	Deaths	Migration	Change
1970	163,683	2,645	858	3,896	5,683
1980	297,761	4,692	1,278	15,908	19,322
1990	393,708	6,182	1,771	-205	4,206
2000	490,743	6,887	2,639	5,189	9,437
2001	501,846	7,355	2,848	6,596	11,103
2002	508,235	7,357	2,992	2,024	6,389
2003	513,310	7,050	3,220	1,244	5,075
2010	550,852	6,906	3,587	1,601	4,921
2020	596,265	7,333	4,356	1,344	4,321

Boulder County

Year	Population	Births	Deaths	Migration	Change
1970	133,432	2,309	780	4,903	6,432
1980	190,695	2,644	897	1,749	3,496
1990	226,042	3,275	1,080	1,493	3,688
2000	292,598	3,747	1,396	6,323	8,674
2001	297,838	3,840	1,442	2,842	5,240
2002	302,626	3,950	1,372	2,210	4,788
2003	306,365	3,828	1,814	1,725	3,740
2010	341,001	3,852	2,038	3,587	5,401
2020	392,720	4,453	2,585	2,811	4,679

146

Vital Statistics – Births, Deaths, Net Migration

Source: Colorado Department of Local Affairs. Data estimated for years 2003, 2010, 2020.

Chaffee County

Year	Population	Births	Deaths	Migration	Change
1970	10,773	159	101	265	323
1980	13,295	253	119	142	276
1990	12,688	133	114	110	129
2000	16,298	137	134	359	362
2001	16,522	158	146	212	224
2002	16,806	162	144	266	284
2003	16,958	138	174	187	152
2010	18,536	140	191	305	254
2020	21,275	176	217	305	265

Costilla County

Year	Population	Births	Deaths	Migration	Change
1970	3,080	49	26	-63	-40
1980	3,069	55	32	-107	-84
1990	3,182	47	25	-117	-95
2000	3,675	40	37	-7	-4
2001	3,723	47	36	37	48
2002	3,759	43	36	30	36
2003	3,772	41	38	10	12
2010	3,949	44	40	18	22
2020	4,178	46	41	18	23

Cheyenne County

Year	Population	Births	Deaths	Migration	Change
1970	2,396	38	22	-80	-64
1980	2,164	40	25	26	-11
1990	2,396	36	29	75	82
2000	2,230	23	15	-57	-49
2001	2,228	18	15	-5	-2
2002	2,230	19	18	1	2
2003	2,226	21	26	0	-5
2010	2,267	27	22	5	10
2020	2,383	28	21	5	12

Crowley County

Year	Population	Births	Deaths	Migration	Change
1970	3,085	38	46	-27	-35
1980	2,983	41	35	159	165
1990	3,927	41	38	23	26
2000	5,504	45	34	495	506
2001	5,446	43	40	-61	-58
2002	5,444	41	61	18	-2
2003	5,435	39	43	-5	-8
2010	5,431	51	42	-1	8
2020	5,392	54	43	-19	-9

Clear Creek County

Year	Population	Births	Deaths	Migration	Change
1970	4,993	82	37	598	643
1980	7,349	155	36	240	359
1990	7,628	110	35	-114	-39
2000	9,355	93	37	116	172
2001	9,485	108	37	59	130
2002	9,664	98	24	105	179
2003	9,780	97	54	73	116
2010	11,174	115	65	228	279
2020	14,792	180	87	296	389

Custer County

Year	Population	Births	Deaths	Migration	Change
1970	1,131	14	13	20	21
1980	1,535	32	8	-47	-23
1990	1,947	19	11	-8	0
2000	3,540	34	21	163	176
2001	3,686	28	15	133	146
2002	3,852	27	22	161	166
2003	3,945	23	32	104	94
2010	4,904	37	42	175	171
2020	6,574	60	58	160	162

Conejos County

Year	Population	Births	Deaths	Migration	Change
1970	7,829	153	57	-357	-261
1980	7,776	183	59	-138	-14
1990	7,465	133	59	-232	-158
2000	8,400	140	84	36	92
2001	8,401	132	73	-58	1
2002	8,420	124	53	-52	19
2003	8,444	117	78	-15	24
2010	8,697	138	77	-12	49
2020	9,306	142	75	-5	61

Delta County

Year	Population	Births	Deaths	Migration	Change
1970	15,316	213	213	-184	-184
1980	21,477	336	227	724	833
1990	21,036	234	268	-135	-169
2000	28,009	302	331	638	609
2001	28,709	322	313	691	700
2002	29,410	305	351	747	701
2003	29,820	296	358	473	411
2010	34,013	365	364	685	686
2020	40,334	455	387	546	614

Vital Statistics – Births, Deaths, Net Migration

Source: Colorado Department of Local Affairs. Data estimated for years 2003, 2010, 2020.

Denver County

Year	Population	Births	Deaths	Migration	Change
1970	515,985	9,802	5,275	-2,542	1,985
1980	493,385	8,201	4,525	-6,554	-2,878
1990	466,998	8,443	4,402	-9,828	-5,787
2000	555,631	10,457	4,553	4,210	10,114
2001	559,610	11,357	4,466	-2,912	3,979
2002	564,327	11,286	4,460	-2,108	4,717
2003	569,453	11,972	4,462	-2,385	5,125
2010	603,186	10,664	4,450	-1,762	4,452
2020	647,484	11,082	4,584	-1,312	5,185

Elbert County

Year	Population	Births	Deaths	Migration	Change
1970	3,912	39	41	54	52
1980	6,904	97	43	649	703
1990	9,754	139	54	-56	29
2000	20,186	200	89	988	1,099
2001	21,441	248	82	1,089	1,255
2002	22,515	241	66	900	1,074
2003	23,255	218	108	629	739
2010	30,844	297	147	1,139	1,289
2020	45,522	454	238	1,349	1,566

Dolores County

Year	Population	Births	Deaths	Migration	Change
1970	1,628	31	15	-118	-102
1980	1,662	35	10	123	148
1990	1,507	18	14	-38	-34
2000	1,844	21	18	30	33
2001	1,844	23	20	-3	0
2002	1,870	25	38	40	26
2003	1,882	21	20	10	12
2010	2,038	23	19	23	27
2020	2,350	28	17	22	32

El Paso County

Year	Population	Births	Deaths	Migration	Change
1970	238,384	5,270	1,363	9,477	13,384
1980	311,995	5,769	1,705	-1,438	2,626
1990	397,289	7,478	2,153	-4,350	975
2000	520,248	8,279	2,915	6,069	11,433
2001	533,526	8,328	2,984	7,934	13,278
2002	542,382	8,456	3,106	3,506	8,856
2003	549,456	8,276	3,243	2,041	7,074
2010	608,247	9,224	3,707	3,498	9,015
2020	700,815	10,695	4,612	3,093	9,177

Douglas County

Year	Population	Births	Deaths	Migration	Change
1970	8,594	129	66	711	774
1980	25,627	355	93	2,264	2,526
1990	61,614	1,169	153	3,434	4,450
2000	180,690	3,302	439	15,504	18,367
2001	200,385	3,648	485	16,532	19,695
2002	210,013	3,603	510	6,535	9,628
2003	216,775	3,357	796	4,202	6,763
2010	278,279	3,973	1,140	6,393	9,226
2020	362,655	5,955	1,805	3,176	7,325

Fremont County

Year	Population	Births	Deaths	Migration	Change
1970	22,110	298	331	643	610
1980	28,847	402	347	202	257
1990	32,230	339	414	191	116
2000	46,358	471	461	1,204	1,214
2001	47,209	446	479	884	851
2002	47,607	438	493	453	398
2003	47,866	392	461	328	260
2010	50,505	450	467	458	441
2020	55,327	528	507	461	482

Eagle County

Year	Population	Births	Deaths	Migration	Change
1970	7,689	169	42	1,042	1,169
1980	13,411	280	48	-104	128
1990	22,182	418	42	925	1,301
2000	42,027	777	79	1,420	2,118
2001	43,497	782	64	752	1,470
2002	45,067	786	69	853	1,570
2003	46,260	822	155	527	1,193
2010	55,493	791	221	755	1,326
2020	69,091	911	358	801	1,354

Garfield County

Year	Population	Births	Deaths	Migration	Change
1970	14,965	253	150	462	565
1980	23,000	429	148	1,098	1,379
1990	30,338	469	199	1,259	1,529
2000	44,219	740	247	1,035	1,528
2001	45,931	801	273	1,184	1,712
2002	47,253	801	305	826	1,322
2003	48,254	765	297	534	1,002
2010	57,479	811	346	1,003	1,469
2020	72,872	1,014	457	1,044	1,601

Vital Statistics – Births, Deaths, Net Migration

Source: Colorado Department of Local Affairs. Data estimated for years 2003, 2010, 2020.

Gilpin County

Year	Population	Births	Deaths	Migration	Change
1970	1,301	21	14	144	151
1980	2,477	36	13	223	246
1990	3,073	38	11	-68	-41
2000	4,775	63	16	190	237
2001	4,845	58	16	28	70
2002	4,927	55	28	55	82
2003	4,991	48	23	38	63
2010	5,542	55	29	69	95
2020	6,580	70	38	83	115

Huerfano County

Year	Population	Births	Deaths	Migration	Change
1970	6,527	95	88	-80	-73
1980	6,417	95	84	-150	-139
1990	5,975	60	79	-136	-155
2000	7,861	72	95	57	34
2001	7,857	74	89	11	-4
2002	8,101	83	87	248	244
2003	8,229	72	90	147	129
2010	9,449	72	95	178	155
2020	10,617	81	104	99	76

Grand County

Year	Population	Births	Deaths	Migration	Change
1970	4,236	72	27	301	346
1980	7,530	149	33	206	322
1990	8,010	115	36	-247	-168
2000	12,535	150	57	447	540
2001	12,909	151	62	285	374
2002	13,303	160	48	282	394
2003	13,586	166	75	192	283
2010	16,355	175	98	390	466
2020	22,012	235	149	543	629

Jackson County

Year	Population	Births	Deaths	Migration	Change
1970	1,850	36	12	36	60
1980	1,895	33	9	100	124
1990	1,592	22	12	-69	-59
2000	1,586	12	7	-1	4
2001	1,620	17	18	35	34
2002	1,644	15	18	27	24
2003	1,657	17	14	10	13
2010	1,828	22	14	22	29
2020	2,163	29	16	20	34

Gunnison County

Year	Population	Births	Deaths	Migration	Change
1970	7,714	123	40	311	394
1980	10,686	135	35	619	719
1990	10,316	127	42	-278	-193
2000	13,967	154	53	130	231
2001	14,012	187	65	-77	45
2002	14,361	189	63	224	349
2003	14,581	180	75	115	220
2010	16,655	165	82	227	310
2020	19,718	189	100	196	285

Jefferson County

Year	Population	Births	Deaths	Migration	Change
1970	237,712	3,963	1,286	10,035	12,712
1980	374,709	5,551	1,836	1,301	5,016
1990	439,524	6,619	2,319	-681	3,619
2000	527,876	6,799	3,153	3,420	7,066
2001	531,155	6,606	3,133	-194	3,279
2002	535,364	6,626	3,280	863	4,209
2003	539,232	6,433	3,714	1,149	3,868
2010	568,476	6,787	4,112	1,563	4,238
2020	612,743	7,378	4,979	2,105	4,503

Hinsdale County

Year	Population	Births	Deaths	Migration	Change
1970	203	5	3	-8	-6
1980	417	4	3	-88	-87
1990	469	4	4	-7	-7
2000	791	12	1	-4	7
2001	794	6	4	1	3
2002	815	8	20	33	21
2003	826	7	6	10	11
2010	927	10	7	12	15
2020	1,091	13	8	11	16

Kiowa County

Year	Population	Births	Deaths	Migration	Change
1970	2,022	32	23	-47	-38
1980	1,948	34	24	70	80
1990	1,678	18	19	-19	-20
2000	1,617	16	14	-17	-15
2001	1,598	13	23	-9	-19
2002	1,600	11	15	6	2
2003	1,598	14	20	4	-2
2010	1,632	20	18	5	7
2020	1,732	19	16	7	10

Vital Statistics – Births, Deaths, Net Migration

Source: Colorado Department of Local Affairs. Data estimated for years 2003, 2010, 2020.

Kit Carson County

Year	Population	Births	Deaths	Migration	Change
1970	7,579	131	71	9	69
1980	7,582	134	65	-73	-4
1990	7,128	111	68	-116	-73
2000	8,010	100	84	93	109
2001	8,007	106	69	-40	-3
2002	8,009	105	73	-29	2
2003	8,021	88	81	5	11
2010	8,142	95	73	7	30
2020	8,544	103	69	10	44

Las Animas County

Year	Population	Births	Deaths	Migration	Change
1970	15,803	252	209	-540	-497
1980	14,943	233	168	261	326
1990	13,746	182	172	-224	-214
2000	15,276	192	160	102	134
2001	15,550	162	208	320	274
2002	15,915	154	251	463	365
2003	16,150	147	183	271	235
2010	18,184	194	184	257	267
2020	20,273	207	194	133	146

Lake County

Year	Population	Births	Deaths	Migration	Change
1970	8,313	196	58	535	673
1980	8,861	218	39	-165	14
1990	6,028	92	34	74	132
2000	7,825	145	39	-103	3
2001	7,878	136	44	-39	53
2002	8,290	140	31	303	412
2003	8,569	124	38	194	279
2010	11,404	143	47	360	457
2020	15,951	202	64	365	503

Lincoln County

Year	Population	Births	Deaths	Migration	Change
1970	4,861	62	64	53	51
1980	4,632	70	65	67	72
1990	4,514	58	50	-43	-35
2000	6,093	56	50	-9	-3
2001	6,117	50	59	33	24
2002	6,175	55	99	102	58
2003	6,181	55	61	13	7
2010	6,450	59	56	37	40
2020	6,962	64	55	45	54

La Plata County

Year	Population	Births	Deaths	Migration	Change
1970	19,316	340	189	-535	-384
1980	27,464	472	194	785	1,063
1990	32,453	438	194	400	644
2000	44,248	435	242	1,298	1,491
2001	45,475	469	215	973	1,227
2002	46,668	460	215	948	1,193
2003	47,467	483	310	626	799
2010	54,676	528	371	912	1,069
2020	62,861	551	478	607	680

Logan County

Year	Population	Births	Deaths	Migration	Change
1970	18,881	302	166	-155	-19
1980	19,797	343	154	336	525
1990	17,508	239	180	-276	-217
2000	20,787	245	195	448	498
2001	21,920	269	199	1,063	1,133
2002	22,430	250	223	483	510
2003	22,729	250	207	256	299
2010	25,857	306	203	401	503
2020	30,606	346	210	315	451

Larimer County

Year	Population	Births	Deaths	Migration	Change
1970	91,179	1,578	655	4,556	5,479
1980	150,115	2,324	798	3,058	4,584
1990	187,046	2,717	1,033	1,764	3,448
2000	253,137	3,213	1,430	5,198	6,981
2001	259,707	3,306	1,521	4,785	6,570
2002	265,230	3,278	1,470	3,716	5,523
2003	269,466	3,246	1,794	2,783	4,235
2010	303,163	3,527	1,990	3,305	4,842
2020	352,529	3,865	2,425	3,456	4,895

Mesa County

Year	Population	Births	Deaths	Migration	Change
1970	54,548	816	555	387	648
1980	82,644	1,434	607	5,114	5,941
1990	93,727	1,264	819	2,689	3,134
2000	116,998	1,485	1,109	2,049	2,425
2001	119,968	1,506	1,181	2,645	2,970
2002	122,350	1,480	1,183	2,086	2,382
2003	124,086	1,458	1,184	1,462	1,736
2010	141,175	1,772	1,252	2,346	2,867
2020	175,465	2,233	1,394	2,859	3,698

Vital Statistics – Births, Deaths, Net Migration

Source: Colorado Department of Local Affairs. Data estimated for years 2003, 2010, 2020.

Mineral County

Year	Population	Births	Deaths	Migration	Change
1970	794	13	6	51	58
1980	825	14	6	26	34
1990	551	7	5	-62	-60
2000	833	5	9	31	27
2001	843	5	5	10	10
2002	861	7	5	17	18
2003	865	6	8	6	4
2010	917	8	10	11	9
2020	1,015	10	11	12	11

Moffat County

Year	Population	Births	Deaths	Migration	Change
1970	6,569	111	61	-211	-161
1980	13,240	311	63	460	708
1990	11,399	168	56	-239	-127
2000	13,185	181	97	76	160
2001	13,190	198	100	93	5
2002	13,387	192	98	103	197
2003	13,494	183	92	16	107
2010	14,565	182	94	71	159
2020	16,373	201	106	95	191

Montezuma County

Year	Population	Births	Deaths	Migration	Change
1970	13,040	238	127	-171	-60
1980	16,728	309	137	277	449
1990	18,706	297	161	138	274
2000	23,864	312	237	265	340
2001	23,999	308	243	70	135
2002	24,514	299	261	477	515
2003	24,881	284	219	303	368
2010	28,260	335	241	449	543
2020	33,870	410	284	415	542

Montrose County

Year	Population	Births	Deaths	Migration	Change
1970	18,357	308	188	-163	-43
1980	24,490	454	186	781	1,049
1990	24,466	314	233	104	185
2000	33,666	430	295	783	918
2001	34,601	464	313	784	935
2002	35,411	468	343	685	810
2003	35,937	440	352	438	526
2010	41,048	490	368	700	823
2020	49,745	607	418	690	878

Morgan County

Year	Population	Births	Deaths	Migration	Change
1970	20,268	356	184	596	768
1980	22,498	434	204	403	633
1990	21,933	364	211	-115	38
2000	27,261	463	233	78	308
2001	27,623	476	277	163	362
2002	28,084	460	293	294	461
2003	28,429	495	245	95	345
2010	31,579	550	235	188	502
2020	36,794	625	241	139	522

Otero County

Year	Population	Births	Deaths	Migration	Change
1970	23,398	409	271	-740	-602
1980	22,559	400	253	-162	-15
1990	20,110	309	224	-443	358
2000	20,244	283	228	-210	-155
2001	19,976	301	217	-352	-268
2002	20,168	302	222	112	192
2003	20,226	296	212	-26	58
2010	21,288	283	200	97	180
2020	22,698	285	196	11	100

Ouray County

Year	Population	Births	Deaths	Migration	Change
1970	1,543	23	19	-71	-67
1980	1,951	30	14	-54	-38
1990	2,306	23	13	34	44
2000	3,771	26	20	147	153
2001	3,888	40	24	101	117
2002	4,039	38	22	136	151
2003	4,112	35	31	68	73
2010	4,739	37	34	76	80
2020	5,578	50	40	74	84

Park County

Year	Population	Births	Deaths	Migration	Change
1970	2,208	23	20	95	98
1980	5,461	110	23	821	908
1990	7,224	91	28	107	170
2000	14,679	148	65	696	779
2001	15,301	166	57	513	622
2002	17,144	168	57	1,733	1,843
2003	18,399	155	83	1,183	1,255
2010	33,974	298	137	3,179	3,340
2020	80,953	790	290	6,625	7,125

Vital Statistics – Births, Deaths, Net Migration

Source: Colorado Department of Local Affairs. Data estimated for years 2003, 2010, 2020.

Phillips County

Year	Population	Births	Deaths	Migration	Change
1970	4,085	55	59	-231	-235
1980	4,533	60	54	104	110
1990	4,185	56	52	-68	-64
2000	4,486	65	50	-47	-32
2001	4,511	53	55	27	25
2002	4,521	58	39	-8	10
2003	4,525	51	59	12	4
2010	4,670	60	49	20	31
2020	5,079	68	45	21	44

Rio Blanco County

Year	Population	Births	Deaths	Migration	Change
1970	4,828	77	45	-64	-32
1980	6,381	144	44	227	327
1990	5,942	83	34	-218	-169
2000	5,986	64	47	-122	-105
2001	5,986	65	57	-8	0
2002	6,125	62	53	130	139
2003	6,217	54	46	85	92
2010	7,146	68	49	133	152
2020	8,694	80	58	127	149

Pitkin County

Year	Population	Births	Deaths	Migration	Change
1970	6,342	121	25	586	682
1980	10,256	106	36	-347	-277
1990	12,714	150	24	173	299
2000	14,943	167	38	-19	110
2001	15,227	159	41	166	284
2002	15,660	158	49	324	433
2003	15,963	175	85	213	303
2010	18,482	193	103	284	374
2020	22,083	234	132	239	341

Rio Grande County

Year	Population	Births	Deaths	Migration	Change
1970	10,453	192	118	-421	-347
1980	10,581	193	117	-70	6
1990	10,746	175	98	-440	-363
2000	12,434	192	113	66	145
2001	12,518	171	132	45	84
2002	12,653	178	183	140	135
2003	12,713	168	121	13	60
2010	13,525	162	117	91	136
2020	14,363	171	119	-19	33

Prowers County

Year	Population	Births	Deaths	Migration	Change
1970	13,274	265	128	137	274
1980	13,075	292	123	-491	-322
1990	13,329	214	115	-489	-390
2000	14,434	239	136	-41	62
2001	14,240	269	141	-322	-194
2002	14,352	258	145	-1	112
2003	14,413	254	123	-69	62
2010	15,188	244	118	4	129
2020	16,449	245	118	-10	117

Routt County

Year	Population	Births	Deaths	Migration	Change
1970	6,733	109	58	512	563
1980	13,419	244	53	252	443
1990	14,216	209	52	109	266
2000	19,862	226	51	463	638
2001	20,551	204	78	563	689
2002	21,091	220	98	418	540
2003	21,433	226	96	211	342
2010	24,644	251	114	426	562
2020	29,786	309	151	252	409

Pueblo County

Year	Population	Births	Deaths	Migration	Change
1970	118,533	2,206	1,035	-2,638	-1,467
1980	125,745	2,053	1,092	-1,149	-188
1990	123,053	1,698	1,190	-818	-310
2000	142,054	1,928	1,380	1,788	2,336
2001	144,383	2,003	1,392	1,718	2,329
2002	146,140	2,001	1,344	1,100	1,757
2003	147,427	1,865	1,412	833	1,287
2010	159,234	1,964	1,457	1,434	1,941
2020	180,763	2,311	1,543	1,474	2,241

Saguache County

Year	Population	Births	Deaths	Migration	Change
1970	3,833	82	36	-43	3
1980	3,969	96	38	-41	17
1990	4,642	81	32	-46	3
2000	5,954	84	51	156	189
2001	6,100	79	45	112	146
2002	6,194	89	38	43	94
2003	6,240	89	45	2	46
2010	6,764	90	49	43	84
2020	7,620	100	57	40	83

Vital Statistics – Births, Deaths, Net Migration

Source: Colorado Department of Local Affairs. Data estimated for years 2003, 2010, 2020.

San Juan County

Year	Population	Births	Deaths	Migration	Change
1970	822	24	6	-21	-3
1980	862	23	3	-8	12
1990	750	12	4	-4	4
2000	558	3	3	1	1
2001	560	4	4	2	2
2002	575	4	0	11	15
2003	584	5	3	8	9
2010	654	7	4	9	11
2020	765	9	5	8	11

Teller County

Year	Population	Births	Deaths	Migration	Change
1970	3,392	61	27	88	122
1980	8,155	140	46	173	267
1990	12,535	188	57	-70	61
2000	20,809	203	94	521	630
2001	21,827	207	81	892	1,018
2002	22,529	226	79	556	702
2003	22,954	216	118	326	424
2010	25,904	246	145	213	314
2020	29,299	292	184	203	311

San Miguel County

Year	Population	Births	Deaths	Migration	Change
1970	1,973	40	18	1	23
1980	3,187	62	12	275	325
1990	3,726	50	10	74	114
2000	6,666	67	13	79	133
2001	6,956	64	15	241	290
2002	7,128	70	8	110	172
2003	7,265	83	27	81	137
2010	8,693	84	37	182	229
2020	10,796	98	53	150	195

Washington County

Year	Population	Births	Deaths	Migration	Change
1970	5,520	70	51	-179	-160
1980	5,287	80	66	402	416
1990	4,768	56	49	190	-183
2000	4,920	46	54	-96	104
2001	4,898	48	43	-27	-22
2002	4,909	52	55	15	11
2003	4,910	46	55	9	1
2010	5,006	55	54	21	23
2020	5,316	59	51	26	34

Sedgwick County

Year	Population	Births	Deaths	Migration	Change
1970	3,406	45	41	-148	-144
1980	3,256	44	36	-165	-157
1990	2,674	29	31	-58	-60
2000	2,742	30	42	35	23
2001	2,722	33	36	-17	-20
2002	2,740	32	33	20	18
2003	2,733	29	37	1	-7
2010	2,792	29	34	19	15
2020	2,985	33	31	20	22

Weld County

Year	Population	Births	Deaths	Migration	Change
1970	90,033	1,578	668	1,923	2,833
1980	123,564	2,124	762	1,959	3,321
1990	131,981	2,183	842	-1,227	114
2000	183,625	2,980	1,045	4,425	6,360
2001	194,382	3,204	1,205	8,758	10,757
2002	200,940	3,164	1,169	4,564	6,558
2003	206,307	3,095	1,267	3,539	5,367
2010	253,667	3,692	1,461	5,557	7,788
2020	346,492	4,867	1,929	7,329	10,266

Summit County

Year	Population	Births	Deaths	Migration	Change
1970	2,794	47	14	531	564
1980	8,926	156	15	222	363
1990	13,059	202	15	154	341
2000	23,705	275	40	902	1,137
2001	24,335	331	45	344	630
2002	25,252	333	58	642	917
2003	25,942	326	88	453	690
2010	31,943	297	134	728	891
2020	39,374	316	217	566	666

Yuma County

Year	Population	Births	Deaths	Migration	Change
1970	8,501	119	112	-256	-249
1980	9,697	177	92	-7	78
1990	8,925	116	96	-306	-286
2000	9,853	93	91	28	30
2001	9,900	142	113	18	47
2002	9,976	122	138	93	76
2003	10,000	117	108	14	23
2010	10,424	124	98	51	77
2020	11,354	136	95	56	96

CHAPTER

6 Famous Folks

Vance Brand

Born in Longmont, Colo., May 9, 1931, Vance Brand is one of many University of Colorado products to become a space pioneer.

He was one of 19 Navy pilot astronauts selected by NASA in 1966. He went on to fly four missions. On his first flight to space, July 15, 1975, he was the Apollo command module pilot on the historic Apollo-Soyuz Test Project. It was the first meeting of Americans and Soviets in space. Alexey Leonov was the Soviet commander for Soyuz.

Brand also was commander of STS-5, the first fully operational flight of the Space Shuttle Columbia on Nov. 11, 1982. Brand commanded the 10th flight of the Shuttle Challenger Feb. 3, 1984, and again Commanded Columbia on its 38th flight, this time with a crew of seven, on Dec. 2, 1990.

Saint Frances Xavier Cabrini

"Mother Cabrini," America's first canonized Saint, was born July 15, 1850 in St. Angelo, Italy, the youngest of 13 children. She grew up dreaming of a missionary life and in 1880 founded the Institute of the Missionary Sisters of the Sacred Heart of Jesus. At the request of Pope Leo XIII, Mother Cabrini went to New York in 1889 to help Italian immigrants. In 1902 she accepted an invitation from Bishop Nicholas Matz to come to Denver where she continued her work. She died in 1917 in Chicago. The Mother Cabrini Shrine on Lookout Mountain reflects the pious works of a woman who founded 67 missions including schools, hospitals, orphanages and child-care centers. The shrine remains a pilgrimage for thousands each year.

Scott Carpenter

Known best as an astronaut, Scott Carpenter was also an aquanaut, a true pioneer of modern exploration.

Carpenter was born May 1, 1925, in Boulder, Colo. He attended the University of Colorado where he received a degree in aeronautical engineering. He joined the U.S. Navy in 1949 where he eventually became one of the famed test pilots of his era.

Carpenter was selected as one of the original seven astronauts on April 9, 1959. He served as backup pilot for John Glenn during preparation for the first manned orbital flight. He flew America's second manned orbital flight on May 24, 1962. He piloted the Aurora 7 spacecraft through three revolutions of the earth and reached a maximum altitude of 164 miles. The flight lasted 4 hours, 54 minutes.

On leave from NASA, Carpenter also participated in the Navy's Man In The Sea program as an aquanaut. In the summer of 1965, he spent 30 days living and working on the ocean floor. He was team leader for two of the three teams of Navy men and researchers who lived at a depth of 204 feet over 45 days. It is through such studies the Navy developed its deep ocean search, rescue and salvage and research capabilities.

He now makes his home in the Los Angeles, Calif. area.

Christopher "Kit" Carson

A trapper, scout, Indian agent, soldier and guide, Kit Carson was a frequent visitor to, and resident of, Colorado long before Colorado was Colorado. Born on Christmas Eve, 1809 in Boone's Lick, Mo., Carson never received a formal education. By age 14 he was apprenticed to a saddle-maker but left home shortly after for Santa Fe, New Mexico. Carson used Taos, N.M. as his base for several fur-trapping expeditions that often led him north to the Rocky Mountains of Colorado. For a time in the early 1840s, he worked as a hunter for William Bent at

Figure 6.1 – Kit Carson. (Denver Public Library, Western History Collection. D.F. Barry photograph of a portrait. B-695.)

Bent's Fort. In 1842, he met John C. Fremont who hired him as a guide for his fabled surveying expeditions across Colorado and the rest of the West. His exploits as Fremont's guide were duly recorded in Fremont's widely read journals. Carson was noted for his daring and competence, yet other than being able to sign his name, he could neither read nor write. Still, he became a major figure in the building of the American West.

Carson worked as a guide and soldier in California's Bear-Flag rebellion and also participated in the Mexican-American War. He returned to New Mexico and started a career in ranching before organizing the New Mexico volunteer infantry during the Civil War. It was during this time he became a famous Indian fighter, helping to fight the Navajo.

After the Civil War, Carson moved to Colorado in hopes of expanding his ranching empire. He died the following year. His body was returned to Taos, where it is buried in a small cemetery near his old home.

Thomas R. Cech

The University of Colorado's first Nobel Prize was earned in chemistry in 1989 by a young research scientist in the school's Department of Molecular, Cellular and Developmental Biology. Thomas Cech was 42 when he won the world-famous award for his discovery of the catalytic properties of RNA – ribonuclaic acid. The discovery changed conceptions about the basic working properties of the cell. A research summary explains: "RNA was long thought to function solely as a genetic messenger, as a component of the ribosome, and as a carrier of amino acids. Now, largely because of research done at the University of Colorado, it is just as common to think of RNA participating directly in cellular catalysis...A major goal of the work carried out by Professor Cech and his research group is to understand mechanisms of RNA catalysis at both the chemical and biological levels. The work integrates organic and physical chemistry, enzymology, molecular biology and structural biology."

Lon Chaney

As Hollywood's first great master of make-up and monsters, Lon Chaney scared millions during his almost four-decade performing career.

Chaney was born April 1, 1883 in Colorado Springs, Colo. The son of deaf mute parents, he learned early to communicate through pantomime, sign language and facial expressions. He entertained his family by observing people in town then returning to enact mimicking pantomimes of the local residents. He worked as a Pikes Peak guide for tourists where he developed a love for the outdoors, and also learned the wallpaper, drapery and carpet trades. Among his early jobs was assisting his brother who was property boy, scene painter and stage hand at the Colorado Springs Opera House. There he witnessed many of America's great stage stars.

At age 19, he joined a traveling road show as an actor in the play "The Little Tycoon." Thus started his theatrical career. By 1918, he had more than 100 film credits for Universal Studios. In 1919 he earned his reputation as master of make-up, disguise and the acting that goes with it. In "The Frog," he played a con man who pretends to be a cripple miraculously healed. In "The Penalty," he had his legs tightly bound behind him to play an amputee. As Quasimodo in "The Hunchback of Notre Dame," he wore a hump and harness reported to weigh more than 50 pounds that twisted his torso and allowed him to feel the pain of Quasimodo. His performance garnered worldwide fame. In 1925, his portrayal of Erik in the "Phantom of the Opera," secured him film immortality. Such performances earned him the nickname "The Man of a Thousand Faces."

Chaney played his last movie roll, and his first in a non-silent film, in 1930 in "The Unholy Three." In the film, he used five different voices in the roll of a crook ventriloquist. Chaney died shortly after release of the film on Aug. 26, 1930.

Mary Coyle Chase

Mary Coyle Chase wrote many plays and two novels for children, but she always will be remembered for her box office hit and 1945 Pulitzer Prize-winning play, "Harvey."

Chase was born Feb. 25, 1907, in Denver. She graduated high school at age 15 and attended both the University of Denver and the University of Colorado before working as a reporter for the Rocky Mountain News for 14 years.

Chase wrote "Harvey" after meeting a woman whose son had been killed in the Pacific theater during World War II. Struck by the woman's sorrow, Chase set out to write something to make the woman laugh again. Chase spent two years writing "Harvey," the story of a friendly tippler and his imaginary six-foot rabbit. She re-wrote the play 50 times, trying versions on family, friends and the cleaning lady. The play was accepted by New York producer Brock Pemberton. It opened on Broadway to rave reviews and played there for 4.5 years, ranking it as one of the five longest-running plays on Broadway. "Harvey" continues to run in theaters around the country with regularity.

Among the play's long list of critical achievements was a call to Chase from the woman whose son had been killed in the Pacific. She said she had seen the play and laughed. Chase received many other letters from around the country from parents of children killed in the war. The parents wrote to say they, too, had seen the play and laughed.

Chase lived in Denver until her death in 1981.

William F. "Buffalo Bill" Cody

Buffalo Bill's fame for western skill and bravery is part fact, part fiction, all of it colorful. He was born in Iowa in 1846 where he first worked for

a wagon freight company as a mounted messenger and wrangler. In 1859 he joined the gold rush to Pikes Peak in Colorado where he tried his luck as a prospector. He abandoned prospecting after one year to become a rider for the short-lived Pony Express.

He first served as a Union scout during the Civil War and later as an enlisted man with the Seventh Kansas Cavalry. He continued to work for the Army as a scout and dispatch carrier after the war. In 1867 he took a job as a buffalo hunter to feed the construction crews of the Kansas Pacific Railroad, during which time he claims to have killed 4,280 buffalo in 17 months. Hence the name

Figure 6.2 — An 1889 portrait of William "Buffalo Bill" Cody probably taken in Paris. (Denver Public Library, Western History Collection. NS-15)

"Buffalo" Bill. In 1868, he again became a scout for the Army where he engaged in a variety of Indian battles. He was present during the Cheyenne defeat at Summit Springs, Colo. in 1869.

His status as a folk hero was as much his doing as the doing of dime-store novelist Ned Buntline who wrote under the name E.Z.C. Judson. It is Buntline who created a fictitous and exaggerated version of Buffalo Bill. Buntline eventually asked Cody to play the starring role in his play "The

Scouts of the Plains." Cody proved a natural showman and self promoter. He continued as an actor for 11 years. He published an autobiography in 1879 and also supervised the production of his own Buffalo Bill dime novels, most of which he did not write.

Not all a showman, Cody continued his visits to the West on hunting expeditions, and even served again with the Army as a scout following the Battle at Little Bighorn.

In 1883, he organized his own traveling extravaganza, Buffalo Bill's Wild West Show. The success of his productions solidified his colorful reputation in America's consciousness. Buffalo Bill's Wild West Show toured America and even Europe for 30 years. He made a fortune in show business, but also lost it.

He was a frequent visitor to Colorado and to Denver where his sister lived. He died Jan. 10, 1917, and is buried on Lookout Mountain above the Front Range city of Golden.

Jack Dempsey

Born in Manassa, Colo., June 24, 1895, William Harrison "Harry" Dempsey toughened himself in the rough mining towns of Colorado before becoming a legendary boxing heavyweight champion.

His first matches were informal affairs in the bars and saloons of Colorado's mining towns where he fought under the name "Kid Blackie." Dempsey promoted his own first professional fight at the 1912 Montrose County Fair. He defeated Fred Wood. Thus started one of the most storied boxing careers of all time. Dempsey was gifted with great speed, agility and pure power that made him one of the biggest box office attractions of all time. Many of his victories came just seconds or a few minutes into a fight.

Dempsey won his first world championship in 1919 in a bout with Jess Willard. His nickname, "The Manassa Mauler," named after his birthplace, became known around the country. He successfully defended his title six times over the next seven years. It wasn't until Sept. 23, 1926, that he was defeated by Gene Tunney. Dempsey lost again to Tunney in a rematch in 1927 during a fight that has since been known as the "Battle of the Long Count." The referee in that fight ruled Dempsey did not return to a neutral corner after knocking down Tunney. Tunney won the match three rounds later.

Figure 6.3 – Jack Dempsey, third from left, poses at Denver's Union Station with a group of unidentified men and his wife, Estelle Taylor. (Denver Public Library, Western History Collection. Harry Mellon Rhoads photographer. Rh-192)

Dempsey continued fighting in exhibitions after his defeat. He retired in 1940 and became a successful restaurateur in New York. He died May 31, 1983 in New York.

Mamie Doud Eisenhower

Mamie Doud Eisenhower was born Nov. 14, 1896 in Boone, Iowa. Her family moved to Denver seven years later where she grew up with three sisters in a large home.

With her father retired from business, the family often took extended winter vacations to visit relatives in San Antonio, Texas. It was on one of the vacations in 1915 she met Dwight D. Eisenhower, a young second lieutenant stationed at Fort Sam Houston. By Valentine's Day 1916, they were engaged. They were married in the Doud Denver home on July 1.

Even through the Eisenhower presidency, the family continued to visit Colorado on a regular basis.

Mamie became the consummate military wife. By her accounting, the family moved 27 times in 37 years as Dwight climbed the military ladder. She raised two sons, Doud "Icky" Dwight who died at age 4 of scarlet fever, and John. John's son, David, is the namesake for the famous presidential retreat Camp David. David later married Julie Nixon, daughter of President Richard Nixon.

When Eisenhower was elected president, Mamie proved an admirable leader of the White House staff. The couple entertained an unprecedented number of guests at the White House during the Eisenhower presidency. Dwight Eisenhower died in 1969, Mamie in 1979. They are buried side by side in a small chapel on the grounds of the Eisenhower Library in Abilene, Kan.

Douglas Fairbanks Sr.

America's biggest silent film star, Douglas Fairbanks Sr. was born Douglas Elton Ulman in Denver, Colo., May 23, 1883. He was the son of a successful New York attorney who moved west to manage mining interests. The senior Ulman was a fan of theater and introduced young Douglas to the stage. He took Douglas backstage at theater productions and often opened his home to traveling troupes of actors. At a very young age, Douglas could recite Shakespeare from memory. Ulman's mining interests eventually failed. He became an alcoholic and left his family in Denver for New York when Douglas was age 5.

Douglas remained in Denver. His mother, Ella, was furious with her husband for leaving the family and legally changed the name of her three children to Fairbanks. By age 11, Douglas

Figure 6.4 -- Douglas Fairbanks Sr. and wife Mary Pickford pose in Denver Nov. 24, 1926. (Denver Public Library, Western History Collection. Harry Mellon Rhoads photographer. Rh-139.)

Fairbanks was performing on stage in the Denver area, including shows at Elitch Gardens Theatre. Fairbanks was a local sensation by the time he was a teenager. He dropped out of high school as a senior and made his way to New York. His New York stage debut was in 1902, but he struggled as a stage actor. By 1915, Fairbanks was in Hollywood where he went on to become one of the great early Hollywood stars and idols.

Eugene Field

Loved as the "Children's Poet" and one of America's first personal newspaper columnists, Eugene Field was born in St. Louis, Mo. He did not spend a great deal of time in Colorado, but it was as a newspaper reporter for the Denver Tribune that Field in 1889 penned one of his most famous poems, *Wynken, Blynken, and Nod.*

Robert Ford

Robert Ford shot Jesse James in the back while a guest in the James home April 3, 1882. Following a murder trial, conviction and full pardon from the governor of Missouri, Ford left Missouri and headed west.

Ford's reputation as the man who killed Jesse James preceded him. For a time he earned a living by posing for photographs in dime museums. He traveled through New Mexico and up to Walsenburg, Colo. When silver was discovered near Creede, Ford moved there to be where the money was.

He opened The Exchange, or Ford's Exchange, a combination gambling and dance hall. The Exchange was short-lived, but Ford simply opened another dance hall. Fire destroyed that building, but Ford set up shop once again in a tent. Into the new business walked Edward O. Kelly with a sawed-off shotgun. Kelly shot Ford dead. Ford was buried in Creede, but later exhumed and reburied in his home state of Missouri.

Ruth Handler

Famous fashion doll and American icon Barbie (and Ken) can trace their roots to Denver, Colo. Ruth Handler, inventor of the doll, was born in Denver June 26, 1938. After getting married and having children of her own, she in 1959 created the original Barbie doll after watching her own daughter at play. More than 1 billion Barbies and family members have since been sold. Handler, with Barbie as the anchor, became a co-founder of Mattel Corp. The dolls are named after Handler's children, Barbie and Ken. Handler died in California in 2002.

John Henry "Doc" Holliday

A dentist by education, Doc Holliday may have hurt more people than he healed. Born Aug. 14, 1851 in Griffin, Ga., Holliday was the product of a prosperous and educated family. In that tradition he earned a degree in dentistry in 1872 from the Pennsylvania College of Dental Surgery. He might have lived a sedate life as a dentist had he not been diagnosed with tuberculosis soon after opening his practice. Under advice to move west, he set up a new office in Dallas, but horrible coughing fits from the disease prevented him from successfully building his practice.

He took up gambling for a living. He shot and killed over a card game for the first time in Dallas. Running from the law, he killed again in a neighboring county, but this time it was a soldier from nearby Fort Richardson. On the run again, this time from federal officials, Holliday made his way to Colorado and Apache country. His stops included Pueblo, Leadville, Georgetown and Central City. Three more men died along the way before he ever reached Denver where he worked for a short time before more trouble chased him on to Wyoming, New Mexico, back to Texas and to Dodge City, Kan.

In his travels, Holliday befriended Wyatt Earp, noted gunslinger and sometimes lawman. Another acquaintance was Bat Masterson. Holliday tried dentistry again in Dodge City. It didn't last. He ended up a faro dealer in the famous Long Branch Saloon. Not long after, he saved Earp's life by stopping a gun battle.

From there it was back to Trinidad, Colo., but his shooting of another gambler had him on the run again. Eventually he found himself in Tombstone, Ariz., where he and Wyatt Earp participated in the famous shootout at the OK Corral.

Holliday left Arizona for Colorado once again where he spent time in Denver, Pueblo and Leadville before traveling to Glenwood Springs to try the sulfur vapor caves for his failing health. He died peacefully in Glenwood Springs on Nov. 8, 1887, and is buried there.

Willard Libby

Grand Valley High School in Parachute, Colo., launched a distinguished research career for Libby at the University of Chicago. In 1960, he won the Nobel Prize for Chemistry for his development of the Carbon 14 dating method, now used widely throughout the world. He is the only Nobel Prize recipient to graduate from a Colorado high school.

Ted Mack

Born in Greeley, Colo., 1904, Ted Mack was no amateur entertainer.

Mack became the host of the Original Amateur Hour in 1948 when the program was aired on both radio and television. The radio version of the show lasted to 1952, while the television version played until 1970. Over almost 20 years, the television version was broadcast at one time or another on all four major networks, eventually settling in on CBS on Sunday afternoons for the last 10 years. Through it all, Mack conducted rambling interviews and cracked corny jokes with contestants between acts. While most acts vanished into obscurity, the show launched several successful entertainment careers. Mack died in 1976,

Glenn Miller

He is the man most associated with the Swing and Big Band Era in American music. Born Alton Glenn Miller March 1, 1904, in Clarinda, Iowa, Miller made his Colorado connection when his family moved to Greeley, Colo. He later attended the University of Colorado for two years. It was there his musical talents flourished. He played with Denver's Boyd Senter band and eventually left college to pursue music as a career.

In 1934, Miller helped Ray Noble build an orchestra that gained recognition through radio broadcasts. In 1937, he started his own band, but that ensemble struggled and soon disbanded. In 1938, he formed a second group, The Glenn Miller Orchestra. With such musical standards as "Chattanooga Choo Choo," "String of Pearls," and "Moonlight Serenade," Miller and his band became one of the most famous and popular groups in America.

Miller disbanded his orchestra in 1942 to join the U.S. Army Air Force with the rank of captain. There he formed another dance band to perform for the troops. On Dec. 15, 1944, Miller boarded a flight from England to Paris where his band was to perform. The plane never arrived. Miller's death was mourned worldwide, but his music endures.

Alfred Packer

Alfred Packer is the first and only person ever convicted of a cannibal-related crime in the United States. His legacy endures throughout Colorado – usually in the form of humor, such as the many restaurants or dinner dishes named in his honor.

He was born in Allegheny County, Penn., in 1842. He worked for a time at shoemaking, but enlisted in the army during the Civil War. Epilepsy earned him a discharge from the service on two separate occasions. In 1862, he went west and found employment as a guide in Utah and Colorado.

In 1873, he was hired by a Utah group of roughly 20 men to lead them on a prospecting trip through the Colorado Rockies. By January 1874, the group had traveled to the camp of Ute Indians led by Chief Ouray near modern day Delta, Colo. They were warned to stay out of the mountains, but five of the group, plus Packer, proceeded into the harsh mountain winter. Two

Figure 6.5 – Alfred Packer. (Photo courtesy Grand Junction Daily Sentinel. File photo.)

months later, only Packer returned. He looked fit and well-fed, carrying more money than was customary, and possessing items belonging to the other men in his party. Under scrutiny, Packer eventually confessed to how four of the men had died in turn from the elements and had been eaten by the rest. Packer said he killed the last man, Shannon Bell, in self-defense before eating him, too. Skeletons of the five men were soon found at a single camp, which disproved Packer's first version of the story. (Packer reportedly changed his story more than once.)

Packer was charged with the murder of Israil Swan, but escaped from jail prior to trial. He remained at large for nine years before his re-capture in Wyoming in 1883 and subsequent return to Colorado. Upon his return, he signed a new confession, this time stating all men were alive but too weak to travel. He said he left the camp to scout a trail. When he returned, Shannon Bell had gone mad and killed the other four men with a hatchet. Bell, he said, was boiling the flesh from one of the men. Packer said Bell charged him with the hatchet, forcing him to shoot him dead. After several more days, Packer said he resorted to cannibalism to stay alive.

Packer was tried for murder, convicted and sentenced to hang. The sentence was later changed to manslaughter and he was sentenced to serve 40 years at the prison in Canon City.

A campaign by the Denver Post and reporter Polly Pry argued for his innocence so successfully that Packer was paroled in 1901. He spent his remaining years as an unofficial guard at the Denver Post before his death by natural causes in 1907. He is buried in the Littleton, Colo., cemetery. On his tombstone his name is spelled "Alferd Packer," causing some confusion over the correct spelling of his name. Historians recently have found evidence to support Packer's final version of the story.

Theodore Puck, Ph.D

A resident of Denver for more than 50 years, Theodore Puck has become a living legend in the fields of genetics and biomedical research. He earned his undergraduate degree in 1937 and his Ph.D. in 1940 from the University of Chicago. During World War II he served as a member of the Commission on Air-Borne Infections, the Army Epidemiological Board and Office of the Surgeon General.

Puck is now the senior scientist at the Eleanor Roosevelt Institute in Denver, the distinguished professor in the Department of Medicine at the University of Colorado Health Sciences Center and a research professor in the Department of Biochemistry in the Department of Biochemistry and Molecular Genetics for the University of Colorado Medical Center. He is a visiting fellow with the Los Alamos National Laboratory and has been a professor and fellow at the California Institute of Technology.

Among his many achievements, he created the incubator technique of growing human cells in cultures, drastically reducing the need for the use of live animals in medical research. His procedure, called "somatic cell genetics," enables experimentation in human genetics and biochemistry not previously possible. The procedure also led to the technique known as amniocentesis. Puck also organized the creation of the classification system by which all scientists study chromosomes, called the Denver Chromosome Classification System. In addition, Puck pioneered the study of toxicity in chemotherapy and radiology by identifying and proving the amount of X-ray dosage needed to destroy cancer cells. Prior to his work, the dosage used was 1,000 times greater than was needed.

Damon Runyon

One of America's great newspapermen arrived in Pueblo, Colo., in 1887 at age 7. The son of a Manhattan, Kan. newspaper publisher, Damon Runyon (born Alfred Damon Runyan) was moved with the rest of the family to Colorado where it was hoped the dry climate would help his mother's health. His father went to work as a printer for the Pueblo Chieftan.

In the family tradition, Runyon later signed on as a cub reporter for the Pueblo Evening Press at age 15. He soon embraced a taste for fancy nightlife, fine clothes and booze. A typographical error at the Evening News is responsible for the changed spelling of his name from Runyan to Runyon.

Following the Spanish-American War, Runyon returned to Denver via various newspaper jobs in Basalt, Glenwood Springs, Trinidad, Pueblo and Colorado Springs. He landed a job at the Denver Post in 1905, but was fired in 1906. His next job was at the Rocky Mountain News during the heyday of the newspaper wars. Runyon teamed with artist Frank Finch. Finch drew and Runyon wrote to the delight of readers and his editors. Finishing each assignment quickly, Runyon also drank, and drank, and drank, mostly at the Denver Press Club, which remains the nation's oldest continuously operating press club.

In an effort to break alcohol's grip on his life, Runyon left Denver for New York and the New York American. He didn't drink anymore, but he still loved the nightlife, the gangsters, the dames, the shysters and the sportsmen. All came alive in his copy. His social circle included the likes of Al Capone, Babe Ruth, Walter Winchell and many other famous and infamous characters he encountered in his beat around the Polo Grounds, Yankee Stadium, Madison Square Garden, Ebbets Field and the various speakeasies of the time. America came to know the characters as The Lemon Drop Kid, Last Card Louie, Harry the Horse, Dave the Dude and Miss Sarah Brown. His writings expanded to national magazines and books. Originally a collection of stories, his book *Guys and Dolls*, gained him international fame. In 1950, two of the stories from *Guys and Dolls* were adapted in to one Broadway play, "Guys and Dolls," still widely performed. His work eventually spread to Hollywood and the silver screen.

Runyon died Dec. 10, 1946.

Jack Swigert

Born Aug. 30, 1931 in Denver, John L. "Jack" Swigert was one of 19 selected by NASA for its fifth astronaut class in 1966. He was appointed backup command module pilot for Appolo 13. When the original command pilot, Thomas Mattingly, became exposed to German measles only days before lift-off, Swigert was given the job.

The 1970 Apollo 13 flight ranks as among the most harrowing space flights in history. An oxygen tank explosion crippled the space craft in space as it approached the moon. Jim Lovell, Fred Haise and Swigert were more than 200,000 miles from Earth when the explosion crippled their spacecraft. Since the explosion happened while Lovell and Haise were approaching the moon for a landing in the lunar module, the lunar module was not harmed by the explosion. Lovell and Haise aborted their lunar landing and retreated to Swigert and the command module. Working with ground crews, the astronauts were able to convert the lunar module into what amounted to a space-based lifeboat. For more than three days, the three astronauts struggled to conserve energy and supplies necessary to make it back to earth. The three returned safely after what must be considered one of the great scientific adventure stories of all time.

Swigert attended Regis and East High Schools in Denver. He received his mechanical engineering degree from the University of Colorado in 1953, a Master of Science in aerospace science from the Rensselaer Polytechnic Institute in 1965 and an MBA degree from the University of Hartford in 1967.

Swigert was elected to the U.S. House of Representatives from Colorado's new 6th Congressional District in 1982. On Dec. 27, 1982, one week before taking office, Swigert died of cancer.

Byron "Whizzer" White

Rarely has a man proved so capable in the fields of brains and brawn. Byron "Whizzer" White is among Colorado's most admired citizens.

He was born June 8, 1917, in Fort Collins, Colo., and raised in nearby Wellington. He entered the University of Colorado in 1934. In 1937 he earned a reputation as one of the finest football players in the land. As an All-American halfback he rushed for a national record 1,121 yards in only eight games while scoring 122 points. He finished second in the Heisman Trophy voting.

After his graduation, White signed what then was the largest professional football contract in history – $15,800 to play for Pittsburgh. He took a year off football in 1939 to accept a Rhodes Scholarship. He resumed his football career in 1940 and was the National Football League's leading rusher. He retired from football in 1941.

White served in the Navy during World War II in the South Pacific. After his service he completed his legal studies at Yale University, graduating in 1946. He was appointed as clerk to Chief Justice Fred M. Vinson of the U.S. Supreme

Figure 6.6 – Byron "Whizzer" White, right, stands with an unidentified man at a University of Colorado event honoring the football star. (Denver Public Library, Western History Collection. Harry Mellon Rhoads photographer. Rh-1285.)

Court and served the 1946-47 term. He then returned to Denver and practiced law for 14 years. In 1961 President John F. Kennedy appointed White Deputy U.S. Attorney General, a post he held until Kennedy nominated him to the U.S. Supreme Court on March 30, 1962. The U.S. Senate confirmed White's appointment April 11, 1962. He was sworn in April 16. He retired as U.S. Supreme Court Justice 31 years later on June 28, 1993. White died in Colorado in the summer of 2002.

White was the second University of Colorado product to serve as a Supreme Court Justice. **Wiley B. Rutledge** earned his law degree from the University of Colorado in 1922. He practiced law for two years in Boulder before deciding on an academic career. President Franklin D. Roosevelt appointed Rutledge to the Supreme Court in 1943. He served for six years before his death in 1949 at age 55.

Paul Whiteman

Paul Whiteman came by his musical talents naturally. Born in Denver, March 28, 1890, his father was the superintendent of musical education for Denver's schools. Whiteman started on the violin and viola, playing first with the Denver Symphony Orchestra before moving to San Francisco.

He discovered jazz in San Francisco and soon formed his own orchestra. His band went on to become the most successful and most popular ensemble of the 1920s. He billed himself as the King of Jazz. His dance music was the most influential of the 1920s, and the band's influence continued in to the 1930s. As Whiteman's popularity declined in the 1940s and 1950s, he became the musical director for the American Broadcasting Company. He formed orchestras from time to time and played Las Vegas regularly during the early 1960s prior to his retirement. He died December 29, 1967.

Carl E. Wieman and Eric Cornell

Physicists Carl Wieman and Eric Cornell shared the 2001 Nobel Prize in physics for creating Bose-Einstein condensate, a new form of matter that occurs just a few hundred billionths of a degree above absolute zero. The Bose-Einstein condensate was previously theorized, but never achieved until the University of Colorado pair created it in 1995.

7 Famous Places

National Parks, Monuments, Recreation Areas, Historic Sites

Colorado boasts four national parks, five national monuments, one national recreation area and one national historic site. Each represents a landscape, ecosystem or history stunningly different from all the others. They are as remarkable for beauty or historical significance as they are for their diversity. Six are managed by the U.S. National Park Service, one by the Bureau of Land Management.

Bent's Old Fort National Historic Site

Brothers William and Charles Bent were an enterprising pair. Together with Ceran St. Vrain, they built a fort and trading post in 1833 on the Santa Fe Trail near La Junta, Colo. The fort became the center of the Bent, St. Vrain Co.'s trading empire that extended north to the St. Vrain River near present day Longmont, and south to the Mexican towns of Taos and Santa Fe. The fort and trading post operated for 16 years, nearly always as the only white settlement on the Sante Fe Trail between Missouri and the Taos, Santa Fe area. The fort's commerce was based on trade with the Southern Cheyenne and Arapaho Indians for buffalo robes. Many of the West's famous frontiersmen and explorers used the fort for needed supplies, repairs, livestock, food, water, rest and protection. The U.S. Army later used the fort as a staging ground in its war against Mexico. The fort was abandoned in 1849. Archeological excavations and original sketches, paintings and diaries were used in its reconstruction in 1976.

Total acreage 2002: 798.8 acres
2002 Total Recreation Visits: 29,709
2001 Budget: $882,000
2002 Budget: $1,000,000
2003 Budget: $1,000,000

Black Canyon of the Gunnison National Park

This is America's newest National Park, gaining the distinction on October 21, 1999. It isn't the biggest canyon in the west, it isn't the longest, deepest or narrowest, but it is without question among the most spectacular. The canyon was formed by the Gunnison River slowly cutting down through hard, Proterozoic crystalline rock. Due to the narrowness, depth and sheer walls, little sunlight hits the walls. Thus, Black Canyon. The canyon boasts Colorado's highest rock wall. Black Canyon in its entirety is 53 miles long, but only the deepest and most spectacular 14 miles lies within park boundaries. About one-third of the park (10,000 acres) has been devoted to wilderness area, while another 58,000 adjacent acres, managed by the Bureau of Land Management, receives similar protection.

Total acreage 2002: 32,770 acres
2002 Total Recreation Visits: 174,346
2001 Budget: $734,000
2002 Budget: $1,026,000
2003 Budget: $1,026,000

Colorado National Monument

Established in 1911, Colorado National Monument sits on the outskirts of Grand Junction, Colo., near the Utah border. It is a land of piñon and juniper forests, abrupt sandstone canyons and large, elegant rock formations carved by wind and water. Wildlife includes bighorn sheep, golden eagles, mule deer and mountain lion. On the eastern flanks of the Colorado Plateau, the monument displays impressive geologic features wrought by erosion. The Monument might also be considered an eastern gateway to the spectacular canyon country of Southern Utah.

Total acreage 2002: 20,534 acres
2002 Total Recreation Visits: 292,750
2001 Budget: $994,000
2002 Budget: $954,000
2003 Budget: $954,000

Curecanti National Recreation Area

Three reservoirs on the Gunnison River are the heart of this recreation area. Established in 1965, the area boasts views of mesas, man-made fjords, and deep narrow canyons. Blue Mesa Reservoir is Colorado's largest

Figure 7.1 – Black Canyon of the Gunnison. (Photo courtesy Grand Junction Daily Sentinel. File photo.)

body of water and the nation's largest Kokanee Salmon fishery. Black Canyon begins at Morrow Point Reservoir, while Crystal Reservoir is the site of the Gunnison Diversion Tunnel, a National Historic Civil Engeneering Landmark (see Chapter 10). Dinosaur fossils have recently been found in the area while traces of 6,000-year-old dwellings are protected in an archaeological district.

Total acreage 2002: 41,972
2002 Total Recreation Visits: 892,408
2001 Budget: $2,924,000
2002 Budget: $2,971,000
2003 Budget: $2,971,000

Dinosaur National Monument

While this national monument is most famous for its fabulous Dinosaur Quarry Visitor Center, where large-scale excavations are in full view, it also is home to a diverse desert river landscape. The Yampa River, Colorado's only free-flowing river, converges with the Green River in the monument's Echo Park where stunning Steamboat Rock has captivated ancient people, early explorers, trappers and the likes of Ansel Adams. The desert piñon and juniper landscape is jumbled in the park by terrific geologic upheavals and faults plainly seen from the Green River and in the canyons surrounding the Split Mountain area. The Monument is in the northwest corner of the state near the small burg of Dinosaur. To reach the Dinosaur Quarry, enter through Jensen, Utah.

Total acreage 2002: 210,278 acres
2002 Total Recreation Visits: 299,622
2001 Budget: $2,528,000
2002 Budget: $2,782,000
2003 Budget: $2,782,000

Florissant Fossil Beds National Monument

The Florissant Fossil Beds became part of the national park system in 1969. Near Pikes Peak, this mountain valley holds important evidence of a very different, very ancient Colorado. An enormous volcanic eruption some 35 million years ago buried a lush valley and petrified the native redwood trees. A lake formed in the valley and in its fine, lake-bottom sediments were deposited plants and insects. As the sediments compacted into layers of shale, the delicate features of the organisms were preserved as fossils.

Total acreage 2002: 5,998 acres
2002 Total Recreation Visits: 63,944
2001 Budget: $609,000
2002 Budget: $630,000
2003 Budget: $630,000

Great Sand Dunes National Park and Preserve

Colorado's San Luis Valley is home to North America's tallest sand dunes. The 700-foot dunes of Great Sand Dunes National Monument make a stark contrast to the alpine majesty of the Sangre De Cristo mountain range that rises directly east of the dunes. The wind-swept dunes can be seen for miles against their mountain backdrop. In all, there are 39 square miles of sand dunes available for long walks and dune climbing. The area became a national monument in 1932, but with passage of the Great Sand Dunes National Park and Preserve Act of 2000, resources now include alpine lakes and tundra, six peaks more than 13,000 feet high, ancient spruce and pine forests, large stands of aspen and cottonwood, grasslands and wetlands, all of which makes for very diverse wildlife habitat.

Total acreage 2002: 83,958 acres
2002 Total Recreation Visits: 235,535
2001 Budget: $964,000
2002 Budget: $1,455,000
2003 Budget: $1,455,000

Hovenweep National Monument

Designated a national monument in 1923, Hovenweep is five prehistoric, Puebloan-era villages on Cajon Mesa along the state of Utah-Colorado border. Architecture of the standing ruins is typical of the area and was built roughly 800 years ago by ancestors of the Puebloan people. Hovenweep is noted for its solitude and undeveloped, natural character. The Square Tower is best seen on ranger-led tours. Outlying ruins include Holly, Horseshoe, Hackberry, Cuththroat Castle and Cajon. The land surrounding Hovenweep is owned by the Navajo Nation, Bureau of Land

Management, State of Utah and private landowners.
  Total acreage 2002: 785 acres
  2002 Total Recreation Visits: 32,817
  2001 Budget: $208,000
  2002 Budget: $280,000
  2003 Budget: $280,000

Mesa Verde National Park

Mesa Verde National Park is the only national park established to pre-serve the works of people. It contains the finest examples of ancestral Puebloan structures and cliff dwellings in the world. The structures date from roughly 550 A.D. to 1300 A.D. Through the roughly 700 years represented by the dwellings, people lived and flourished throughout the area. The society eventually built the elaborate stone villages in the sheltering cliffs. Known generically as cliff dwellings, the shelters are thought to represent only the last 75 to 100 years of Mesa Verde occupation. It is a mat-

Figure 7.2 – Cliff dwellings at Mesa Verde National Park. (Photo courtesy Grand Junction Daily Sentinel. File photo.)

ter of great debate and speculation as to why the residents of the cliff dwellings abandoned the structures. There is no conclusive evidence of where the people went or even if they survived once leaving the cliff villages. It is believed the dwellings were abandoned in the late 1200s within one or two generations. Descendants of the people who once lived in the dwellings continue to live throughout Southwest Colorado and the Southwest U.S.

The park was originally established in 1906. Boundary changes were made in 1913, 1932 and 1963. About one-sixth of the park – 8,100 acres – was designated as wilderness area in 1978, when it also was designated a World Heritage Site.

Total acreage 2002: 52,122 acres
2002 Total Recreation Visits: 411,399
2001 Budget: $4,670,000
2002 Budget: $4,806,000
2003 Budget: $4,806,000

Rocky Mountain National Park

Rocky Mountain National Park, established in 1915 might best epitomize what many think of when they think of Colorado – densely packed, towering and craggy mountains. More than 110 peaks stand more than 10,000 feet, 60 exceed 12,000 feet, dozens more are higher than 13,000. Longs Peak, at 14,255 feet, is the highest in the park. Overall, elevations in the 416-square-mile park range from roughly 8,000 feet to more than 14,000 feet.

The park straddles the Continental Divide and includes roughly 150 lakes, 364 miles of hiking trails and Trail Ridge Road – the highest, continuous paved road in North America. For those not ready for the rugged hiking in the park, Trail Ridge Road, summiting at 12,183 feet, affords fantastic views of the park and the more than 100 square miles of the park that is above timberline.

Roughly 450 miles of streams are within the park that serve as the headwaters for some of Colorado's most important waterways. Great stands of ponderosa pine, Douglas fir, lodgepole pine, aspen, subalpine fir and spruce adorn the peaks, as do mountain meadows filled with wildflowers. Roaming the meadows and forests is an array of wildlife including one of the highest concentrations of elk anywhere.

Figure 7.3 – A 1946 photograph of Bear Lake in Rocky Mountain National Park. (Denver Public Library, Western History Collection. Donald Campbell Kemp photographer. K-237.)

Almost 90% of the park is designated and managed as wilderness. It was designated as a biosphere reserve in 1976.

Total acreage 2002: 265,765 acres
2002 Total Recreation Visits: 3,005,524
2001 Budget: $9,647,000
2002 Budget: $10,082,000
2003 Budget: $10,082,000

Yucca House National Monument

Yucca House, near Cortez, Colo., in the southwest corner of the state, is the smallest of the state's lands managed by the National Park Service. It was designated a national monument in 1919. The 34 acres of this monument house a large unexcavated Ancestral Puebloan surface site. The site is a cluster of mounds suggesting much archaeological treasure when excavated. The two most prominent mounds are known as Upper House and Lower House. There are no fees or facilities at the monument. The dirt

road leading to the area is to be avoided in wet weather.
Total acreage 2002: 34 acres
2002 Total Recreation Visits: not counted
2001 Budget: $100,000
2002 Budget: $100,000
2003 Budget: $100,000

Canyons of the Ancients National Monument

President Bill Clinton signed a proclamation June 9, 2000 creating the Canyons of the Ancients National Monument under management of the Bureau of Land Management.

The 164,000-acre area contains the highest known density of archaeological sites in the United States. It is believed hunter/gatherer cultures inhabited the region more than 10,000 years ago. A farming culture later developed between 450 and 1300 A.D. when the Ancestral Northern Pueblo People lived in the area. Villages were established which evolved to the famous cliff-dwelling pueblos found in Mesa Verde. More than 20,000 archaeological sites preserve clues to past human life. Among the sites are villages, field houses, check dams, reservoirs, great kivas, cliff dwellings, shrines, sacred springs, agricultural fields, petroglyphs and sweat lodges. Some of the area has more than 100 sites per square mile.

The monument is in the Four Corners area of the state near Mesa Verde National Park. The Bureau of Land Management designated the area as the Anasazi Area of Critical Environment Concern in 1985.

Alpine Ski Areas

With 28 ski hills (29 if Arrowhead is separated from Beaver Creek), Colorado earns its slogan, "Ski Country USA." It isn't just the mountains, terrain or amount of snow that makes Colorado skiing special. It's the kind of snow that falls. High altitude and low humidity create a lighter brand of snow known as champagne powder.

A billion-dollar industry, Colorado's ski hills have transformed quiet mountain valleys into developed playgrounds. A million-dollar second home in Aspen, Vail or Telluride isn't unusual, and often the norm. The ski industry has also brought people to the high country. In only 40 years, the Eagle Valley, home of Vail, has changed from a sheep ranching community to a bustling tourist mecca with more than 41,000 year-round residents.

The size of the industry can best be described by considering it as a whole – one gigantic mountain.

• If Colorado's ski mountains were stacked on top of each other, they'd have a vertical drop of 64,128 feet – almost 12 miles – or more than twice the height of Mt. Everest.

• Skiable terrain totals more than 36,300 acres, or just shy of 56 square miles. If all that terrain is stretched to form one run 150 feet wide, it would stretch from Denver to just outside Boston – nearly 2,000 miles.

• Total uphill lift capacity is about 400,000 people per hour, enough to transport the entire state of Wyoming (population 479,602) to the top of the hill in just more than 60 minutes.

Following drought periods of the late 1970s and early 1980s, ski areas began investing heavily in artificial snowmaking. Ski resorts report snowmaking on roughly 7,200 acres statewide. The amount of water used in snowmaking varies greatly depending on temperatures and how wet or dry the resort wants to make snow on any given day. By using one example of 9,000 gallons used to make 3,100 cubic feet of snow, it computes that Colorado snowmaking guns will use 2,760 acre-feet of water to cover 7,110 acres with one foot of snow. Should three feet of artificial snow go down, that's 8,280 acre-feet of water. Some is lost, but most is returned to rivers and streams during the spring thaw – a form of water storage.

Arapahoe Basin

Where . . . . .Summit County
Base Elevation . . . . .10,780 feet
Summit Elevation . . . . . .13,050 feet
Vertical Drop . . . . .2,270 feet
Skiable Area . . . . .490 acres
Number of Trails 69
Longest Run . . . . .1.5 miles
Easiest 15%
More Difficult 40%
Most Difficult 25%

Expert Only 20%
Uphill Lift Capacity . . . . .8,700 per hour
Number of Lifts 6

Avg. Annual Snowfall . . . . . . .367 inches
Snowmaking . . . . .125 acres

Telephone 888-272-7246
Snow Phone 888-ARAPAHOE
Internet . . . . . .arapahoebasin.com

❄ ❄ ❄ ❄ ❄

Aspen Highlands

Where . . . . .Pitkin County
Base Elevation . . . . .8,040 feet
Summit Elevation . . . . . . .11,675 feet
Vertical Drop . . . . .3,635 feet
Skiable Area . . . . .790 acres
Number of Trails 131
Easiest 18%
More Difficult 30%
Most Difficult 16%
Expert Only 36%

Uphill Lift Capacity . . . . .5,400 per hour
Number of Lifts 4

Avg. Annual Snowfall . . . . . . .300 inches
Snowmaking . . . . .110 acres

Telephone 970-925-1220
Snow Phone 888-277-3676
Internet . . . . .aspensnowmass.com

❄ ❄ ❄ ❄ ❄

Aspen Mountain

Where . . . . .Pitkin County
Base Elevation . . . . .7,945 feet
Summit Elevation . . . . . . .11,212 feet
Vertical Drop . . . . .3,267 feet
Skiable Area . . . . .673 acres
Number of Trails 76
Easiest 0%
More Difficult 48%
Most Difficult 26%
Expert Only 26%

Uphill Lift Capacity . . . . . . .10,755 per hour
Number of Lifts 8

Avg. Annual Snowfall . . . . . . .300 inches
Snowmaking . . . . .210 acres

Telephone 970-925-1220
Snow Phone 888-277-3676
Internet . . . . .aspensnowmass.com

Beaver Creek

Where	Eagle County	Uphill Lift Capacity	24,739 per hour
Base Elevation	8,100 feet	Number of Lifts	14
Summit Elevation	11,440 feet		
Vertical Drop	4,040 feet	Avg. Annual Snowfall	310 inches
Skiable Area	1,625 acres	Snowmaking	605 acres
Number of Trails	146		
Longest Run	2.8 miles	Telephone	970-845-2500
Easiest	34%	Snow Phone	970-476-4888
More Difficult	39%	Internet	vailresorts.com
Most Difficult	27%		

❄ ❄ ❄ ❄ ❄

Breckenridge

Where	Summit County	Uphill Lift Capacity	36,680 per hour
Base Elevation	9,600 feet	Number of Lifts	27
Summit Elevation	12,998 feet		
Vertical Drop	3,398 feet	Avg. Annual Snowfall	300 inches
Skiable Area	2,208 acres	Snowmaking	540 acres
Number of Trails	146		
Longest Run	3.5 miles	Telephone	970-453-5000
Easiest	13%	Snow Phone	888-404-3535
More Difficult	32%	Internet	vailresorts.com
Most Difficult	55%		

❄ ❄ ❄ ❄ ❄

Buttermilk Mountain

Where	Pitkin County	Expert Only	0%
Base Elevation	7,870 feet	Uphill Lift Capacity	7,500 per hour
Summit Elevation	9,900 feet	Number of Lifts	7
Vertical Drop	2,030 feet		
Skiable Area	427 acres	Avg. Annual Snowfall	200 inches
Number of Trails	41	Snowmaking	108 acres
Longest Run	3 miles		
Easiest	35%	Telephone	970-925-1220
More Difficult	39%	Snow Phone	888-277-3676
Most Difficult	26%	Internet	skiaspen.com

Copper Mountain Resort

Where . . . . .Summit County
Base Elevation . . . . .9,712 feet
Summit Elevation . . . . . .12,313 feet
Vertical Drop . . . . .2,601 feet
Skiable Area . . . . .2,450 acres
Number of Trails 125
Longest Run . . . . .2.8 miles
Easiest 21%
More Difficult 25%
Most Difficult 36%

Expert Only 18%
Uphill Lift Capacity . . . . . . .32,088 per hour
Number of Lifts 23

Avg. Annual Snowfall . . . . .284 inches
Snowmaking . . . . .440 acres

Telephone 970-968-2882
Snow Phone 970-789-7609
Internet . . . . .coppercolorado.com

❅   ❅   ❅   ❅   ❅

Crested Butte Mountain Resort

Where . . . . .Gunnison County
Base Elevation . . . . .9,375 feet
Summit Elevation . . . . . . .12,162 feet
Vertical Drop . . . . .3,062 feet
Skiable Area . . . . .1,058 acres
Number of Trails 85
Longest Run . . . . .2.6 miles
Easiest 10%
More Difficult 25%
Most Difficult 8%

Expert Only 57%
Uphill Lift Capacity . . . . . . .18,160 per hour
Number of Lifts 14

Avg. Annual Snowfall . . . . .300 inches
Snowmaking . . . . .300 acres

Telephone 800-544-8448
Snow Phone 970-349-2323
Internet . . . . .skiCB.com

❅   ❅   ❅   ❅   ❅

Cuchara Mountain Resort *(Not operating 2003-2004 season)*

Where . . . . .Huerfano County
Base Elevation . . . . .9,248 feet
Summit Elevation . . . . . . .10,810 feet
Vertical Drop . . . . .1,562 feet
Skiable Area . . . . .230 acres
Number of Trails 28
Easiest 40%
More Difficult 40%
Most Difficult 10%
Expert Only 0%

Uphill Lift Capacity . . . . .5,000 per hour
Number of Lifts 6

Avg. Annual Snowfall . . . . .254 inches
Snowmaking 85%

Telephone 888-CUCHARA
Snow Phone . . .888-CUCHARA x250
Internet . . . . .cuchara.com

Durango Mountain Resort

Where	.La Plata County	
Base Elevation	.8,793	feet
Summit Elevation	.10,822	feet
Vertical Drop	.2,029	feet
Skiable Area	.1,200	acres
Number of Trails	.85	
Longest Run	.2.3	miles
Easiest	.23%	
More Difficult	.51%	
Most Difficult	.26%	

Expert Only	.0%	
Uphill Lift Capacity	.15,600	per hour
Number of Lifts	.11	
Avg. Annual Snowfall	.260	inches
Snowmaking	.250	acres
Telephone	.970-247-9000	
Snow Phone	.970-247-9000	
Internet	.DurangoMountainResort.com	

❄ ❄ ❄ ❄ ❄

Eldora Mountain Resort

Where	.Boulder County	
Base Elevation	.9,300	feet
Summit Elevation	.10,800	feet
Vertical Drop	.1,500	feet
Skiable Area	.680	acres
Number of Trails	.53	
Easiest	.30%	
More Difficult	.50%	
Most Difficult	.20%	
Expert Only	.0%	

Uphill Lift Capacity	.11,500	per hour
Number of Lifts	.12	
Avg. Annual Snowfall	.300	inches
Snowmaking	.90%	
Telephone	.303-440-8700	
Snow Phone	.303-440-8700	
Internet	.eldora.com	

❄ ❄ ❄ ❄ ❄

Hesperus Ski Area

Where	.Durango County	
Base Elevation	.8,100	feet
Summit Elevation	.8,880	feet
Vertical Drop	.700	feet
Skiable Area	.80	acres
Number of Trails	.13	
Longest Run	.5,500	feet
Easiest	.30%	
More Difficult	.20%	
Most Difficult	.30%	

Expert Only	.20%	
Uphill Lift Capacity	.2,000	per hour
Number of Lifts	.2	
Avg. Annual Snowfall	.150	inches
Snowmaking	.0%	
Telephone	.970-259-3711	
Snow Phone		
Internet	.durango.com	

Howelsen Hill Ski Area

Where . . . . .Routt County
Base Elevation . . . . .6,696 feet
Summit Elevation . . . . . . , , ,7,136 feet
Vertical Drop . . . . .440 feet
Skiable Area . . . . .150 acres
Number of Trails 15
Longest Run . . . . .5,280 feet
Easiest 20%
More Difficult 30%
Most Difficult 50%

Expert Only 0%
Uphill Lift Capacity . . . . .2,057 per hour
Number of Lifts 3

Avg. Annual Snowfall . . . . .250 inches
Snowmaking 30%

Telephone 970-879-2043
Snow Phone 970-879-8499

❄ ❄ ❄ ❄ ❄

Kendall Mountain

Where . . . .San Juan County
Skiable Area . . . . .35 acres
Number of Trails 11
Number of Lifts 1
Telephone . .970-387-5522
Internet . . . . . .Silverton.org

❄ ❄ ❄ ❄ ❄

Keystone Resort

Where . . . . .Summit County
Base Elevation . . . . .9,300 feet
Summit Elevation . . . . . . .12,200 feet
Vertical Drop . . . . .2,900 feet
Skiable Area . . . . .1,861 acres
Number of Trails 116
Longest Run . . . . .3 miles
Easiest 12%
More Difficult 34%
Most Difficult 54%

Expert Only 0%
Uphill Lift Capacity . . . . . . .34,564 per hour
Number of Lifts 21

Avg. Annual Snowfall . . . . .230 inches
Snowmaking . . . . .956 acres

Telephone 800-842-8087
Snow Phone 970-496-4111
Internet . . . . . .Keystoneresort.com

Loveland Ski Area

Where . . . . .Clear Creek County
Base Elevation . . . . .10,600 feet
Summit Elevation . . . . .12,700 feet
Vertical Drop . . . . .2,410 feet
Skiable Area . . . . .1,365 acres
Number of Trails 70
Longest Run . . . . .2 miles
Easiest 17%
More Difficult 42%
Most Difficult 41%

Expert Only 0%
Uphill Lift Capacity . . . . . . .14,293 per hour
Number of Lifts 11

Avg. Annual Snowfall . . . . .400 inches
Snowmaking 17%

Telephone 800-736-3SKI
Snow Phone 303-571-5554
Internet . . . . .Skiloveland.com

❄   ❄   ❄   ❄   ❄

Monarch Ski and Snowboard Area

Where . . . . .Gunnison County
Base Elevation . . . . .10,790 feet
Summit Elevation . . . . .11,961 feet
Vertical Drop . . . . .1,171 feet
Skiable Area . . . . .670 acres
Number of Trails 54
Longest Run . . . . .10,560 feet
Easiest 21%
More Difficult 37%
Most Difficult 42%

Expert Only 0%
Uphill Lift Capacity . . . . .6,000 per hour
Number of Lifts 5

Avg. Annual Snowfall . . . . .350 inches
Snowmaking 0

Telephone 888-996-7669
Snow Phone 800-228-7943
Internet . . . . .Skimonarch.com

❄   ❄   ❄   ❄   ❄

Powderhorn Resort

Where . . . . .Mesa County
Base Elevation . . . . .8,200 feet
Summit Elevation . . . . .9,850 feet
Vertical Drop . . . . .1,650 feet
Skiable Area . . . . .510 acres
Number of Trails 29
Longest Run . . . . .2.2 miles
Easiest 20%
More Difficult 50%
Most Difficult 15%

Expert Only 15%
Uphill Lift Capacity . . . . .4,370 per hour
Number of Lifts 4

Avg. Annual Snowfall . . . . .220 inches
Snowmaking 15%

Telephone 970-268-5700
Snow Phone 970-268-5700
Internet . . . . .Powderhorn.com

Silverton Mountain

Where . . . . .San Juan County
Base Elevation . . . . .10,400 feet
Summit Elevation . . . . . . .13,300 feet
Vertical Drop . . . . .2,900 feet
Skiable Area . . . . .n/a
Number of Trails . . .All backcountry
Longest Run . . . . .n/a
Easiest 0%
More Difficult 0%
Most Difficult 100%

Maximum 475 visitors per day
Number of Lifts 1

Avg. Annual Snowfall . . . . .400 inches
Snowmaking 0%

Telephone 970-387-5706
Internet . . .Silvertonmountain.com

❄ ❄ ❄ ❄ ❄

Ski Cooper

Where . . . . .Fremont County
Base Elevation . . . . .10,500 feet
Summit Elevation . . . . . . .11,700 feet
Vertical Drop . . . . .1,200 feet
Skiable Area . . . . .400 acres
Number of Trails 26
Longest Run . . . . .1.4 miles
Easiest 30%
More Difficult 40%
Most Difficult 30%

Expert Only 0%
Uphill Lift Capacity . . . . .3,300 per hour
Number of Lifts 5

Avg. Annual Snowfall . . . . .250 inches
Snowmaking 0

Telephone 719-486-3684
Snow Phone 719-486-2277
Internet . . . . .Skicooper.com

❄ ❄ ❄ ❄ ❄

Snowmass Mountain

Where . . . . .Pitkin County
Base Elevation . . . . .8,104 feet
Summit Elevation . . . . . . .12,510 feet
Vertical Drop . . . . .4,406 feet
Skiable Area . . . . .3,010 acres
Number of Trails 84
Longest Run . . . . .4.2 miles
Easiest 7%
More Difficult 55%
Most Difficult 18%

Expert Only 20%
Uphill Lift Capacity . . . . . . .27,968 per hour
Number of Lifts 21

Avg. Annual Snowfall . . . . .300 inches
Snowmaking . . . . .180 acres

Telephone 970-923-1220
Snow Phone 888-277-3676
Internet . . . . .Aspensnowmass.com

187

Sol Vista Golf and Ski Ranch

Where ....Grand County
Base Elevation ....8,202 feet
Summit Elevation ....9,202 feet
Vertical Drop ....1,000 feet
Skiable Area ....406 acres
Number of Trails 33
Longest Run ....1.5 miles
Easiest 30%
More Difficult 50%
Most Difficult 20%

Expert Only 0%
Uphill Lift Capacity ....6,000 per hour
Number of Lifts 5

Avg. Annual Snowfall ....220 inches
Snowmaking ....244 acres

Telephone 866-SOLVISTA
Snow Phone 800-754-7458
Internet ....Solvista.com

❄ ❄ ❄ ❄ ❄

Steamboat Ski Resort

Where ....Routt County
Base Elevation ....6,900 feet
Summit Elevation ....10,568 feet
Vertical Drop ....3,668 feet
Skiable Area ....2,939 acres
Number of Trails 142
Longest Run ....15,840 feet
Easiest 13%
More Difficult 56%
Most Difficult 31%

Expert Only 0%
Uphill Lift Capacity ....32,158 per hour
Number of Lifts 20

Avg. Annual Snowfall ....363 inches
Snowmaking 15%

Telephone 970-879-6111
Snow Phone 970-879-7300
Internet ......Steamboat-ski.com

❄ ❄ ❄ ❄ ❄

Sunlight Mountain Resort

Where ....Garfield County
Base Elevation ....7,885 feet
Summit Elevation ....9,895 feet
Vertical Drop ....2,010 feet
Skiable Area ....460 acres
Number of Trails 66
Longest Run ....13,200 feet
Easiest 20%
More Difficult 55%
Most Difficult 20%

Expert Only 5%
Uphill Lift Capacity ....4,600 per hour
Number of Lifts 4

Avg. Annual Snowfall ....300 inches
Snowmaking 12%

Telephone 970-945-7491
Snow Phone 800-445-7931
Internet ....Sunlightmtn.com

Telluride

Where	Telluride County	
Base Elevation	8,725	feet
Summit Elevation	12,260	feet
Vertical Drop	3,535	feet
Skiable Area	1,700	acres
Number of Trails	84	
Longest Run	4.6	miles
Easiest	24%	
More Difficult	38%	
Most Difficult	38%	

Expert Only	0%	
Uphill Lift Capacity	21,186	per hour
Number of Lifts	16	
Avg. Annual Snowfall	309	inches
Snowmaking	15%	
Telephone	970-728-6900	
Snow Phone	970-728-7425	
Internet	Tellurideskiresort.com	

❄ ❄ ❄ ❄ ❄

Vail

Where	Eagle County	
Base Elevation	8,120	feet
Summit Elevation	11,570	feet
Vertical Drop	3,450	feet
Skiable Area	5,289	acres
Number of Trails	193	
Longest Run	3	miles
Easiest	18%	
More Difficult	29%	
Most Difficult	53%	

Expert Only	0%	
Uphill Lift Capacity	53,381	per hour
Number of Lifts	34	
Avg. Annual Snowfall	347	inches
Snowmaking	390	acres
Telephone	970-845-2602	
Snow Phone	970-476-4888	
Internet	vailresorts.com	

❄ ❄ ❄ ❄ ❄

Winter Park Resort

Where	GrandCounty	
Base Elevation	9,000	feet
Summit Elevation	12,060	feet
Vertical Drop	3,060	feet
Skiable Area	2,762	acres
Number of Trails	134	
Longest Run	5.1	miles
Easiest	9%	
More Difficult	21%	
Most Difficult	57%	

Expert Only	13%	
Uphill Lift Capacity	35,510	per hour
Number of Lifts	21	
Avg. Annual Snowfall	359	inches
Snowmaking	294	acres
Telephone	970-726-5514	
Snow Phone	303-572-SNOW	
Internet	skiwinterpark.com	

Wolf Creek Ski Area

Where . . . . .Mineral County

Base Elevation . . . . .10,300 feet

Summit Elevation . . . . . . .11,904 feet

Vertical Drop . . . . .1,604 feet

Skiable Area . . . . .1,600 acres

Number of Trails 77

Longest Run . . . . .2 miles

Easiest 20%

More Difficult 35%

Most Difficult 25%

Expert Only 20%

Uphill Lift Capacity . . . . .4,200 per hour

Number of Lifts 6

Avg. Annual Snowfall . . . . .465 inches

Snowmaking 0

Telephone 970-264-5639

Snow Phone 800-SKI-WOLF

Internet . . . . .wolfcreekski.com

Figure 7.4 — Skiers enjoy Winter Park Resort with the Continental Divide as a backdrop. (Photo courtesy Winter Park Resort.)

Colorado Skier Days per year

Compiled by Colorado Ski Country USA. Only CSCUSA member resorts reported.

Destination Resorts

	93-94	94-95	95-96	96-97	97-98	98-99	99-00	00-01	01-02
Aspen Highlands	106,197	159,288	153,764	157,053	149,963	142,090	127,389	140,640	136,136
Aspen Mtn	359,846	329,535	322,338	334,512	345,351	334,536	331,121	319,343	310,381
Buttermilk Mtn	172,948	168,439	175,940	154,028	180,006	178,089	158,194	148,826	145,683
Crested Butte	530,088	485,840	507,309	519,250	549,660	462,478	414,642	367,263	336,483
Cuchara Mtn.	17,300	not open	19,735	not open	39,760	21,678	32,154	DNO	DNO
Durango Mtn	302,103	382,839	307,442	341,643	328,705	304,735	235,000	321,600	250,500
Howelsen Hill	16,171	14,095	17,768	18,736	14,946	14,475	14,000	14,000	15,208
Monarch	158,148	162,982	136,074	145,733	148,160	140,000	127,215	147,266	138,850
Powderhorn	61,202	80,241	52,466	71,689	88,196	55,613	71,941	70,118	76,456
Snowmass	814,852	767,509	690,067	788,620	884,066	777,140	707,600	740,241	676,505
Steamboat	1,021,140	1,013,606	1,017,342	1,102,751	1,053,145	1,013,254	1,024,832	1,003,317	1,001,003
Sunlight	88,251	93,952	91,078	102,096	102,389	78,290	77,047	84,104	82,742
Telluride	300,388	301,748	270,916	306,507	375,027	382,467	309,737	334,506	341,370
Wolf Creek	140,456	157,995	124,478	152,971	158,235	202,053	114,802	187,116	170,847
Sub Total	4,089,099	4,118,069	3,886,717	4,195,589	4,417,609	4,106898	3,745,674	3,878,340	3,682,164

Front Range Destination Resorts

	93-94	94-95	95-96	96-97	97-98	98-99	99-00	00-01	01-02
Arapahoe Basin	257,358	262,240	241,435	234,257	215,296	267,406	220,945	240,406	151,678
Arrowhead	23,721	28,641	21,729	not open	not open	not open	not open	not open	not open
Beaver Creek	504,516	538,897	554,443	644,451	668,520	614549	586,004	676,528	675,956
Breckenridge	1,215,013	1,227,357	1,357,790	1,341,179	1,300,883	1,385,927	1,444,365	1,422,783	1,468,518
Copper Mtn	842,210	770,973	967,074	943,713	921,065	867,394	803,312	922,888	1,005,913
Keystone	1,095,857	1,042,171	1,057,568	1,217,359	1,149,270	1,253,192	1,192,198	1,230,100	1,069,111
Sol Vista	93,516	92,547	91,016	95,401	107,399	90,330	92,514	71,303	62,837
Vail	1,527,698	1,568,360	1,652,247	1,686,790	1,597,932	1,334,939	1,371,702	1,645,902	1,536,024
Winter Park	1,008,040	986,077	1,012,580	991,393	1,042,290	980,408	902,827	978,539	975,256
Sub Total	6,567,929	6,517,263	6,955,882	7,154,543	7,002,655	6,752,798	6,612,922	7,258,449	6,945,293

Front Range Resorts

	93-94	94-95	95-96	96-97	97-98	98-99	99-00	00-01	01-02
Berthoud Pass	not open	not open	not open	not open	10,735	20,101	16,870	20,160	0
Eldora Mtn	145,011	145,370	171,073	174,237	202,136	175,939	229,785	233,741	250,000
Loveland	295,000	258,000	307,200	251,855	264,532	230,333	225,896	209,757	199,781
Ski Cooper	67,193	66,404	66,186	68,299	82,052	62,145	60,171	66,225	68,893
Sub Total	507,204	469,774	544,459	494,391	559,455	506,669	532,722	529,883	518,674

| Total All Areas | 11,164,232 | 11,105,106 | 11,387,058 | 11,844,523 | 11,979,719 | 11,366,365 | 10,891,318 | 11,666,672 | 11,146,131 |

+ / - from previous year

	93-94	94-95	95-96	96-97	97-98	98-99	99-00	00-01	01-02
	52,942	(59,126)	281,952	457,465	135,196	(613,354)	(475,047)	775,354	(520,541)
Percent +/-	0.48%	(0.53%)	2.54%	4.02%	1.33%	(5.12%)	(4.18%)	7.12%	(5.0%)

191

8 Military

Influence and impact of the United States military on Colorado remains substantial despite the recent closing, or planned closing, of three bases – Lowry Air Force Base, Fitzsimons Army Medical Center and Rocky Mountain Arsenal.

Today, nine military installations operate in Colorado. They employ 29,733 military personnel and 10,183 civilians (fiscal year 2002). The bases cover 477,457 acres. U.S. Department of Defense spending in Colorado totals more than $5.3 billion annually. More than $2.6 billion represent Department of Defense contracts awarded to Colorado-based companies that supply services such as aircraft, missile defense, satellite or weapons designs, equipment and supplies.

Colorado's most significant contribution to national defense is its status as home to the United States Space Command, an arm of the military that concerns itself primarily with space-based technologies such as navigation, communication and spy satellites, North American Aerospace Defense Command and weapons systems. It is an ultra-high technology command that incorporates all branches of the military. Many of the activities are highly classified.

United States Space Command is based at Peterson Air Force Base near Colorado Springs. Air Force Space Command also is based at Peterson, along with the newly formed Northern Command. Associated with Space Command activities are Schriever Air Force Base, Buckley Air Force Base and the Cheyenne Mountain complex. Activity at Schriever is centered around the nation's satellite systems: the Global Positioning System (GPS), and the military's spy and communications satellite system. Cheyenne Mountain is home to NORAD, a broad-based surveillance system that patrols the skies and space. NORAD is jointly staffed by the United States and Canada. Activity at Buckley is highly classified. Virtually no public information is available.

The Air Force Academy – one of three national service academies in the U.S. – is just north of Colorado Springs. The 18,000-acre campus at the base of the Rocky Mountains is a major tourist attraction and one of the finest academic institutions in America. Approximately 4,000 cadets are enrolled.

The United States Army opened Fort Carson south of Colorado Springs in 1942. The huge 373,300-acre base has served as an important training post for Army personnel ever since. Today more than 14,000 soldiers are on base, while more than 2,000 civilians are employed there. Other Army posts in the state include the largely dormant Rocky Mountain Arsenal and the Pueblo Chemical Depot. Fitzsimons Army Medical Center near Denver has been decommissioned, but activities are under way to eventually transfer the University of Colorado Health Sciences center to the site east of Denver.

Fort Carson

World War II created the need for trained soldiers. Camp Carson, named for frontiersman Brig. Gen. Christopher "Kit" Carson, opened in 1942 on 60,048 acres south of Colorado Springs. 5,533 acres were donated by the city of Colorado Springs, 29,676 were purchased from private land owners, 262 were acquired from the Department of the Interior and 24,577 were leased from the state of Colorado. The original cost of construction was $30,054,390. At the peak of construction, nearly 11,500 workers were employed to build the much-needed war-training post. During World War II, 104,165 soldiers trained at Camp Carson. In 1943, approximately 43,000 military personnel were stationed at the camp.

Figure 8.1 -- Group portrait of the 87th Mountain Infantry Battalion (Reinforced), Company C, taken at Fort Carson in 1942. (Denver Public Library, Western History Collection. TMD-199.)

Sharing the post were nearly 9,000 German, Italian and some Japanese prisoners of war.

Camp Carson grew quiet after World War II. Troop strength in 1946 dropped to roughly 600. Another 320 were patients in the hospital. The camp began to build again from this low point. During the Korean War, another 100,000 soldiers passed through Carson. Activity again increased during the Vietnam conflict. 14,000 Carson-trained soldiers were sent to Vietnam in 1966, 9,000 in 1967, 6,000 in 1968. When the 1st Brigade of the 5th Infantry Division was airlifted to Da Nang in July 1968, it was the second largest airlift in history. Peak troop strength at Carson during Vietnam was 24,735

Camp Carson became a permanent Fort Carson in 1954. The facility continues to evolve and expand. It now covers 373,300 acres and is staffed by nearly 17,000 people.

Rocky Mountain Arsenal

Construction of Rocky Mountain Arsenal began June 30, 1942, in response to World War II. Its purpose was to manufacture chemical weapons. The facility northeast of Denver was selected as much for Denver's transportation hub capabilities as it was for its distance – and therefore safety – from the east and west coasts. Construction costs were more than $50 million and production of weapons was started only six months after groundbreaking. The production of chemical weapons was considered a deterrent. Axis powers were producing chemical weapons and it was thought America could prevent them from using them by promising immediate retaliation. During the first year of production, Rocky Mountain Arsenal outproduced Axis nations by 150%.

Three main chemicals were manufactured at Rocky Mountain Arsenal: mustard gas, Lewisite and chlorine gas. Chlorine gas, used in World War I, had become ineffective due to protective measures available, but it was manufactured as part of the recipe for mustard gas and Lewisite. Mustard gas is said to smell like mustard or garlic. The more-lethal Lewisite is said to smell like geraniums. It is made by combining chlorine, acetylene and arsenic.

Incendiary bombs were another Rocky Mountain Arsenal product. The most common type was the napalm bomb, used during the campaign in the Pacific against the Japanese in World War II. On March 9 and 10, 1945, U.S. forces bombed Tokyo with 1,500 tons of napalm bombs, all produced at Rocky Mountain Arsenal. Napalm, an explosive mix of jellied gasoline, went on to gain dubious notoriety for its use in Vietnam.

The Rose Hill POW camp housed as many as 300 German soldiers during World War II on Arsenal land.

Production was decreased after World War II, but increased again in 1950 in response to the communist threat and the Korean War. By 1953 a secret installation was completed to produce deadly GB nerve gas. For the next four years, Rocky Mountain Arsenal was the major production site for GB nerve gas in the free world.

Waste liquids associated with the production of chemical weapons at the plant – more than 250 million gallons worth – were stored in evaporation ponds, some of them unlined. This contaminated legacy would create what is today one of the largest and most expensive superfund clean-up sites in the United States.

By 1952, the Army had leased part of the facility to private interests to produce pesticides. The Army spent the next 20 years slowly demilitarizing the plant, even though production of GB nerve gas continued through the 1960s. In 1962, the plant was used to manufacture rocket fuel for Titan rockets.

As it became clear the serious environmental and health problems were resulting from plant by-products, the government started pumping 175 million gallons of treated waste into a 12,000-foot well to rid itself of the problem. A series of earthquakes subsequently hit the Denver area. Many geologists blamed the well and the activity was ended.

Through the 1970s and 1980s the focus at Rocky Mountain Arsenal shifted from manufacturing chemical weapons to destroying chemical weapons. Through it all, massive clean-up studies and efforts were initiated. Those efforts continue today with cumulative costs of many billions of dollars. A silver lining to the ghastly Rocky Mountain Arsenal story is found in a small wildlife preserve and viewing area now open on Arsenal land.

Pueblo Depot

This 23,121-acre site 15 miles east of Pueblo has historically been used as a storage site for many of the chemical agents produced at the Rocky Mountain Arsenal. At least 780,000 mustard gas munitions are stored at the plant in specially designed igloos. The Department of Defense is studying technologies for destroying the gas.

Peterson Air Force Base

What started as a small Army Air Base to train photo reconnaissance specialists has become the headquarters for United States Space Command, Air Force Space Command, and the nascent Northern Command.

The 1,278-acre base south and east of Colorado Springs is the hub of operations for perhaps the most sophisticated and technologically advanced portion of the U.S. military complex. From Peterson the fantastic operations of three other Colorado Air Force bases are directed.

All missile warning, space surveillance and satellite control units operate under the umbrella of Peterson AFB. And while many might regard this high-tech world as the domain only of spy novels and Hollywood movies, technologies employed here touch lives everyday. The Global Positioning System (GPS) of satellites is used by every facet of civilian transportation from shipping and trucking lines right down to afternoon hikers. Technologies employed in communications and surveillance satellites spill over to the private sector. Military use of these space-age technologies has changed the face of war. The Persian Gulf War in the early 1990s, the ongoing conflict in Afghanistan, Central Asia and the Iraq War have shown that war can be waged and won almost entirely from the air and from space.

The three Colorado arms of Space Command under Peterson are Schriever Air Force Base in Colorado Springs, North American Aerospace Defense Command (NORAD) in the Cheyenne Mountain complex near Colorado Springs, and Buckley Air Force Base near Denver.

In general, Schriever handles satellite control, while NORAD handles air and deep-space surveillance and tracking. Activities at Buckley remain highly classified.

The newly formed Northern Command is charged with finding and destroying terrorist threats in North America and to providing assistance to civilian agencies in matters of terrorist threats or disaster response. Northern Command is expected to employ 400 in a new, $90 million, 157,000-square-foot headquarters at Peterson.

Schriever Air Force Base

Schriever is the base of satellite control under the auspices of the 50th Space Wing. Both GPS satellite constellations and communication satellite constellations are managed here on 4,102 acres by 2,329 military personnel and 369 civilians.

Navstar Global Positioning System

The Navstar Global Positioning System (GPS) is a 24-satellite system that provides 24-hour navigation data to military and civilian users all over the world. The following capabilities of the system were provided by Air Force Space Command.

• Extremely accurate, three-dimensional location information (latitude, longitude and altitude), velocity and precise time.
• A worldwide common grid easily converted to any local grid.
• Passive all-weather operations.
• Continuous real-time information.
• Support to an unlimited number of users and areas.
• Support to civilian users at a slightly less accurate level.

GPS satellites orbit Earth every 12 hours, emitting continuous navigation signals. With proper equipment, users can receive these signals to calculate time, location and velocity. The signals are so accurate, time can be figured to within a millionth of a second, velocity within a fraction of a mile-per-hour and location to within 1 meter. Receivers are used in aircraft, ships, land vehicles and handheld devices.

The GPS constellation is designed and operated as a 24-satellite system. The Delta II expendable launch vehicle is used to launch GPS satellites from Cape Canaveral into nearly 11,000-mile circular orbits. While orbiting, the systems transmit signals on two different L-band frequencies. Satellite design life is 7.5 years.

The GPS-dedicated ground system consists of five monitor stations and four ground antennas around the world. The monitor stations use receivers to passively track the navigation signals on all satellites. Information is then processed and used to update the navigation messages.

Crews send updated navigation information to GPS satellites through ground antennas.

The general characteristics of each satellite are:

Weight:	1,860 pounds in orbit.
Orbit Altitude:	10,900 nautical miles.
Power Plant:	Solar panel array generating 800 watts.
Dimensions:	5 feet wide, 17.5 feet long including wingspan.

Milstar Satellite Communications System

Air Force Space Command has provided the following information.

Milstar is a joint service satellite communications system that provides secure, jam-resistant, worldwide communications to meet essential wartime requirements for high-priority military users. The multi-satellite constellations will link command authorities with resources including ships, submarines, aircraft and ground stations.

The operational Milstar satellite constellation will consist of four satellites positioned around the earth in geosynchronous orbits. Each mid-latitude satellite weighs approximately 10,000 pounds and has a design life of 10 years.

The first Milstar satellite was launched in 1994, the second in 1995, the third in 1999. A total of six launches are planned.

Each Milstar satellite serves as a "smart switchboard in space" by directing traffic from terminal to terminal anywhere on Earth. Since the satellite actually processes the communications signal and can link with other Milstar satellites through crosslinks, the requirement for ground-controlled switching is significantly reduced. The satellite establishes, maintains, reconfigures and disassembles required communications circuits as directed by the users. Milstar terminals provide encrypted voice, data, teletype or facsimile communications.

The general characteristics of each satellite are:

Weight: About 10,000 pounds.

Orbit Altitude: 22,250 nautical miles (inclined geostationary orbit).

Power Plant: Solar panel generating 8,000 watts.

Payload: Low data rate communications (voice, data, teletype, facsimile) at 75 bits per second to 2,400bps. Medium data rate communications (voice, data, teletype, facsimile) at 4.8 kilobits per second to 1.54 Megabits per second (satellites 3 through 6 only).

Launch vehicle: Titan IVB/Centaur upper stage.

Cheyenne Mountain Operation Center

Surrounded by 2,000 feet of solid granite, the Cheyenne Mountain Operation Center is deep inside Cheyenne Mountain near Colorado Springs. The center contains operational elements of United States Space

Command, Air Force Space Command and the North American Aerospace Defense Command. Air Force personnel account for more than half of the 1,100-person staff, but all of the armed forces are represented, as are Canadian forces.

The idea of an underground, hardened command-and-control center was first broached in 1956 as a defense against Soviet bombers. Following the 1957 launch of Sputnik, the focus was changed to concentrate on early warning and the ballistic missile threat. Cheyenne Mountain was selected as the site because of its central North American position, the area's low seismic activity and the already established military presence in Colorado Springs.

Construction began in June of 1961. 1.5 million pounds of dynamite were used to excavate approximately 700,000 tons of granite. The complex was completely operational on April 20, 1966 at a cost of $142 million dollars. The Government Accounting Office reports the facility would cost approximately $20 billion to construct today.

The underground campus was designed to ensure a 70% probability of continuing operation against a five megaton weapon detonated within three miles. The 4.5-acre complex, 2,000 feet underground, contains 15 buildings, 12 of which are three stories high. Each building has its own tunnel and functions independently of the other structures. The complex entrance is protected by three blast doors each made of steel, 3.5 feet thick and weighing 25 tons. The entire complex is mounted on 1,319, 1,000-pound springs that allow the complex to sway up to 12 inches in any direction. A total of 110,000 rock bolts reinforce the tunnel structure.

Primary power is provided by the city of Colorado Springs. Back-up power comes from a series of six 2,800-horsepower diesel engines and an array of 3,500 batteries. Four water reservoirs have a capacity of six million gallons of water. A natural spring under one of the buildings supplies the complex with between 30,000 and 120,000 gallons of water a day, of which up to 15,000 gallons is needed for daily operations.

Annual operating costs of the facility is roughly $23 million.

The primary operations components of the facility include the Space Control Center, the Air Warning Center and the Missile Warning Center. Supporting those missions are the Command Center, Combined Intelligence Watch, the Systems Center and Weather Center.

Space Control Center

The Space Control Center's (SCC) primary objective is to detect, track, identify and catalog all man-made objects orbiting earth. The SCC maintains a current computerized catalog of all orbiting man-made objects, charts preset positions, plots future orbital paths and forecasts times and general location of objects re-entering the atmosphere.

Since 1957, more than 26,000 man-made objects have been catalogued, many of which have re-entered the atmosphere. At present, the SCC tracks more than 8,300 man-made objects. About 7% of those are functional payloads or satellites.

An important aspect of the tracking mission is to avoid in-space collisions for the Space Shuttle and the International Space Station. The SCC constructs a theoretical box around a high-interest object such as the Space Shuttle and projects its flight 36 to 72 hours out. If any of the 8,300 catalogued objects intersect the theoretical box, SCC alerts NASA to the danger. Between 1981 and December, 2001, NASA moved the Space Shuttle 11 times and the Space Station four times based on SCC tracking.

The SCC relies on three Ground-Based Electro-Optical Deep Space Surveillance sites to monitor the heavens. These tracking stations are in Socorro, N.M., Maui, Hawaii, and Diego Garcia, British Indian Ocean Territories. The tracking system can track objects as small as a basketball more than 20,000 miles in space.

Air Warning Center

The Air Warning Center is the hub of air defense for North America. It provides command-and-control of the air surveillance and defense network using air and ground-based radars around North America. The AWC closely monitors the periphery of Canada and the United States to detect any aircraft or cruise missile violating sovereign airspace or that might represent a threat.

Roughly 7,000 aircraft per day, or 2.5 million a year, enter North American Airspace. A small percentage are classified as unknown. In year 2000, the total number of unknowns was 115. It is AWC's mission to determine the identity of each. Radar and airborne interceptors are used to identify unknown aircraft.

Missile Warning Center

The Missile Warning Center (MWC) uses a worldwide communications and sensor network to provide warning of missile attacks against North America or against friendly forces overseas. The MWC is divided into strategic and theater missions. Strategic missions focus on missiles launched anywhere on Earth that are a potential threat to North America. The theater mission is primarily concerned with protecting forces overseas.

Command Center

The Command Center is the fusion point of all operations inside Cheyenne Mountain. The Command Director and crew serve as NORAD's and USSPACECOM's direct representative for monitoring, processing and interpreting missile, space or air events that threaten North America or overseas operations.

The Command Center fuses data from other centers and passes it to national command authorities of the United States and Canada. Regional command centers overseas also have access to this intelligence.

Military personnel in Colorado, FY 2002

Source Washington Headquarters Service, Department of Defense
(Includes retired military personnel)

	Total	Army	Navy and Marine Corps	Air Force	Other Defense
Personnel - Total	60,752	26,621	4,668	26,975	2,488
Active Duty Military	29,735	14,951	908	13,874	0
Civilian	10,183	2,682	48	4,965	2,488
Reserve / National Guard	20,836	8,988	3,712	8,136	0

Payroll Expenditures, 2002 ($000)

	Total	Army	Navy and Marine Corps	Air Force	Other Defense
Payroll Outlays - Total	2,686,331	991,903	172,777	1,372,854	148,797
Active Duty Military Pay	1,119,988	523,285	36,935	559,768	0
Civilian Pay	498,696	116,632	2,192	231,075	148,797
Reserve / National Guard Pay	127,966	49,234	10,403	68,329	0
Retired Military Pay	939,681	302,752	123,247	513,682	0

Contracts, 2002 ($000)

	Total	Army	Navy and Marine Corps	Air Force	Other Defense
Total	2,623,565	657,501	99,752	1,583,965	282,347
Supply and Equip. Contracts	317,229	68,116	56,406	90,053	102,654
RDT and E Contracts	940,091	108,861	22,467	795,397	13,366
Service Contracts	1,207,106	321,960	20,879	697,940	166,327
Construction Contracts	133,204	132,629,0	0	575	0
Civil Function Contracts	25,935	25,935	0	0	0
Grants	32,009	19,029	6,742	6,032	206

Total Colorado Department of Defense Expenditures, 2002 ($000)

	Total	Army	Navy and Marine Corps	Air Force	Other Defense
Expenditures - Total	5,341,905	1,668,433	279,271	2,962,851	431,350

Summary of contract dollars awarded in Colorado, 2002 ($000)
Source Washington Headquarters Service, Department of Defense

	Total	Army	Navy and Marine Corps	Air Force	Other Defense
Fiscal Year					
2001	2,302,817	498,138	71,209	1,472,520	260,949
2000	2,214,033	488,735	77,713	1,383,427	264,158
1999	2,441,790	417,496	58,870	1,715,261	250,164
1998	2,380,692	387,826	61,866	1,722,008	208,991
1997	1,900,224	369,664	67,407	1,350,648	112,505
1996	2,045,074	366,110	47,192	1,486,413	145,360
1995	2,260,461	409,299	70,385	1,498,432	282,345
1994	2,619,907	481,670	67,122	1,937,279	133,836

Top 10 expenditures by location, 2002 ($000)

Location	Total	Payroll Outlays	Grants/ Contracts
Colorado Springs	1,197,567	450,093	747,474
Denver	761,720	258,434	503,286
Fort Carson	714,735	585,335	129,400
Peterson AFB	375,576	265,084	110,492
Air Force Academy	361,371	294,294	67,077
Schriever AFB	268,481	104,208	164,273
Littleton	203,961	40,035	163,926
Aurora	186,878	165,366	21,512
Boulder	186,122	14,270	171,852
Englewood	134,656	20,198	114,458

Top 10 military and civilian personnel by location, 2002
(Does not include retired military personnel)

Location	Total	Military	Civilian
Fort Carson	16,084	14,219	1,865
Air Force Academy	7,754	6,284	1,470
Peterson AFB	5,413	3,484	1,929
Denver	2,908	1,166	1,742
Schriever AFB	2,454	1,965	489
Buckley AGB	1,396	1,352	44
Aurora	1,151	138	1,013
Colorado Springs	571	215	356
Cheyenne Mtn.	527	527	0
Lowry AFB	308	0	308

Active duty military and civilian Department of Defense employees, Sept. 30, 2002

INST./CITY	Army Military	Navy Military	Marine Military	Air Force Military	Subtotal Military	Army Civilian	Navy / Marine Civilian	Air Force Civilian	Other Civilian	Subtotal Civilian	Total All DoD
Air Force Academy	0	0	0	6,284	6,284	6	0	1,398	66	1,470	7,754
Aurora	0	19	107	12	138	169	2	609	233	1,013	1,151
Buckley AGB	255	0	0	1,097	1,352	0	0	44	0	44	1,396
Cheyenne Mtn	0	0	0	527	527	0	0	0	0	0	527
Colorado City	235	0	0	0	235	0	0	0	0	0	235
Colorado Springs	0	111	1	103	215	189	16	30	91	356	571
Denver	162	485	83	436	1,166	67	19	23	1,633	1,742	2,908
Englewood	0	0	0	2	2	84	0	14	78	176	178
Fort Carson	14,115	9	0	95	14,219	1,744	0	6	115	1,865	16,084
Greeley	0	0	0	6	6	0	0	110	0	110	115
Lowry AFB	0	0	0	0	0	0	0	308	0	308	308
Peterson AFB	171	0	46	3,267	3,484	6	1	1,823	99	1,929	5,413
Pueblo	0	0	0	3	3	172	0	0	4	176	179
Schriever AFB	0	0	0	1,965	1,965	0	0	489	0	489	2,454
Other	7	1	0	34	42	243	8	80	161	492	534
State Total	14,951	647	261	13,874	29,733	2,682	48	4,965	2,488	10,183	39,916

Top 10 Colorado defense contractors by award, 2002 ($000)
Source: Washington Headquarters Services, Department of Defense

Contractor Name	Amount
Lockheed Martin Corp.	854,216
ITT Industries Inc.	257,684
Ball Corp.	141,184
Northrop Gruman	112,723
Foster Wheeler Ltd.	83,954
CH2M Hill Companies Ltd	49,454
Berkshire Hathaway	47,372
Space Imaging LLC	44,455
Agilent Technologies Inc	38,425
SI International LLC	32,986

Where the military buys by county and armed service FY 2002 ($000)
Source: Department of Defense, Directorate for Information Operations and Reports, Statistical Information Analysis Division.

	Total	Army	Navy	Air Force	Defense Logistics	Corp of Eng.	Other
Colorado	2,623,545	631,564	99,746	1,583,956	29,540	25,935	252,804
Adams	226,385	139,535	4,260	21,773	11,739	231	48,847
Alamosa	84	0	60	0	0	24	0
Arapahoe	327,532	65,138	27,018	208,082	1,701	3,340	22,252
Archuleta	20	0	0	0	0	20	0
Bent	3,099	151	0	0	0	2,948	0
Boulder	206,617	32,370	14,381	134,155	521	406	24,784
Chaffee	25	25	0	0	0	0	0
Clear Creek	2	0	0	0	0	2	0
Costilla	69	0	0	0	69	0	0
Delta	888	0	0	41	761	86	0
Denver	515,494	25,016	7,129	446,023	2,116	9,634	25,574
Douglas	8,068	174	953	1,306	4,367	5	1,263
Eagle	647	607	0	32	0	8	0
El Paso	1,251,269	329,162	28,358	758,421	3,669	3,100	128,560
Fremont	321	0	0	273	0	0	50
Garfield	94	5	0	26	62	0	0
Gilpin	14	0	14	0	0	0	0
Gunnison	105	4	70	0	0	31	0
Jefferson	20,441	9,055	6,110	4,598	80	280	318
La Plata	670	105	0	485	29	6	45
Lake	167	0	0	0	167	0	0
Larimer	15,644	1,016	1,884	6,432	362	5,302	648
Las Animas	4,262	946	3,175	0	0	141	0
Mesa	17,121	7,602	5,548	293	3,652	0	26
Montezuma	358	0	0	358	0	0	0
Montrose	871	282	433	154	0	0	0
Otero	4	0	0	0	0	0	4
Park	46	0	46	0	0	0	0
Pueblo	21,510	19,612	306	1,183	72	298	38
Rio Grande	192	0	0	0	171	20	0
Routt	135	135	0	0	0	0	0
Summit	484	484	0	0	0	0	0
Teller	373	54	0	317	0	3	0
Washington	16	0	0	0	0	0	16
Weld	517	84	0	4	0	51	378

Department of Defense contract awards by major procurement program, 2002 ($)

Source: Washington Headquarters Services, Department of Defense

Procurement Program	Total	Army	Navy	Air Force	Logistics	Engineer	Other
Aircraft engines and spares	1,023,492	95,649	0	688,835	239,008	0	0
Airframes and spares	79,899,805	89,308	1,918,709	76,548,663	1,306,617	0	36,508
Other supplies and equipment	188,900,211	29,986,967	20,224,380	62,713,735	5,258,098	3,354,905	67,362,126
Ammunition	12,042,983	6,907,920	5,135,063	0	0	0	0
Building supplies	29,901	29,901	0	0	0	0	0
Combat vehicles	456,462	365,002	0	0	91,460	0	0
Construction	284,661,639	154,054,106	9,375,066	115,037,971	0	6,140,617	53,879
Construction equipment	281,898	281,898	0	0	0	0	0
Containers and handling equipment	127,473	127,473	0	0	0	0	0
Electronics and communications equip.	370,381,867	93,309,094	29,351,287	243,184,969	1,649,042	56,459	2,831,016
Materials handling equipment	129,473	129,473	0	0	0	0	0
Medical, dental supplies and equip.	3,242,455	2,478,527	349,066	296,771	113,191	4,900	0
Missile and space systems	671,799,794	14,828,746	6,968,886	645,371,506	0	0	3,630,656
Non-combat vehicles	205,788	205,788	0	0	0	0	0
Other aircraft equipment	53,459,135	438,882	731,696	48,542,333	3,746,224	0	0
Other fuels and lubricants	3,527,729	3,630	70,000	0	3,454,099	0	0
Petroleum	10,927,065	0	0	0	10,927,065	0	0
Photographic supplies and equip.	2,352,324	247,841	590,800	(938,460)	124,020	7,656	2,320,467
Production equipment	531,047	2,727	286,955	0	220,365	21,000	0
Services	916,797,684	326,201,443	21,745,399	382,250,363	147,706	16,349,558	170,103,215
Ships	3,348,257	0	2,998,407	0	349,850	0	0
Subsistence	8,675,889	636,450	0	0	1,573,222	0	6,466,217
Textiles, clothing and equipage	740,710	529,113	0	139,063	72,534	0	0
Transportation equipment	41,908	41,908	0	0	0	0	0
Weapons	9,959,912	572,080	0	9,119,993	267,839	0	0

CHAPTER

9 Transportation

While Colorado has 79 public airports, Amtrak rail service and a variety of historic passenger train lines, the automobile remains king of transportation. Colorado motorists drive a combined total of nearly 70 million miles each day – about 17 miles for each resident. If the average car on the road achieves gas mileage of 20 miles per gallon, roughly 3.5 million gallons of gasoline are burned each day.

To accommodate this mobile population, the Colorado Department of Transportation operated on a nearly $1 billion budget in 2002.

In all, 72,699 miles of roadway criss-cross the state. Only 946 miles are part of the interstate highway system. The roads range from world-class engineered superhighways such as Interstate 70 to rural county roads – some not even graveled. Not included in the state and county counts are hundreds of miles of forest roads and four-wheel-drive-only mountain passes.

Colorado's 79 public airports range from dirt runways to the bustling Denver International Airport. DIA, one of the busiest airports in the world, is an important air transportation hub in the nation's commercial airline industry. Almost 8,000 takeoffs and landings are recorded everyday in Colorado, about one-third of which are handled at only two airports: DIA and Centennial Airport just south of Denver.

The aeronautics division of the Colorado Department of Transportation estimates that Colorado's 79 public-use airports generate an annual economic impact of $14.3 billion, some $4.6 billion of which is paid as wages to the 246,000 jobs associated with aviation, including medical transport, fire fighting, public safety, agriculture, tourism and recreation and shipping.

Railway buffs have an interesting array of passenger train service. Amtrak offers two daily long-distance trains. They are the California Zephyr (Chicago-Denver-Oakland) and the Southwest Chief (Chicago-

Kansas City-La Junta-Albuquerque-Los Angeles). One eastbound and one westbound train are scheduled each day.

Three different historic narrow-gauge lines transport passengers through Colorado's spectacular alpine scenery. These include the Georgetown Loop just west of Denver, the Durango to Silverton run through the San Juan Mountains and the Cumbres and Toltec line from Antonito to Chama, N.M. Another scenic tour runs from Canon City up the narrow Royal Gorge and back. A cog railway transports 200,000 people each year to the summit of Pikes Peak near Colorado Springs. In all, Colorado tourist trains host almost 1 million passengers a year.

The Denver area's Regional Transportation Disrict operates a light rail railroad on 15.8 miles of track with 24 stations.

Freight, specifically coal, is the backbone of Colorado's railroad industry. Of the 36 million tons of freight originated in the state each year, 73% is coal. Twelve freight railroads operate in the state on 3,662 miles of track. They carry a combined total of 143 million tons of freight on almost 2.3 million rail cars each year. Wages paid annually to the 3,329 railroad workers living in the state total more than $201 million, with an additional $95.6 million in retirement pay.

Figure 9.1 – A passenger train crosses the High Bridge over Clear Creek some time between 1899 and 1910 as part of the Georgetown Loop. The train will loop around and travel under the bridge. Denver Public Library, Western History Collection. Louis Charles McClure photographer. MCC-1394.)

Colorado Freight Railroads

Class 1 Railroads
(operating revenue of at least $261.9 Million)   Track Miles
Burlington Northern and Santa Fe Railroad Co.   1,304
Union Pacific Railroad   1,810

Regional Railroads
(350 miles or more, revenues of at least $40 million)
Central Kansas Railway   5   (In Colorado)
Kyle Railroad   89   (In Colorado)
Nebraska, Kansas and Colorado RailNet Inc.   63   (In Colorado)

Local Railroads
Colorado, Kansas and Pacific Railway Co.   122
Great Western Railway of Colorado   80
Rock and Rail Inc.   53
San Luis Central Railroad   12

Switching and Terminal Railroads
Cimarron Valley Railroad   28
Colorado & Wyoming Railway   85
Denver Rock Island Railroad   11

TOTAL   3,662

Colorado Freight Railroad Traffic

Tons Originated (2001)			Tons Terminated (2001)		
	Tons	%		Tons	%
Coal	26,432,920	73%	Coal	15,061,350	51%
Food Products	2,414,760	7%	Lumber / Wood	2,213,042	8%
Farm Products	2,028,739	6%	Glass, Stone	2,177,652	7%
Nonmetal Minerals	1,400,064	4%	Nonmetal Minerals	1,496,440	5%
Petroleum	772,392	2%	Food Products	1,345,408	5%
Other	3,114,316	9%	Other	7,053,815	24%
TOTAL	36,163,191	100%	TOTAL	29,347,707	100%

Colorado Passenger Railroads

	Track Miles	Passengers / Year
Amtrak	432 (between stations)	243,000
Cumbres & Toltec Scenic RR	64	70,000
Durango & Silverton Narrow Gauge RR	45	200,000
Georgetown Loop	4.2	120,000
Manitou and Pikes Peak Cog Railway	8.9	200,000
Royal Gorge Line	12	80,000
TOTAL	566.10	913,000

Source: Association of American Railroads

Colorado Public Use Airports

Airport	Elevation (Feet)	Longest Runway (Feet)	Runway Surfaces	Aircraft Operations per day	Transient General Aviation	Local General Aviation	Air Taxi	Commercial	Military
Akron / Washington Co.	4,714.0	7,000.0	Asphalt	48.0	79%	17%	2%	1%	<1%
Akron / Gebauer	4,509.0	3,000.0	Turf / gravel	0.1	50%	50%	-	-	-
Alamosa / San Luis Valley Regional	7,539.0	859.0	Asphalt / dirt	81.0	49%	25%	15%	9%	3%
Aspen-Pitkin / Sardy field	7,820.0	7,000.0	Asphalt	128.0	63%	18%	13%	5%	100%
Aurora Airpark	5,680.0	4,840.0	Asphalt	60.0	90%	10%	-	-	-
Blanca	7,720.0	6,150.0	Dirt	5.0	77%	23%	-	-	-
Boulder Municipal	5,288.0	4,100.0	Asphalt	281.0	73%	27%	1%	-	<1%
Brush Municipal	4,280.0	4,300.0	Asphalt	3.0	80%	18%	2%	-	-
Buena Vista / Central Colo. Regional	7,946.0	8,300.0	Asphalt	9.0	60%	40%	-	-	-
Burlington / Kit Carson Co. Airport	4,219.0	5,201.0	Concrete	21.0	56%	39%	5%	-	-
Calhan	6,450.0	4,565.0	Turf / dirt	12.0	60%	40%	-	-	-
Canon City / Fremont Co. airport	5,439.0	5,399.0	Asphalt / turf	38.0	56%	33%	1%	-	9%
Center / Leach Airport	7,598.0	7,000.0	Asphalt	15.0	75%	25%	-	-	-
Colo. Springs Municipal	6,184.0	13,500.0	Concrete / asphalt	514.0	27%	40%	8%	1<%	11%
Colo. Springs / Meadow Lake	6,874.0	6,000.0	Asphalt / turf	160.0	19%	51%	-	-	51%
Cortez Municipal	5,918.0	7,205.0	Asphalt	41.0	34%	42%	-	2%	<1%
Craig / Moffat Airport	6,193.0	5,600.0	Asphalt	6.0	24%	76%	-	-	-
Crawford Airport	6,470.0	5,100.0	Gravel	14.0	13%	87%	-	-	-
Creede / Mineral Co. Memorial	8,680.0	6,880.0	Asphalt	5.0	25%	75%	-	-	-
Del Norte Muni. and Co. Airport	7,949.0	6,015.0	Asphalt / turf	7.0	20%	80%	-	-	-
Delta / Blake Field	5,193.0	5,600.0	Asphalt	20.0	31%	69%	-	-	-

Colorado by the Numbers

Colorado Public Use Airports (continued)

Airport	Elevation (Feet)	Longest Runway (Feet)	Runway Surfaces	Aircraft Operations per day	Transient General Aviation	Local General Aviation	Air Taxi	Commercial	Military
Delta / Hawkins Field	5,000.0	5,000.0	Dirt / turf	5.0	-	100%	-	-	-
Denver International	5,431.0	12,000.0	Concrete	1,362.0	4%	-	26%	69%	<1%
Denver / Centennial	5,883.0	10,002.0	Asphalt	1,194.0	42%	51%	7%	1%	<1%
Denver / Jefferson Co.	5,670.0	9,000.0	Asphalt	464.0	54%	45%	1%	-	1%
Denver / Front Range	5,512.0	8,000.0	Asphalt	327.0	39%	59%	1%	-	<1%
Dove Creek	6,975.0	4,200.0	Dirt	1.5	40%	60%	-	-	-
Durango / La Plata Co.	6,685.0	9,201.0	Asphalt	130.0	25%	49%	4%	5%	2%
Durango / Animas Air Park	6,684.0	5,010.0	Asphalt	25.0	34%	65%	1%	-	-
Eads Municipal	4,245.0	3,860.0	Asphalt	7.0	80%	20%	-	-	-
Eagle Co. Regional Airport	6,535.0	8,000.0	Asphalt	108.0	54%	14%	14%	10%	9%
Ellicott / Colo. Springs East	6,145.0	4,500.0	Gravel	24.0	20%	80%	-	-	-
Erie / Tri-County	5,130.0	4,700.0	Concrete/asphalt	197.0	40%	60%	-	-	1%
Fort Collins Downtown	4,939.0	5,300.0	Asphalt	48.0	50%	50%	-	-	1%
Fort Collins / Loveland Municipal	5,016.0	8,500.0	Asphalt	225.0	61%	36%	2%	<1%	<1%
Fort Morgan Municipal	5,467.0	5,050.0	Concrete / turf	125.0	73%	25%	-	-	2%
Glenwood Springs Municipal	5,916.0	3,305.0	Asphalt	38.0	14%	79%	6%	-	<1%
Granby / Grand Co.	8,203.0	5,095.0	Asphalt	7.0	70%	30%	-	-	-
Grand Junction / Walker Field	4,858.0	10,501.0	Asphalt	292.0	42%	29%	8%	14%	6%
Greeley / Weld Co.	4,697.0	10,000.0	Asphalt	370.0	37%	58%	-	-	5%
Greeley / Valley View	4,820.0	4,000.0	Turf / dirt	8.0	23%	76%	<1%	-	-

Colorado Public Use Airports (continued)

Airport	Elevation (Feet)	Longest Runway (Feet)	Runway Surfaces	Aircraft Operations per day	Transient General Aviation	Local General Aviation	Air Taxi	Commercial	Military
Gunnison Co.	7,678.0	9,400.0	Asphalt / turf	98.0	25%	56%	10%	9%	-
Haxtun Municipal	4,035.0	3,860.0	Asphalt / turf	0.7	60%	40%	-	-	-
Hayden / Yampa Valley	6,602.0	10,000.0	Asphalt	33.0	35%	47%	2%	-	<1%
Holly	3,390.0	4,140.0	Gravel	4.0	40%	60%	-	-	-
Holyoke	3,730.0	5,000.0	Asphalt	18.0	30%	69%	-	-	1%
Hudson / Plate Valley Airpark	4,965.0	4,100.0	Asphalt / turf	11.3	24%	73%	-	-	2%
Julesburg Municipal	3,520.0	3,700.0	Asphalt	0.7	60%	40%	-	-	-
Kremmling / McElroy Field	7,411.0	5,540.0	Asphalt	10.4	67%	29%	4%	-	-
La Junta Municipal	4,238.0	6,848.0	Asphalt/concrete	19.0	67%	28%	-	-	5%
La Veta / Cuchara Valley	7,153.0	5,798.0	Asphalt	1.8	45%	16%	-	-	39%
Lamar Municipal	3,706.0	6,304.0	Asphalt/concrete	37.0	35%	30%	16%	10%	9%
Las Animas City and County	3,915.0	3,870.0	Asphalt	8.1	16%	83%	-	-	<1%
Leadville / Lake Co.	9,927.0	6,400.0	Asphalt/concrete	27.0	50%	28%	2%	-	20%
Limon Municipal	5,365.0	4,700.0	Concrete	12.3	44%	56%	-	-	-
Longmont Vance Brand	5,052.0	4,800.0	Concrete / turf	274.0	30%	70%	-	-	<%
Mack Mesa	4,724.0	2,600.0	Asphalt	16.5	17%	83%	-	-	<1%
Meeker	6,421.0	6,500.0	Asphalt	32.0	84%	15%	-	-	<1%
Monte Vista Municipal	7,608.0	5,900.0	Asphalt / dirt	18.0	40%	60%	-	-	<1%
Montrose Regional Airport	5,759.0	10,000.0	Asphalt	39.0	39%	33%	-	27%	<1%
Nucla / Hopkins Field	5,936.0	4,600.0	Asphalt / turf	4.5	65%	34%	-	-	1%

Colorado Public Use Airports (continued)

Airport	Elevation (Feet)	Longest Runway (Feet)	Runway Surfaces	Aircraft Operations per day	Transient General Aviation	Local General Aviation	Air Taxi	Commercial	Military
Pagosa Springs / Stevens Field	7,700.0	8,500.0	Asphalt	46.0	59%	36%	1%	-	4%
Paonia / North Fork Valley	5,798.0	4,500.0	Asphalt	11.0	50%	50%	-	-	-
Pueblo Memorial	4,726.0	10,496.0	Asphalt	230.0	38%	30%	6%	<1%	26%
Rangely	5,274.0	6,400.0	Asphalt	82.0	17%	83%	-	-	-
Rifle / Garfield Co. Regional	5,544.0	7,000.0	Asphalt	23.0	44%	20%	36%	<1%	<1%
Rocky Ford / Melon Field	4,260.0	3,780.0	Asphalt / dirt	12.1	40%	59%	-	-	1%
Saguache Municipal	7,826.0	7,745.0	Gravel	3.6	100%	-	-	-	-
Salida / Harriet Alexander Field	7,489.0	7,350.0	Concrete/asphalt	18.7	65%	35%	-	-	-
Springfield Municipal	4,387.0	5,000.0	Concrete	7.0	20%	80%	-	-	-
Steamboat Sprgs. / Bob Adams Field	6,878.0	4,452.0	Asphalt	30.0	64%	28%	9%	-	<1%
Sterling Municipal	4,038.0	4,730.0	Concrete/ gravel	9.0	67%	29%	-	-	4%
Telluride Regional	9,078.0	6,870.0	Asphalt	81.0	37%	6%	49%	8%	<1%
Trinidad / Perry Stokes	5,762.0	5,500.0	Asphalt / turf	37.0	55%	32%	8%	-	5%
Walden / Jackson Co.	8,149.0	5,900.0	Asphalt / turf	2.8	80%	20%	-	-	-
Walsenburg / Spanish Peaks	6,050.0	4,900.0	Asphalt / turf	9.6	29%	71%	-	-	-
Westcliffe / Silver West	8,290.0	7,000.0	Asphalt	2.2	40%	60%	-	-	-
Wray Municipal	3,667.0	5,400.0	Asphalt	40.0	53%	47%	-	-	-
Yuma Municipal	4,136.0	4,200.0	Concrete/ gravel	11.7	44%	56%	-	-	-
TOTAL				7,747.6					

Colorado State and Interstate Highway Miles and Daily Vehicle Miles Traveled (Year 2000)

Numbers may not add due to rounding. Source: Colorado Department of Transportation

County	Total Interstate Miles	Total Other Miles	Total All Centerline Miles	Total Lane Miles	2000 Daily Vehicle Miles Traveled	1997 Daily Vehicle Miles Traveled	97-00 % change
Adams	.58	.138	.196	.675	5,432,060	5,783,856	-6%
Alamosa	0	.88	.88	.184	317,579	286,531	11%
Arapahoe	.48	.120	.168	.642	4,911,154	4,521,967	9%
Archuleta	0	.93	.93	.199	300,596	271,297	11%
Baca	0	.150	.150	.305	184,134	136,556	35%
Bent	0	.81	.81	.177	183,850	172,237	7%
Boulder	0	.213	.213	.578	3,273,755	2,943,580	11%
Chaffee	0	.96	.96	.228	418,015	385,340	8%
Cheyenne	0	.130	.130	.263	164,969	133,840	23%
Clear Creek	.33	.64	.97	.318	1,172,307	1,031,529	14%
Conejos	0	.101	.101	.202	177,491	163,359	9%
Costilla	0	.83	.83	.175	168,175	164,477	2%
Crowley	0	.66	.66	.131	74,942	63,987	17%
Custer	0	.81	.81	.162	74,907	74,927	0%
Delta	0	.110	.110	.244	522,602	504,171	4%
Denver	.29	.64	.93	.489	7,269,336	6,868,984	6%
Dolores	0	.43	.43	.98	92,139	82,478	12%
Douglas	.31	.104	.135	.408	3,407,965	2,872,824	19%
Eagle	.59	.86	.146	.424	1,591,864	1,438,697	11%
El Paso	.47	.182	.229	.720	5,226,324	5,008,483	4%
Elbert	.27	.76	.103	.262	448,229	377,191	19%
Fremont	0	.146	.146	.357	709,878	661,561	7%
Garfield	.65	.109	.174	.518	1,410,657	1,279,272	10%
Gilpin	0	.32	.32	.65	174,299	171,575	2%
Grand	0	.172	.172	.361	565,387	460,315	23%
Gunnison	0	.189	.189	.399	484,270	406,589	19%
Hinsdale	0	.38	.38	.77	30,585	24,159	27%
Huerfano	.29	.116	.145	.360	477,867	438,538	9%
Jackson	0	.129	.129	.259	95,056	84,465	13%
Jefferson	.25	.203	.228	.843	7,253,039	6,713,648	8%
Kiowa	0	.136	.136	.272	143,354	103,546	38%
Kit Carson	.60	.116	.176	.473	596,271	564,175	6%
La Plata	0	.157	.157	.382	970,775	869,668	12%
Lake	0	.68	.68	.140	180,235	175,926	2%
Larimer	.39	.260	.299	.793	3,117,818	2,756,902	13%
Las Animas	.39	.224	.263	.604	476,734	447,467	7%

Colorado State and Interstate Highway Miles and Daily Vehicle Miles Traveled Year 2000 *continued*

Numbers may not add due to rounding. Source: Colorado Department of Transportation

County	Total Interstate Miles	Total Other Miles	Total All Centerline Miles	Total Lane Miles	2000 Daily Vehicle Miles Traveled	1997 Daily Vehicle Miles Traveled	97-00 % change
Lincoln	.30	.165	.195	.461	.440,167	.390,628	.13%
Logan	.47	.156	.203	.531	.614,741	.501,130	.23%
Mesa	.66	.195	.261	.705	1,691,134	1,549,755	.9%
Mineral	.0	.62	.62	.146	.118,663	.97,227	.22%
Moffat	.0	.246	.246	.505	.263,538	.244,249	.8%
Montezuma	.0	.170	.170	.378	.675,571	.632,691	.7%
Montrose	.0	.193	.193	.437	.529,299	.464,473	.14%
Morgan	.38	.150	.188	.464	.643,627	.564,659	.14%
Otero	.0	.187	.187	.423	.384,044	.353,268	.9%
Ouray	.0	.48	.48	.101	.204,361	.189,768	.8%
Park	.0	.164	.164	.339	.452,263	.404,302	.12%
Phillips	.0	.96	.96	.195	.91,595	.86,616	.6%
Pitkin	.0	.55	.55	.122	.373,015	.359,849	.4%
Prowers	.0	.152	.152	.324	.328,861	.270,001	.22%
Pueblo	.48	.201	.249	.718	2,243,914	2,058,800	.9%
Rio Blanco	.0	.143	.143	.292	.154,399	.146,579	.5%
Rio Grande	.0	.92	.92	.192	.315,294	.277,535	.14%
Routt	.0	.112	.112	.240	.402,260	.338,982	.19%
Saguache	.0	.158	.158	.318	.208,562	.176,745	.18%
San Juan	.0	.40	.40	.84	.86,159	.80,751	.7%
San Miguel	.0	.99	.99	.200	.181,270	.172,561	.5%
Sedgwick	.27	.63	.90	.235	.190,573	.174,826	.9%
Summit	.24	.72	.96	.280	1,054,822	.991,980	.6%
Teller	.0	.55	.55	.118	.387,479	.362,148	.7%
Washington	.11	.201	.211	.447	.329,579	.263,945	.25%
Weld	.67	.400	.466	1,247	4,059,744	3,489,968	.16%
Yuma	.0	.202	.202	.411	.248,903	.229,424	.8%
Total	.946	.8,140	.9,086	.22,699	.68,772,454	.63,316,977	.9%

Colorado County Roads and Bridges (Year 2000)

Numbers may not add due to rounding. Source: Colorado Department of Transportation

	Paved Centerline Miles	Unpaved Centerline Miles	Total Centerline Miles	Paved Lane Miles	Unpaved Lane Miles	Total Lane Miles	Bridge Deck Sq. Feet
Adams	.397	.714	1,112	1,213	1,721	2,934	.264,874
Alamosa	.172	.471	.643	.419	1,214	1,633	.30,103
Arapahoe	.588	.281	.870	2,076	.687	2,763	.229,067
Archuleta	.48	.494	.542	.118	.932	1,050	.37,041
Baca	.12	1,878	1,889	.29	4,163	4,192	.134,841
Bent	.69	.680	.749	.161	1,504	1,665	.80,281
Boulder	.375	.275	.650	.963	.561	1,525	.163,062
Chaffee	.140	.371	.511	.317	.607	.924	.64,260
Cheyenne	.16	1,075	1,091	.44	2,449	2,494	.92,787
Clear Creek	.59	.144	.203	.132	.281	.413	.12,828
Conejos	.66	.537	.603	.147	1,144	1,290	.76,614
Costilla	.68	1,434	1,502	.154	3,362	3,516	.39,970
Crowley	.52	.412	.463	.123	.950	1,073	.24,782
Custer	.43	.316	.358	.90	.650	.740	.7,762
Delta	.269	.439	.708	.616	.806	1,422	.84,726
Dolores	.11	.553	.564	.28	1,099	1,126	.9,607
Douglas	.667	.367	1,034	2,211	.930	3,141	.181,670
Eagle	.131	.378	.509	.288	.594	.882	.44,349
El Paso	.848	1,121	1,970	2,328	2,672	5,000	.95,223
Elbert	.82	1,121	1,202	.214	2,612	2,826	.394,651
Fremont	.201	.388	.590	.486	.799	1,284	.110,914
Garfield	.263	.467	.731	.674	.801	1,475	.85,582
Gilpin	.1	.146	.147	.3	.307	.310	.8,214
Grand	.29	.722	.751	.71	1,462	1,533	.78,108
Gunnison	.99	.712	.810	.228	1,222	1,449	.81,320
Hinsdale	.4	.242	.246	.10	.412	.421	.13,529
Huerfano	.13	.653	.666	.31	.990	1,021	.61,462
Jackson	.40	.483	.522	.97	.724	.821	.33,812
Jefferson	.879	.368	1,247	2,689	.881	3,571	.224,625
Kiowa	.48	1,128	1,176	.115	2,681	2,795	.27,693
Kit Carson	.79	2,039	2,117	.190	5,080	5,270	.123,497
La Plata	.206	.474	.679	.486	.963	1,449	.840
Lake	.64	.81	.145	.158	.163	.321	.81,791
Larimer	.483	.601	1,084	1,286	1,300	2,586	.359,733
Las Animas	.50	1,516	1,567	.140	3,240	3,380	.160,806
Lincoln	.98	1,360	1,458	.231	3,237	3,468	.231,473
Logan	.228	1,624	1,852	.506	3,819	4,326	.262,526
Mesa	.625	.763	1,389	1,490	1,228	2,717	.223,186
Mineral	.3	.189	.191	.6	.325	.331	.17,964

Colorado County Roads and Bridges (Year 2000) *continued*

Numbers may not add due to rounding. Source: Colorado Department of Transportation

	Paved Centerline Miles	Unpaved Centerline Miles	Total Centerline Miles	Paved Lane Miles	Unpaved Lane Miles	Total Lane Miles	Bridge Deck Sq. Feet
Moffat	127	1,544	1,671	304	2,855	3,159	87,265
Montezuma	151	644	795	359	1,228	1,587	44,974
Montrose	245	1,074	1,319	583	1,997	2,579	95,425
Morgan	202	883	1,085	487	2,161	2,647	290,895
Otero	226	428	654	505	851	1,357	137,256
Ouray	9	234	242	22	419	442	27,880
Park	143	1,480	1,623	326	3,282	3,608	18,521
Phillips	7	1,000	1,007	15	2,274	2,289	35,048
Pitkin	104	171	275	219	238	456	43,150
Prowers	83	1,179	1,261	193	2,642	2,834	129,956
Pueblo	442	763	1,205	1,074	1,717	2,791	167,634
Rio Blanco	173	748	921	417	1,309	1,726	60,733
Rio Grande	215	355	570	525	783	1,308	99,112
Routt	131	718	849	333	1,251	1,583	109,967
Saguache	145	752	897	363	1,670	2,033	16,253
San Juan	1	148	149	2	197	199	9,160
San Miguel	42	611	653	98	1,073	1,171	43,236
Sedgwick	38	594	632	93	1,361	1,454	73,960
Summit	78	144	222	196	299	495	13,123
Teller	63	491	554	150	975	1,125	15,696
Washington	60	2,281	2,341	157	5,594	5,751	127,004
Weld	692	2,464	3,155	1,676	6,237	7,913	624,664
Yuma	53	2,228	2,282	150	5,833	5,983	110,313
TOTAL	**10,954**	**47,948**	**58,902**	**28,815**	**104,816**	**133,631**	**6,636,798**

Colorado City Street Miles Year 2000

Numbers may not add due to rounding. Source: Colorado Department of Transportation

	Paved Centerline Miles	Unpaved Centerline Miles	Total Centerline Miles		Paved Centerline Miles	Unpaved Centerline Miles	Total Centerline Miles
Aguilar	1.61	6.4	8.01	Commerce City	118.37	11.06	129.43
Akron	12.47	3.49	15.96	Cortez	41.32	6.72	48.04
Alamosa	44.62	2.48	47.1	Craig	45.63	6.92	52.55
Alma	0	2.55	2.55	Crawford	1.68	2.37	4.05
Antonito	2.25	7.72	9.97	Creede	2.3	2.8	5.1
Arriba	1.4	3.86	5.26	Crested Butte	6.56	1.86	8.42
Arvada	372.47	1.06	373.53	Crestone	1.12	2	3.12
Aspen	27.34	0.31	27.65	Cripple Creek	12.29	3.72	16.01
Ault	5.43	1.41	6.84	Crook	0.23	2.89	3.12
Aurora	771.57	33.58	805.15	Crowley	3.56	0	3.56
Avon	18.62	0	18.62	Dacono	11.39	9	20.39
Basalt	14.76	0.16	14.92	De Beque	3.59	0.76	4.35
Bayfield	9.28	0.84	10.12	Deer Trail	1.2	5.57	6.77
Bennett	15.12	0.65	15.77	Del Norte	5.28	7.93	13.21
Berthoud	23.65	2.91	26.56	Delta	45.07	2.07	47.14
Dethune	0.17	3.3	3.47	Denver	1,624.41	24.84	1,649.25
Black Hawk	3.49	1.02	4.51	Dillon	6.87	0.41	7.28
Blanca	3.66	23.06	26.72	Dinosaur	6.55	0.6	7.15
Blue River	3.79	11.06	14.85	Dolores	2.17	4.97	7.14
Bonanza	0	2.67	2.67	Dove Creek	8.61	0.42	9.03
Boone	0.08	3.53	3.61	Durango	58.92	1.38	60.3
Boulder	272.87	4.02	276.89	Eads	8.02	0.63	8.65
Bow Mar	9.22	0	9.22	Eagle	19.01	0.6	19.61
Branson	0.2	2.71	2.91	Eaton	18.49	0	18.49
Breckenridge	27.86	1.21	29.07	Eckley	0.75	6.09	6.84
Brighton	92.54	5.37	97.91	Edgewater	13.66	0	13.66
Brookside	1.56	1.5	3.06	Elizabeth	4.27	5.98	10.25
Broomfield	143.48	6.67	150.15	Empire	0.61	1.79	2.4
Brush	23.2	2.52	25.72	Englewood	118.54	1.11	119.65
Buena Vista	19.34	2.76	22.1	Erie	60.53	3.76	64.3
Burlington	25.74	2.84	28.58	Estes Park	48.21	0.23	48.44
Calhan	5.02	3.51	8.53	Evans	49.04	5	54.04
Campo	3.18	0.66	3.84	Fairplay	3.16	5.43	8.59
Canon City	71.44	14.96	86.4	Federal Heights	14.86	0.3	15.16
Carbondale	20.75	0	20.75	Firestone	24.36	7.93	32.29
Castle Rock	125.99	15.64	141.63	Flagler	7.1	4.57	11.67
Cedaredge	14.11	1.23	15.34	Fleming	1.42	4.98	6.4
Center	11.37	2.07	13.44	Florence	17.08	7.09	24.17
Central City	6.39	5.37	11.76	Fort Collins	413.98	7.45	421.43
Cheraw	2.18	0	2.18	Fort Lupton	28.16	3.54	31.7
Cherry Hills Village	42.9	6.32	49.22	Fort Morgan	48.98	0.73	49.71
Cheyenne Wells	10.18	3.85	14.03	Fountain	60.63	2.51	63.14
Coal Creek	1.61	3.36	4.97	Fowler	9.31	0.14	9.45
Cokedale	0	1.95	1.95	Foxfield	1.98	10.03	12.01
Collbran	2.96	0.27	3.23	Fraser	4.6	0.77	5.37
Colo. Spgs.	1,321.28	45.23	1,366.51	Frederick	32.66	6.33	38.99
Columbine Valley	7.49	0	7.49	Frisco	16.88	0.14	17.02

Colorado City Street Miles Year 2000 *continued*

Numbers may not add due to rounding. Source: Colorado Department of Transportation

	Paved Centerline Miles	Unpaved Centerline Miles	Total Centerline Miles		Paved Centerline Miles	Unpaved Centerline Miles	Total Centerline Miles
Fruita	36.58	1.89	38.47	Lake City	0.87	7.91	8.78
Garden City	2.2	0	2.2	Lakewood	470.15	4.69	474.84
Genoa	0.76	3.06	3.82	Lamar	53.03	3.14	56.17
Georgetown	5.69	5.61	11.3	Larkspur	2.37	1.59	3.96
Gilcrest	3.49	3.3	6.79	Las Animas	22.34	3.12	25.46
Glendale	5.98	0.04	6.02	Leadville	19.84	0.63	20.47
Glenwood Springs	37.71	0.97	38.68	Limon	12.65	4.83	17.48
Golden	67.51	0.89	68.4	Littleton	148.33	0.92	149.25
Granada	3.35	3.98	7.33	Lochbuie	6.21	2.54	8.75
Granby	9.6	1.13	10.73	Log Lane Village	4.08	0.16	4.24
Grand Junction	254.53	3.39	257.92	Lone Tree	21.51	0.5	22.01
Grand Lake	6.2	5.91	12.11	Longmont	273.24	1.38	274.62
Greeley	280.07	6.73	286.8	Louisville	83.4	1.28	84.68
Green Mtn. Falls	2.79	6.44	9.23	Loveland	241.43	3.81	245.24
Greenwood Village	84.94	3.31	88.25	Lyons	6.4	1.35	7.75
Grover	0.43	5.19	5.62	Manassa	2.69	12.48	15.17
Gunnison	27.49	4.02	31.51	Mancos	0.48	5.52	6
Gypsum	22.65	0.42	23.07	Manitou Springs	21.97	7.06	29.03
Hartman	0.21	2.87	3.08	Manzanola	3.81	0.18	3.99
Haswell	2.47	1.14	3.61	Marble	0	4.33	4.33
Haxtun	9.01	2.14	11.15	Mead	13.68	5.23	18.91
Hayden	8.84	1.66	10.5	Meeker	18.69	0.35	19.04
Hillrose	0	2.31	2.31	Merino	0.61	2.77	3.38
Holly	7.44	1.29	8.73	Milliken	14.41	4.91	19.32
Holyoke	16.07	3.26	19.33	Minturn	3.9	0.61	4.51
Hooper	1.22	3.47	4.69	Moffat	1.66	4.85	6.51
Hot Sulphur Springs	3.09	3.76	6.85	Monte Vista	21.1	5.8	26.9
Hotchkiss	6.26	0.71	6.97	Montrose	92.29	5.27	97.56
Hudson	4.86	6.37	11.23	Monument	15.97	0.38	16.35
Hugo	5.03	2.7	7.73	Morrison	2.51	0.17	2.68
Idaho Springs	8	2.08	10.08	Mountain View	2.31	0	2.31
Ignacio	4.46	0.1	4.56	Mountain Village	17.51	0	17.51
Iliff	0	3.7	3.7	Mt. Crested Butte	11.8	0.65	12.45
Jamestown	1.53	2.17	3.7	Naturita	4.5	2.09	6.59
Johnstown	24.64	3.35	27.99	Nederland	2.87	14.5	17.37
Julesburg	13.86	1.66	15.52	New Castle	10.96	0.9	11.86
Keenesburg	8.1	0.66	8.76	Northglenn	100.94	0	100.94
Kersey	6.28	0.74	7.02	Norwood	3.22	0.93	4.15
Kim	0.86	3.43	4.29	Nucla	6.21	1.98	8.19
Kiowa	2.28	0	2.28	Nunn	0	7.92	7.92
Kit Carson	1.95	4.98	6.93	Oak Creek	0.99	4.32	5.31
Kremmling	12.68	1.49	14.17	Olathe	6.44	3.94	10.38
La Jara	3.12	2.09	5.21	Olney Springs	2.5	2.4	4.9
La Junta	42.24	1.42	43.66	Ophir	0	1.83	1.83
La Salle	8.35	1.58	9.93	Orchard City	26.42	5.8	32.22
La Veta	2.47	12.57	15.04	Ordway	10.61	0.76	11.37
Lafayette	88.42	1.1	89.52	Otis	0.12	6.88	7

Colorado City Street Miles Year 2000 *continued*

Source: Colorado Department of Transportation

	Paved Centerline Miles	Unpaved Centerline Miles	Total Centerline Miles		Paved Centerline Miles	Unpaved Centerline Miles	Total Centerline Miles
Ouray	1.01	7.33	8.34	South Fork	7.25	6.81	14.06
Ovid	0.52	3.36	3.88	Springfield	14.29	5.9	20.19
Pagosa Springs	11.72	6.65	18.37	Starkville	0.73	0.95	1.68
Palisade	9.59	0.65	10.24	Steamboat Springs	61.5	2.15	63.65
Palmer Lake	6.63	14.02	20.66	Sterling	62.73	2.32	65.05
Paoli	1.45	1.06	2.51	Stratton	6.7	1.29	7.99
Paonia	9.36	0.73	10.09	Sugar City	5.39	0.3	5.69
Parachute	6.76	0.24	7	Superior	31.83	3.12	34.95
Parker	72.82	0.47	73.29	Swink	4.24	0	4.24
Peetz	0.8	2.97	3.77	Telluride	13.36	0.39	13.75
Pierce	3.69	4.81	8.5	Thornton	254.78	10.17	264.95
Pitkin	0.89	2.4	3.29	Timnath	1.64	0.18	1.82
Platteville	9.17	3.02	12.19	Trinidad	61.06	8.24	69.3
Poncha Springs	0.97	6.06	7.03	Two Buttes	3.03	1.63	4.66
Pritchett	3.04	0.14	3.18	Vail	30.64	0.21	30.85
Pueblo	443.43	9.36	452.79	Victor	0.65	4.41	5.06
Ramah	0.45	3.05	3.5	Vilas	2.29	0.22	2.51
Rangely	17.92	2.66	20.58	Vona	0.3	2.84	3.14
Raymer	0	4.34	4.34	Walden	4.58	1.7	6.28
RedCliff	2.32	0.22	2.54	Walsenburg	20.17	9.17	29.34
Rico	0	6.31	6.31	Walsh	8.27	1.1	9.37
Ridgeway	1.4	9.06	10.46	Ward	1.45	1.83	3.28
Rifle	29.36	2.69	32.05	Wellington	14.7	1.82	16.52
Rockvale	2.95	6.99	9.94	Westcliffe	6.14	1.13	7.27
Rocky Ford	26.12	1.56	27.68	Westminster	298.41	5.18	303.59
Romeo	0.49	4.14	4.63	Wheat Ridge	130.16	0.49	130.65
Rye	1.22	0.29	1.51	Wiggins	2.48	5.96	8.44
Saguache	5.96	2.17	8.13	Wiley	3.15	0.98	4.13
Salida	33.6	1.23	34.83	Williamsburg	3.8	8.87	12.67
San Luis	3.94	2.86	6.8	Windsor	55.5	1.26	56.76
Sanford	2.92	22.77	25.69	Winter Park	9.1	4.74	13.84
Sawpit	0	0.46	0.46	Woodland Park	50.69	0.59	51.28
Sedgwick	0.41	4.08	4.49	Wray	18.01	6.08	24.09
Seibert	0.67	3.41	4.08	Yampa	0.63	3.3	3.93
Severance	16.77	2.84	19.61	Yuma	20.06	8.05	28.11
Sheridan	19.6	0.97	20.57				
Sheridan Lake	0.28	2.01	2.29	**TOTAL**	**11,586.73**	**1,015.60**	**12,602.35**
Silt	17.32	0.57	17.89				
Silver Cliff	1.52	17.77	19.29				
Silver Plume	0.02	2.36	2.38				
Silverthorne	18.98	0.08	19.06				
Silverton	0	8.83	8.83				
Simla	0.7	6.84	7.54				
Snowmass Village	29.47	3.15	32.62				

Transportation Highlights

Sometimes in Colorado, getting there is as spectacular as being there. The rough mountain terrain has sorely tested transportation engineers, but they have responded by building roads, bridges tunnels and railways that still rank among the world's most spectacular. Many of the transportation corridors are destinations in their own right. Following are brief descriptions of some of the most interesting transportation opportunities in the world.

Narrow-Gauge Railroads

Narrow-gauge railroads were common in Colorado where steeper grades and tighter corners made the narrower rails an advantage. The narrow gauge refers to the distance between rails. The standard gauge of American railroads is four-feet, 8.5-inches. Narrow gauge rails are three feet apart. Three narrow gauge railroads continue to operate in Colorado.

Cumbres and Toltec Railroad

Owned jointly by Colorado and New Mexico, and managed by a non-profit entity, the Cumbres and Toltec is the longest narrow-gauge line in the state. It travels from Antonito, Colo., through the San Juan Mountains to Chama, N.M.

The line was built in 1880 by the Denver and Rio Grande Railroad. The 64-mile stretch is a portion of a longer network of narrow gauge rails that once connected Denver to Santa Fe and Silverton. The line finds its roots in the gold and silver mining boom and was built to service the mountain mines of southwestern Colorado.

The entire railroad is designated a National Historic Site. It is one of the longest narrow-gauge railway lines in North America and its peak elevation of 10,015 at the summit of Cumbres Pass ranks it as the highest narrow-gauge railway in North America.

Cumbres is the Spanish word for "crest" or "summit." The line passes through Toltec Gorge as part of its route that also includes remote backcountry of the San Juan Mountains. Spring snow gives way to summer flowers, which give way to spectacular fall color in late September. The line includes the 137-foot Cascade Trestle and passes through two tunnels.

To contact the Cumbres & Toltec Railroad, call 1-888-286-2737, or visit cumbrestoltec.com on the Internet.

Georgetown Loop Railroad

Another mining era relic, the Georgetown Loop Railroad runs between the towns of Georgetown and Silver Plume – a scant two miles. But what makes this line remarkable isn't the horizontal distance between the towns, it's the 638 vertical feet that separates Georgetown and Silver Plume.

Because the mountain valley between Georgetown and Silver Plume is too narrow for switchbacks, Union Pacific engineer Robert Blickensderfer designed a rail line that loops back over itself and uses two hairpin turns. The result is a 4.47-mile length of track that literally spirals up 638 vertical feet in the two-horizontal tmiles to Silver Plume.

The most spectacular portion of the line is Devils Gate Bridge, or the High Bridge. The bridge spans a 300-foot gap in the valley, is 96 feet above Clear Creek and 75 feet above the track that runs beneath it. About one mile beyond the bridge is a 28-degree hairpin curve which crosses Clear Creek two more times. Another quarter mile along is "Big Fill," a 30-degree horseshoe curve. The result is a railroad line that completes 3.5 circles on its way from 8,476-foot Georgetown to 9,114-foot Silver Plume.

For information, call 303-569-2403, 800-691-4FUN, or visit georgetownloop.com on the Internet.

Durango & Silverton Narrow Gauge Railroad

The Durango & Silverton Narrow Gauge Railroad holds the distinction for most years of operation. It opened in 1882 amid promotion as a scenic route for passengers, even though it's estimated the line has hauled more than $300 million in gold and silver out of the San Juan Mountains. The line has endured a remarkable number of hardships in its 120 years: Economic woes in the form of the Silver Panic of 1893, floods, snowslides, world wars, the Great Depression and even a 1918 flu epidemic that killed 10% of Silverton's population in just six weeks. Through it all the line has proved resolute in its ability to survive. Such tenacity is due in large part to the scenic splendor of the 45-mile trip. Mine closings and economics proved almost fatal many times. Through it all, Hollywood might be credited for keeping the line alive. Just after World War II, when survival prospects look most grim, seven Hollywood films were shot on location between 1950 and 1957. Titles included "Ticket to Tomahawk," "Across the Wide Missouri," "Denver and Rio Grande," "Viva Zapata," Maverick Queen," "Around the World in 80 Days" and "Night Passing." In 1962, film crews from "How the West Was Won" made use of the line, as did crews from "Butch Cassidy and the Sundance Kid" almost 100 years after the line was built.

The line was designated a National Historic Landmark in 1967 and a National Historic Civil Engineering Landmark in 1968.

Today, the Durango & Silverton Narrow Gauge railroad offers year-round service using historical trains and rolling stock indigenous to the line.

For more information, visit durangotrain.com on the Internet.

Royal Gorge Route

The 12-mile standard-gauge passenger train route operating from Canon City through Royal Gorge to Parkdale and back is spectacular for its canyon and river views, the hanging bridge and the famed Royal Gorge Bridge (see Chapter 10). Building of the line, however, also sparked a war.

Silver was discovered in the upper reaches of the Arkansas River Valley in the 1870s. Two competing railroads, the Rio Grande and the Santa Fe, both immediately sought rail line routes to the mines. The route followed the Arkansas River from Canon City through the 1,000-foot-deep Royal Gorge Canyon.

The railroads engaged in a construction race. By day they put down sections of track. At night, crews often sabotaged the work of opposing crews, sometimes using dynamite to obliterate the previous day's work. Construction crews built rock forts in the canyon for the fight. Gunfire was common.

The war eventually moved to the courts with the Santa Fe railroad prevailing at first. When the court battle started again in 1879 and rights were returned to the Rio Grande, the Santa Fe railroad hired gunslinger Bat Masterson and some of his Kansas gang to take back what they had lost in court. The move forced Colorado Governor A.C. Hunt to form a 200-man militia to roust out the Santa Fe troops over a 10-day battle in the canyon. A final agreement was reached in December of 1879. The Rio Grande was given control of the canyon for good. The Santa Fe Railroad was forced to pay $1.4 million to its rival and was banished from operating in the Denver or Leadville area for 10 years. By July of 1880, the Rio Grande had completed its line through the gorge.

By 1882, the Royal Gorge Route had become a transcontinental rail link between Denver and Salt Lake. In the 1890s, four transcontinental passenger trains a day passed through the gorge, over Marshall Pass, through Gunnison and Grand Junction. When Tennessee Pass opened, the primary transcontinental route changed to Leadville to Minturn to Glenwood Springs to Grand Junction.

The opening of the Moffat Tunnel in 1928 gave Denver a more direct and reliable route to Salt Lake City.

July 27, 1967 marked the last regularly scheduled passenger train through the Royal Gorge.

Today, the Canon City & Royal Gorge Route retraces the most spectacular section of the trip with daily scenic tours of 12 miles to Parkdale and back. Highlights of the trip include a stop at the famed Hanging Bridge where the canyon narrows to only 30 feet, the river roars underneath, and straight up more than 1,000 feet, is the world's highest suspension bridge, the Royal Gorge Bridge.

For more information, call 303-569-2403 or visit royalgorgeroute.com on the Internet.

Manitou and Pikes Peak Cog Railway

Reaching the summit of one of Colorado's 14,000-foot peaks normally is an athletic and sometimes challenging ordeal. Pikes Peak, however, has a passenger train to the 14,110-foot summit.

Zalmon Simmons, founder of the Beautyrest Mattress Co., gets credit for this spectacular rail line. He visited Pikes Peak in the late 1880s and took a two-day mule trip to the summit. He returned with the notion there must be a better way to the top and later agreed to finance plans to build a rail line to the summit.

Track construction began in 1889. Limited service began in 1890. In 1891, the first passenger train, under steam power, chugged up the 8.9 miles of track to the summit with a church choir from Denver. So began rail service to the summit of Pikes Peak.

The cog railroad uses a gear wheel that meshes with a rack rail between the rails and thus can climb much steeper grades than ordinary trains. Maximum grades on the Pikes Peak line are 25% with a top speed of nine miles per hour. Traditional locomotives can typically pull up grades no steeper than 6%, and a modest 2% grade is more common for freight hauling.

The Swiss-made railroad cars of the Pikes Peak line are self-contained, diesel electric locomotives powered by two Cummins diesel engines. In mid-summer, eight trains a day make the trip up the mountain.

For travel information, call 719-685-5401, or visit cograilway.com on the Internet.

Pikes Peak Toll Road

Lt. Zebulon M. Pike was unable to climb the peak during his exploration mission in 1806, but millions of visitors have since gained the summit by foot, by rail and by automobile.

The first carriage road to the top of 14,110-foot Pikes Peak was completed in 1889, built by the Cascade and Pikes Peak Toll Road Co. The toll for using the road was $1. In 1893, Katherine Lee Bates made the 16-

Figure 9.2 – Near the summit of Pikes Peak on the Manitou and Pikes Peak Cog Railway. (Photo courtesy Manitou and Pikes Peak Cog Railway).

mile trip in a prairie wagon. The trip inspired the writing of the lyrics for "America the Beautiful." In 1895, the lyrics were set to music and published.

In 1901, the first automobile made the famous trip to the top of Pikes Peak. The machine was an interesting contraption called a Locomobile, powered by a two-cylinder steam engine. The locomobile took nine hours to reach the summit, a pace most hikers could easily surpass.

In 1915, the road was purchased by mining millionaire Spencer Penrose who improved the carriage road and opened it to automobiles. To publicize the opening, he organized the Pikes Peak Auto Hill Climb race in 1916. The race to this day continues to draw the world's top racing teams. Modern racers are able to finish the treacherous 12.5-mile course in just more than 10 minutes. Racers attain speeds of more than 110 mph in some sections of the course.

Slower drivers have the chance to enjoy a journey through four distinct ecosystems. In a 16-mile drive from Colorado Springs to the summit of Pikes Peak, one passes through four separate ecosystems – Grassland, Montane Forest, Subalpine Forest and Alpine Tundra. To pass through similar life zones without gaining altitude, one would have to drive as far north as northern Alaska. Many of the plants and animals living in Colorado between 9,000 and 11,500 feet, in the spruce-fir forest life-zones, thrive at 1,000 feet in northern Canada. The low tundra vegetation above timberline (approx. 11,000 feet) is similar to plant life found in the Arctic tundra.

The road continues to be a toll road, but is now run by the city of Colorado Springs under a special-use permit from the U.S. Forest Service.

Mountain Passes

One definition of a mountain pass is the low point on a watershed divide that is the simplest route over that divide. Colorado abounds in passes due to its substantial mountainous terrain. Ed and Gloria Helmuth, in their book, *The Passes of Colorado*, identify 469 named passes, some only for foot traffic. Passes for automotive travel range from interstate highways all the way down to rough four-wheel-drive-only, two-track trails. An excellent guide to Colorado's backcountry motor passes is the *Colorado Pass Book* by Don Koch, but there is much material available on the subject. Following is a list of Colorado automotive passes.

Pass	County	Summit Elevation
Arapahoe	Boulder-Grand	11,905
Argentine	Clear Creek-Summit	13,207
Baxter	Garfield	8,422
Berthoud	Clear Creek-Grand	11,315
Black Bear	San Juan-San Miguel	12,840
Black Sage	Gunnison	9,745
Boreas	Park-Summit	11,481
Breakneck	Park	10,910
Browns	Park	11,372
Buffalo	Jackson-Routt	10,180
Cameron	Jackson-Larimer	10,276
Cinnamon	Hinsdale-Ouray	12,620
Cochetopa	Saguache	10,030
Columbine	Montrose	9,120
Cordova	Huerfano-Las Animas	11,248
Corona or Rollins	Grand-Boulder	11,671
Cottonwood	Chaffee-Gunnison	12,126
Crooked Creek	Eagle	10,020
Cucharas	Huerfano-Las Animas	9,941
Cumberland	Gunnison	12,020
Cumbres	Conejos	10,015
Dallas Divide	Ouray-San Miguel	8,970
Douglas	Mesa	8,268
Elwood	Mineral-Rio-Grande	11,631
Engineer Mountain	Hinsdale-Ouray	12,750
Fall River	Larimer	11,796
Fremont	Lake	11,318
Georgia	Park-Summit	11,585
Gore Pass	Grand	9,527
Guanella	Clear Creed-Park	11,669
Gunsight	Gunnison	12,090
Gypsum Gap	San Miguel	6,100
Hagerman	Lake-Pitkin	11,925
Hancock	Chaffee-Gunnison	12,140
Hayden	Fremont-Saguache	10,709
Hermit	Custer-Saguache	13,020
Hoosier Pass	Park-Summit	11,541
Imogene	Ouray-San Miguel	13,114
Independence	Lake-Pitkin	12,095
Jones	Clear Creek-Grand	12,453
Kebler	Gunnison	10,000
Kenosha	Park	10,001
La Manga	Conejos	10,230
La Salle	Park	9,733
La Veta	Costilla-Huerfano	9,382
Lizard Head	Dolores-San Miguel	10,222
Los Pinos	Hinsdale-Saguache	10,500
Loveland	Clear Creek-Summit	11,992
Marshall	Chaffee-Saguache	10,846
McClure	Gunnison-Pitkin	8,755
Medano	Huerfano-Saguache	9,950
Milner	Grand-Larimer	10,758
Molas	San Juan	10,910
Monarch	Chaffee-Gunnison	11,312
Mosca	Alamosa-Huerfano	9,713
Mosquito	Lake-Park	13,188
Muddy	Grand-Jackson	8,772
Music	Custer-Saguache	11,380
No Name	Huerfano	10,100
North	Saguache	10,149
North La Veta	Costilla-Huerfano	9,413
Ohio	Gunnison	10,003
Old Monarch	Chaffee-Gunnison	11,375
Ophir	San Juan-San Miguel	11,789
Owl Creek	Ouray-Gunnison	10,114
Pass Creek	Costilla-Huerfano	9,400
Pearl	Gunnison-Pitkin	12,705
Poncha	Chaffee-Saguache	9,010
Ptarmigan	Eagle-Summit	11,777
Rabbit Ears	Grand-Jackson	9,426
Red Cone	Park-Summit	12,600
Red Hill	Park	9,993
Red Mountain	Ouray-San Juan	11,018
Ripple Creek	Rio Blanco	10,343
Schofield	Gunnison-Pitkin	10,707
Shrine	Eagle-Summit	11,089
Slumgullion	Hinsdale	11,361
Spring Creek	Hinsdale	10,901
Squaw	Clear Creek	9,807
Stoney	Jefferson	8,560
Stony	Hinsdale-San Juan	12,588
Stunner	Conejos	10,541
Taylor	Gunnison-Pitkin	11,928
Tennessee	Eagle-Lake	10,424
Tincup	Chaffee-Gunnison	12,154
Tomichi	Gunnison	11,979
Trail Ridge Road	Grand-Larimer	12,183
Trout Creek	Chaffee-Park	9,346
Ute	Grand	9,524
Ute	Teller	9,165
Vail	Eagle-Summit	10,666
Waunita	Gunnison	10,303
Webster	Park-Summit	12,096
West Cottonwood	Eagle	8,280
Weston	Lake-Park	11,921
Weston	Lake-Park	11,900
Wilkerson	Chaffee-Gunnison	9,507
Williams	Chaffee-Gunnison	11,762
Willow Creek	Grand-Jackson	9,621
Wolf Creek	Mineral	10,850
Yvonne	Hinsdale-Ouray	12,800

CHAPTER

10 Man-Made Marvels

Colorado's rugged terrain long has played the role of encouraging technological and engineering inventions. New technology was needed to move men and materials across the mountains. Miners were among the first to innovate, followed by railroad engineers, water engineers and highway engineers. Following are the abbreviated stories of the men and technologies that changed life in Colorado, and in some cases, the world.

Tesla and Nunn Electrify the World

Croatia-born scientist and inventor Nikola Tesla quite literally electrified the world. His list of inventions include the rotating magnetic field principle, polyphase alternating-current generating and transmission systems, a telephone repeater, the induction motor, the Tesla coil transformer and wireless communication.

It was in his laboratory in Colorado Springs that he worked from early 1899 to early 1900 to become the first and still only man to create man-made lightning. He used 40,000 feet of wire in a giant transformer to send millions

Figure 10.1 – Nikola Tesla.
(Tesla Museum photo.)

of volts of electricity to a 30-inch copper ball atop an 80-foot wood tower. When power was applied to his invention, sharp cracking sounds were heard 15 miles away in Cripple Creek as the current built. Soon, enough power was generated to send lightning bolts 135 feet to the ground. No doubt the experiment could have produced even greater results, but the overload on the Colorado Springs Electric Co. power plant caused a fire, which resulted in a complete blackout of the town.

While the man-made lightning was spectacular, Tesla's impact on Colorado and the world started several years earlier with his invention and patent of an alternating-current power and transmission system.

Tesla in 1885 sold the patents for his alternating-current generating and transmission systems to George Westinghouse and the Westinghouse Electric Company. What followed was an epic business battle between Westinghouse and Thomas Edison (Tesla once worked for Edison) over the superiority of Tesla's alternating-current system and Edison's direct-current system. It took a banker and attorney in Telluride, Colo. to help settle the issue.

L.L. Nunn

Lucien L. Nunn moved to Telluride in 1881 as an entrepreneur. He built the town's first bath and operated a rental house. He practiced law and eventually bought the San Miguel Basin Bank – the bank Butch Cassidy robbed to start his infamous criminal career. With the bank in hand, Nunn ventured into mining when hired by the Keystone Placer and Gold King Mines.

The business challenge facing Nunn at the mines was the potentially ruinous high cost of transporting energy up the mountain to run the mine equipment.

Nunn had heard of Tesla's alternating-current power system and believed it to be superior to Edison's direct-current system, which lost substantial power during transmission. With $100,000 in gold from his mines, he traveled to Pittsburgh where he met with Westinghouse. A partnership was formed.

While others had generated and transmitted alternating current to light lightbulbs, Nunn's construction of an alternating-current power plant, and the resulting transmission of power three miles and 900 feet in elevation to his mine, proved to be the world's first commercial application of an alternating power plant and transmission system.

The power system gave Tesla and Westinghouse evidence to argue for the superiority of alternating current. In 1893 Westinghouse exhibited the AC system next to Edison's DC power exhibit at the Columbian Exposition in Chicago where the superiority of AC power was given ample

Figure 10.2 — L.L. Nunn's power plant near Ames, Colo., in San Miguel County. George Westinghouse and Nikola Tesla were contracted to build the alternating-current generating and transmission plant. When completed, it was the world's first commercial transmission of high-pressure, alternating-current electricity. (Denver Public Library, Western History Collection. X-6589.)

exposure. Edison's DC power system soon became an also-ran.

Tesla and Nunn subsequently were granted the right to build a power plant at Niagara Falls to power most major cities of the industrial Northeast. The abundant and inexpensive power supply played a major factor in America's leap to industrial powerhouse.

World's Highest Suspension Bridge

The Arkansas River, in its 1,450-mile journey from Colorado's Continental Divide to the Mississippi River, cuts a spectacular, 1,000-foot canyon through a massive granite upthrust at the base of the Rocky Mountains. The canyon, now called Royal Gorge, is an access point for travel in to the high mountains. By the 1870s, the Denver and Rio Grande Railroad was transporting silver from the mines in Leadville to the world through the Royal Gorge. Passenger trains also proved popular on the route as tourists flocked to see the spectacular canyon from the bottom up.

Lon Piper, a San Antonio, Texas, entrepreneur, by 1920 had recognized the value of the canyon as a tourist attraction. In 1929, he convinced the nearby town of Canon City that an automobile bridge be constructed over the gorge. Such a bridge would enhance the area's appeal to tourists. Piper put up $60,000 of his own money to construct the bridge. Construction was started in the summer of 1929. Only six months later, the world's highest suspension bridge – 1,053 feet above the Arkansas River – was completed at a cost of $350,000. No major accidents or injuries were recorded.

The bridge today is no less spectacular, although it doesn't serve any particular transportation purpose. It crosses the Royal Gorge, yes, but not on a transportation route. It doesn't go anywhere. Still, it draws more than 500,000 visitors each year, and now is accompanied by a 35-passenger aerial tramway and an incline railway that offer tourists yet more views of the Royal Gorge. A passenger tourist train runs through the bottom of the gorge (see Transportation chapter), while the river itself hosts thousands of whitewater enthusiasts enjoying the views and the challenging river run. In total, it is one of the busiest tourist centers in the state.

The first step in building the bridge was construction of the two concrete abutments to hold the bridge towers on either side of the canyon. Next, the two steel towers were erected. The south tower is 110 feet high, the north tower 150 feet. Spanning the first cables across the canyon was accomplished by lowering two ends from either side of the canyon rim to the bottom where the ends were spliced before the cable was hauled back up as a single piece across the gorge. Trolley cables were hung first, which allowed the suspension cable to be put in place.

Each suspension cable consists of 2,100 individual #9 wires woven around a three-quarter-inch core wire into a cable nine inches in diameter. Each suspension cable weighs more than 300 tons. Each of the 4,200 #9 wires was pulled across the canyon one at a time. The bridge will support more than 2 million pounds.

Total length of the bridge is 1,260 feet, its width is 18 feet. The span of the bridge between towers is 880 feet. There is 1,000 tons of steel in the floor of the bridge, while the deck consists of 1,292 planks, of which roughly 250 are replaced each year.

Replacement cost of the bridge is estimated at more than $10 million.

First of the Great Irrigation Tunnels

Early settlers of the Uncompahgre Valley near the towns of Delta and Montrose on Colorado's far Western Slope by 1883 had almost everything needed for a thriving community. A narrow-gauge railroad had arrived from Gunnison in 1882. A standard-gauge spur connected the area to Grand Junction to the north. What the valley didn't have was water for irrigation. The Uncompahgre River was not big enough nor reliable enough for farmers.

The saga of designing and building the 5.8-mile Gunnison tunnel is one of high adventure and perseverance. While the tunnel was considered an engineering marvel in its day, it also played an important political role in shaping the American West. Efforts to secure funding for the project can claim some credit – or bear some responsibility – for the creation of the U.S. Bureau of Reclamation and its nearly century-long efforts to transform the American West.

A tunnel running from the Gunnison River at the bottom of fearsome Black Canyon, under Vernal Mesa and into the Uncompahgre Valley was first proposed by French gold miner and farmer F.C. Lauzon. He knew in 1890 of the much greater supply of water locked deep in the canyon, and proposed the community figure a way of getting that water to the Uncompahgre.

What followed was a long battle by local community leaders, state politicians and Colorado senators and congressmen to secure financing for the project. Eventually, the U.S. Department of the Interior set aside $2.4

million for the tunnel project from a new reclamation fund, a precursor to the Bureau of Reclamation.

Design and engineering of the project was an adventurous endeavor. The first attempt to survey the canyon ended with sunken boats, lost provisions, a difficult climb out of the canyon and not enough information. A second more successful attempt was made by local men in 1901 who used rubber mattresses to negotiate the rough river.

Work began in 1901, but the first site selected for a three-mile tunnel proved unworkable when crews encountered difficult and very expensive mining conditions. By 1904, construction had started on a longer tunnel, 30,582 feet, but simpler to engineer and able to deliver more water. This tunnel would deliver 1,300 cubic feet per second through the 10.5-foot-by-11.5-foot tunnel into a 15-mile canal before being deposited in the Uncompahgre River south of Montrose.

Work on the tunnel was slow and dangerous. Crews encountered soft conditions which required costly reinforcements of the tunnel. Rugged fault zones spewed both hot and cold water. In 1906, the tunnel struck a huge underground water supply that flooded the tunnel with an estimated 25 million gallons of water every 24 hours. With the water came deadly amounts of carbon dioxide. Construction halted while water was pumped out and a 680-foot ventilation shaft could be built to vent the tunnel. Later in 1906, a cave-in killed six workers.

Pay for the workers averaged $2.36 per day.

The tunnel holed through in June of 1909. President William Howard Taft dedicated the tunnel later that year while on a whistlestop tour. Despite Taft's 1909 dedication, the tunnel was not fully operational until 1912.

Some 25 years later, the ever-growing reclamation project was finalized with the construction of Taylor Park Dam on the Taylor River near Gunnison. The dam stored 106,200 acre-feet of water which guarantees irrigation water for 146,000 acres of land in Delta and Montrose Counties. The system includes 170 miles of canals, 400 miles of lateral ditches and 205 miles of drainage ditches. Total cost of the project in 1938 was just shy of $9 million. Users today pay $13 per acre for irrigation water.

Other dams have since been built and added to the system. They include Blue Mesa Dam, Curecanti Dam, Crystal Dam and Ridgeway Reservoir. Blue Mesa Reservoir is the largest body of water in Colorado and helps supply water to Arizona, California and other thirsty down-stream members of the Colorado River Compact.

Colorado-Big Thompson Project

The largest of Colorado's several large-scale irrigation projects is the Colorado - Big Thompson Project. A massive trans-basin project, the CBTP moves water from Colorado's water-rich Western Slope under the Continental Divide to provide supplemental water to 30 Front Range cities and towns. The roughly 230,000 acre-feet of water moved under the mountains each year also irrigates approximately 615,000 acres of fertile northeastern Colorado farmland.

Over an area of roughly 9,750 square miles, the CBTP system is comprised of 35 miles of water tunnels, 95 miles of canals, 700 miles of electricity transmission lines and 12 reservoirs. The system collects water from the Upper Colorado River Basin in Grand County at elevations generally above 8,000 feet. Water is pumped from lower-elevation reservoirs such as Windy Gap and Lake Granby before gravity takes over at Grand Lake and the 13.1-mile Alva B. Adams tunnel under the Continental Divide.

As water travels down from the Adams Tunnel to the cities and farms at elevations around 5,000 feet, it is used to generate electricity. Five power plants capture the water's energy on the way down and generate 670 million kilowatt hours sold annually through the U.S. Department of Energy.

Reservoirs on the West Slope side of the system include Willow Creek, Lake Granby, Shadow Mountain, Windy Gap and Green Mountain. Grand Lake is also utilized, but is a natural lake.

Water is collected in Grand County in Willow Creek, Lake Granby and Windy Gap Reservoirs where pumping stations move it uphill to Shadow Mountain Reservoir. From there, water flows down into Grand Lake before moving through the Adams Tunnel to the east side of the Continental Divide. Green Mountain Reservoir stores water to be released into the Colorado River System when water is drawn out through the Adams Tunnel system.

On the east side, a series of reservoirs store water for use by municipalities and farmers. They include Mary's Lake (a natural basin), Lake Estes, Pinewood Reservoir, Horsetooth Reservoir, Carter Lake and Boulder Reservoir.

An extensive system of pipelines and canals moves the water from the reservoirs to the users.

10.3 – Lake Granby is the primary water storage reservoir for the Colorado-Big Thompson Project and the second-largest body of water in the state. Note the famous silhouette of Abraham Lincoln in repose created by the Indian Peaks. (Photo courtesy of Grand County Newspapers. File photo.)

The idea for the massive water moving project was first proposed in 1884, but preliminary surveys indicated the project wasn't feasible. By 1890, a small trans-basin diversion imported a small amount of water from the West Slope to the Poudre River Basin.

With the creation of the U.S. Reclamation Service in 1902, and the subsequent creation of the Bureau of Reclamation, it became possible by the 1930s to organize the Northern Colorado Water Conservancy District to oversee construction and management of the massive project. Construction started in 1938 with Green Mountain Reservoir to satisfy demands of downstream users in the Colorado River system. Lake Granby dam followed in 1941, then came Shadow Mountain Reservoir in 1944. The Adams Tunnel was holed through in 1944. By 1947 the first of the West Slope water flowed east, but the entire system was an ongoing project that continued through the 1980s when Windy Gap Reservoir was completed.

Cost to end users was $1.50 per acre-foot when applications were first accepted in 1937 and 1938. One acre foot will supply one to two average urban households for one year.

Denver Water Collection System

With more than one million customers, Denver Water provides water to roughly 25% of the state's population. Unlike many other large water collection and distribution systems, Denver Water is not used for agricultural irrigation. Rather it is used for municipal purposes. Some 54% of the water delivered to residential customers, however, is used for landscaping.

Almost all of Denver Water's supply comes from mountain snowmelt. A vast collection system in Summit and Grand Counties on the Western Slope, and on the South Platte drainage system on the Front Range, draws snowmelt from roughly 4,000 square miles of winter snowpack.

Denver water maintains almost 657,000 acre feet of water storage in 13 reservoirs, the largest and most important being Dillon Reservoir in Summit County with a capacity of 254,036 acre feet. Water for Dillon Reservoir is collected from the Blue River and its tributaries. It is piped under the Continental Divide for use on the Front Range via the Harold D. Roberts Tunnel.

The Roberts Tunnel is an engineering marvel in its own right. At 23.3 miles, it is the world's longest major underground water tunnel, and is nearly the same length as the "Chunnel" running from England to France under the English Channel. The tunnel, at 4,465 feet below the surface, took 16 years to build and today is valued at nearly $60 million.

The deep bore presented numerous engineering problems that eventually were overcome by digging from four headings on three courses. At capacity, the tunnel can move 2,023 acre-feet of water a day, or roughly 680 million gallons. The water is deposited in the North Fork of the South Platte River where it becomes part of the multi-reservoir collection and storage system on the South Platte drainage.

In Grand County, Denver Water engages in more West Slope water collection. The tributaries of the Fraser River are a maze of small diversion dams and canals, all collecting and funneling water to the Moffat Tunnel, a 6.2-mile tunnel under the Continental Divide from Winter Park Resort to South Boulder Creek. The Moffat Tunnel was another major engineering achievement in its day. It is the pilot bore of the famous railroad tunnel. At capacity, it can carry 1,280 cubic feet per second.

One of the more interesting aspects of the Denver Water West Slope collection system is the multi-basin journey of water from the Williams Fork Valley as it makes its way to Front Range homes. Snowmelt in the high portions of the Williams Fork Valley is collected and transported

Figure 10.4 – An inspection crew at Roberts Tunnel in 1956. At 23.3 miles, the tunnel is the world's longest major underground water tunnel. (Photo courtesy Denver Water.)

through he Gumlick Tunnel under the Continental Divide, west to east. From there the water runs through the Vasquez Tunnel, back under the Continental Divide, east to west. Now in the Fraser River collection system, the water is transported once again under the Continental Divide, west to east, this time through the Moffat Tunnel.

Denver Water was established in 1918. It is the oldest and largest water utility in the state.

Reservoirs adding storage to the Denver Water system are:

Reservoir	Capacity acre-feet
Dillon	254,0364
Eleven-Mile	97,7791
Cheesman	79,0641
Gross	41,811
Antero	20,015
Marston	19,796
Ralston	10,749
Strontia Springs	7,863
Long Lakes	1,807

```
Platte Canyon  . . . . . . . . . . . . . .910
Soda Lakes  . . . . . . . . . . . . . . .645
Williams Fork  . . . . . . . . . . . .96,822 . . . . . . . . . . . . . . . . .Exchange
Wolford Mountain . . . . . . . . .25,606 . . . . . . . . . . . . . . . . .Exchange
```

Denver Water trans-basin diversion tunnels:

Tunnel	Length	Capacity
Harold D. Roberts	23.3 miles	1,020 cubic feet/second
August P. Gumlick	2.9 miles	550 cubic feet/second
Vasquez	.3 miles	550 cubic feet/second
Moffat	6.1 miles	1,280 cubic feet/second

Denver Water uses two canals to move water. The High Line Canal runs through Denver and selected suburbs for 68 miles. It can carry 600 cubic feet per second. City Ditch runs from Chatfield Dam, 27.5 miles to Denver's City Park with a capacity of 86 cubic feet per second.

As water flows from the mountains to Denver, Denver Water uses the energy to produce electricity at five different power plants. The Williams Fork Dam and Power Plant has a generator capacity of 3 megawatts; Strontia Springs Dam, 1 megawatt; Foothills Treatment Plant, 3 megawatts; Dillon Dam, 1.7 megawatt; and Roberts Tunnel, 5.5 megawatts. One megawatt is equal to 1 million watts.

Three treatment plants are used in the Denver Water System. The Marston Treatment Plant and the Moffat Treatment Plant each can treat 200 million gallons per day. Foothills Treatment Plant can treat 270 million gallons of water each day.

Eisenhower Tunnel

Efforts to construct an automobile tunnel under the Continental Divide at Loveland Pass date back to 1943 when a pioneer bore was completed and construction bids sought by the Colorado Department of Highways. When only one bid was received, the $10 million bid so far exceeded engineer estimates the idea was shelved. Bids were sought again in 1956, but once again only one bid was received and no contract award was made.

A Denver to Cove Fort, Utah route for Interstate 70 was designated by the Bureau of Public Roads in 1957. Even with the route designation federal funds did not become available for construction of the Denver to Utah leg of Interstate 70 until 1962. To complete an interstate through the Colorado mountains, engineers agreed a tunnel under or near Loveland Pass would be necessary. The severity of Loveland Pass makes it an impossible route for an interstate-caliber roadway.

With federal funds secured, a pioneer bore was finished in late 1964. With information gained from the pioneer bore, preliminary engineering commenced. Actual tunnel construction on the first of two bores was started on March 15, 1968.

The original plan called for the first bore to be completed in three years, but opening ceremonies weren't held on the first bore until March 8, 1973. By then, the tunnel, which originally was called the Straight Creek tunnel, named for the drainage at the west portal, had been renamed in honor of President Dwight D. Eisenhower.

Contractors struggled throughout the five-year construction phase. Building at 11,000 feet proved less efficient for man and machines. A brief summer construction season at such an elevation also complicated matters. But it was the mountain itself that caused the most trouble. Engineers based construction techniques on data from the pioneer bore. Conditions 115 feet to 230 feet north, where the tunneling was underway, did not match those found in the pioneer bore. The result was a five year battle between engineers and the mountain.

During the peak of construction, 1,140 workers were employed in three shifts, 24 hours a day, six days a week. The final cost of the first tunnel was $108 million, 91% of that coming from federal funds.

From portal to portal, the length of the tunnel is 8,941 feet, or 1.693 miles. The shape of the tunnel varies from a straight-leg horseshoe to an oval, the oval used where stress is greatest. The rough bore is at maximum 48-feet high, 40-feet wide. Vehicles travel through a finished section of only 16-feet, four inches by 26-feet wide. The portion of the tunnel not dedicated to vehicles is dedicated to structure and ventilation.

East portal elevation of the tunnel is 11,012 feet, the west portal is at 11,112 feet. The Continental Divide crosses over the roadway at 12,608 feet, 1,496 feet above. It is the highest vehicular tunnel in the world.

While the tunnel saves motorists an estimated 30 minutes drive-time from traveling over Loveland Pass, weather still plays a major factor in traveling up the steep approaches to the high-altitude portals. It is not uncommon for more than 300 inches of snow to fall in a winter at the west portal. Consider that the summit of Berthoud Pass, another trans-Continental Divide automobile route, is 11,315 feet, a scant 203 feet higher than the tunnel.

Construction statistics for the first bore were compiled by Colorado

Department of Transportation:

```
Excavation in tunnel .............. .524,000 cubic yards
Portal excavation .................. .90,000 cubic yards
Other excavation ..........     ......177,000 cubic yards
Concrete in tunnel lining ........... .190,000 cubic yards
Concrete in buildings .............. .34,000 cubic yards
Steel reinforcing bars in tunnel ............. .10,000 tons
Structural steel in tunnel ................. .23,400 tons
Structural steel in buildings ................ .2,600 tons
Reinforcing steel in buildings ............... .2,100 tons
```

Construction of the Edwin C. Johnson bore, the second bore of the tunnel, went considerably smoother.

The Johnson bore is, essentially, a twin to the Eisenhower tunnel. Centerline to centerline, the two tunnels are 115 feet apart at the east ventilation building entrance, 120 feet apart at the west entrance and 230 feet at the widest point. The length of the Johnson tunnel is slightly longer at 1.697 miles. Both tunnels have an average grade of 1.64% from east to west.

Construction was started on the Johnson bore in August of 1975. More than 800 workers were employed, 480 in actual drilling operations. Workers encountered many of the same mining problems in the second tunnel, but this time were able to shorten the construction time to four years. The second tunnel was opened to traffic Dec. 29, 1979, allowing for the first time two-lane travel in both directions under the Continental Divide. The cost of the Johnson Tunnel was $110.5 million.

Even with modern construction techniques, the building of the Eisenhower Tunnel proved dangerous. Three workers were killed during construction of the first bore, six died while building the second bore.

Traffic through the Eisenhower Tunnel and on I-70 has steadily increased. Long traffic delays caused by the steep tunnel approaches and volume are common. As the following traffic statistics show, traffic through the tunnel from 1990 to 2002 increased a staggering 54%, due primarily to a boom in population and the increasing popularity of outdoor recreation.

Eisenhower Tunnel Traffic Counts 1990

	Eastbound	Westbound	Monthly Total	Avg. Daily Total
January	281,956	268,455	550,411	17,755
February	269,484	274,408	543,892	19,425
March	325,731	328,739	654,470	21,112
April	236,666	216,207	452,873	15,096
May	229,044	229,065	458,109	14,777
June	295,487	308,386	603,873	20,129
July	378,475	368,492	746,967	24,096
August	379,624	377,834	757,458	24,434
September	326,170	311,280	637,450	21,248
October	246,909	245,819	492,728	15,894
November	222,834	228,140	450,974	15,032
December	266,895	284,963	551,758	17,799
Annual Total 1990			**6,900,963**	**18,899**

Eisenhower Tunnel Traffic Counts 2002

	Eastbound	Westbound	Monthly Total	Avg. Daily Total
January	476,643	457,885	934,528	30,146
February	434,558	442,567	877,125	31,326
March	538,355	539,007	1,077,362	34,754
April	382,373	357,670	740,043	24,668
May	382,410	382,483	764,893	24,674
June	449,820	457,369	907,189	30,240
July	541,493	543,945	1,085,438	35,014
August	531,502	547,708	1,079,210	34,813
September	459,250	432,661	891,911	29,730
October	378,086	375,794	753,880	24,319
November	387,547	406,098	793,645	26,455
December	469,902	497,215	967,117	31,197
Annual Total for 2002			**10,872,341**	**29,787**

Eisenhower Tunnel Traffic Counts 2003

	Eastbound	Westbound	Monthly Total	Avg. Daily Total
January	489,803	475,355	965,158	31,134
February	421,590	428,256	849,846	30,352
March	480,229	470,986	951,215	30,684
April	376,586	361,558	738,144	24,604
May	370,039	371,876	741,915	23,932
June	435,555	433,386	868,941	28,964
July				
August				
September				
October				
November				
December				
Annual Total 2003				

The Moffat Railroad Tunnel

David H. Moffat spent a lifetime pursuing his dream of building an efficient railroad route from Denver, through the Rocky Mountains, and on to Salt Lake City and the Pacific. At one time reputed as the richest man in Colorado, he died penniless after sinking his entire fortune in his railroad dream. While he did succeed in building a spectacular route over the Continental Divide at Rollins Pass, the route never showed a profit due to harsh winter conditions. His dreamed-of tunnel wouldn't become a reality until more than a decade after his 1911 death.

Moffat's Rollins Pass route was North America's highest railroad pass at 11,660 feet. This proved as spectacular as it did expensive to operate. With much of the route above timberline, heavy snowfall or drifting snow harassed the route and workers for the nearly 25 years of its operation. So frequent were winter delays on the pass, workers coined a favorite slogan when the Moffat Tunnel finally opened in February of 1928. The tunnel, it was said, took "23 miles off the route and 23 days off the schedule."

Denver political interests had tried many times to secure public financing to make a western railroad route from Denver possible. Since southern Colorado towns had access through the mountains via Marshall and Tennessee Passes, legislators from those areas would block Denver's efforts in the name of competitive advantage. It took a catastrophic flood in Pueblo on June 3, 1921 to turn the tide in Denver's favor. The flood destroyed downtown Pueblo, killing more than 100 people and causing more than $16 million in damage. Pueblo citizens immediately sought emergency funds from the state. Governor Oliver Shoup called a special session of the state legislature to help in the aftermath of the flood. While flood relief funding was passed for Pueblo, so too, was the Moffat Tunnel Bill.

The Moffat Tunnel Bill created a public board, the Moffat Tunnel Commission. The Commission was given the power to collect taxes in nine counties from Denver to the Utah border, and was charged with building the Moffat Tunnel.

An initial bond issue was floated for $6.72 million. Construction commenced in 1923 on what was at the time the sixth-longest railroad tunnel in the world. A pilot bore construction technique was used. The pilot bore would later become the Moffat Water Tunnel, an important element to Denver Water's collection system.

Work progressed from the east and west portals. Elevation of the East

241

Figure 10.5 – An eastbound Denver and Rio Grande Western train exits the east portal of the Moffat Tunnel in the winter of 1993. (Doug Freed photo.)

Portal is 9,198 feet, elevation of the West Portal is 9,085. The elevation of the apex 9,239 feet. The slight gradients sloping down to each portal allow for natural drainage of the tunnel. At the apex, the tunnel is 2,400 feet below the Continental Divide.

Workers tunneling from the east found good hard rock and made rapid progress. On the west side, however, workers found bad rock and tremendous underground pressures which caused significant delays and budget-busting conditions. By November of 1925 two more bond issues totaling another $6 million had been sold to continue construction.

On Feb. 26, 1926, workers from the east portal were suddenly deluged with a massive pour of water. Having passed the apex of the tunnel, the tunnel quickly filled with water and mud. By the time the water had subsided, it was necessary to re-excavate several thousand feet of the tunnel.

Engineers continued to struggle on the west side. On July 30, 1926, more than 100 tons of rock collapsed in the tunnel, killing six workers. It was the project's worst catastrophe. In all, 28 workers were killed during construction of the tunnel, a safety record considered quite good.

The pilot bore of the tunnel was holed through Feb. 12, 1926, with official ceremonies held Feb. 18. The holing-through ceremonies were conducted with the usual pomp of the day. A series of blasts were set off via telegraph by President Calvin Coolidge from the White House. The sound of the blasts were broadcast over the radio.

With the pilot bore holed through, work on the railroad tunnel progressed rapidly. The railroad tunnel was holed through on July 7, 1926. Another $2.75 million in bonds were sold to complete the project.

The first train to pass through the Moffat Tunnel carried lumber from the West Slope on Feb. 24, 1928. Official opening ceremonies were held Feb. 26, 1928. The ceremony was broadcast nationwide on KOA radio.

The tunnel bore is 24-feet high, 18-feet wide. During construction, 750,000 cubic yards of rock was removed with the assistance of 2.5 million pounds of dynamite. That equates to three billion pounds of rock, enough to fill 1,600 freight trains of 40 cars each. More than 700 miles of blasting holes were drilled using 800,000 pounds of drill steel. Workers sharpened 1,500 drill bits every day. To shore up the tunnel, more than 11-million board feet of timber was used, an amount equal to 2,000 miles of one-inch-by-12-inch plank. Workers were paid an average of $5.15 for an eight-hour shift.

Glenwood Canyon

Federal funds for Interstate 70 from Denver to Cove Fort, Utah were authorized in 1962. It would take 32 years to finish this section, the last segment being a 12.5-mile stretch through Glenwood Canyon.

The scenic splendor of Glenwood Canyon posed a double threat to highway engineers. A narrow canyon of towering rock walls and the Colorado River predicated a number of engineering challenges. But it was the beauty of the canyon, and those who sought to protect it, that caused the most substantial construction delays.

As early as 1965, when twin tunnels were built to accommodate four lanes just east of Glenwood Springs, protesters starting making their voices heard. While the tunnels proved useful from a traffic engineer's viewpoint, critics attacked the design as unimaginative and detrimental to the beauty of the canyon. Thus started a long struggle to accomplish a goal outlined in a 1968 Colorado General Assembly resolution: to blend "the wonders of human engineering" with the "wonders of nature."

By the 1960s, the canyon had become a focal point for preservationists and environmental groups. Some, such as the Sierra Club, vowed to block construction of the interstate through the canyon. The effort even drew the attention of celebrities from nearby Aspen. Singer John Denver became a vocal opponent of the construction project.

In an effort to reach some consensus, a citizen's advisory council was established to liaison with the public and provide critical review of the construction process. Before plans were finalized, they had been reviewed by more than 60 government agencies, environmental groups or advisory committees.

While time-consuming, the final design reached never-before-seen levels of environmental sensitivity and architectural design. The project garnered international attention for its efforts to preserve the beauty and ecosystem of the canyon. Once the final design had been completed, engineers spent an additional 800,000 hours developing the construction techniques that would have the least amount of environmental impact in the canyon.

Construction started in April 1980. Approximately 500 workers were employed on a daily basis by various contractors associated with the project.

To build the 39 bridges and 6.5 miles of viaduct found in the canyon, a 350-foot, eight-legged gantry was used to allow overhead construction once abutments and piers were placed. Several portions of viaduct or bridges were put in place simply to allow wildlife unfettered access to the river. More than 20 miles of retaining walls needed to be built, some are 40 feet high. An estimated 150,000 trees and shrubs were planted in a revegetation effort. Where rock walls were blasted during construction, the scarred portions were artificially stained to match the patina of surrounding weathered rock.

Each of the four rest areas employ the latest in environmental engineering. The buildings are heated with passive solar technology. The septic systems convert human waste to fertilizer in all but the Bair Ranch area.

Inside the 3,900-foot twin bores of the Hanging Lake Tunnel is where engineers displayed the latest in highway technology. Between the two tunnels is a four-story control center. From the control center engineers can monitor the temperature, moisture, ice or carbon monoxide present in the tunnel. Every car can be tracked with 20 video cameras. A radio rebroadcast system allows motorists uninterrupted radio reception even when deep in the tunnel. Technicians can use the rebroadcast system to broadcast emergency messages to cars via the car radios. The control center also can monitor traffic and send messages to much of the interstate system west of Vail Pass.

The construction effort continued for 12 years. The end result is a highway that draws almost as much attention as the canyon it travels through. For many, the graceful sweep of curves actually enhances the beauty of the canyon. For that reason alone, the canyon stretch of Interstate 70 should be applauded and imitated.

Opening ceremonies were held on Oct. 14, 1992. Final cost of the project was $490,348,000, 90% of that from federal funds. Three workers were killed during construction.

The project in 1993 received the "Outstanding Civil Engineering Achievement" award from the American Society of Civil Engineers.

Materials used during construction included 1.62 billion pounds of concrete, 30 million pounds of reinforcing steel and 30 million pounds of structural steel.

Shoshone Dam and Power Plant

Long before engineers built an interstate highway through Glenwood Canyon, there were engineers boldly damming the Colorado River to make electricity for an electricity-craving Western Slope population.

Work started on the Shoshone Dam, power plant and a bridge across the river at Shoshone Falls in 1906. Up to 1,000 workers toiled on the $3 million project. The dam is roughly eight miles from the west entrance to Glenwood Canyon.

The concrete diversion dam still stops the flow of the river, diverting water through a 12-foot-high by 16-foot-wide, 2.7-mile tunnel through the north canyon wall to the downstream power plant. At the power plant, the water falls 287 feet from the tunnel to turbines near river level. When the power plant opened in 1909, it had a production rating of 14.4 megawatts. The water, after turning the twin 9,000-horsepower turbines, re-enters the river channel. When power is being produced, the stretch of river between the dam and the power plant to this day runs almost dry. It is a twist of irony that this dry stretch of river draws much credit for keeping the rest of the river flowing with enough water to maintain recreation and fisheries. Shoshone Power Plant water rights are senior to virtually all those upstream, and that, even in the driest of years, keeps the water flowing in the Colorado River as upstream users must maintain reservoir releases to satisfy the senior water right.

World's Longest Conveyor System

At $500 million, the Henderson Mine and Mill is the largest privately financed construction project in Colorado. It is owned by Climax Molybdenum Co., a subsidiary of Phelps Dodge Corp.

Development of Henderson Mine began in 1967 when exploration revealed 300 million tons of molybdenum-rich ore about 50 miles west of Denver near the southeast flank of Berthoud Pass at the base of Jones Pass. The mine is in Clear Creek County, but the mill is 60 highway miles away in Grand County, high up in the environmentally preferred Williams Fork drainage.The tailing impoundment boasts a closed-loop water recycling system.

Moving the ore from mine to mill for more than 20 years involved a 9.6-mile railroad tunnel – the longest railroad tunnel in North America. Another five miles of surface rail connected the mine to the mill.

Replacing the railroad tunnel in 2002 is another engineering marvel. Rather than rail cars, the ore now is transported the 15 miles to the mill via a massive conveyor system. The ore travels one mile on a conveyor from the crusher to the old railroad tunnel. From there it is transferred to a 10-mile conveyor that runs through the old tunnel. This conveyor is the longest single-flight conveyor in the world. Another four-mile overland conveyor then transports the ore to the mill. Climax Molybdenum supplies the following data concerning the 10-mile conveyor, known as Production Conveyor 2.

Length: . . . . .55,195 feet
Lift: . . . . .1,556 feet
Belt Width: . . . . .48 inches
Speed: . . . .1,200 feet per minute max.
Capacity: . . . . .2,500 tons per hour
Installed Power: . . . . .11,000 hp

Pueblo's Transportation Technology Center

The Transportation Technology Center outside Pueblo, Colo. is a rail transit test facility owned by the U.S. Department of Transportation and operated by the Transportation Technology Center.

The center is home to 48 miles of test track, divided into three primary testing programs.

The Railroad Test Track is a 13.5-mile oval track used for testing trains at speeds up to 125 miles per hour.

The Facility for Accelerated Service Testing is a 4.8-mile loop dedicated to testing rail components and cars under high axle loads.

The Transit Test Track is a 9.1 mile oval with overhead electrical and third-rail electrical used for testing rapid transit vehicles at speeds up to 80 miles per hour.

On the Railroad Test Track is being developed a GPS-based tracking and reporting system able to track and communicate with on-track and off-track vehicles, and detect broken or damaged rails with far more accuracy than anything available to date.

11 Business and Economy

Once dependent on agriculture and mining, Colorado entered the new millennium with a diversified economy not matched in its history. Tourism, long important to the state, now ranks second to a broad-based and multi-faceted service industry. Manufacturing, thanks to the state's popularity as a high-technology corridor, has gained importance.

The state's service economy is dominated by business services such as software development, temporary employment agencies and advertising. Professional services such as health services, legal services and engineering remain important components of the state's economy.

Farm market receipts hover near $5 billion a year. The U.S. Department of Defense spends more than $5 billion annually in the state. Extractive industries – mining and oil and gas production – add roughly $3 billion to the economy. Employment in these sectors continues to decline, but technological improvements have kept production high.

Tourism's impact on the economy is more difficult to quantify. No economic subgroup specific to tourism exists (hotels and lodging, for instance, are reported as part of the service industry). Still, the governor's office for economic development estimates roughly $7 billion is generated from domestic travelers, another $900 million from international tourists. Many of the jobs generated by the tourism industry, however, are among the lowest-paying jobs in the state.

Thanks to the state's status as a high-technology manufacturing center, international exports hover near $6 billion a year.

Continued strong population growth points to continued expansion of the state's economy.

Top 40 Employers – Non-Government

Source: Denver Post, August 11, 2002

Rank	Employer	Type of Business	Number of Employees
1	Wal-Mart	Retail	19,600
2	Kroger (King Soopers/City Market)	Grocery	17,039
3	Qwest Communications	Telecommunications	15,000
4	Centura Health	Health Care	12,350
5	Vail Resorts	Ski / Resort	12,000
6	Safeway Inc.	Grocery	11,500
7	Staffing Solutions	Employment Contractor	11,000
8	Columbia / Health One	Health Care	9,000
9	Lockheed Martin Space Systems	Aerospace / Defense	8,700
10	United Airlines	Airline	7,876
11	Worldcom Inc.	Communications	7,245
12	Home Depot	Home Improvement Retail	7,000
13	Target	Discount Retail	6,694
14	Hewlett-Packard Co.	Computer	6,500
15	IBM Corp.	Computer	6,000
16	Wells Fargo	Banking	6,000
17	AT&T	Telecommunications	6,000
18	Exempla Healthcare	Hospital	5,324
19	ConAgra Inc.	Meat Products	5,000
20	Agilent Technologies	Diversified Technologies	4,700
21	United Parcel Service	Delivery Service	4,561
22	EchoStar Communications	Satellite Television	4,500
23	Xcel Energy	Utility	4,100
24	Coors Brewing Co.	Brewer	4,012
25	Albertsons	Grocery	4,000
26	Kmart Corp.	Discount Retailer	4,000
27	Sears Roebuck & Co.	Retail	4,000
28	Kaiser Permanente	Health Care Provider	3,900
29	Resource Management Systems	Employment Leasing	3,750
30	Sun Microsystems	Computers	3,600
31	Avaya Inc.	Communications systems	3,300
32	May Department Stores	Retail	3,100
33	Great-West Life & Annuity	Insurance	3,097
34	EDS Corp.	Computing / Neodata	2,931
35	Ball Corp.	Containers / Aerospace	2,900
36	7-Eleven Inc.	Convenience stores	2,800
37	Storage Technology Corp.	Computer Storage Systems	2,770
38	U.S. Bancorp	Bank	2,700
39	First Data Corp.	Financial Services	2,600
40	Children's Hospital	Hospital	2,557

Colorado's Top Export Products (2001)
Source: Office of Economic Development

Products	2001 Annual Exports
Total All Commodities	$6,125,493,907
Automatic data process machines	990,460,193
Office machines	656,147,958
Electronic integrated circuits	632,957,628
Oscilloscopes, spectrum analyzers	329,989,548
Medical equipment	206,011,761
Photo plates, film, etc.	175,970,709
Electric apparatus for line telephony	147,574,109
Aircraft, spacecraft, balloon parts	109,780,324
Instrument measure, check flow	80,098,173
Total Top 10 Products	$3,423,510,462

Colorado's Top 10 Trading Partners (2001)
Source: Office of Economic Development

Country	2001 Annual Exports
Canada	$1,046,065,506
Japan	764,723,162
United Kingdom	385,926,479
Singapore	356,972,202
Germany	341,016,840
France	339,555,440
Mexico	335,421,248
Netherlands	312,483,813
Hong Kong	261,618,226
Republic of Korea	248,046,401

National Rank in Technology Economy (2001)
Source: Office of Economic Development

Measure	U.S. Rank	Description
Technology companies	1	Percent of jobs in high-tech industries
New business job growth	6	Percent employment growth for firms less than 5 years old
Patents issued	10	# patents issued per 1 million population
University research & development	10	University research $ granted per capita
Federal research & development	8	Federal research $ granted per capita
Small business innovation research	3	SBIR grant money awarded per worker
Households with computers	3	Percent of households with computers

Federal Laboratories in Colorado

Laboratory / Research Center	Location
Bureau of Reclamation Research Laboratory	Denver
Climate Monitoring & Diagnostics Laboratory	Boulder
Dept. of Energy Grand Junction Projects Office	Grand Junction
Environmental Technology Laboratory	Boulder
Forecast Systems Laboratory	Boulder
Institute for Telecommunications Sciences	Boulder
National Center for Atmospheric Research	Boulder
National Geomagnetic Information Center	Denver
National Institute of Standards and Technology	Boulder
National Renewable Energy Laboratory	Golden
National Seed Storage Laboratory	Ft. Collins
National Wildlife Research Center	Ft. Collins
Natural Hazards Research & Applications Info. Center	Boulder
Rocky Mountain Research Station	Ft. Collins
Space Environment Laboratory	Boulder
Transportation Test Center	Pueblo

Education

The 2000 Census ranks Colorado third nationally in percentage of population with a college degree and ninth in percentage of population with a high school diploma.

The public K-12 education system is comprised of 176 school districts. The combined fall 2001 enrollment of those districts was 742,145. Because of a high concentration of students in metropolitan areas, the 10 largest districts enroll 56% of all students. Total K-12 funding approaches $4 billion, 58% of which is from the state, the balance primarily from local property taxes.

Colorado boasts 13 four-year colleges and universities in the state system with a 2001-2002 full-time enrollment of 104,369 students. Fifteen two-year colleges accounted for another 46,562 students. The United States Air Force Academy, one of America's four service academies, adds another 4,000. An estimated 23,000 students are enrolled in private universities, of which the largest are University of Denver, Regis University, Colorado Christian University and Colorado College. Another 23,000 students attend Colorado's vocational schools.

Two-Year Public Colleges (2002)
Source: Colorado Commission on Higher Education

College	Location	Full-time Enrollment
Aims Community College	Greeley	3,953
Arapahoe Community College	Littleton	4,318
Colorado Mountain College	Glenwood Springs	2,954
Colorado Northwestern College	Rangely	872
Community College of Aurora	Aurora	2,814
Community College of Denver	Denver	4,189
Front Range Community College	Westminster	8,125
Lamar Community College	Lamar	683
Morgan Community College	Fort Morgan	987
Northeastern Junior College	Sterling	1,594
Otero Junior College	La Junta	1,092
Pikes Peak Community College	Colorado Springs	5,679
Pueblo Community College	Pueblo	3,610
Red Rocks Community College	Lakewood	4,204
Trinidad State Junior College	Trinidad	1,488
Two-Year Institution Total		**46,562**

Four-Year Public Colleges and Universities (2002)
Source: Colorado Commission on Higher Education

College	Location	Full-time Enrollment
Adams State College	Alamosa	2,294
Colorado School of Mines	Golden	3,216
Colorado State University	Fort Collins	21,468
Fort Lewis College	Durango	4,169
Mesa State College	Grand Junction	4,461
Metropolitan State College	Denver	13,277
University of Colorado - Boulder	Boulder	23,920
University of Colorado - Colorado Springs	Colo. Springs	5,324
University of Colorado - Denver	Denver	7,892
University of Colorado Health Sciences Center	Denver	2,411
University of Northern Colorado	Greeley	10,328
University of Southern Colorado	Pueblo	3,515
Western State College	Gunnison	2,094
Four-Year Institution Total		**104,369**

Correction

Four-Year Colleges
Outside State System (2002)
Source: Colorado Commission on Higher Education

College	Location
Beth-El College of Nursing	Colorado Springs
Colorado Christian University	Lakewood
Colorado College	Colorado Springs
Colorado Technical College	Colorado Springs
Denver Technical College	Denver
Denver University	Denver
Jones International University	Denver
Naropa Institute	Boulder
National Technological University	Denver
Nazarene Bible College	Colorado Springs
Regis University	Denver
Rocky Mountain College of Art & Design	Denver
St. Thomas Theological Seminary	Denver
Teikyo Loretto Heights University	Denver
University of Phoenix	Denver
United States Air Force Academy	Colorado Springs
Yeshiva Tora Chaim Talmudical Seminary	Denver

Four-Year Colleges Outside State System (2002)
Source: Colorado Commission on Higher Education

College	Location
Beth-El College of Nursing	Colorado Springs
Colorado Christian University	Lakewood
Colorado College	Colorado Springs
Colorado Technical College	Colorado Springs
Denver Technical College	Denver
Jones International University	Denver
Naropa Institute	Boulder
National Technological University	Denver
Nazarene Bible College	Colorado Springs
Regis University	Denver
Rocky Mountain College of Art & Design	Denver
St. Thomas Theological Seminary	Denver
Teikyo Lorctto Heights University	Denver
University of Phoenix	Denver
United States Air Force Academy	Colorado Springs
Yeshiva Tora Chaim Talmudical Seminary	Denver

Two-Year Colleges Outside State System (2002)
Source: Colorado Commission on Higher Education

College	Location
Bel-Rae Institute of Animal Technology	Denver
Blair Junior College	Colorado Springs
Colorado Institute of Art	Denver
Columbia College	Aurora
Denver Automotive and Diesel College	Denver
Denver Conservative Baptist Seminary	Denver
Denver Institute of Technology	Denver
National College	Denver
Parks College	Denver

Public Higher Education Degrees Conferred
Source: Colorado Commission on Higher Education (2001)

Major	Degrees Conferred	Major	Degrees Conferred
Ag. Science / Ag. Business	619	Interdisciplinary Studies	373
Architecture	335	Law & Public Affairs	553
Arts & Humanities	6,905	Library Science	62
Business & Management	6,036	Mathematics & Science	2,423
Education	1,359	Parks	888
Engineering & Technologies	3,019	Protective Services	727
Health Care	3,349	Social & Behavioral Sciences	4,516
Home Economics	361	Vocational Programs	987
		Total	**32,450**

253

Technology

An estimated 6,000 high-tech businesses call Colorado home. They employ 183,559, enough to rank 10th nationally and easily No. 1 as a percentage of population. A variety of independent groups estimate Colorado is among the states best positioned to enjoy strong growth in the high-technology sector.

Colorado ranked 5th nationally in 2001 in venture capital investment when roughly $1.5 billion was invested in 111 Colorado companies. This amount was a sharp drop from previous years due to the national dot-com bust, but still was the third best year in Colorado history. Telecommunications once dominated the venture capital market, but 30% went to biotech firms in 2001, 33% to software companies.

The vast majority of Colorado's high-tech firms are small companies. Nearly half employ 10 or fewer, more than 75% employ 50 or fewer. Half see sales of $1 million or less, another 25% fall in the $3 million-or-under category.

Colorado ranks 7th nationally in computer and office equipment manufacturing, and fifth in software services and photonics manufacturing.

Biotechnology, an industry dominated by state-funded universities, remains strong. It is ranked 12th nationally with 665 workers generating $1 billion in annual revenue. The industry is expected to receive a boost with the $2 billion transformation of the former Fitzsimons Army Medical post to a life-science research, education and patient-care facility. The site will host the new 217-acre campus of the University of Colorado Health Sciences Center, and a 160-acre Colorado Bioscience Park. The bioscience park is expected to feature 3 million square feet of office space with an eventual workforce of 4,000.

Only California and Florida outpace Colorado in the aerospace, satellite and space industry. Colorado hosts more than 100 companies working in the space industry. They employ between 115,000 and 130,000 workers and generate between $4 and $5 billion annually. The state ranks 9th in per-capita U.S. Department of Defense spending, and 14th in per-capita defense contracts.

Colorado Springs has been awarded the command post for the newly created Northern Command at Peterson Air Force Base. Northern Command is expected to create up to 1,000 new jobs.

The 2002 Rocky Mountain High Technology Directory lists the following Colorado high-tech businesses by category. The directory is not a census of the businesses, as companies must voluntarily choose to be included.

Product	Number of Companies
Aerospace, Aircraft and Equipment	53
Analytical and Testing Equipment	118
Biotechnology	5
Chemicals	73
Communications Equipment and Service	137
Components	158
Computer Hardware Systems	50
Computer Peripherals	51
Electronics Production Equipment	20
Energy	7
Environmental	78
Industrial Equipment	137
Lasers, Optics and Photonics	47
Material Handling Equipment	29
Medical Equipment and Devices	100
Microelectronics	137
Military Equipment and Services	15
Monitoring and Controlling Equipment	63
Non-Industrial Electrical Products	25
Pharmaceutical	38
Plastics and Advanced Materials	64
Power Devices and Systems	37
Research, Development and Testing	189
Robotics and Factory Automation	22
Software Development	207
Software-Related Services	447

Tourism and Recreation

The vast majority of this book is dedicated to what makes Colorado such a popular tourist destination. It's density of national parks, national monuments, state parks and ski areas cannot be matched. The splendor of its natural beauty needs no explanation.

Of the $7 billion spent in Colorado in 2001 on tourism and recreation, $1.9 billion was spent for accommodations, $1.6 billion on eating and drinking, $1.2 billion in retail outlets, $1.3 billion for transportation and $1 billion for recreation.

Personal Income by County (in 1,000 dollars)

Source: U.S. Department of Commerce Bureau of Economic Affairs

	1970	1980	1990	2000	Avg. Annual Growth Rate
Colo. total	9,018,240	31,442,298	65,094,513	140,224,394	9.7
Adams	669,279	2,334,464	4,281,276	9,209,856	9.1
Alamosa	30,296	97,920	190,906	317,586	8.2
Arapahoe	802,499	3,900,422	9,646,137	21,614,876	11.6
Archuleta	8,755	32,494	69,925	182,923	9.9
Baca	22,483	36,937	86,677	104,069	5.9
Bent	17,664	38,838	73,024	101,480	6.3
Boulder	571,222	2,215,358	5,022,353	11,521,469	10.6
Chaffee	34,313	123,024	169,228	345,662	8.4
Cheyenne	9,644	19,652	46,427	54,116	6.1
Clear Creek	21,864	91,346	139,503	316,231	9.4
Conejos	15,469	38,297	73,059	126,913	7.7
Costilla	5,633	19,242	37,448	65,406	8.6
Crowley	9,679	28,155	47,521	86,859	.8
Custer	3,962	15,050	29,055	75,098	10.2
Delta	46,213	164,342	271,275	546,609	8.4
Denver	2,471,037	6,245,295	11,057,760	22,331,252	7.8
Dolores	3,704	14,608	21,368	35,482	6.8
Douglas	43,378	361,546	1,532,101	6,391,260	18.1
Eagle	28,752	176,847	495,984	1,466,217	14
Elbert	13,423	71,038	171,527	572,959	12.8
El Paso	891,848	2,946,450	7,072,264	14,956,694	10
Fremont	65,927	227,829	400,419	838,580	9
Garfield	56,925	235,360	513,287	1,137,121	10.5
Gilpin	3,992	26,394	50,106	142,856	12.7
Grand	13,670	79,310	137,112	301,972	10.7
Gunnison	18,020	80,336	141,358	300,962	9.8
Hinsdale	745	3,106	8,359	17,614	12.1
Huerfano	17,193	44,806	68,406	138,128	7.4
Jackson	5,159	17,039	22,358	32,567	6.5
Jefferson	1,088,822	4,582,046	9,391,939	19,245,697	10.2
Kiowa	12,256	27,056	39,836	55,312	5.1
Kit Carson	36,568	62,655	140,996	194,450	6.3
Lake	29,587	99,145	89,598	172,729	6.4
La Plata	58,001	241,472	524,128	1,171,655	10.5
Larimer	297,196	1,405,927	3,310,760	7,376,369	11.4
Las Animas	39,166	119,340	168,163	289,291	6.8
Lincoln	16,737	48,218	75,374	110,555	6.5
Logan	72,514	179,743	311,479	513,358	6.9
Mesa	185,109	811,712	1,447,971	2,884,697	9.6

Personal Income by County *continued*

Source: U.S. Department of Commerce Bureau of Economic Affairs

	1970	1980	1990	2000	Avg. Annual Growth Rate
Mineral	3,013	9,798	9,009	17,435	6.5
Moffat	22,005	121,460	183,273	283,066	8.9
Montezuma	34,155	137,993	265,604	507,080	9.2
Montrose	54,278	187,101	353,867	709,283	8.9
Morgan	74,708	196,653	363,865	594,685	7.4
Otero	71,198	182,155	280,716	445,381	6.3
Ouray	5,704	17,694	39,098	91,117	9.7
Park	9,038	51,861	125,545	388,280	13.7
Phillips	20,884	39,577	79,621	111,436	6.4
Pitkin	35,166	176,585	408,741	1,014,080	12
Prowers	42,853	98,833	207,245	337,590	7
Pueblo	396,969	1,108,346	1,768,897	3,145,555	7.2
Rio Blanco	19,403	92,800	93,986	155,714	7.2
Rio Grande	29,453	111,799	167,582	253,040	7.7
Routt	26,090	172,392	301,301	629,997	11.4
Saguache	9,501	31,183	57,411	88,282	8.5
San Juan	2,228	7,367	12,555	12,761	6.3
San Miguel	5,403	22,045	72,547	202,116	12.7
Sedgwick	13,967	27,680	47,341	66,393	5.1
Summit	8,363	112,442	295,979	806,193	16.6
Teller	14,376	75,432	217,032	562,358	13.2
Washington	22,914	60,614	94,419	101,062	5.5
Weld	322,906	1,042,664	2,071,600	4,125,887	9.2
Yuma	34,961	95,005	200,812	228,673	6.7

Metropolitan Areas

All Colo. Metro	7,740,265	26,954,230	56,603,058	122,803,612	9.8
Non-Metro Areas	1,277,975	4,488,068	8,491,455	17,420,782	9.2
Boulder/Longmont	571,222	2,215,358	5,022,353	11,521,469	10.6
Colo. Springs	891,848	2,946,450	7,072,264	14,956,694	10
Denver	5,075,015	17,423,773	35,909,213	78,792,941	9.7
Ft. Collins/Loveland	297,196	1,405,927	3,310,760	7,376,369	11.4
Grand Junction	185,109	811,712	1,447,971	2,884,697	9.6
Greeley	322,906	1,042,664	2,071,600	4,125,887	9.2
Pueblo	396,969	1,108,346	1,768,897	3,145,555	7.2
Denver/ Boulder/Greeley	5,969,143	20,681,795	43,003,166	94,440,297	9.8

Per Capita Income by County (dollars)

Source: U.S. Department of Commerce Bureau of Economic Affairs

	1970	1980	1990	2000	State Rank
Colorado total	4,055	10,809	19,680	32,434	
Adams	3,578	9,446	16,057	25,124	22
Alamosa	2,634	8,249	14,035	21,232	45
Arapahoe	4,902	13,119	24,489	44,081	2
Archuleta	3,258	8,688	12,992	18,214	55
Baca	3,972	6,844	19,155	23,126	33
Bent	2,719	6,538	14,523	16,984	60
Boulder	4,284	11,603	22,186	39,347	4
Chaffee	3,340	9,271	13,329	21,221	46
Cheyenne	4,022	9,069	19,385	24,322	27
Clear Creek	4,393	12,428	18,279	33,916	10
Conejos	1,973	4,933	9,769	15,089	62
Costilla	1,832	6,274	11,765	17,778	58
Crowley	3,132	9,416	12,043	15,698	61
Custer	3,488	9,811	14,961	21,310	43
Delta	3,021	7,656	12,885	19,590	52
Denver	4,793	12,636	23,621	40,203	3
Dolores	2,268	8,795	14,198	19,221	53
Douglas	5,027	14,112	24,844	35,452	6
Eagle	3,743	13,113	22,244	34,997	7
Elbert	3,421	10,289	17,589	28,463	16
El Paso	3,745	9,442	17,792	28,804	15
Fremont	2,980	7,910	12,415	18,111	57
Garfield	3,804	10,223	16,896	25,748	21
Gilpin	3,076	10,721	16,279	29,799	13
Grand	3,234	10,535	17,052	24,195	28
Gunnison	2,339	7,499	13,671	21,556	41
Hinsdale	3,688	7,502	17,861	22,381	36
Huerfano	2,631	6,952	11,407	17,659	59
Jackson	2,790	9,151	14,035	20,612	49
Jefferson	4,579	12,234	21,345	36,442	5
Kiowa	6,055	13,918	23,768	34,270	8
Kit Carson	4,820	8,247	19,772	24,373	26
Lake	3,561	11,221	14,802	22,105	38
La Plata	3,001	8,803	16,125	26,517	18
Larimer	3,262	9,367	17,676	29,178	14
Las Animas	2,476	7,995	12,224	18,928	54
Lincoln	3,437	10,387	16,657	18,198	56
Logan	3,839	9,069	17,734	24,942	24
Mesa	3,398	9,804	15,444	24,693	25

Per Capita Income by County *continued*

Source: U.S. Department of Commerce Bureau of Economic Affairs

	1970	1980	1990	2000	State Rank
Mineral	3,819	11,963	16,262	20,880	48
Moffat	3,374	9,208	16,065	21,485	42
Montezuma	2,618	8,280	14,179	21,234	44
Montrose	2,956	7,629	14,439	21,122	47
Morgan	3,685	8,739	16,568	21,806	40
Otero	3,039	8,068	13,953	22,003	39
Ouray	3,711	9,102	16,933	24,124	30
Park	4,055	9,570	17,401	26,414	19
Phillips	5,111	8,719	18,962	24,958	23
Pitkin	5,555	17,061	32,038	68,761	1
Prowers	3,224	7,564	15,538	23,355	31
Pueblo	3,348	8,796	14,366	22,174	37
Rio Blanco	4,013	14,616	15,636	26,039	20
Rio Grande	2,816	10,574	15,569	20,326	51
Routt	3,873	12,819	21,160	31,810	11
Saguache	2,472	7,871	12,394	14,738	63
San Juan	2,701	8,718	16,762	22,828	34
San Miguel	2,757	6,906	19,392	30,476	12
Sedgwick	4,102	8,493	17,678	24,134	29
Summit	2,994	12,549	22,552	34,136	9
Teller	4,236	9,270	17,327	27,212	17
Washington	4,135	11,473	19,736	20,433	50
Weld	3,587	8,424	15,675	22,539	35
Yuma	4,104	9,823	22,490	23,256	32

Metropolitan Areas

	1970	1980	1990	2000
All Colo. Metro	4,210	11,118	20,284	33,854
Non-Metro Areas	3,314	9,266	16,423	25,029
Boulder/Longmont	4,284	11,603	22,186	39,347
Colo. Springs	3,745	9,442	17,792	28,804
Denver	4,561	12,110	22,026	37,153
Ft. Collins/Loveland	3,262	9,367	17,676	29,178
Grand Junction	3,398	9,804	15,444	24,693
Greeley	3,587	8,424	15,675	22,539
Pueblo	3,348	8,796	14,366	22,174
Denver/ Boulder/Greeley	4,468	11,794	21,622	36,370

Per Capita Personal Income as Percent of U.S.

Source: U.S. Department of Commerce Bureau of Economic Affairs

	1970	1980	1990	2000
Colorado total	99	106	101	110
Adams	87	93	82	85
Alamosa	64	81	72	72
Arapahoe	120	129	125	150
Archuleta	80	85	66	62
Baca	97	67	98	78
Bent	66	64	74	58
Boulder	105	114	113	134
Chaffee	82	91	68	72
Cheyenne	98	89	99	83
Clear Creek	107	122	93	115
Conejos	48	48	50	51
Costilla	45	62	60	60
Crowley	76	92	62	53
Custer	85	96	76	72
Delta	74	75	66	66
Denver	117	124	121	136
Dolores	55	86	73	65
Douglas	123	139	127	120
Eagle	91	129	114	119
Elbert	84	101	90	97
El Paso	91	93	91	98
Fremont	73	78	63	61
Garfield	93	100	86	87
Gilpin	75	105	83	101
Grand	79	103	87	82
Gunnison	57	74	70	73
Hinsdale	90	74	91	76
Huerfano	64	68	58	60
Jackson	68	90	72	70
Jefferson	112	120	109	124
Kiowa	148	137	121	116
Kit Carson	118	81	101	83
Lake	87	110	76	75
La Plata	73	86	82	90
Larimer	80	92	90	99
Las Animas	60	79	62	64
Lincoln	84	102	85	62
Logan	94	89	91	85
Mesa	83	96	79	84

Per Capita Personal Income as Percent of U.S.

Source: U.S. Department of Commerce Bureau of Economic Affairs

	1970	1980	1990	2000
Mineral	.93	117	.83	.71
Moffat	.82	.90	.82	.73
Montezuma	.64	.81	.72	.72
Montrose	.72	.75	.74	.72
Morgan	.90	.86	.85	.74
Otero	.74	.79	.71	.75
Ouray	.91	.89	.87	.82
Park	.99	.94	.89	.90
Phillips	125	.86	.97	.85
Pitkin	136	168	164	233
Prowers	.79	.74	.79	.79
Pueblo	.82	.86	.73	.75
Rio Blanco	.98	144	.80	.88
Rio Grande	.69	104	.80	.69
Routt	.95	126	108	108
Saguache	.60	.77	.63	.50
San Juan	.66	.86	.86	.77
San Miguel	.67	.68	.99	103
Sedgwick	100	.83	.90	.82
Summit	.73	123	115	116
Teller	103	.91	.89	.92
Washington	101	113	101	.69
Weld	.88	.83	.80	.76
Yuma	100	.96	115	.79

Metropolitan Areas

	1970	1980	1990	2000
All Colo. Metro	103	109	104	115
Non-Metro Areas	.81	.91	.84	.85
Boulder/Longmont	105	114	113	134
Colo. Springs	.91	.93	.91	.98
Denver	111	119	113	126
Ft. Collins/Loveland	.80	.92	.90	.99
Grand Junction	.83	.96	.79	.84
Greeley	.88	.83	.80	.76
Pueblo	.82	.86	.73	.75
Denver/Boulder/Greeley	109	116	110	123

Colorado by the Numbers

Wage / Salary Employment – Number of Jobs

Source: U.S. Department of Commerce Bureau of Economic Affairs

	1970	1980	1990	2001
Colorado total	860,245	1,367,172	1,655,348	2,378,037
Adams	40,720	81,766	101,240	155,840
Alamosa	3,292	4,788	5,675	8,255
Arapahoe	42,067	116,728	189,090	305,343
Archuleta	819	1,127	1,774	3,448
Baca	1,364	1,525	1,338	1,549
Bent	1,639	1,906	1,574	1,677
Boulder	46,582	92,400	128,603	198,921
Chaffee	2,343	3,763	4,429	6,816
Cheyenne	575	775	816	953
Clear Creek	2,023	3,837	2,545	3,065
Conejos	1,438	1,664	1,682	1,817
Costilla	722	700	904	825
Crowley	520	662	948	1,295
Custer	142	320	396	924
Delta	3,246	5,246	5,530	8,450
Denver	348,957	439,454	417,915	495,199
Dolores	338	361	463	511
Douglas	1,719	5,452	15,049	67,977
Eagle	3,059	8,849	15,897	30,454
Elbert	623	1,090	1,421	3,646
El Paso	101,579	141,596	194,929	281,111
Fremont	5,379	7,944	9,540	14,626
Garfield	4,224	8,643	13,064	21,536
Gilpin	226	380	435	5,762
Grand	1,193	3,665	4,644	7,240
Gunnison	2,058	4,864	5,342	8,360
Hinsdale	62	109	165	334
Huerfano	1,253	1,415	1,455	2,238
Jackson	504	756	640	630
Jefferson	58,025	123,786	174,837	225,018
Kiowa	588	591	581	744
Kit Carson	2,132	2,800	3,027	3,358
Lake	4,071	5,504	2,010	2,131
La Plata	5,550	10,725	14,563	23,162
Larimer	28,188	58,175	81,912	133,286
Las Animas	4,002	4,852	4,212	5,931
Lincoln	1,341	1,612	1,833	2,404
Logan	6,148	8,340	7,516	9,812
Mesa	18,081	33,783	37,711	54,996

Wage / Salary Employment – Number of Jobs

Source: U.S. Department of Commerce Bureau of Economic Affairs

	1970	1980	1990	2001
Mineral	282	669	292	492
Moffat	2,050	5,501	4,701	5,223
Montezuma	3,580	5,234	7,043	9,813
Montrose	5,078	8,412	9,555	14,105
Morgan	5,680	8,721	9,154	11,917
Otero	7,243	8,128	7,353	7,879
Ouray	705	530	805	1,426
Park	423	917	1,064	2,284
Phillips	1,154	1,405	1,476	1,874
Pitkin	3,553	9,609	13,752	17,108
Prowers	3,797	4,961	5,232	6,011
Pueblo	40,576	45,953	47,134	59,262
Rio Blanco	1,738	3,785	2,685	2,982
Rio Grande	2,928	3,867	4,187	4,719
Routt	2,032	7,630	9,140	14,497
Saguache	687	1,306	1,386	1,686
San Juan	320	402	465	291
San Miguel	533	1,199	2,372	5,055
Sedgwick	1,337	1,206	1,000	1,054
Summit	664	6,651	12,153	20,077
Teller	728	1,634	2,259	7,081
Washington	1,138	1,449	1,547	1,555
Weld	25,120	42,815	51,777	78,088
Yuma	2,107	3,235	3,111	3,914

Metropolitan Areas

	1970	1980	1990	2001
All Colo. Metro	751,614	1,181,908	1,440,197	2,055,041
Non-Metro Areas	108,631	185,264	215,151	322,996
Boulder/Longmont	46,582	92,400	128,603	198,921
Colo. Springs	101,579	141,596	194,929	281,111
Denver	491,488	767,186	898,131	1,249,377
Ft. Collins/Loveland	28,188	58,175	81,912	133,286
Grand Junction	18,081	33,783	37,711	54,996
Greeley	25,120	42,815	51,777	78,088
Pueblo	40,576	45,953	47,134	59,262
Denver/ Boulder/Greeley	563,190	902,401	1,078,511	1,526,386

263

Average Wage Per Job (dollars)

Source: U.S. Department of Commerce Bureau of Economic Affairs

	1970	1980	1990	2001
Colorado total	6,661	14,225	22,428	37,189
Adams	6,877	14,351	21,802	34,296
Alamosa	4,693	10,552	15,328	23,011
Arapahoe	6,499	14,493	24,693	44,455
Archuleta	5,910	10,131	13,904	22,120
Baca	3,982	8,710	11,999	16,717
Bent	5,658	11,507	18,478	25,528
Boulder	6,708	13,070	22,306	43,220
Chaffee	5,174	11,282	15,163	22,265
Cheyenne	4,555	9,277	16,651	23,608
Clear Creek	7,343	17,165	19,963	28,357
Conejos	3,892	8,856	12,687	20,166
Costilla	3,557	8,176	12,431	20,034
Crowley	3,942	7,591	17,341	25,236
Custer	4,359	7,378	11,192	21,571
Delta	4,600	10,789	14,343	21,979
Denver	7,470	16,429	26,042	45,481
Dolores	4,589	8,853	15,292	17,988
Douglas	5,796	12,320	19,905	34,804
Eagle	5,645	12,045	18,628	31,364
Elbert	4,438	8,496	14,004	27,891
El Paso	5,923	12,137	20,936	34,051
Fremont	5,230	11,852	16,868	27,396
Garfield	6,180	11,888	19,402	29,770
Gilpin	4,858	8,461	13,687	30,287
Grand	4,563	10,301	14,537	22,533
Gunnison	5,353	11,256	14,418	22,728
Hinsdale	4,048	8,376	12,236	17,530
Huerfano	4,006	8,697	13,371	20,721
Jackson	4,960	12,685	15,747	19,046
Jefferson	6,966	14,785	24,589	37,057
Kiowa	4,114	8,535	12,864	23,289
Kit Carson	4,317	9,492	13,517	20,877
Lake	7,689	19,291	18,481	22,528
La Plata	5,154	10,519	16,522	25,925
Larimer	5,746	12,608	20,513	32,247
Las Animas	5,098	11,476	16,054	22,877
Lincoln	4,778	8,533	14,020	24,332
Logan	5,318	11,726	16,210	23,639
Mesa	5,647	13,556	18,641	27,187

Average Wage Per Job (dollars)
Source: U.S. Department of Commerce Bureau of Economic Affairs

	1970	1980	1990	2001
Mineral	7,628	16,830	13,178	18,083
Moffat	5,230	14,779	22,491	28,670
Montezuma	5,039	11,278	16,813	22,633
Montrose	5,660	11,114	15,986	24,816
Morgan	5,326	11,924	15,069	25,072
Otero	5,207	10,814	14,349	21,960
Ouray	5,817	8,211	12,880	22,391
Park	4,988	10,446	16,301	24,906
Phillips	4,343	9,449	13,533	20,591
Pitkin	5,747	13,048	20,482	34,367
Prowers	4,547	9,691	14,775	24,621
Pueblo	6,594	14,287	18,138	26,785
Rio Blanco	5,664	17,341	21,246	27,061
Rio Grande	4,650	9,899	15,330	23,234
Routt	5,224	14,300	18,412	27,854
Saguache	4,325	8,139	12,925	20,771
San Juan	6,597	12,806	22,256	19,512
San Miguel	5,886	10,114	16,067	27,861
Sedgwick	4,654	9,251	12,709	19,621
Summit	5,083	10,955	16,110	26,664
Teller	4,341	8,103	13,423	23,758
Washington	4,374	9,946	13,793	20,541
Weld	5,654	12,209	19,473	29,517
Yuma	4,168	8,985	14,006	22,613

Metropolitan Areas

	1970	1980	1990	2001
All Colo. Metro	6,868	14,620	23,299	38,929
Non-Metro Areas	5,228	11,706	16,604	26,117
Boulder/Longmont	6,708	13,070	22,306	43,220
Colo. Springs	5,923	12,137	20,936	34,051
Denver	7,272	15,618	24,894	41,737
Ft. Collins/Loveland	5,746	12,608	20,513	32,247
Grand Junction	5,647	13,556	18,641	27,187
Greeley	5,654	12,209	19,473	29,517
Pueblo	6,594	14,287	18,138	26,785
Denver/ Boulder/Greeley	7,154	15,196	24,326	41,305

Gross State Product by Industry Component
(Million of dollars)
Source: U.S. Department of Commerce Bureau of Economic Affairs

	1980	1990	2000
Total Gross State Product	139,860	152,202	167,918
Private industries	122,619	133,942	148,605
Agriculture, forest, fish	2,190	2,284	2,261
Farms	1,405	1,354	1,225
Agricultural services	785	930	1,036
Mining	2,299	2,349	2,913
Metal mining	276	230	208
Coal mining	219	235	221
Oil & gas	1,685	1,757	2,335
Nonmetalic minerals	119	127	150
Construction	8,282	9,548	11,084
Manufacturing	14,633	15,303	16,257
Durable goods	8,739	9,005	9,572
Lumber & wood	293	322	324
Furniture and fixtures	204	217	232
Stone, clay, glass	655	800	833
Primary metals	117	73	77
Fabricated metals	888	947	992
Industrial machinery	2,283	2,275	2,498
Electronic equipment	1,205	1,122	1,315
Motor vehicles	213	205	243
Other transport. equip.	1,530	1,586	1,470
Instruments and related	1,122	1,182	1,304
Misc. manufacturing	230	276	285
Electronic equip. + Instr.	2,327	2,304	2,618
Nondurable goods	5,894	6,298	6,685
Food & kindred products	2,061	2,208	2,338
Tobacco products	0	0	0
Textile mill products	11	12	12
Apparel & textile	106	91	88
Paper products	198	198	215
Printing & publishing	1,966	2,179	2,339
Chemicals	777	871	887
Petroleum products	167	130	167
Rubber & plastics	492	495	527
Leather products	115	114	111
Transportation & utilities	16,585	18,437	20,376
Transportation	4,565	4,881	5,037
Railroad transportation	376	372	365

Gross State Product by Industry Component
(Million of dollars)

Source: U.S. Department of Commerce Bureau of Economic Affairs

	1980	1990	2000
Local & interurban	240	228	255
Trucking and warehousing	1,518	1,594	1,668
Water transportation	4	4	4
Transportation by air	2,007	2,200	2,202
Pipelines, ex. nat. gas	27	35	42
Transportation services	392	448	500
Communications	9,355	10,761	12,385
Electric, gas, & sanitary	2,664	2,796	2,955
Wholesale trade	8,903	9,474	10,726
Retail trade	13,566	14,596	15,911
F.I.R.E.	24,425	26,598	28,734
Depository institutions	3,048	3,494	3,996
Nondepository institution	1,155	1,109	1,113
Security brokers	1,418	1,614	1,867
Insurance carriers	2,636	2,844	2,945
Insurance agents	819	944	968
Real estate	15,149	16,642	18,061
Holding and investment	200	-49	-215
Depository + Nondepository	4,203	4,603	5,109
Services	31,736	35,353	40,342
Hotels & lodging	1,448	1,581	1,701
Personal services	917	938	1,006
Business services	9,797	11,328	13,930
Auto repair & parking	1,422	1,609	1,723
Misc. repair services	384	401	439
Motion pictures	260	536	618
Amusement and recreation	1,789	1,934	2,127
Health services	6,567	6,849	7,444
Legal services	1,463	1,550	1,727
Educational services	654	739	842
Social services	803	888	982
Other services	5,079	5,781	6,483
Membership organizations	971	1,050	1,139
Private households	182	168	181
Business serv. + Other serv	14,876	17,109	20,413
Government	17,241	18,260	19,313
Federal civilian	3,879	4,058	4,268
Federal military	1,991	2,055	2,167
State and local	11,371	12,147	12,878

Employee Compensation by Industry
(Million of dollars)

Source: U.S. Department of Commerce Bureau of Economic Affairs

	1980	1990	2000
Total Gross State Product	82,619	90,839	101,564
Private industries	67,738	75,152	84,950
Agriculture, forest, fish	860	951	1,056
Farms	355	358	406
Agricultural services	504	593	650
Mining	950	1,026	974
Metal mining	193	271	154
Coal mining	161	156	142
Oil & gas	519	512	583
Nonmetalic minerals	77	87	95
Construction	5,466	6,279	7,368
Manufacturing	10,024	10,469	11,488
Durable goods	6,870	7,215	8,014
Lumber & wood	194	219	232
Furniture and fixtures	199	213	232
Stone, clay, glass	488	523	565
Primary metals	130	114	116
Fabricated metals	577	596	643
Industrial machinery	1,991	2,098	2,355
Electronic equipment	1,083	1,185	1,523
Motor vehicles	111	109	129
Other transport. equip.	742	712	662
Instruments and related	1,201	1,290	1,394
Misc. manufacturing	154	155	162
Electronic equip. + Instr.	2,285	2,475	2,917
Nondurable goods	3,153	3,254	3,474
Food & kindred products	1,073	1,077	1,144
Tobacco products	0	0	0
Textile mill products	11	11	12
Apparel & textile	103	94	90
Paper products	142	154	164
Printing & publishing	1,124	1,206	1,324
Chemicals	279	311	313
Petroleum products	53	50	53
Rubber & plastics	312	294	319
Leather products	57	57	55
Transportation & utilities	7,319	8,404	9,488
Transportation	2,661	2,843	3,115
Railroad transportation	not available		

Employee Compensation by Industry
(Million of dollars)
Source: U.S. Department of Commerce Bureau of Economic Affairs

	1980	1990	2000
Local & interurban	166	158	178
Trucking and warehousing	871	899	951
Water transportation	(D)	3	3
Transportation by air	1,064	1,181	1,349
Pipelines, ex. nat. gas	(D)	(D)	(D)
Transportation services	260	299	336
Communications	3,690	4,548	5,361
Electric, gas, & sanitary	968	1,013	1,012
Wholesale trade	5,326	5,826	6,735
Retail trade	7,992	8,674	9,400
F.I.R.C.	6,787	7,748	8,666
Depository institutions	1,070	1,146	1,241
Nondepository institution	924	916	869
Security brokers	992	1,344	1,811
Insurance carriers	1,478	1,598	1,613
Insurance agents	523	548	569
Real estate	1,129	1,234	1,375
Holding and investment	670	965	1,188
Depository + Nondepository	1,995	2,062	2,110
Services	23,016	25,774	29,775
Hotels & lodging	880	945	1,007
Personal services	424	458	488
Business services	7,059	8,317	10,565
Auto repair & parking	683	772	831
Misc. repair services	217	225	241
Motion pictures	210	436	491
Amusement and recreation	1,074	1,190	1,320
Health services	5,235	5,386	5,809
Legal services	942	1,005	1,126
Educational services	580	658	748
Social services	757	836	928
Other services	3,856	4,391	4,964
Membership organizations	917	989	1,077
Private households	182	168	181
Business serv. + Other serv	10,915	12,708	15,529
Government	14,881	15,687	16,614
Federal civilian	3,419	3,557	3,794
Federal military	1,684	1,729	1,811
State and local	9,778	10,401	11,009

Employment by Industry (Number of Jobs)

Source: U.S. Department of Commerce Bureau of Economic Affairs

	1970	1980	1990	2000
Employment by place of work				
Total employment	1,031,728	1,654,180	2,054,770	2,960,920
By type				
Wage / salary employment	860,245	1,367,172	1,655,348	2,363,304
Proprietors' employment	171,483	287,008	399,422	597,616
Farm proprietors' employment	29,083	26,820	27,225	29,119
Nonfarm proprietors' employ.	142,400	260,188	372,197	568,497
By industry				
Farm employment	46,852	45,801	43,690	44,406
Nonfarm employment	984,876	1,608,379	2,011,080	2,916,514
Private employment	751,690	1,314,695	1,678,660	2,534,168
Ag. services, forest, other	5,934	12,909	20,189	39,364
Mining	17,758	43,389	31,384	22,634
Construction	55,831	102,472	97,386	226,475
Manufacturing	120,809	185,430	197,879	217,473
Transportation/public utilities	55,544	84,623	107,235	162,241
Wholesale trade	48,264	80,223	92,254	121,306
Retail trade	163,925	274,739	344,149	493,168
F.I.R.E	89,357	160,250	179,826	304,660
Services	194,268	370,660	608,358	946,847
Government	233,186	293,684	332,420	382,346
Federal, civilian	45,494	51,665	56,920	54,116
Military	60,584	51,507	52,077	42,559
State and local	127,108	190,512	223,423	285,671
State	(N)	54,904	66,924	83,043
Local	(N)	135,608	156,499	202,628

Appendix

Colorado's 13ers

Bill Graves in the 1960s was first to publish the Centennial list of Colorado Peaks – Colorado's hightst 100 peaks. The effort to rank Colorado Mountains has continued with many others adding to and refining the list. Mike Garratt and Bob Martin are responsible for a widely used and authoritative list of Colorado 13ers. Gerry Roach, in his book *Colorado's High Thirteeners*, has added and refined Garratt and Martin's list to arrive at 584 ranked peaks more than 13,000 feet, plus another 154 points that either do not qualify under Graves' 300-foot saddle rule (see Page 11) or are considered "soft" summits by Roach.

Colorado 13ers

Rank	Elev.	Summit Name	7.5' Quad
1	13,988	Grizzly Pk A	Independence Pass
2	13,983	Stewart Pk	Stewart Pk
3	13,980	"Kat Carson"	Crestone Pk
4	13,972	Pigeon Pk	Snowdon Pk
5	13,971	Ouray, Mt	Mt Ouray
6	13,951	Fletcher Mtn	Copper Mtn
7	13,951	Ice Mtn	Winfield
8	13,950	Pacific Pk	Breckenridge
9	13,943	Cathedral Pk	Hayden Pk
10	13,940	French Mtn	Mt Massive
11	13,933	Hope, Mt	Mt Elbert
12	13,932	"Thunder Pyramid"	Maroon Bells
13	13,931	Adams, Mt	Horn Pk
14	13,913	Gladstone Pk	Mt Wilson
15	13,911	Meeker, Mt	Allens Park
16	13,908	Casco Pk	Mt Elbert
17	13,908	Red Mtn A	Culebra Pk
18	13,904	Emerald Pk	Winfield
19	13,898	Horseshoe Mtn	Mt Sherman
20	13,895	"Phoenix Pk"	Halfmoon Pass
21	13,894	Vermillion Pk	Ophir
22	13,870	"North Carbonate"	Saint Elmo
23	13,865	Buckskin, Mt	Climax
24	13,864	Vestal Pk	Storm King Pk
25	13,860	Jones Mtn A	Handies Pk
26	13,860	North Apostle	Winfield
27	13,857	Clinton Pk	Climax
28	13,855	Dyer Mtn	Mt Sherman
29	13,852	Crystal Pk	Breckenridge
30	13,850	Edwards, Mt	Grays Pk
31	13,849	California Pk	Blanca Pk
32	13,845	Oklahoma, Mt	Mt Champion
33	13,841	Atlantic Pk	Copper Mtn
34	13,841	Hagerman Pk	Snowmass Mtn
35	13,841	Half Pk	Pole Creek Mtn
36	13,835	Turret Pk	Snowdon Pk

Colorado 13ers *continued*

Rank	Elev.	Summit Name	7.5' Quad
37	13,832	Point 13,832	Redcloud Pk
38	13,831	Holy Cross Ridge	Mt of the Holy Cross
39	13,830	Jupiter Mtn	Columbine Pass
40	13,828	"Huorfano Pk"	Blanca Pk
41	13,824	Jagged Mtn	Storm King Pk
42	13,823	"Lackawanna"	Independence Pass
43	13,822	Silverheels, Mt	Alma
44	13,821	Rio Grande Pyramid	Rio Grande Pyramid
45	13,819	Teakettle Mtn	Mt Sneffels
46	13,811	Point 13,811	Redcloud Pk
47	13,809	Dallas Pk	Telluride
48	13,807	Niagara Pk	Handies Pk
49	13,806	"American Pk"	Handies Pk
50	13,805	Trinity Pk	Storm King Pk
51	13,803	Arrow Pk	Storm King Pk
52	13,803	"Castleabra"	Maroon Bells
53	13,801	Organ Mtn A	San Luis Pk
54	13,799	"Obstruction Pk"	Crestone Pk
55	13,795	Arkansas Mt	Climax
56	13,795	Point 13,795	Redcloud Pk
57	13,794	Rito Alto Pk	Rito Alto Pk
58	13,794	Square Top Mtn	Montezuma
59	13,786	Animas Mtn	Snowdon Pk
60	13,786	Potosi Pk	Ironton
61	13,783	Rinker Pk	Mt Elbert
62	13,781	Mosquito Pk	Climax
63	13,780	Garfield Pk	Independence Pass
64	13,780	Golden Horn	Ophir
65	13,768	Point 13,768	Mt of the Holy Cross
66	13,767	US Grant Pk	Ophir
67	13,765	Trinity Pk West	Storm King Pk
68	13,762	Point 13,762	Mt Harvard
69	13,761	Bull Hill	Mt Elbert
70	13,761	Deer Mt	Mt Champion
71	13,752	San Miguel Pk	Ophir
72	13,752	Storm King Pk	Storm King Pk
73	13,748	Sheridan, Mt	Mt Sherman
74	13,745	Aetna, Mt	Garfield
75	13,745	Trinity Pk East	Storm King Pk
76	13,738	Argentine Pk	Montezuma
77	13,738	Grizzly Pk B	Ophir
78	13,738	Pilot Knob	Ophir
79	13,738	Sayers BM	Mt Elbert
80	13,736	Point 13,736	Mt Champion
81	13,735	"T 0"	Telluride
82	13,723	Vermejo Pk	Culebra Pk
83	13,722	"Animas Forks Mtn"	Handies Pk
84	13,722	Point 13,722	Maroon Bells
85	13,716	Pole Creek Mtn	Pole Creek Mtn
86	13,714	Silver Mtn A	Uncompahgre Pk
87	13,712	Point 13,712	Mt Antero
88	13,711	Twining Pk	Mt Champion
89	13,708	Grizzly Mtn	Saint Elmo

Colorado 13ers *continued*

Rank	Elev.	Summit Name	7.5' Quad
90	13,705	Colony Baldy	Crestone Pk
91	13,705	Six, Pk	Storm King Pk
92	13,700	Fifteen, Pk	Snowdon Pk
93	13,700	Grizzly Pk C	Columbine Pass
94	13,698	Baldy Alto	Stewart Pk
95	13,695	Monitor Pk	Storm King Pk
96	13,694	Gilpin Pk	Telluride
97	13,693	Rolling Mtn	Ophir
98	13,691	Point 13,691	Redcloud Pk
99	13,690	Wheeler Mtn	Copper Mtn
100	13,688	Point 13,688 A	Redcloud Pk
101	13,688	Point 13,688 B	Handies Pk
102	13,686	Cirque Mtn	Mt Sneffels
103	13,684	Bald Mtn	Boreas Pass
104	13,684	Oso, Mt	Emerald Lake
105	13,682	Seven, Pk	Storm King Pk
106	13,681	Point 13,681	Uncompahgre Pk
107	13,676	Purgatoire Pk	Culebra Pk
108	13,674	Point 13,674	Redcloud Pk
109	13,672	Tweto, Mt	Climax
110	13,670	Jackson, Mt	Mt Jackson
111	13,667	White, Mt	Mt Antero
112	13,663	Carbonate Mtn	Saint Elmo
113	13,661	Lookout Pk	Ophir
114	13,660	Point 13,660 A	Twin Pks
115	13,660	Point 13,660 B	Pole Creek Mtn
116	13,660	Wood Mtn	Handies Pk
117	13,657	Carson Pk	Pole Creek Mtn
118	13,656	Coxcomb Pk	Wetterhorn Pk
119	13,651	Taylor Mtn	Garfield
120	13,646	Champion, Mt	Mt Champion
121	13,646	Point 13,646	Saint Elmo
122	13,642	Redcliff	Wetterhorn Pk
123	13,641	Bard Pk	Grays Pk
124	13,635	"Electric Pk"	Hayden Pk
125	13,633	Pk 10	Breckenridge
126	13,631	Point 13,631 A	New York Pk
127	13,631	Point 13,631 B	Maroon Bells
128	13,628	Silex, Mt	Storm King Pk
129	13,627	White Dome	Storm King Pk
130	13,626	Point 13,626	Mt Yale
131	13,626	West Spanish Pk	Spanish Pks
132	13,617	Guardian, The	Storm King Pk
133	13,616	Point 13,616	Mt Elbert
134	13,614	North Star Mtn	Breckenridge
135	13,611	Pico Asilado	Crestone Pk
136	13,604	Tijeras Pk	Crestone Pk
137	13,602	Gray Wolf Mtn	Mt Evans
138	13,598	Electric Pk A	Electric Pk
139	13,596	Cyclone Mtn	Saint Elmo
140	13,590	Matterhorn Pk	Uncompahgre Pk
141	13,589	One, Pk	Storm King Pk
142	13,588	Cottonwood Pk	Valley View Hot Spgs

Colorado 13ers *continued*

Rank	Elev.	Summit Name	7.5' Quad
143	...13,581	Emma, Mt	Telluride
144	...13,581	Point 13,581	Pole Creek Mtn
145	...13,580	Clark Pk	Capitol Pk
146	...13,580	Point 13,580 A	Pole Creek Mtn
147	...13,580	Point 13,580 B	Horn Pk
148	...13,580	Powell, Mt (Pk B)	Mt Powell
149	...13,580	Twin Pks A	Twin Pks
150	...13,579	Chiefs Head Pk	Isolation Pk
151	...13,577	Evans B, Mt	Climax
152	...13,577	Point 13,577	Blanca Pk
153	...13,575	Greylock Mtn	Columbine Pass
154	...13,575	Rosalie Pk	Harris Park
155	...13,574	Parnassus, Mt	Grays Pk
156	...13,573	Broken Hand Pk	Crestone Pk
157	...13,568	West Apostle	Winfield
158	...13,566	Point 13,566	Redcloud Pk
159	...13,565	Point 13,565	El Valle Creek
160	...13,560	Hagues Pk	Trail Ridge
161	...13,555	Wasatch Mtn	Telluride
162	...13,554	Fluted Pk	Horn Pk
163	...13,554	McCauley Pk	Columbine Pass
164	...13,553	Gibbs Pk	Electric Pk
165	...13,553	Pettingell Pk	Loveland Pass
166	...13,552	Tower Mtn	Howardsville
167	...13,550	Point 13,550	Gothic
168	...13,546	Point 13,546	Horn Pk
169	...13,542	Whitecross Mtn	Redcloud Pk
170	...13,541	Point 13,541	Crestone Pk
171	...13,540	Eleven, Pk	Storm King Pk
172	...13,540	Point 13,540 A	Dolores Pk
173	...13,540	Point 13,540 B	Redcloud Pk
174	...13,540	"V 4"	Ophir
175	...13,540	White Rock Mtn	Gothic
176	...13,538	Emma Burr Mtn	Cumberland Pass
177	...13,537	Point 13,537	Maroon Bells
178	...13,535	"K49"	Mt Champion
179	...13,535	Point 13,535	Handies Pk
180	...13,531	Point 13,531	Mt Elbert
181	...13,530	"Epaulie"	Harris Park
182	...13,528	Boulder Mtn	Saint Elmo
183	...13,528	Leviathan Pk	Storm King Pk
184	...13,528	Treasure Mtn	Snowmass Mtn
185	...13,528	"V 3"	Ophir
186	...13,524	Point 13,524 A	Pole Creek Mtn
187	...13,524	Point 13,524 B	Rito Alto Pk
188	...13,522	Milwaukee Pk	Crestone Pk
189	...13,521	Star Pk	Pearl Pass
190	...13,517	Point 13,517 A	Winfield
191	...13,517	Trinchera Pk	Trinchera Pk
192	...13,516	Keefe Pk	Maroon Bells
193	...13,514	Ypsilon Mtn	Trail Ridge
194	...13,513	Point 13,513	Electric Pk
195	...13,510	Point 13,510 A	Baldy Cinco

Colorado 13ers *continued*

Rank	Elev.	Summit Name	7.5' Quad
196	.13,510	.Point 13,510 B	.Ironton
197	.13,510	."T 11"	.Telluride
198	.13,507	.Eureka Mtn	.Rito Alto Pk
199	.13,505	.Point 13,505	.New York Pk
200	.13,502	.Fairchild Mtn	.Trail Ridge
201	.13,502	.North Arapaho Pk	.Monarch Lake
202	.13,500	.Point 13,500	.Independence Pass
203	.13,498	.Point 13,498	.Dolores Pk
204	.13,497	.Hunter Pk	.Maroon Bells
205	.13,497	.Pagoda Mtn	.Isolation Pk
206	.13,496	.Mears Pk	.Mt Sneffels
207	.13,492	.Whitehouse Mtn	.Ouray
208	.13,490	.Marcy, Mt	.Electric Pk
209	.13,490	.Point 13,490	.Rito Alto Pk
210	.13,489	.Graystone Pk	.Storm King Pk
211	.13,487	.Cuatro Pk	.Trinchera Pk
212	.13,487	.Storm Pk A	.Silverton
213	.13,481	.Three Needles	.Telluride
214	.13,478	.Canby Mtn	.Howardsville
215	.13,478	.Three, Pk	.Storm King Pk
216	.13,477	."T 10"	.Ironton
217	.13,475	.Two, Pk	.Storm King Pk
218	.13,475	."V 10"	.Ophir
219	.13,472	.La Junta Pk	.Telluride
220	.13,472	.Point 13,472 A	.Mt Ouray
221	.13,470	.Silver Mtn B	.Telluride
222	.13,468	.Ridgeway, Mt	.Mt Sneffels
223	.13,466	."Alamosito"	.Culebra Pk
224	.13,463	.Point 13,463	.Independence Pass
225	.13,462	.Point 13,462 A	.Winfield
226	.13,462	.Point 13,462 B	.Winfield
227	.13,462	.Treasury Mtn	.Snowmass Mtn
228	.13,461	.Quail Mtn	.Mt Elbert
229	.13,460	.Point 13,460	.Independence Pass
230	.13,460	.San Joaquin Ridge	.Telluride
231	.13,460	.Sleeping Sexton	.Maroon Bells
232	.13,455	.Ute Ridge	.Rio Grande Pyramid
233	.13,454	.Hanson Pk	.Handies Pk
234	.13,454	."Campbell Creek Pk"	.Redcloud Pk
235	.13,451	.Kendall Pk	.Howardsville
236	.13,450	.Horn Pk	.Horn Pk
237	.13,450	.Point 13,450	.Pole Creek Mtn
238	.13,441	.Apache Pk	.Monarch Lake
239	.13,441	."S 6"	.Mt Sneffels
240	.13,436	."T 5"	.Telluride
241	.13,435	."Mascot Pk"	.Mt Yale
242	.13,435	.Taylor Pk A	.Pearl Pass
243	.13,434	.Point 13,434	.Howardsville
244	.13,433	.Point 13,433	.Mt Jackson
245	.13,432	.Jenkins Mtn	.Pieplant
246	.13,432	."Sundog"	.Redcloud Pk
247	.13,432	.Twin Sister East	.Ophir
248	.13,428	.Vallecito Mtn	.Storm King Pk

Appendix

Colorado 13ers *continued*

Rank	Elev.	Summit Name	7.5' Quad
249	13,427	Grizzly Pk D	Grays Pk
250	13,427	Point 13,427	Handies Pk
251	13,425	Mummy Mtn	Estes Park
252	13,423	Spread Eagle Pk	Electric Pk
253	13,420	Eagles Nest (Pk A)	Mt Powell
254	13,420	"Siberia Pk"	Snowmass Mtn
255	13,417	"SoSo, Mt"	Emerald Lake
256	13,416	Little Giant Pk	Howardsville
257	13,414	Cleveland Pk	Crestone Pk
258	13,411	"Heisshorn"	Wetterhorn Pk
259	13,410	Four, Pk	Storm King Pk
260	13,409	Hilliard Pk	Maroon Bells
261	13,409	Navajo Pk	Monarch Lake
262	13,408	Wilcox, Mt	Montezuma
263	13,405	Mariquita Pk	El Valle Creek
264	13,402	Nine, Pk	Storm King Pk
265	13,402	Point 13,402	Halfmoon Pass
266	13,402	Rhoda, Mt	Howardsville
267	13,401	Point 13,401	Crestone Pk
268	13,401	White BM	Gothic
269	13,400	Bartlett Mtn	Copper Mtn
270	13,393	Bent Pk	Pole Creek Mtn
271	13,391	Parry Pk	Empire
272	13,391	Rogers Pk	Harris Park
273	13,385	Chicago Pk	Ironton
274	13,384	Point 13,384	Crestone Pk
275	13,384	Prize BM	Pieplant
276	13,383	Baldy Cinco	Baldy Cinco
277	13,382	Gold Dust Pk	Mt Jackson
278	13,382	Williams Mtn	Mt Champion
279	13,380	Geissler Mtn East	Mt Champion
280	13,380	Music Mtn	Crestone Pk
281	13,380	Point 13,380	Gothic
282	13,380	Precarious Pk	Maroon Bells
283	13,380	South Lookout Pk	Ophir
284	13,378	Italian Mtn	Pearl Pass
285	13,377	Point 13,377	Wetterhorn Pk
286	13,375	Lakes Pk	Electric Pk
287	13,374	Point 13,374	Mt Harvard
288	13,374	Twin Sister West	Ophir
289	13,370	Buckskin BM	Maroon Bells
290	13,370	Dome Mtn	Howardsville
291	13,370	Guyot, Mt	Boreas Pass
292	13,369	Monumental Pk	Garfield
293	13,368	Sultan Mtn	Silverton
294	13,362	De Anza Pk A	Electric Pk
295	13,362	Englemann Pk	Grays Pk
296	13,362	Pearl Mtn	Pearl Pass
297	13,359	"T 7"	Ironton
298	13,357	"Silverthorne, Mt"	Willow Lakes
299	13,352	Hoosier Ridge	Breckenridge
300	13,350	Hermit Pk	Rito Alto Pk
301	13,348	Malemute Pk	Hayden Pk

277

Colorado 13ers *continued*

Rank	Elev.	Summit Name	7.5' Quad
302	13,346	"North Gold Dust"	Mt Jackson
303	13,345	"Tincup Pk"	Cumberland Pass
304	13,342	Beattie Pk	Ophir
305	13,342	Point 13,342	Rio Grande Pyramid
306	13,340	Herard, Mt	Medano Pass
307	13,340	Owen A, Mt	Electric Pk
308	13,340	Point 13,340 A	Emerald Lake
309	13,340	Point 13,340 B	Uncompahgre Pk
310	13,339	Brown Mtn	Ironton
311	13,338	Kendall Mtn	Silverton
312	13,336	Point 13,336	Maroon Bells
313	13,334	Coney BM	Finger Mesa
314	13,334	Venable Pk	Rito Alto Pk
315	13,333	De Anza Pk B	El Valle Creek
316	13,330	"Proposal Pk"	Handies Pk
317	13,328	Cinnamon Mtn	Handies Pk
318	13,327	McHenrys Pk	McHenrys Pk
319	13,326	West Buffalo Pk	Marmot Pk
320	13,325	Point 13,325	Silverton
321	13,322	Point 13,322	Pieplant
322	13,321	Sunshine Mtn	Handies Pk
323	13,321	Trico Pk	Ironton
324	13,317	Point 13,317	Saint Elmo
325	13,315	"T 8"	Ironton
326	13,313	Point 13,313	Baldy Cinco
327	13,312	Point 13,312 A	Redcloud Pk
328	13,312	Point 13,312 B	Pearl Pass
329	13,312	Point 13,312 C	Pieplant
330	13,312	Williams Mtn South A	Thimble Rock
331	13,310	Alice, Mt	Isolation Pk
332	13,310	Aztec Mtn	Columbine Pass
333	13,310	Point 13,310	Emerald Lake
334	13,309	"V 2"	Ophir
335	13,308	Point 13,308	Rio Grande Pyramid
336	13,307	Warren, Mt	Mt Evans
337	13,302	Point 13,302	Storm King Pk
338	13,301	Geissler Mtn West	Mt Champion
339	13,300	Daly, Mt	Capitol Pk
340	13,300	East Buffalo Pk	Marmot Pk
341	13,300	"El Punto"	Uncompahgre Pk
342	13,300	Galena Mtn	Howardsville
343	13,300	Middle Pk	Dolores Pk
344	13,300	Point 13,300 A	New York Pk
345	13,300	Point 13,300 B	Mt Champion
346	13,300	Point 13,300 C	Wetterhorn Pk
347	13,300	Point 13,300 D	Columbine Pass
348	13,300	Summit Pk	Summit Pk
349	13,300	"V 8"	Ophir
350	13,295	Point 13,295	Pieplant
351	13,294	"Citadel"	Loveland Pass
352	13,294	James Pk	Empire
353	13,292	Electric Pk B	Storm King Pk
354	13,292	Sheep Mtn A	Howardsville

Colorado 13ers *continued*

Rank	Elev.	Summit Name	7.5' Quad
355	13,290	Dolores Pk	Dolores Pk
356	13,286	Bonita Pk	Handies Pk
357	13,285	Point 13,285	San Luis Pk
358	13,284	Point 13,284	Mt Champion
359	13,283	Five, Pk	Storm King Pk
360	13,282	Point 13,282	New York Pk
361	13,282	Truro Pk	New York Pk
362	13,281	Grizzly Pk E	Pieplant
363	13,281	Lady Washington, Mt	Longs Pk
364	13,278	Point 13,278	Weminuche Pass
365	13,277	Comanche Pk	Horn Pk
366	13,277	Ruby Mtn	Montezuma
367	13,276	Kiowa Pk	Ward
368	13,274	Seigal Mtn	Handies Pk
369	13,271	Whitney Pk	Mt of the Holy Cross
370	13,270	"Crestolita"	Crestone Pk
371	13,269	Antora Pk	Bonanza
372	13,266	Geneva Pk	Montezuma
373	13,266	Marble Mtn	Crestone Pk
374	13,266	Wildhorse Pk	Wetterhorn Pk
375	13,265	Knife Point	Storm King Pk
376	13,262	Heisspitz, The	Storm King Pk
377	13,261	Point 13,261	Weminuche Pass
378	13,260	"Pk G"	Vail East
379	13,260	Point 13,260 A	Handies Pk
380	13,260	Point 13,260 B	Maroon Bells
381	13,260	Point 13,260 C	Finger Mesa
382	13,260	"V 9"	Ophir
383	13,256	Broken Hill	Uncompahgre Pk
384	13,255	Point 13,255	Winfield
385	13,254	Henry Mtn	Fairview Pk
386	13,253	Point 13,253	Winfield
387	13,252	"S 8"	Sams
388	13,248	Point 13,248	Mt of the Holy Cross
389	13,245	"Pk Z"	Willow Lakes
390	13,244	Point 13,244	Highland Pk
391	13,244	Spring Mtn	Horn Pk
392	13,242	"S 4"	Mt Sneffels
393	13,241	"U 3"	Wetterhorn Pk
394	13,235	Point 13,235	Pieplant
395	13,234	Sniktau, Mt	Grays Pk
396	13,233	Belleview Mtn	Maroon Bells
397	13,233	Turner Pk	Tincup
398	13,232	Hesperus Mtn	La Plata
399	13,232	Point 13,232 A	Maroon Bells
400	13,232	Point 13,232 B	Pieplant
401	13,230	"Pk Q"	Vail East
402	13,230	Point 13,230 A	Rio Grande Pyramid
403	13,229	Point 13,229	El Valle Creek
404	13,229	Red Mtn C	Breckenridge
405	13,223	Audubon, Mt	Ward
406	13,222	Point 13,222 A	Uncompahgre Pk
407	13,222	Point 13,222 B	Emerald Lake

Colorado 13ers *continued*

Rank	Elev.	Summit Name	7.5' Quad
408	13,220	Greenhalgh Mtn	Howardsville
409	13,220	Hagar Mtn	Loveland Pass
410	13,220	Lavender Pk	La Plata
411	13,220	"Pk C"	Vail East
412	13,220	"Weminuche Pk"	Emerald Lake
413	13,220	"S 7"	Sams
414	13,218	Engineer Mtn	Handies Pk
415	13,218	Irving Pk	Columbine Pass
416	13,218	Jones Mtn B	Tincup
417	13,216	Point 13,216	Maroon Bells
418	13,215	"Hassell Pk"	Loveland Pass
419	13,214	Fairview Pk	Fairview Pk
420	13,213	"Pk L"	Vail East
421	13,212	Point 13,212	Mt Champion
422	13,209	Gladstone Ridge	Mt Yale
423	13,209	Homestake Pk	Homestake Reservoir
424	13,208	Powell Pk	McHenrys Pk
425	13,208	Teocalli Mtn	Gothic
426	13,206	Hayden Mtn South	Ironton
427	13,206	Point 13,206	Wetterhorn Pk
428	13,205	Eagle Pk A	Electric Pk
429	13,205	Jacque Pk	Copper Mtn
430	13,205	Nebo, Mt	Storm King Pk
431	13,204	Lenawee Mtn	Grays Pk
432	13,203	Bennett Pk	Jasper
433	13,203	"Leaning South Pk"	Trinchera Pk
434	13,203	Tuttle Mtn	Handies Pk
435	13,203	Williams Mtn South B	Mt Champion
436	13,202	Point 13,202	Mt Champion
437	13,201	Point 13,201	Wetterhorn Pk
438	13,198	Point 13,198	Independence Pass
439	13,195	Pk 9	Breckenridge
440	13,194	London Mtn	Climax
441	13,192	"Fancy Pk"	Mt Jackson
442	13,189	Red Pk B	Willow Lakes
443	13,185	Valois, Mt	Columbine Pass
444	13,184	Beaubien Pk	El Valle Creek
445	13,180	Babcock Pk	La Plata
446	13,180	Grand Turk	Silverton
447	13,180	Point 13,180 A	Maroon Bells
448	13,180	Point 13,180 B	Redcloud Pk
449	13,180	Santa Fe Pk	Montezuma
450	13,180	"Valhalla, Mt"	Willow Lakes
451	13,176	Copeland Mtn	Isolation Pk
452	13,172	Conejos Pk	Platoro
453	13,169	Point 13,169	Rio Grande Pyramid
454	13,168	Sheep Mtn C	Sheep Mtn
455	13,165	Amherst Mtn	Columbine Pass
456	13,165	"Stony Pass Pk"	Howardsville
457	13,164	Kelso Mtn	Grays Pk
458	13,164	Point 13,164	Pole Creek Mtn
459	13,162	Point 13,162 A	Baldy Cinco
460	13,162	Point 13,162 B	Gothic

Colorado 13ers *continued*

Rank	Elev.	Summit Name	7.5' Quad
461	13,159	Point 13,159	Ophir
462	13,158	Point 13,158	Uncompahgre Pk
463	13,158	Twilight Pk	Snowdon Pk
464	13,157	"Window Pk"	Rio Grande Pyramid
465	13,156	"V 5"	Ophir
466	13,155	Point 13,155	San Luis Pk
467	13,153	Point 13,153 A	Medano Pass
468	13,153	Point 13,153 B	Horn Pk
469	13,153	Taylor Pk B	McHenrys Pk
470	13,151	Pomeroy Mtn	Saint Elmo
471	13,150	Arikaree Pk	Monarch Lake
472	13,150	Montezuma Pk	Summit Pk
473	13,148	South River Pk	South River Pk
474	13,147	Point 13,147	Garfield
475	13,145	Point 13,145 A	Telluride
476	13,144	Precipice Pk	Wetterhorn Pk
477	13,143	Little Horn Pk	Horn Pk
478	13,143	Willoughby Mtn	Highland Pk
479	13,140	Point 13,140 A	Winfield
480	13,140	Point 13,140 B	Pieplant
481	13,140	Point 13,140 C	New York Pk
482	13,140	Twelve, Pk	Storm King Pk
483	13,139	Hayden Mtn North	Ironton
484	13,139	Savage Pk	Mt Jackson
485	13,138	Ogalalla Pk	Isolation Pk
486	13,136	Hunchback Mtn	Storm King Pk
487	13,135	Francisco Pk	El Valle Creek
488	13,134	"S 9"	Sams
489	13,132	Flora, Mt	Empire
490	13,132	"Darley Mtn"	Handies Pk
491	13,130	Eva, Mt	Empire
492	13,130	Point 13,130	Maroon Bells
493	13,128	Lomo Liso Mtn	El Valle Creek
494	13,126	Pika Pk	Mt Jackson
495	13,123	Point 13,123 A	Dolores Pk
496	13,123	Point 13,123 B	Electric Pk
497	13,122	Peters Pk	Emerald Lake
498	13,122	Point 13,122	Rito Alto Pk
499	13,121	"Pk N"	Mt Powell
500	13,121	Point 13,121	Columbine Pass
501	13,118	Isolation Pk	Isolation Pk
502	13,117	"Cupid"	Grays Pk
503	13,113	Lizard Head	Mt Wilson
504	13,112	Fitzpatrick Pk	Cumberland Pass
505	13,111	Cow BM	Wetterhorn Pk
506	13,111	Point 13,111	San Luis Pk
507	13,110	Point 13,110	Storm King Pk
508	13,109	Point 13,109	Howardsville
509	13,108	Williams Mtn North	Mt Champion
510	13,106	Point 13,106	Uncompahgre Pk
511	13,105	Bushnell Pk	Bushnell Pk
512	13,105	Point 13,105	Columbine Pass
513	13,102	Point 13,102	Garfield

Colorado 13ers *continued*

Rank	Elev.	Summit Name	7.5' Quad
514	13,100	"Baldy Lejos"	Baldy Cinco
515	13,100	"Corbett Pk"	Ouray
516	13,100	Middle Mtn A	Independence Pass
517	13,100	Point 13,100 A	Sheep Mtn
518	13,100	Point 13,100 B	Mt Jackson
519	13,095	Kreutzer, Mt	Tincup
520	13,095	"Tomboy Pk"	Telluride
521	13,093	Point 13,093	Handies Pk
522	13,091	Point 13,091	Uncompahgre Pk
523	13,090	Point 13,090	New York Pk
524	13,090	"Solitude, Mt"	Vail East
525	13,088	Paiute Pk	Monarch Lake
526	13,088	Virginia Pk	Winfield
527	13,085	Keller Mtn	Willow Lakes
528	13,085	"Pk X"	Vail East
529	13,085	Point 13,085	Mt Jackson
530	13,082	Boreas Mtn	Boreas Pass
531	13,081	"Huerfanito"	Blanca Pk
532	13,079	"North Traverse Pk"	Willow Lakes
533	13,078	Point 13,078	Saint Elmo
534	13,078	Whale Pk	Jefferson
535	13,077	Snowdon Pk	Snowdon Pk
536	13,075	North Twilight Pk	Snowdon Pk
537	13,075	Point 13,075	Handies Pk
538	13,074	Garfield, Mt	Snowdon Pk
539	13,074	Point 13,074	New York Pk
540	13,073	Blackwall Mtn	Wetterhorn Pk
541	13,071	Hunts Pk	Wellsville
542	13,070	Point 13,070	Saint Elmo
543	13,070	Sheep Mtn D	Columbine Pass
544	13,069	Point 13,069	Howardsville
545	13,062	Point 13,062 A	Snowmass Mtn
546	13,062	Point 13,062 B	Rito Alto Pk
547	13,062	West Needle Mtn	Snowdon Pk
548	13,060	Point 13,060 A	Capitol Pk
549	13,060	Point 13,060 B	Rito Alto Pk
550	13,058	Owen B, Mt	Oh Be Joyful
551	13,057	"East Partner Pk" (Pk V)	Vail East
552	13,055	"Chalk Rock Mtn"	Tincup
553	13,054	Point 13,054	Rito Alto Pk
554	13,052	Houghton Mtn	Handies Pk
555	13,051	Point 13,051	Uncompahgre Pk
556	13,050	"Dead Man Pk"	Crestone Pk
557	13,050	Point 13,050	Cumberland Pass
558	13,046	Point 13,046	Snowdon Pk
559	13,042	Point 13,042	Silverton
560	13,041	"Grand Traverse Pk"	Willow Lakes
561	13,041	"West Partner Pk" (Pk U)	Vail East
562	13,039	Point 13,039	Maroon Bells
563	13,038	"Old Baldy"	Monarch Lake
564	13,035	West Elk Pk	West Elk Pk
565	13,034	Point 13,034	Baldy Cinco
566	13,033	Williams Mtn South C	Thimble Rock

Colorado 13ers *continued*

Rank	Elev.	Summit Name	7.5' Quad
567	13,032	Organ Mtn B	Columbine Pass
568	13,028	Point 13,028	Rito Alto Pk
569	13,026	Point 13,026	Mt Champion
570	13,024	"Snow Pk"	Willow Lakes
571	13,020	Point 13,020 A	Maroon Bells
572	13,020	Point 13,020 B	Crestone Pk
573	13,020	"S 10"	Sams
574	13,020	"Unicorn Pk"	Summit Pk
575	13,017	Point 13,017	Rio Grande Pyramid
576	13,016	Point 13,016	Uncompahgre Pk
577	13,015	Point 13,015	Halfmoon Pass
578	13,014	Chief Mtn	Little Squaw Creek
579	13,012	Twin Sisters	Bushnell Pk
580	13,010	"Golden Bear Pk"	Loveland Pass
581	13,010	Point 13,010	Cimarrona Pk
582	13,006	Pennsylvania Mtn	Climax
583	13,003	Point 13,003	Mt Champion
584	13,001	Point 13,001	Mt Champion

Selected Bibliography

Books

Abbot, Carl; Leonard, Stephen J. and McComb, David. *Colorado: A History of the Centennial State.* Colorado Associated University Press. Boulder, Colorado. 1982.

Albi, Charles and Forrest, Kenton. *The Moffat Tunnel: A Brief History.* Colorado Railroad Museum. Golden, Colorado. 1984.

Bailey, Alfred M. and Niedrach, Robert J. *Pictorial Checklist of Colorado Birds.* Denver Museum of Natural History. Denver, Colorado. 1967.

Beckman, William C. *Guide to the Fishes of Colorado.* University of Colorado Museum. Boulder, Colorado. 1963.

Borneman, Walter R. and Lampert, Lyndon J. *A Climbing Guide to Colorado's Fourteeners.* Pruett Publishing Company. Boulder, Colorado. 1998.

Brewer, Robyn. *Colorado Camping.* Foghorn Outdoors Avalon Travel Publishing, Inc. Emeryville, California. 2000.

Bright, William. *Colorado Place Names.* Johnson Books. Boulder, Colorado. 1993.

Cheney, Margaret. *Tesla: Man Out of Time.* A Touchstone Book published by Simon and Schuster. New York, New York. 1981.

Crutchfield, James A. *It Happened in Colorado.* Falcon Press Publishing Co., Helena and Billings, Montana. 1993.

DeLorme Publishing. *Colorado Atlas and Gazatteer.* Delorme Publishing. Yarmouth Maine. 1998.

Bibliography

Druger, Frances A. and Meaney, Carron A. *Explore Colorado, A Naturalist's Notebook.* Denver Museum of Natural History and Westcliffe Publishers. Denver, Colorado. 1995.

Erickson, Kenneth A. and Smith, Albert W. Research assistants: Stafford Binder, Kathryn Ingaham and Jennifer Nash. *Atlas of Colorado.* Colorado Associated University Press. 1985.

Fay, Abbot. *I Never Knew That About Colorado: A Quaint Volume of Forgotten Lore.* Western Reflections, Inc. Ouray, Colorado. 1999.

Fay, Abbott. *Beyond the Great Divide: 101 True Stories of Western Colorado.* Western Reflections, Inc. Ouray, Colorado. 1999.

Fitzgerald, James P.; Meaney, Carron A. and Armstrong, David M. *Mammals of Colorado.* Denver Museum of Natural History and University Press of Colorado. Niwot, Colorado. 1994.

Garratt, Mike and Martin, Bob. *Colorado's High Thirteeners: A Climbing and Hiking Guide.* Cordillera Press. Louisville, Colorado. 1984.

Guild, Thelma S. and Carter, Harvey L. *Kit Carson: A Pattern for Heroes.* University of Nebraska Press. Lincoln, Nebraska. 1984

Hammerson, Geoffrey A. *Amphibians and Reptiles in Colorado.* University Press of Colorado and Colorado Division of Wildlife. Boulder, Colorado. 1999.

Harrington, Harlod D. and Thornton, Bruce J. *Weeds of Colorado.* Agriculture Experiment Station, Colorado State University. 1963 [?].

Helmuth, Ed and Helmuth, Gloria. *The Passes of Colorado: An Encyclopedia of Watershed Divides.* Pruett Publishing Company. Boulder, Colorado. 1994

Jones, Stephen R. and Cushman, Ruth Carol. *Colorado Nature Almanac, A Month-by-Month Guide to Wildlife and Wild Places.* Pruett Publishing Co. Boulder, Colorado. 1998.

Kingery, Hugh E., editor. Radeaux, illustrator. *Colorado Breeding Bird Atlas*. Colorado Bird Atlas Partnership and Colorado Division of Wildlife. 1998.

Knowles, Richard and Scott, Evelyn D. *Reference Sourcebook of Colorado*. Hi Willow Research and Publishing. Castle Rock, Colorado. 1994.

Koch, Don. *The Colorado Pass Book: A Guide to Colorado's Backroad Mountain Passes*. Pruett Publishing Company. Boulder, Colorado. 2000.

Midwest Research Institute and Capper Press. *The Colorado Quick-Fact Book*.Capper Press. Topeka, Kansas. 1992.

National Oceanic and Atmospheric Administration. New material by James A. Ruffner. *Climates of the States*. Gale Research Company. Detroit, Michigan. 1974.

Nelson, Mike and the 9News Weather Team. *The Colorado Weather Book*. Westcliffe Publishers. Englewood, Colorado. 1999.

Noel, Thomas J. *The Colorado Almanac: Facts About Colorado*. WestWinds Press. Portland, Oregon. 2001.Rennicke, Jeff. *The Rivers of Colorado*. Falcon Press, Helena and Billings, Montana. 1985.

Noel, Thomas J.; Mahoney, Paul F. and Stevens, Richard E. *Historical Atlas of Colorado*. University of Oklahoma Press. Norman, Oklahoma. 1994.

Pearson, Mark. *The Complete Guide to Colorado's Wilderness Areas*. Westcliffe Publishers, Englewood, Colorado. 1994.

Rennicke, Jeff. *Colorado Mountain Ranges*. Falcon Press, Helena and Billings, Montana. 1986.

Roach, Gerry. *Colorado's Fourteeners: From Hikes to Climbs*. Fulcrum Publishing. Golden, Colorado. 1982

Sauder, Richard, Ph.D. *Underground Bases and Tunnels: What is the Government Trying to Hide?* Adventures Unlimited Press. Kempton, Illinois. 1995.

Schader, Conrad F. Glenwood Canyon: From Origin to Interstate. Regio Alta Publications. Golden, Colorado. 1996.

van der Leeden, Fritz. *The Water Encyclopedia.* Lewis Publishers, Inc. Chelsea, Michigan. 1990

Wood, Richard Ph.D., editor. *Weather of U.S. Cities: A guide to the recent weather histories of 268 key cities and weather observation stations in the United States and its territories.* Gale Research. Detroit, Michigan. 1996.

Reports, Periodicals
and Government Papers

Carmichael, Tess. "Shoo Away the Snakes, Prairie Dogs and Rabbits; Let's Make the Desert Bloom: The Uncompahgre Project 1890-1909." Journal of the Western Slope. Mesa State College. Vol. 8 No. 4. Fall 1993.

Colorado Office of Economic Development and International Trade. "Colorado Data Book." 2001.

Graves, William A. "14,000 Foot Mountains." Trail and Timberline Magazine, the official monthly publication of the Colorado Mountain Club. February, 1968.

Horizons 2000: Colorado State Parks 2000-2004. Prepared by Colorado State Parks Staff. 2000.

Kendall, Wilson D. "A Brief Economic History of Colorado." Center for Business and Economic Forecasting Inc. Prepared for the Demography Section, Colorado Department of Local Affairs. September 15, 2002.

Lyndon, Paula, editor. "Pikes Peak: America's Mountain." Published by the City of Colorado Springs. Colorado Springs, Colorado. Vol. 3 No. 1. Springs/Summer 2000.

McKee, Thomas B. Doesken, Nolan J., Kleist, John. Colorado Climate Center, Atmospheric Science Department, Colorado State University and Shrier, Catherine J., Colorado Water Resources Research Institute in collaboration with Stanton, William P., Colorado Water Conservation Board. "A History of Drought in Colorado: Lessons Learned and What Lies Ahead." February, 2000.

Unknown. "Dillon Dam to Almost Double System Water Storage Capacity." Denver Water News. Vol. 29, No. 7. July 1960.

Walton, Andy. "Cheyenne Mountain: America's Underground Watch Tower." Cable News Network Interactive. www.cnn.com/specials/coldwar/experience/the bomb/route/01.cheyenne

Electronically Published Information and Organization Websites providing information

All Web pages checked for accuracy 10/29/03

AmericanWest. "'Doc' Holiday" Biography. www.americanwest.com/pages/docholid.htm 1996.

Association of American Railroads. "Railroad Service in Colorado." www.aar.org/PubCommon/Documents/AboutTheIndustry/RRState_CO .pdf?states=RRState_CO.pdf

Brief by *Colorado Central* Staff. "The Lowest Point Isn't on the Arkansas, after all." Colorado Central Magazine. www.cozine.com. October, 2000. No. 80, Page 4.

Bureau of Land Management - Colorado. www.co.blm.gov

Central Regional Headquarters, National Weather Service. "Severe Weather...Stats and Facts." www.crh.noaa.gov/den/stats00.html

Cheyenne Mountain Operations Center. Formerly found at www.cheyennemountain.af.mil

Bibliography

City of Littleton, Colorado Home Page. "Littleton History: Alfred Packer." www.littletongov.org/history/biographies/packer.asp

City of Colorado Springs. "Fun Facts About Pikes Peak." www.pikespeakcolorado.com

Climate Diagnostice Center, National Oceanic and Atmospheric Administration. "Colorado Tornado info." www.cdc.noaa.gov/boulder/tornado.html

Climax Molybdenum, a Subsidiary of Phelps Dodge Corp. "Henderson 2000 Conveyor System." www.climaxmolybdenum.com.conveyor.htm

Climb.mountains.com. "Peak Lists of Colorado thirteeners"

CMG Worldwide Inc. The Official Glenn Miller Web Site. "Biography." www.glennmillerstore.com

Colorado Avalanche Information Center. www.caic.state.co.us

Colorado Department of Natural Resources. www.dnr.state.co.us

Colorado by the Numbers (CBN). Developed in 1996 by Margaret M. Jobe and Deborah R. Hollis. Developed under grants from the U.S. Department of Education, U.S. Department of Commerce and National Telecommunications and Information Administration. www.colorado.edu/libraries/govpubs/online.htm

Colorado Department of Local Affairs. www.dlg.oem2.state.co.us

Colorado Department of Local Affairs. "Colorado Demography Section." www.dola.state.co.us/demog/demog.htm

Colorado Department of Transportation Aeronautics Division. www.colorado-aeronautics.org

Colorado Department of Transportation. "Roadway Statistics and Data." www.dot.state.co.us/App_DTD_DataAccess/index.cfm

Colorado Division of Wildlife. http://wildlife.state.co.us
Colorado Ski Country USA. www.skicolorado.org

Colorado Ski Resort Guide. Mountain Resort Guides.
www.coloradoskicountry.com ©2003

Colorado State Archives. www.colorado.gov/dpa/doit/archives

Colorado State University. Colorado Water Knowledge.
www.waterknowledge.colostate.edu

Cumbres & Toltec Scenic Railroad. "About the Cumbres & Toltec
Scenic Railroad." www.cumbrestoltec.com/History.shtml

Department of Defense, Washington Headquarters Services, Directorate
for Information Operations and Reports. web1.whs.osd.mil

Denver Metro Convention and Visitors Bureau. www. denver.org

Denver Press Club Online. "The Story of Damon Runyon."
www/pressclub.org/about/history/drunyon.htm

Denver Water. www.water.denver.co.gov

Department of Neurological Surgery at the University of Pittsburgh.
"Nikola Tesla: A Short Biography."
www.neurosurgery.pitt.edu/~bogdan/tesla/bio.htm

Douglas Fairbanks Sr. Home Page. "Douglas Fairbanks Sr."
www.fortunecity.com/lavendar/wargames/154/bio.htm
Colorado Division of Water Resources. www.water.state.co.us

Durango and Silverton Narow Gauge Railroad and Musuem. "History
Tour." www.durangotrain.com/historytour

Ekwall, Steve. Colorado ODDities.
www.diac.com/~ekwall2/info/coloddity.shtml

Bibliography

Eleanor Roosevelt Institute. University of Health Sciences Center
www-eri.uchsc.edu/faculty/puck
Eugene Field House The, and St. Louis Toy Museum. "The History of
the Field Family." www.eugenefieldhouse.org/history.html ©2000-2003

Environmental Protection Agency. "Surf Your Watershed."
www.epa.gov/surf/watershed.html

Fort Carson. The Mountain Post. United States Army.
www.carson.army.milPeakware World Mountain Encyclopedia.
www.peakware.com. ©2002

Gracyk, Tim. "Paul Whiteman (28 March, 1890 - 29 December, 1967)"
www.garlic.com/~tgracyk/whiteman

Great Idea Finder, The: Celebrating the Spirit of Innovation. Ruth
Handler biography.
www.ideafinder.com/history/inventors/handler.htm

Headwaters Hill Home Page. www.geocities.com/CapitolHill/3162/3RP.
1999.

Howard Hughes Medical Institute. "Enzymatic RNA Molecules and the
Replication of Chromosome Ends."
www/hhmi.org/research/investigators/cech.html

Legal Information Institute. Cornell Law School. Roster of United States
Supreme Court justices with biographies.
www.law.cornell.edu

Lon Chaney Entertainment. Lon Chaney biography.
www.lonchaney.com

Manitou and Pike's Peak Railway. "History of the Manitou & Pikes Peak
Railway." www.cograilway.com/history.htm

Manley, Donna. Empire:Zine: A Writers Cookbook. "Eugene Field – A Look Into." www.empirezine.com/spotlight/field/field1.htm

Morgan, Gary. "The Georgetown Loop: Colorado's Scenic Wonder." The Georgtown Loop Railroad. www.georgetownloop.com/history.htm

Mother Cabrini Shrine. "Saint Francis Xavier Cabrini." Originally found 9/14/01:
www.den-cabrini-shrine.org/saintfrancisxaviercabrinihistory.htm

Museum of Broadcast Communications, The. www.museum.tv

National Aeronautics and Space Administration. www.nasa.gov

National Oceanic and Atmospheric Administration. www.noaa.gov

National Park Service. www.nps.gov

National Weather Service. www.nws.noaa.gov

Northern Colorado Water Conservancy District. "Colorado-Big Thompson by the Numbers." www.ncwcd.org

Official Jack Dempsey Web Site, The. Biography. www.cmgww.com/sports/dempsey/jdbio

Penrose Library. University of Denver. Special Collections: Mary Coyle Chase Manuscript Collection, Special Collections/Archives. "Biographical Sketch of Mary Coyle Chase." www.penlib.du.edu/specoll/chase/chasebio.html. ©2002

Peterson Air Force Base. www.peterson.af.mil

Public Broadcasting Service. "New Perspectives on The West: William F Cody." www.pbs.org/weta/thewest/people/a_c/buffalobill.htm ©2001 The West Film Project.

Bibliography

Public Broadcasting Service. "New Perspectives on The West: Kit Carson" www.pbs.org/weta/thewest/people/a_c/carson.htm ©2001 The West Film Project.

Red Hot Jazz Archive, The: "A History of Jazz Before 1930." www.redhotjazz.com

Rocky Mountain Arsenal. www.pmrma.army.mil

Royal Gorge Bridge Co. www.royalgorgebridge.com.

Royal Gorge Route Railroad, The. www.royalgorgeroute.com

Schriever Air Force Base. www.schriever.af.mil

Sangres.Com: For Your Daily Dose of the Mountains. CristoMedia. ©1997-2003. www.sangre.com

Silverton Mountain. www.silvertonmountain.com

Telluride Tech Fest. "...Birth of Alternating Current Electricity." www.Telluridetechfestival.com/history.html and "L.L. Nunn Biography." www.Telluridetechfestival.com/about_techfestNunn.html

Traywick, Ben T. *From the book The Chronicles of Tombstone.* Owlhoots of the Old West. "The Dirty Little Coward: aka Robert Ford." www.mtnguy.com/owlhoots/ford.htm

USA Today. "What Happens When People and Lightning Converge." June 18, 1999. www.usatoday.com/weather/news/1999/w0618lit.htm

United States Air Force Academy. www.usafa.af.mil

U.S. Bureau of Reclamation. "DataWeb." www.usbr.gov/dataweb

United States Census Bureau. www.census.gov.

United States Department of Defense, Defense Link.
www.defenselink.mil

United States Forest Service. United States Department of Agriculture.
www.fs.fed.us
United States General Services Administration. www.gsa.gov

U.S. Naval Observatory Astronomical Applications Department.
http://aa.usno.navy.mil/

United States Space Command. "Cheyenne Mountain Fact Sheet."
Originally found at www.spacecom.af.mil

United States Space Command. Orginally found at
www.spacecom.af.mil.

United States White House Home Page. Mamie Doud Eisenhower biography. www.whitehouse.gov/history/firstladies/me34.html

University of Colorado. News Release. "Wieman and Cornell win 2001
Nobel Prize in Physics." www.Colorado.edu/newsservices/newsreleases/2001/1429.html. Oct. 9, 2001.

Volpe Center for GPS Activities. "Mobile Tracking System for
Locomotives." www.volpe.dot.gov/gps/gpsmts.html
The Disaster Center. "Colorado Tornadoes."
www.disastercenter.com/colorado/tornado.html

Western Regional Climate Center. Desert Research Institute.
www.wrcc.dri.edu

Index

Colorado by the Numbers

Index

Index